LITERATURE OLD AND NEW FOR CHILDREN

Materials for a College Course

BY

ANNIE E. MOORE, M.A.

FORMERLY ASSOCIATE PROFESSOR OF EDUCATION
TEACHERS COLLEGE, COLUMBIA UNIVERSITY
AUTHOR OF *The Primary School*

HOUGHTON MIFFLIN COMPANY

BOSTON · NEW YORK · CHICAGO · DALLAS · ATLANTA · SAN FRANCISCO

The Riverside Press Cambridge

The Riverside Press
CAMBRIDGE · MASSACHUSETTS
PRINTED IN THE U.S.A.

TO

MY STUDENTS

So had I spoken with them everyone,
That I was of their fellowship ...

CHAUCER

PREFACE

THE rapid development of children's literature in recent years and a liberalized school curriculum and policy constitute two factors in the increased need and demand on the part of teachers for guidance and practical help in the subject. Such aid is already available in a number of excellent textbooks, handbooks, and anthologies, but, as in every other growing and expanding subject, new features develop from time to time and others call for enlargement or a changed emphasis. It is hoped that this book, which has grown out of an intimate knowledge of such needs, especially as they reveal themselves in large classes in training schools and teachers colleges, may serve to meet some of them.

The plan has been to present important historical aspects of the subject, the contributions of various leading writers and modern criticism, with sufficient fullness to enable students to enter quickly but with a sense of security and satisfaction into a large field. Particular attention has been given to all kinds of new material and to its evaluation in the light of established standards and contemporary trends. It would seem that many of the most fundamental features are presented in a manner which should be helpful to instructors and students concerned with all grades of the six-year elementary school, although attention is concentrated on the needs of the kindergarten and first four grades. While the extensive lists of books for children of about those years are not organized as a course of study for school use, they might well be regarded as representing a rich core for such a course.

With very few exceptions every book discussed or included in the lists both for teachers and children has been used or carefully examined by me. This is true, not only of recently published books, but of all the old material which has been freshly reviewed either in early editions or reprints. Teachers College has an excellent collection of such books which have been long in use in the course in literature for children out of which this book has grown; Columbia University has other more complete collections; and the New York Public Library offers rare old material as well as a superior collection of modern books for children. I am indebted to all these libraries, but I wish to express in a special way my appreciation of the cheerful and competent service rendered by the librarians at Teachers College, extending on the part of some of them over a good many years.

I am much indebted to my associate, Dr. Jean Betzner, with whom many of the questions in this book have been discussed and who has generously shared with me her choice library of modern books for children. My students too have contributed much. By their responsive attitude, suggestion of profitable lines for special studies and enthusiastic pursuit of these, they helped to shape not only the college course in which they were participants but also this book which is its outgrowth.

Acknowledgment is made of the help rendered by the many carefully compiled book lists now available, and published reviews of current books by specialists in the field. Origins and titles of these will be found in the annotated bibliographies.

One of the great debts of all who are concerned in any way with the full health and happiness of children is to those living authors of children's books who are keeping the stream of literature sparkling and inviting. Any adult whose daily work demands continued acquaintance with this stream is singularly fortunate.

I greatly appreciate and hereby acknowledge the kind co-operation of the following publishers in permitting me to reprint certain passages from copyrighted articles and books: The American-Scandinavian Foundation; *The American Review* (formerly *The Bookman*); Thomas Y. Crowell Company; Doubleday, Doran and Company; E. P. Dutton and Company; Harcourt, Brace and Company; Henry Holt and Company; Houghton Mifflin Company; Little, Brown and Company; The Macmillan Company; G. P. Putnam's Sons.

A. E. M.

CONTENTS

CHAPTER I

APPROACHES TO THE STUDY OF CHILDREN'S LITERATURE

A WELL–SELECTED and representative library for children of elementary school age will contain today some hundreds of books suited to their personal pleasure and entertainment. These will include many well-known classics, not originally written for children, but appropriated by them from generation to generation, as well as the latest products of leading contemporary writers who have addressed themselves directly to the young. Over a relatively short space of time there has been a remarkable production of books designed wholly for pleasure reading and the last two decades in particular have been very fruitful in this field. Not only is there a wealth of new books of all kinds and for varying ages, but much thought and taste have gone into collecting and editing the old material and giving it a more attractive form.

The study of literature from the standpoint of children's needs has long been considered an important part of the preparation of teachers, social workers and home-makers, but in recent years the scope and dignity of the subject have been more fully recognized. Courses in this subject now take rank in colleges and training schools along with offerings in adult literature, and the time has passed when a brief study devoted largely to story-telling and other features of method is at all acceptable. The increasing amount and variety of excellent literary material for children, a fuller knowledge of child psychology, and the great social need for types of school experience which shall enrich life and open up many lines of innocent enjoyment are serving to emphasize the need for an enlargement of the study. Parents and teachers have always counted on literature to contribute to a more sympathetic understanding of human motives and actions and thus to encourage just and generous social attitudes. Nothing in our human inheritance of knowledge and art speaks a clearer language to successive generations than literature, and for the young at least, no other form of art expression makes such a direct appeal to thought and feeling.

Literature has had a long struggle to win and hold a place in elementary education upon the basis of its own intrinsic worth rather than by reason of some specific moral lesson which it is thought to convey or some utilitarian service which it is expected to render in the acquisition of facts and skills. Its unique and independent value is not yet fully recognized in the curriculum, especially in primary grades, for there are not a few schools in which its chief office is that of furnishing material for practice in learning to read. All lovers of literature who also know and understand children realize that immature readers may be so limited and frustrated by their imperfect mastery of technical skill that most of the real values of reading are lost altogether. The children's own stumbling efforts during their early school years must be richly supplemented in order to secure that happy introduction and sustained acquaintance with choice books which is conducive to developing a love for reading and taste in selection.

For these reasons it is highly important that all adults having a personal relation to children should have a broad knowledge of books both old and new and learn to judge the probable response of children to them. Teachers in particular need to develop the art of invitation and incitement to worthwhile reading, for lacking this art, their absorption in the techniques of reading skill will be prejudicial to developing a love of reading in their pupils.

This book is the product of many years of work with college students, most of whom have been preparing to teach, to supervise, to engage in social work, or to participate in curriculum-making in elementary schools from kindergarten through the fourth grade, and it is offered as embracing both materials and guidance for similar courses. The purpose of such a course should be to arouse and satisfy a genuine interest in children's books apart from school textbooks, to aid students to obtain a better working knowledge of this literature and to make them more aware of degrees of excellence in content and form. Since pleasure in books and reading is of prime importance in the case of children, a like consideration should operate in any plan for adult study of the subject. The approach should be conducive to present satisfaction and delight while preparing for some more remote responsibility. Students should have an opportunity to immerse themselves in the best that world literature has to offer to children and to enjoy the books as genuinely as children if not in just the same way. If they can renew acquaintance with old favorites, read much in current literature for sheer pleasure, pursue some lines with intensity and enthusiasm, and slight some which have less appeal, attitudes essential to literary appreciation will be built up which can scarcely be violated in their own work with children.

Next in importance to knowing and thoroughly enjoying the books themselves, we might place an adequate knowledge of the historical and social background out of which distinct types of literature have sprung. No one is equipped to judge the newer trends and to detect recurrent issues who lacks a knowledge of what has gone before. Modes and manners in life and in art have a disconcerting way of repeating themselves in rhythmic cycles, and this is illustrated in waves of approval and disapproval concerning certain types of literature. Some of the latest realistic stories are close kin to the didactic and informational ones of an earlier time, and long lists of stories especially selected for character training so prevalent today would have been welcomed in late eighteenth-century families where the elders were obsessed by this narrow conception of the purpose of literature. However quaint and out of key with modern life much of the old material may seem, there has been a certain continuity in trends and persistence in types which it is interesting and enlightening to trace.

It does not necessarily follow, however, that a course in children's literature should be mapped out in chronological sequence. It may be better to follow a quite independent order somewhat after the manner of the Monk in the *Canterbury Tales*, who announced to his fellow pilgrims that he did not intend to narrate events

> After their ages as men written find,
> But tell them some before and some behind.

Similarly it might be desirable in some situations to begin with the work of contemporary writers and proceed to those which are "behind," in an attempt to understand the relations of the simplest literature to the changing ideals and customs of a people and a period. This book furnishes much material for such comparisons which may be rearranged in a variety of ways according to the judgment, needs, and desires of those using it. Nursery rhymes and folk tales are presented first, partly because it has been found that most students can in the beginning move freely and confidently in this familiar material, and partly because it embodies in a striking way most of the principles which are operative in a great variety of more recent stories and verse. If one can discern what it is that gives charm and holding power to nursery rhymes and folk tales one is in possession of a large part of the secret of later literary successes.

Another question of approach concerns the presentation of a body of principles supposed to govern literary art. Should such a body of principles and standards be formulated and accepted in advance of a direct and pleasurable acquaintance with the literature itself? And should such principles be used as a sort of infallible and universal measure by which all kinds of material shall be weighed and approved or found wanting? Such a plan seems far too simple and neatly academic to be valid and useful where real children and living books are concerned. A better and sounder practice would seem to be for the student to learn to distinguish some of the most distinctive features of beauty and delight in each general type studied and thus in an accumulative way build up a fuller consciousness of the effect of such features wherever they appear. The plan followed here is to let each type stand on its own merits, calling attention to fine individual examples and pointing the way to the discovery of some of the elements which constitute their peculiar attraction for children. Principles of criticism are thus made intrinsic to the discussion and applicable to the solution of questions found at the close of almost every chapter. Integration of this kind ought to render inexperienced critics less liable to the mistake of condemning a fairy tale because it does not reflect everyday life, or discrediting simple little realistic stories because they lack a certain kind of imagination, or ignoring nonsense verse on the ground that it has not the qualities of true poetry.

A full-length portrait and an extended interpretation is offered of only one author — Hans Christian Andersen. The limits of this book and of the usual course in children's literature forbid extensive treatment of many individual writers. The study of Andersen is recommended as an example of method in tracing significant relations between an author's life and personality and whatever is unique in his creative work. This study also yields a wealth of suggestion to all who try to write for children or to become more expert in identifying elements of charm in the work of others. Andersen made a very unusual contribution to children's literature and occupies a unique position in relation to both traditional and modern stories. Whether many of his tales can be used in lower primary grades or not, no story-teller can afford to neglect the work of this wizard in the art.

What is to determine which of the many recently published books should be considered along with established classics, and which living writers should be given special attention? A common-sense answer to this question is the only possible one. We cannot wait for books to become accepted classics before trying to learn about them, nor can we wait for authors to be placed in some Hall of Fame. Beautiful books of quite unequal value are available in large quantity, but happily along with this increased production there have grown up a high intelligence and a new artistry in criticism. Gifted writers have turned critics, and accomplished critics have become successful writers. Leading publishers quite commonly avail themselves of expert advice before publication and several firms employ especially qualified editors for their department of children's books. Prominent artists and designers everywhere have turned their attention to the making of beautiful books for children as they did in England at an earlier period.

Teachers must become intelligent guides in the selection of this new material. This text introduces in the last three chapters and in supplementary lists many familiar names, and others not so well known, of contemporary writers for children — most of them living. There are nearly a hundred of these names. Some who are included have one choice book to their credit, but there are at least twenty-five who have an established reputation resting upon continued production of books which delight children and call out the praise of the best qualified critics. Some of this work will live — some of the books are without doubt the "classics to be"; but we are not so much concerned with opinions of posterity as with supplying the boys and girls of today with the best books of their own time along with those which have survived out of the past.

In organizing and presenting this material, much thought has been given to making it easily adaptable to different conditions and especially to varying stages of experience and knowledge attained by a student-group. Some topics may be given slight attention and others may need to be expanded or given greater emphasis. Many pleasant by-paths are suggested or discoverable which students should be encouraged to follow, and many questions are raised which might lead to fruitful original research — original at least for those pursuing the study. No thoroughly vital and functioning study ever describes the straight line of a highway from "here" to "there." It tends to follow a path much more like those which ramble across fields and hills offering tempting excursions to be pursued or reluctantly passed by.

Another means of adaptation to different types of student groups may be found in the nature and scope of the questions furnished. These may be treated singly in class discussion or several related questions may be combined to give direction to a somewhat extensive study by individual students or by small groups. These questions have arisen out of direct experience with books and people and scarcely one is of the "desk-made" or purely theoretical type. Many of them have been propounded by students. The problems for more extended study vary considerably in scope and in probing quality but practically all of them call for a direct and close acquaintance with the literature itself.

The subject bibliographies offer a wide range from the more basic and indispensable references to those which only the more ambitious and best prepared students may care to read or need to consult in some special piece of work.

Some explanation is called for regarding the grading of the lists of children's books. The placement indicated has little to do with independent reading skill or "reading age." There are very weighty reasons for practically ignoring this feature in a course concerned with the enjoyment and appreciation of literature on the part of the younger children. Books for pleasure and delight cannot be subjected to the rigid control of content and style which a finely graded and standardized vocabulary now imposes upon textbooks in reading. An inquirer has only to examine one of the extensive book lists constructed with a studied regard for degrees of reading skill to see how thin is the offering for lower grades. It is expected that most of the children's books included in the lists found throughout this text will be read to them, at least below third grade, and no assurance is offered that all can be read independently even by fourth grade pupils. Children from seven to ten years of age will be able to read many of these books but that merely implies another and different pleasure at the command of these particular children.

The books listed and described in the following chapters were selected primarily for the guidance of adult students in becoming acquainted with literature for children and developing some skill in discovering their growing and expanding tastes. Probable maturity levels for the enjoyment of books are frequently indicated in annotations but for the extensive lists of less well-known books in Chapters XI and XII some more convenient symbol seemed called for, so that letters A, B, C are used to indicate three predictable levels of understanding and appreciation. This classification should be interpreted in a very flexible way and there will be much overlapping for the reason that æsthetic enjoyment is one of those intangibles which refuse to be standardized.

A. For children about five to seven years of age.
B. For children about seven to nine years of age.
C. For children about eight to ten years of age.

Some books in the C group will be greatly enjoyed by still older children and a few in the A group will be claimed by pre-school children.

CHAPTER II
MOTHER GOOSE

Wisdom of babes — the nursery Shakespeare still —
Cackles she ever with the same good-will.
                                        MRS. A. D. T. WHITNEY

THE history of Mother Goose rhymes, as it relates to the first authentic collections, has been written many times by competent students of the subject. Many of the separate rhymes, also, have been traced back to their source in popular ballads, folk songs, folk games, political satire and doggerel, ancient proverbs, riddles, and real or legendary events. Authorities cited at the close of this chapter may be consulted for a fuller presentation of the historical aspects of this alluring subject, but it seems advisable to restate here, very briefly, some of the main facts concerning several of the oldest collections of Mother Goose which have furnished the core of all later editions.

Mention is made in Chapter IV of the first known use in literature of the name *Mother Goose*. It was used as a sort of sub-title by Charles Perrault for his collection of nursery tales entitled *Histoires ou Contes du Temps Passé, avec des Moralités*, published in 1697. The frontispiece of this book shows an old woman at a spinning wheel entertaining with her tales a group consisting of a man, a girl, a boy, and a cat. Attached to this picture is a placard bearing the legend *Contes de ma Mère l'Oye*. While this is the first known use of the name as a title, Andrew Lang[1] cites ample proof that, previous to this date (1697), the term *Conte de la Mère l'oye* was current in France to de-

[1] Lang, Andrew, Introduction to *Popular Tales* by Charles Perrault.

note, in general, any fabulous tale, particularly a familiar nursery tale.

This collection of Perrault's, consisting of eight nursery tales popular in France, was translated into English about 1729 and thus was the old dame first introduced to English children as a teller of prose tales.

John Newbery, the famous publisher of children's books at Saint Paul's Churchyard, London, soon popularized the name Mother Goose and at some time prior to his death in 1767 published a collection of nursery rhymes called *Mother Goose's Melody*. From that time on, the name Mother Goose became attached wholly to song and rhyme, and the old lady was transformed for all time from a French peasant telling French tales to young and old, to an English grandam or nurse singing old English songs to her infant charges. And so she has come down to us, but during the period of nearly two and a half centuries since this transmutation, how great the increase of her repertoire and how changed her dress!

THE FIRST MOTHER GOOSE COLLECTION

Great interest centers, of course, in the Newbery edition of about 1765 which is believed, on good authority, to be the first collection of English nursery rhymes to bear the name of Mother Goose. According to Charles Welsh [1] not a single copy of the original edition is extant. Fortunately, however, there is available a reprint by the publishing house of Isaiah Thomas, Worcester, Massachusetts, which, undoubtedly, follows the original very closely and which was issued along with many other Newbery books about 1785. Since pirating of English publications by American publishers was a common practice, and since numerous other instances of exact duplication of children's books of the period can be proved,

[1] Welsh, Charles, *A Bookseller of the Last Century*. London, 1885.

it is generally accepted that the book about to be described is virtually the Newbery Mother Goose.

Whitmore [1] says two specimens of the Thomas reprint have been preserved and it was from one of these that he produced his facsimile. The title page was lacking in both specimens but, otherwise, the Whitmore replica brings us very close to Mother Goose the First. The replica will be eagerly examined by any interested person who sees it for the first time. What rhymes were contained in this first collection? What was the form? What sort of illustrations did it have? Do our modern editions contain these rhymes? Which, if any, of the original verses have since been discarded? Some of these questions we shall try to answer, and for the others, adequate sources of information will be given.

Considering this Worcester reprint then as the veritable Newbery *Mother Goose's Melody*, we notice first that it is thoroughly British. There is not a trace of the French Perrault's prose tales and scarcely a suggestion of America. There is a mock-serious preface never intended for children, cast in the form of a literary disquisition by an antiquarian. The Preface is declared to be "By a Very Great Writer of Very Little Books." A few really significant sentences from the opening and closing paragraphs follow:

> Much might be said in favour of this collection, but as we have no room for critical disquisitions we shall only observe to our readers that the custom of singing these songs and lullabies to children is of great antiquity. It is even as old as the time of the ancient *Druids. Caractatus*, King of the *Britons*, was rocked in his Cradle in the Ile of *Mona*, now called *Anglesea*, and tuned to sleep by some of these soporiferous sonnets....

---

[1] Whitmore, W. H., *The Original Mother Goose's Melody*, as first issued by John Newbery of London about A.D. 1760. Reproduced in facsimile from the edition as reprinted by Isaiah Thomas of Worcester, Massachusetts, about A.D. 1785, with Introductory notes by William H. Whitmore, Albany, 1880.

We cannot conclude without observing the great probability there is that the custom of making nonsensical verses in our schools was borrowed from this practice among the old *British* nurses; they have, indeed, been always the first preceptors of the youth of this Kingdom, and from them the rudiments of taste and learning are naturally derived. Let none therefore speak irreverently of this ancient maternity, as they can be considered as the great grandmothers of science and knowledge.

Whitmore [1] and other commentators offer ample evidence that Oliver Goldsmith was contributing extensively to the Newbery publications from 1762 to 1767 and it is generally believed that he was the "Very great writer of very little books" referred to, and that he wrote not only the Preface but had a hand in the imitations of scholarly maxims, footnotes, and titles which characterize this edition.

Although the writer of the Preface evidently speaks "with tongue in cheek," we feel that the part quoted above has a note of sincerity in its tribute to the antiquity of the rhymes and to the part played by British nurses in preserving the old ones and composing new. We wonder, too, just what the writer meant by "the custom of making nonsense verses in our schools." It certainly has a modern ring. Were English schoolboys in mid-eighteenth century composing nonsense verses or is the reference to their halting and unintentionally humorous Latin Verse Composition?

Other evidence that the editor could not throw himself whole-heartedly into the spirit of childhood and prepare a book for children alone, is seen in the absurd and irrelevant titles and maxims. "I won't be my father's Jock" is called "Amphion's Song of Eurydice"; "Plato's Song" proves to be "Ding, Dong, Bell"; "Aristotle's Story" is another hoax; and "Little Tom Tinker's Dog" has the

[1] Whitmore, W. H., *op. cit.*

title "Cæsar." All this seems to be without reason though not without rhyme.

Here are two examples of satirical comment and pseudo-philosophy attached to the simplest of rhymes:

> Hush-a-by, Baby,
> On the Tree Top,
> When the Wind blows,
> The Cradle will rock;
> When the Bough breaks,
> The Cradle will fall;
> Down tumbles baby,
> Cradle and all.

This may serve as a warning to the proud and ambitious, who climb so high that they generally fall at last.

Maxim
Content turns all it touches into gold.

> Shoe the Colt,
> Shoe the Colt,
> Shoe the wild Mare;
> Here a nail,
> There a nail,
> Yet she goes bare.

"Ay, ay, drive the nail when it will go: That's the Way of the World, and is the Method pursued by all our Financiers, Politicians, and Necromancers."

Note that this nonsense is extraneous to the rhymes themselves and is clearly addressed to adults. We suspect that purchasers of children's books and toys in that day consulted their own pleasure to a considerable extent just as they do now.

THE ORIGINAL MOTHER GOOSE'S MELODY

The book was very small, as were all books of the period for children. Reprints and replicas indicate a page not more than four and a quarter inches high by three and a quarter inches wide, with quite small type. The woodcuts were, of course, very small, usually about one inch by two inches, though Betty Winkle's pig which was "not very big" occupies, quite appropriately, a space of only one inch by one and a quarter inches. We marvel that so small a pig could have occasioned such deep woe! There is a picture for each rhyme, and tiny or crude as they are, for the most part, some of them achieve surprising clearness and a story-telling quality which is quite pleasing.

This little book contained fifty-one rhymes, or fifty-two if we include "There was an old woman tossed up in a blanket" which is quoted in the Preface by the learned editor. Of the fifty-two at least thirty-three are very familiar today. Most of them are quite short, usually from four to eight lines, though one runs to three stanzas and another to six. It will be seen, therefore, that the longer nursery favorites, such as "The Queen of Hearts," "Mother Hubbard and Her Dog," "Jenny Wren," and other extended narratives, are not found in the Newbery edition. We discover, however, a goodly number of the best-known short rhymes. Among them are "Ding, Dong, Bell"; "Little Tom Tucker"; "Great A, Little A"; "Ride a Cock Horse"; "Jack and Jill"; "Hush-a-by, Baby"; "Little Jack Horner"; "Pat-a-Cake"; "Jack Sprat"; "This Pig Went to Market"; "Baa, Baa, Black Sheep"; "High Diddle, Diddle"; and "Dickery, Dickery Dock." The absence is noted of certain very popular short rhymes such as "Little Miss Muffet," "Little Boy Blue," "Mistress Mary," and "Humpty-Dumpty."

One of the most surprising things about this old collection is the introduction at the end, of sixteen selections from Shakespeare. An advertisement in the Thomas reprint reads:

MOTHER GOOSE'S MELODY; or Sonnets for the Cradle. In two Parts. Part 1st, contains the most celebrated

Songs and Lullabies of the old British Nurses, calculated to amuse children and excite them to sleep. Part 2nd, those of that sweet Songster and Nurse of Wit and Humour, Master William Shakespeare. Embellished with Cuts, and illustrated with Notes and Maxims, Historical, Philosophical, and Critical.

Here again, the hand of a man of literary taste and discrimination is shown, for the selections from Shakespeare for younger readers could not be improved upon. They are just the selections which have found their way into the best modern anthologies for children. Among them we find: "Where the Bee Sucks"; "You Spotted Snakes"; "When Icicles Hang by the Wall"; "Under the Greenwood Tree"; and "Hark, Hark! the Lark."

Thus, Mother Goose, in her first presentation in verse form to the English nursery, has the high distinction of appearing side by side with England's greatest poet who is, himself, called a "Nurse of Wit and Humor." Modern detractors of the wise old dame, please take notice!

GAMMER GURTON'S GARLAND

In tracing the evolution of our modern collections of Mother Goose rhymes one should not neglect to examine *Gammer Gurton's Garland* by Joseph Ritson. The exact date of his first edition is not known with certainty, but an editorial note in the 1866 reprint [1] states that the probable date of publication was 1784. In 1810 the *Garland* appeared in its final form with four parts. Ritson attributes Parts I and II to a "literary gentleman now deceased" and says he is now publishing this older part "with additions." The title page, according to Whitmore, [2] reads:

Gammer Gurton's Garland: or, the Nursery Parnassus. A choice collection of pretty songs and verses, for the amuse-

---

[1] Ritson, Joseph, *Gammer Gurton's Garland; or, the Nursery Parnassus.* Reprinted for Hugh Hopkins, Glasgow, 1866.

[2] Whitmore, *op. cit.*, p. 8.

ment of all little good children who can neither read nor run. London: printed for R. Triphook, 37 St. James Street, by Harding and Wright, St. John's Square, 1810.

There are 136 rhymes in Ritson's *Garland* as against 52 in the Newbery collection, and we are indebted to Ritson for the addition of many of the more popular ones current today. Among the shorter rhymes which he introduced are: "Boy Blue"; "Little Maid, Pretty Maid": "One, Two, Buckle My Shoe"; "Humpty-Dumpty"; "Goose-a, Goose-a, Gander"; "There was an Old Woman, She Lived in a Shoe"; and one stanza of "Old Mother Hubbard and Her Dog." Ritson added also a number of longer stories in rhyme which, as noted above, had but slight representation in the earliest collection. We find here for the first time, "London Bridge is Broken Down," eight stanzas; "The Merry Bells of London," thirteen couplets; "There was a Frog Lived in a Well," nine stanzas; and the full-length story of "Little Bopeep." Thus, we see well started the practice of including in Mother Goose not only short and more or less fragmentary bits of song and nonsense rhymes, but also ballads, singing games, folk songs, and narrative poems of sufficient length and fullness to develop dramatic plot and action; and this example has been consistently followed by almost all editors of nursery-rhyme books in the century and a quarter that has elapsed since the publication of *Gammer Gurton's Garland*.

EARLY AMERICAN REPRINTS

Following the Thomas reprint, there were two editions of importance published in New England in the early part of the nineteenth century. In 1824 the firm of Monroe and Francis, Boston, brought out a collection called *Mother Goose's Quarto; or, Melodies Complete*. It contained 48 of the Newbery rhymes and many from

Ritson's *Garland*.   There are about 180 different rhymes
in this little book and most of them have the true flavor
of ancient folk verse, though Whitmore [1] says a number of
them are modern.   He cites as one of these the "Pibroch
of Donnel Dhu," by Walter Scott.   The same firm brought
out in 1833 another edition almost identical with the one
of 1824 so far as contents are concerned and, fortunately,
we are not dependent on rare old copies for a close acquaintance with this book, since there is an excellent reproduction [2] easily available.   All later nursery rhyme books
have drawn extensively on the edition of 1833 and it has
constituted one of the chief sources for authentic Mother
Goose material.

OTHER SOURCES

It is not uncommon for modern collections of Mother
Goose rhymes to contain more than four hundred separate
titles.   Where has this material been obtained?   Antiquarians who have collected all kinds of traditional material
— songs, games, ballads, proverbs, riddles, charms, finger-
plays, counting-out rhymes, memorization stunts, and
tongue-twisters — have furnished practically all that cannot
be accounted for by the earliest edition of Mother Goose
already mentioned.   Halliwell in his *Nursery Rhymes of
England* [3] assembled a very large amount of this sort of
material and his collection has furnished many choice bits
of traditional verse suitable for children as well as quite
a number that are not so appropriate.   Compilers of
collections for children sometimes appear to think that
any ancient short nonsense rhyme, epigram, or folk song
from a reliable source is worthy of a place in a child's book.

[1] Whitmore, *op. cit.*, p. 16.
[2] *The Only True Mother Goose*. An exact reproduction of the text and
illustrations of the original edition published and copyrighted in Boston
in the year 1833 by Monroe and Francis. With an Introduction by Edward Everett Hale. Lothrop, Lee and Shepard, 1905.
[3] Halliwell, James O., *The Nursery Rhymes of England*.   1842.

Carelessness is often exhibited in including in Mother Goose books certain familiar poems for children and omitting the names of the authors which should be well known. Those poems thus appear to be anonymous, and not being "modern" in the sense of recently written, they are often regarded as traditional English verse. There are three titles in particular which are frequently attributed incorrectly to Mother Goose: "Twinkle, Twinkle, Little Star," by Jane Taylor; "Mary Had a Little Lamb," by Sara J. Hale; and "Three Little Kittens," by Eliza Lee Follen.

THE BEST-KNOWN RHYMES

In a brief treatment of Mother Goose in *The Primary School* [1] an account is given of an attempt to ascertain whether a certain few rhymes are better known than others, and if so, which they are. The procedure and results are as follows:

Suspecting that general acquaintance with folk verse is limited to about a dozen well-known titles, we tested a group of kindergarten-primary teachers to see what titles came most prominently to mind. Without previous warning and without recent reading or study of Mother Goose, ninety-seven young women taking a course in children's literature were asked to write down as rapidly as possible, titles, or any identifying line, of Mother Goose rhymes in the order in which they came to their minds. They were given just two minutes in which to write.

The results of this experiment in brief were as follows: The largest number of titles given by any one was fourteen, the smallest was two. The total number of different rhymes named was one hundred and five. The frequency with which certain titles were mentioned ranged from one to fifty-one, the rhymes which were listed by fifty per cent of the class being Miss Muffet and Jack and Jill, with fifty-one "votes" each, and Boy Blue, with fifty out of a possible ninety-seven.

---

[1] Moore, Annie E., *The Primary School.* Houghton Mifflin Company, 1925, pp. 261-262.

Jack Horner was just below the fifty per cent mark, being found on forty-six lists.

So far as revealed by this test the following are the best known rhymes; at least they are the selections most readily recalled by these particular people:

	TIMES MENTIONED
Miss Muffet	51
Jack and Jill	51
Boy Blue	50
Jack Horner	46
Old Mother Hubbard	43
Little Bopeep	41
Hey, Diddle, Diddle	40
Humpty-Dumpty	36
Mistress Mary	30
Hickory, Dickory, Dock	29
Baa, Baa, Black Sheep	28

Such charming verses as "I saw a ship a-sailing," and "Lady-bug, lady-bug," are mentioned only once each, and the picturesque little mariner, Bobby Shafto, is recalled by only two. "One misty, moisty morning" finds a place on two lists; "Pat-a-cake" on three; and "I had a little pony," on four.

This experiment has since been tried several times by the author with groups of students similarly constituted and numbering in all 290 people. The results have been almost identical with those of the first experiment. Invariably, the totals of these lists of rhymes quickly recalled show the same five or six in the lead, though the order of frequency shifts slightly with different groups. The frequencies for the whole 290 lists are shown here.

	TIMES MENTIONED IN 290 LISTS
Jack and Jill	172
Boy Blue	169
Jack Horner	160
Miss Muffet	155
Humpty-Dumpty	139
Little Bopeep	131
Old Mother Hubbard	121
Mistress Mary	120

The long life of these particular rhymes is shown by the fact that all but one were in one or both of the two oldest known collections. Miss Muffet seems to have made her appearance by way of the Monroe and Francis edition of 1824.

Miss Alice Gordon tried a similar experiment with thirty-four seventh- and eighth-grade pupils at La Crosse, Wisconsin.[1] It is interesting to note almost the same titles appearing with highest frequency in those quickly recalled by these boys and girls. The following table shows the results when the two grades are combined:

Number of eighth-grade pupils reporting 16
Number of seventh-grade pupils reporting 18
          Total 34

Reports of two grades are here combined.

	TIMES MENTIONED
1. Old Mother Hubbard	16
2. Jack and Jill	15
3. Jack be Nimble	12
4. Little Boy Blue } Miss Muffet }	10
5. Little Jack Horner	9
6. Mistress Mary	8
7. Little Bopeep	7

LEADING CHARACTERS

It is a noticeable fact that the eight leading rhymes in both the adult list and the children's list have interesting central figures of marked individuality and bearing distinctive names. In all but one ("Humpty-Dumpty"), this central figure is a real person performing natural ordinary acts, and with one other exception ("Mother Hubbard and Her Dog"), the leading character is a child vividly portrayed.

Led by these eight picturesque little boys and girls what

[1] Unpublished report.

a procession of children we see dancing, skipping, running, or walking sedately behind old Mother Goose down the centuries! As already suggested, most of these children are known to us by name, often by the full name or by a distinguishing sobriquet. Bobby Shafto, Georgy Porgy, Johnny and Betty Pringle, Bessie Bell and Mary Gray, Polly Flinders, Tommy Tucker, Marjory Daw, Willie Winkie, Lucy Locket, Simple Simon, Curly Locks, Tommy Grace, Betty Blue, and a host of others, named and nameless, each intent on his own vocation or employment, pastime or prank. They pass before us — sailor-boy, farmer's boy, fisherman, shepherdess, milkmaid, gardener, musician, market-man, street-vendor, as well as merry, carefree children at play. Whatever the occupation, most of them are true children, happy, busy, thoughtless, and often quite irresponsible. Their behavior on the whole is natural and rational. We recognize the little girls who do not like spiders, who resent having a beloved pony abused, who lose shoe and pocketbook and get their clothes soiled as soon as they are freshly dressed, who like pretty trinkets, and those who seem to enjoy motherly duties and household tasks. We meet as in real life little boys who tease, who are boastful, self-assured, and sometimes cruel, who go to sleep at a crucial moment, who attempt to get something for nothing, as well as those who are tender-hearted, independent, industrious, and ingenious. There is only one Simple Simon, and if we could give the whole crowd an intelligence test at long range in time and space, we should probably get the normal curve of distribution from dull to very clever.

We see these boys and girls with their elders in the work of kitchen, shop, mill, barn, and field; there is the normal contact with affairs of the grown-up world which attend simple family and village life — courtship, marriage, death, burial, country fair, and festival; echoes of school come to us;

the sound of music from pipe and fiddle is heard; there are journeys "over the water and over the lea," on foot ("Jog on, jog on"), on a gaily decked pony ("Gallop-a-trot"), in boats that are none too seaworthy, in a wheelbarrow.

In many of these activities friendly birds and animals participate or they enjoy among themselves similar experiences. They too make love, quarrel, marry, die and have a grand funeral. They dance and sing and play the fiddle, but between times they fulfill their natural functions in quite a matter-of-fact fashion. Are children of today deceived by all this delightful fooling? Not unless they are more stupid than Simple Simon or more literal than "little Bill Cook who always read his book." Of course care should be taken to insure that babies and toddlers and underprivileged children have opportunities to become acquainted with real animals and birds through first-hand experience, and by means of realistic stories and accurate pictures.

TRUE NATURE OF SOME OF THE NONSENSE

When we understand why many of these old rhymes appear to be such sheer nonsense, we have more respect for them. Many that seem most senseless, are old counting-out rhymes such as:

> Hickery, dickery, six and seven,
> Alabone, crackabone, ten and eleven;
> Spin, span, muskidan;
> Twiddle 'um, twaddle 'um, twenty-one.

> Eeny, meeny, miny-moe
> Crak a-feeny, finy, foe
> Ominooja, poppatooja
> Rick, bick ban doe
> O–U–T, out.

As a means of discovering by chance who shall be "It" in a game, such counting-out rhymes have been invented by children of all nations and have gone through many changes due to oral transmission.

One must recognize riddles also before the charge of empty nonsense is brought.

> Higgledy piggledy, here we lie,
> Picked and plucked and put in a pie.
> (Currants)

> Black within, and red without,
> Four corners round about.
> (Chimney)

> Flour of England, fruit of Spain,
> Met together in a shower of rain;
> Put in a bag tied round with a string,
> If you'll tell me this riddle, I'll give you a ring.
> (A plum-pudding)

> Lives in winter,
> Dies in summer,
> And grows with its root upward.
> (Icicle)

Other apparently meaningless jingles constitute an important part of some old game. Two examples may be cited:

> Buff says Buff to all his men
> And I say Buff to you again;
> Buff neither laughs nor smiles
> But carries his face
> With a very good grace,
> And passes the stick to the very next place!

This rhyme accompanies a game in which a child in the center of the ring points a stick at one child after another making amusing grimaces and trying to cause them to laugh. The one who laughs when thus singled out must be "It."

> A duck and a drake,
> A nice barley-cake,
> With a penny to pay the old baker;

> A hop and a scotch
> Is another notch,
> Slitherum, slotherum, take her.

Ritson [1] calls this rhyme "Water Skimming," and we learn from Wheeler [2] that these lines are probably very old and that they refer to the sport of skimming a stone over water. He gives the translation of a reference in Latin to this kind of play "called a duck and a drake and a halfe-penie cake."

There are numerous gesture plays concerning the baby's face, his toes, his fingers, etc., with which mothers and nurses for ages past have entertained little children. A well-known one concerning the face runs as follows:

Eye-Winker	(touching one eye)
Tom-Tinker	(touching other eye)
Nose-Smeller	(touching nose)
Mouth-Eater	(touching mouth)
Chin-Chopper	(touching chin)
Gullie, gullie, gullie	(tickling under chin)

Wheeler [3] quotes the following variation:

> Brow brinky
> Eye winky
> Chin choppy
> Nose noppy
> Cheek cherry
> Mouth merry

A WORD TO THE WISE

Mother Goose occasionally makes use of direct injunction. More commonly, however, she employs pointed aphorism to prick the bubbles of child and man, or crystallizes cool logic in adage and proverb.

---

[1] Ritson, *op. cit.*, p. 52.
[2] Wheeler, W. A., ed., *Mother Goose's Melodies*. Houghton Mifflin Company, 1878.
[3] *Ibid.*, p. 182, note.

Come when you're called,
Do what you're bid,
Shut the door after you,
　　Never be chid.

Speak when you're spoken to,
　　Come when one call;
Shut the door after you,
　　And turn to the wall.

If ifs and ands
Were pots and pans
There would be no need of tinkers.

If wishes were horses
Beggars would ride,
If turnips were watches
　　I would wear one by my side.

He that by the plough would thrive
Himself must either hold or drive

FOR OLDER CHILDREN

The general impression regarding Mother Goose is that it is intended for very young children only. It is true that the best-known and most frequently published verses are those which appeal especially to the child from two to six or seven years of age. There are, however, a great many verses and longer poems in any full collection which will not be understood by such young children and which depend for real enjoyment upon an appreciation of some clever joke, a play upon words, a numerical trick, a grammatical twist, or an absurd antithesis. One way to discover these is to run through a collection and note how many cause the adult reader to pause and wonder whether there is a hidden meaning or no meaning at all. A good annotated edition such as Wheeler's reveals many very entertaining points which older children enjoy.

> Ten and ten and twice eleven,
> Take out six and put in seven;
> Go to the green and fetch eighteen,
> And drop one a-coming.

This is nothing but the equation of old-time arithmetic books, but how much more engaging in rhyme!

Roman numbers only faintly disguised, array themselves in the stanza —

> When V and I together meet,
> They make the number Six complete.
> When I with V doth meet once more,
> Then 'tis they Two can make but Four.
> And when that V from I is gone,
> Alas! poor I can make but One.

Play with language has produced a number of trick rhymes which amuse children when they "catch on" to the joke. Having grasped the obscure point, they enjoy setting the trap for others.

The mysteries of singular and plural:

> There was a man who had no eyes,
> He went abroad to view the skies;
> He saw a tree with apples on it,
> He took no apples off, yet left no apples on it.

> Elizabeth, Elspeth, Betsy, and Bess [1]
> They all went together to seek a bird's nest.
> They found a bird's nest with five eggs in,
> They all took one and left four in.

Here one is impressed with the importance of correct punctuation:

> Every lady in this land
> Has twenty nails upon each hand
> Five and twenty on hands and feet
> All this is true without deceit.

A familiar trick depending on visualization and hence demonstrated by an earlier generation with slate and

---

[1] Four forms for one name; therefore, one child.

pencil, is described in a rhyme which is itself very "catchy" and pleasing to the ear:

> Make three-fourths a cross
>   And a circle complete;
> And let two semi-circles
>   On a perpendicular meet;
> Next add a triangle
>   That stands on two feet;
> Then two semicircles,
>   And a circle complete.

(Tobacco)

POETIC QUALITY

One basic element in poetry is rhythm, and in nursery rhymes this element is very prominent. Many of them are in reality songs, and almost all can be readily set to simple music because measure and accent are quite regular and marked. When set to music many of them can be adapted easily to two-four or marching time. It is almost as if Bopeep, Jack Horner, Jack and Jill, Lucy Locket, and others of the merry throng led by Tom the Piper's son were keeping step down the road from the long ago, each singing his own song and all to the same tune. Here and there a measure must be repeated or a phrase contracted a bit in order to keep in step, but a regular *left*, *right*, *left*, *right*, is seldom disturbed.

Babies soon respond by clapping in time to the regular beat of "Pat-a-cake, pat-a-cake," and at an older age two children play together with perfect co-ordination the rhythmical game of "Pease porridge hot." "See-saw sacradown" swings lazily to the motion of a see-saw, "Hush-a-by, baby, on the tree top," sways gently and evenly with the wind, while in "Ride a cock horse," one can hear quick hoof-beats accompanied by the tinkle of the lady's rings and bells. That this is not mere imagination is proved by the fact that so many of these little song-stories have been set to appropriate music by composers of reputation.

Alliteration is another factor in securing pleasing sound effects in poetry, and Mother Goose offers many examples of such effects. It is evident that children like this element in poetry because they so frequently invent a series of alliterative syllables or words and reiterate them in a way that is sometimes wearisome to their elders. Some of the following lines from Mother Goose are not unlike children's playful spontaneous rigamaroles.

Deedle, deedle, dumpling,
My son John,

Doodledy, doodledy, doodledy, dan,
I'll have a piper to be my good man.

Hick-a-more, hack-a-more
On the King's kitchen door.

Riddle me, riddle me, ree,
A hawk sat upon a tree

I jump mejerime jee

With a wing, wang, waddle O.

Little John Jiggy Jag
He rode a penny nag
And went to Wiggan to woo.

Rowley powley, pudding and pie.

Old Gammer Hipple-Hopple hopped out of bed.

Alliteration of a higher order is seen in

Little Robin Redbreast
Sat upon a rail.
Niddle, naddle, went his head,
Wiggle, waggle, went his tail.

Bless you, bless you, burnie bee.

My maid Mary
She minds her dairy,
While I go hoeing and mowing each morn.

Pussy-cat, wussy-cat, with a white foot,
When is your wedding? for I'll come to't.
The beer's to brew, the bread's to bake,
Pussy-cat, pussy-cat, don't be too late.

My mother is a dairy maid,
Kind sir, says she,
And it's dabbling in the dew where you'll find me.

I saw a ship a-sailing,
A-sailing in the sea;

One misty, moisty morning.

But sit on a cushion and sew a fine seam,
And feed upon strawberries, sugar and cream.

A string of mere nonsense words used as a refrain often
gives a delightful effect and is a common feature in folk
song and traditional verse. Many old ballads have this
characteristic. The following examples illustrate the
musical refrain:

Sing heigh-ho, the carrion crow,
Fol de riddle, lol de riddle, hi ding do.

My true love lives far from me,
Perrie, Merrie, Dixie, Dominie.
Many a rich present he sends to me,
Petrum, Partrum, Paradise, Temporie,
Perrie, Merrie, Dixie, Dominie.

There was an old couple, and they were poor,
Fa la, fa la la lee!

With a rowley, powley, gammon and spinach,
Heigho, says Anthony Rowley.

A number of verses which possess the beauty of true
poetry as embodied in charming concept, lovely phrase,
and fitting form have been preserved for the storehouse of

Mother Goose.   Some of the choicest ones in this category
are: "The north wind doth blow"; "I had a little nut tree";
"Rock-a-by, baby, thy cradle is green"; "Bless you, bless
you, burnie bee"; "Wee Willie Winkie"; "Rock-a-by,
baby, on the tree top"; "'Twas on a merry time when
Jenny Wren was young"; "Once I saw a little bird";
"Lavender blue and Rosemary green;" "Johnny shall
have a new bonnet"; "My maid Mary"; "Cushy cow
bonny"; "Bobby Shafto"; and "I saw a ship a-sailing."

Where can one find more charming conceptions, delicate
fancy or pleasing elaboration than in the description of
Tom Thumb's apparel and accouterments?   One is
reminded strongly of Mercutio's description of Queen
Mab in *Romeo and Juliet.*

> Come, listen, my boys, sit still and be mum,
> I'll read the apparel of Master Tom Thumb.
> An oaken leaf he had for his crown;
> His shirt, it was by spiders spun;
> His stockings of thistle-down, they tie
> With eye-lash picked from his mother's eye;
> His hat was made of butterfly's wing;
> His boots were wove of gossamer thin;
> His coat and breeches were shaped with pride;
> A needle mounted swung by his side;
> A mouse he rode as his dapple steed;
> His bridle curb an inch of thread;
> His shoes were made of a squirrel's skin,
> Nicely tanned, the hair within.

Many other selections offer picturesque and childlike conceptions of a truly poetic character such as King Boggin's
fine hall built of pie crust and slated with pancakes; John
Jiggy Jag's costume including a hat made of a coat lap and
stockings of pearly blue; monkeys made of gingerbread
and sugar horses painted red; the garden with silver bells
and cockle-shells; the little nut tree with its silver nutmeg
and golden pear; the white dove sat on the castle wall;

the rose is red the violet blue; gathering roses to give to the queen.

HUMOR

The humor in Mother Goose ranges all the way from the crudest sort which depends upon some ludicrous mishap or the absurd and incongruous behavior of animals and people, to that which involves amusing surprise, unexpected turn of events, or clever antithesis.

Crude mishaps are numerous and may be illustrated here by the man who waded in buttermilk up to his chin and got a long icicle on his nose, and the barber who in shaving the mason "cut off his nose and popped it in the basin." Absurd and incongruous behavior which is quite inconsequential forms the basis of most of the fun. Familiar examples are "Hey diddle, diddle"; "A cat came dancing out of the barn"; "There was a piper had a cow"; "Old Mistress McShuttle"; "Peter, Peter, Pumpkin-eater"; "There was a man in our town"; "Simple Simon"; and "Old Mother Hubbard."

A large number of rhymes which cause a laugh depend less upon concrete situations. The humor is of a more delicate sort and demands for appreciation a somewhat more mature mind and quick response to tricks of language. Some rest wholly upon the surprise of antithesis, such as "Three children sliding on the ice upon a summer's day"; "He went by the South and burnt his mouth, With eating cold plum porridge"; "The man in the wilderness asked me, How many strawberries grew in the sea"; and the whole of "Three Jolly Welshmen" detailing a series of amusing misconceptions. A pleasant shock of surprise often comes at the end of a short stanza.

> To make your candles last for aye
> You wives and maids give ear O!
> To put 'em out's the only way,
> Says honest John Boldero.

The mock-seriousness of some of the rhymes is very amusing to children who can appreciate this kind of fooling.

> There was a little guinea-pig
> Who, being little, was not big.
> He always walked upon his feet,
> And never fasted when he eat.
>
> When from a place he ran away,
> He never at that place did stay;
> And while he ran, as I am told,
> He ne'er stood still for young or old.

UNDERLYING MEANING

There are two extreme points of view regarding the inner significance of these old rhymes. One is that as pure flotsam and jetsam of the centuries they are wholly superficial and fragmentary and carry little or no meaning of any kind. The opposite point of view holds that there is a profound philosophical import to many of the verses and that consciousness of this meaning on the part of adults will serve to make children more aware of the "lessons" inherent in the material. There was once a little pamphlet circulated with serious purpose in which a number of Mother Goose rhymes were "interpreted" very much after the manner of Froebel's *Mother-Play Commentaries*, and bordering even more than the latter on metaphysics. Such attempts are amusing and of course quite ephemeral.

A common-sense opinion seems to be that, like any other stories dealing with real child-life and everyday conduct, they will have just as much effect on behavior as can be claimed for other realistic literature and no more. If children can learn through vicarious experience viewed in story and song, then the failure of Boy Blue, the baseless pride of Jack Horner, the carelessness of Polly Flinders,

Betty Blue, and Lucy Locket, the humane act of Johnny Stout, and the cheerful hospitality of Polly and Sukey may possibly help to establish desirable attitudes. That is about all that can be claimed for much more developed literature which shows cause and effect more forcefully than these little incidents can possibly do. It would be very unfortunate if these charming verses should be regarded by adults as chiefly valuable because of the "lessons" they are supposed to contain, and if in consequence they should be made the theme of "character education" talks.

The elucidation of Mother Goose has been accomplished only once in a very clever and delightful way, so far as the present writer knows. *Mother Goose for Grown Folks*,[1] as the title indicates, is intended for adults and not children. It was written wholly for entertainment and the best of Mrs. Whitney's verses are in the spirit of banter or light satire, though a few of them come perilously close to serious admonition. In the section called Introductory, the author pays this tribute to Mother Goose and at the same time sets forth her own intention.

> Somewhere in that uncertain "long ago,"
>   Whose dim and vague chronology is all
> That elfin tales or nursery fables know,
> Rose a rare spirit, keen, and quick, and quaint —
> Whom by the title, whether fact or feint,
>   Mythic or real, Mother Goose we call.
> Wisdom of babes — the nursery Shakespeare still —
> Cackles she ever with the same good-will:
> Uttering deep counsels in a foolish guise,
> That come as warnings, even to the wise;
>
> Full many a rare and subtile thing hath she,
> Undreamed of in the world's philosophy:
> Toss-balls for children hath she humbly rolled,
> That shining jewels secretly enfold;

---

[1] Whitney, Mrs. A. D. T., *Mother Goose for Grown Folks*. Houghton Mifflin Company, 1898.

Sibylline leaves she casteth on the air,
Twisted in fool's caps, blown unheeded by,
That, in their lines grotesque, albeit bear
Words of great truth, and signal prophecy;
And lurking satire, whose sharp lashes hit
A world of follies with their homely wit.

A taste of Mrs. Whitney's ingenious elaboration of a theme may be had in her handling of Little Miss Muffet:

Little Miss Muffet
Sat on a tuffet,
Eating curds and whey:
There came a black spider,
And sat down beside her
And frightened Miss Muffet away.

To all mortal blisses,
From comfits to kisses,
There's sure to be something by way of alloy;
Each new expectation
Brings fresh aggravation,
And a doubtful amalgam's the best of our joy.

You may sit on your tuffet;
Yes — cushion and stuff it;
And provide what you please if you don't fancy whey;
But before you can eat it,
There'll be — I repeat it —
Some sort of black spider to come in the way

CENSORED AND EXPURGATED

In view of this wealth of beauty, charm, gaiety, common sense and high wisdom, how paltry seem the platitudes and fervent warnings of those who see in this verse of infinite variety, nothing but faulty English, bad manners and wrong conduct. One marvels at the presumption of those who at frequent intervals attempt to censor these old treasures in the supposed interest of child morals, manners and habits of speech, who see in this folk literature nothing but coarseness and bad grammar. Still more self-assured are those who attempt definitely to substitute for Mother Goose their own fabricated rhymes having no literary merit and designed to teach facts concerning history, geography, grammar, health, dietetics, safety, prevention of cruelty to animals, cleanliness, and a dozen other subjects.

Perhaps even more objectionable are the numerous efforts to "improve" the old rhymes. Frequently these "weakened and sweetened" versions find their way into print and there are always a few advocates who speak for them through the press. Two examples will serve to show the method by which "objectionable" features are eliminated, and the peculiar results of such expurgation:

> I had a little pony,
> His name was Dapple Gray.
> I lent him to a lady
> To ride a mile away.
> She fed him, she petted him,
> She let him stop to graze.
> I'll always lend my pony now,
> For I like the lady's ways.

> Baa, baa, black sheep,
>   Have you any wool?
> Yes, kind master,
>   Three bags full;
> One for my master,
>   And one for my dame,
> And one for the little boy
>   Who works down the lane.

Thus does the tinker in ethics try to suppress everything negative, and encourage the spread of "sweetness and light."

Perhaps one example will suffice of Mother Goose forced to masquerade as a dispenser of information. In this instance the subject is dental hygiene:

> Little Bopeep has lost her teeth,
>   To brush them she neglected.
> Now hear her moan, and hear her groan!
>   Good teeth should be respected.

And this doggerel is supposed to be *sung!*

Fortunately, such bastard verses die almost at birth. They never find their way into general collections and they are commonly rejected by children (if they have a chance), by parents, teachers, and all who have any part in the selection and preservation of genuine literature.

SUGGESTIONS FOR FURTHER STUDY

In spite of the many excellent appreciations that have been written about Mother Goose and the large amount of critical and historical comment on the subject, there is still a rich mine open for small investigations. For such studies a full collection of the rhymes, preferably in an annotated edition, furnishes almost all material necessary. The only way to arrive at a real knowledge and appreciation of any piece of literature is to dig deeply into the material itself to learn its nature and to catch its true flavor. Having some definite question or questions in mind gives direction to this sort of study and tends to sharpen observation and ripen the judgment and taste.

Since Mother Goose is full of fun and frolic, it is advised that the following proposed topics for papers be taken not too seriously. A treatment best fitting these subjects will be only half-serious or mock-serious and will make copious use of quotations from the rhymes. A light touch is called for, and one should never labor a point, force a relationship, or exaggerate a claim. It is great fun, for example, to run through a collection and pick out all the modes of travel and transportation — quaint, miraculous, commonplace, mysterious; a strange ship, an open boat, a tub; tossed in a blanket higher than the moon; on the back of a gander; on cock horse, pony, or nag; with "heels nimble and fleet"; in a wheelbarrow. In writing such a paper the incidents will be lightly sketched, the situations made vivid, and the whole drawn together by means of the one common element — travel in strange company and by unusual modes. Any discerning person will see that the majority of the topics listed below lend themselves to a similar more or less jocular style.

Longer and more serious papers might be written on subjects marked with an asterisk. More extensive and sustained work also would be called for if several topics were combined. For instance, 29, 30, and 31 might be covered by "Living creatures in Mother Goose"; 33, 34, and 36 could be included in a study of "Mother Goose as true poet"; 17, 35, 37, and 38 might serve as heads under "Mother Goose as playwright"; 42, 43, and 44 could be merged under the topic "Mother Goose and the Censor."

TOPICS FOR PAPERS ON MOTHER GOOSE

1. Mother Goose, the child's book of nature.
2. Mother Goose, the child's book of adventure.
3. Mother Goose, a family portrait gallery.
*4. English life two hundred years ago as reflected in Mother Goose.
5. Village life in Mother Goose.
6. Geographic allusions.
7. A trip with Mother Goose.
8. Transportation in Mother Goose.
9. Mother Goose and the weather.
10. The psychology of Mother Goose.
11. The philosophy of Mother Goose.
12. School and curriculum in Mother Goose.
13. The Rotary roster of Mother Goose.
14. Tradesmen in Mother Goose.
15. Princes and potentates.
16. Class distinctions in Mother Goose.
17. Character types portrayed in Mother Goose.

18. Faults and foibles of Mother Goose characters.
19. Marketing with Mother Goose.
20. Finding the I.Q. of certain characters.
21. Gaffers and Gammers.
22. The course of true love, smooth and otherwise.
23. Mysteries in Mother Goose.
*24. Humor in Mother Goose
25. Childish woe in Mother Goose.
26. Moods, from grave to gay.
27. Animal antics in Mother Goose.
28. The musicians of Mother Goose.
29. Mother Goose's birds.
30. Mother Goose's cats.
31. Domestic animals in Mother Goose.
*32. Play and games in Mother Goose.
*33. True poetic beauty of certain verses.
*34. The lyric quality of certain selections.
*35. The dramatic quality of certain selections.
*36. Poetry patterns in Mother Goose.
*37. Plot in the longer narrative poems.
38. Dialogue in Mother Goose.
39. New dresses for an old friend.
*40 Characteristic features of the work of prominent illustrators of Mother Goose.
*41. Trace the connection of prominent authors, artists and musicians with Mother Goose.
42. Attempts at "improvement" of Mother Goose.
43. Mother Goose and the grammarians.
44. Mother Goose and the moralists.
*45. Mother Goose rhymes found in Reading texts.
*46. An annotated bibliography of about twenty editions of nursery rhymes.

The mock-serious intent of many of these topics will be seen at a glance and most of them should be handled with a light, playful touch in a spirit of jest. The more scholarly aspects, such as origin, history, literary associations, comparison with folk rhymes of other countries, etc., have been fully treated by competent specialists and their findings and opinions can easily be discovered by anyone interested in the subject. The ordinary student will probably get a much fuller appreciation of the richness of these old rhymes by following up one or more of these minor subjects by means of a very careful examination of the material itself. Few if any of the preceding topics can be treated successfully by a mere reading of what some editor or commentator has said about Mother Goose, for aside from historical questions and matters of literary style few writers have offered more than fragmentary bits of internal evidence concerning their nature and quality. The subject matter in particular has been greatly neglected even by most of the warmest admirers and defenders of Mother Goose.

In making these half-jesting studies, it is, of course, necessary to get into the spirit of the rhymes themselves, to sense their gusto and robust jollity, their vivid pictures of rural and village life, their freedom from cant, the tangential way in which they hint at both the serious and comic, their lively nonsense and their eminent commonsense. Their true flavor is perhaps best caught by quickly running through one or two of the best collections, following this with a more careful examination of the contents. In the second examination especially, it is a good plan to have in mind two or three specific things to look for. The reading then takes on something of the spirit of the chase or of a collector's pursuit of treasure and if a playful attitude of mind is maintained, here and there in gratifying number will appear choice examples of the particular feature, trait, character, or situation sought.

REFERENCES

Barnes, Walter. *The Children's Poets.* World, 1925.
    Chapter II, "Mother Goose."
Bett, Henry. *Nursery Rhymes and Tales: Their Origin and History.* Holt, 1924.

Shows the probable origin of different traditional stories and rhymes.

Cammaerts, Emile. *The Poetry of Nonsense*. Dutton, 1926.
Chapter II, "Nonsense and the Child."

Chubb, Percival. "The Child as a Literary Personage." *The Kindergarten Review*, September, 1909. Also in *Annual Report of the International Kindergarten Union*, 1909.
A spirited advocacy of oral presentation of folk verse and ample provision for children's active responses thereto.

Eckenstein, Lina. *Comparative Studies of Nursery Rhymes*. London, Duckworth.
Gives a brief history of early collections and many variations from different countries.

Field, Walter T. *A Guide to Literature for Children*. Ginn, 1928.
Chapter X. "Mother Goose." This book is a revised edition of the author's *Finger Posts to Children's Reading*.

Godfrey, Elizabeth. *English Children in the Olden Time*. London, 1907.
Chapter II, "Nursery Lore."

Halliwell, James O. *Nursery Rhymes of England*. London, 1842.
This old book, now out of print, has been one of the great sources for later collections.

Rankin, Jean S. "Mother Goose and Her English Grammar." *Educational Review*, September, 1926.
A clever and forceful reply to the hypercritical.

COLLECTIONS OF MOTHER GOOSE ESPECIALLY USEFUL TO STUDENTS

The Only True Mother Goose Melodies. Lothrop. Introduction by Rev. Edward Everett Hale.
This small book is an exact reproduction of the edition published in Boston in 1833 by Munroe and Francis. For many students, this will be the closest approach available to the original *Mother Goose*.

Mother Goose's Melodies; or, Songs for the Nursery. Edited by William A. Wheeler. Houghton.
A good full collection with valuable notes on origins. Old-fashioned style of book not attractive to children. Introduction gives in full the story of Mrs. Goose (or Ver-

goose) of Boston and her supposed authorship of "Mother
Goose Rhymes" — a claim never well supported by facts.

Mother Goose.   Illustrated by E. Boyd Smith.   Putnam.

> The foreword gives a brief history of Mother Goose
> rhymes.   The collection includes the fifty rhymes of the
> "original" Newbery edition as reproduced by Isaiah Thomas
> about 1785.   This book is pleasing to children also.

Nursery Rhyme Books

Children's List

Randolph Caldecott's Picture Book No. 2.   Warne.

Randolph Caldecott's The Hey Diddle Diddle Picture Book.
Warne.

> Each of these contains four of the longer nursery rhymes
> with many colored pictures full of humor, by a famous
> English artist.

This Little Pig's Picture Book.   Pictures and decorations by
Walter Crane.   Dodd.

> Contains "This Little Pig," "The Fairy Ship," and "King
> Luckieboy's Party."
> Another noted English artist produced this delightful
> book and many other picture books distinguished for rich-
> ness of color and beauty of design.

A Nursery Rhyme Picture Book No. 1.   Illustrated by L. Leslie
Brooke.   Warne.

A Nursery Rhyme Picture Book No. 2.   Same.

> Each of these books contains a number of well-chosen
> Mother Goose rhymes with pictures in color and black and
> white by an artist whose work is unsurpassed in its appeal
> to young children.

Ring O' Roses: A Nursery Rhyme Picture Book.   Illustrated by
L. Leslie Brooke.   Warne.

> Every small child should have an opportunity to enjoy
> this delightful book.   It contains about twenty favorite
> rhymes.

Mother Goose.   Illustrated by Kate Greenaway.   Warne.

> A small book containing about fifty of the shortest rhymes.
> A little gem of book-making, with typical Kate Greenaway
> pictures.   Very fine print.

The Real Mother Goose. Illustrated by Blanche Fisher Wright. Rand.

> Young children especially like this book with its many gayly colored pictures.

Mother Goose Picture Book. Berta and Elmer Hader. Coward.

> An exceptionally beautiful book, distinctive in style. It includes a good selection of singing games and lullabies set to old familiar tunes.

The Old Mother Goose Nursery Rhyme Book. Illustrated by Anne Anderson. Nelson.

> A beautiful and popular book. This collection may also be had in reduced size.

The Volland Mother Goose. Arranged and edited by Eulalie Osgood Grover. Illustrated by Frederick Richardson. Volland.

> Selections well made but not extensive. Large, attractive pictures.

Mother Goose. Illustrated by Jessie Willcox Smith. Dodd.

> A large collection with many full-page colored pictures in this artist's charming style which often lacks the humorous detail so much enjoyed by young children.

Mother Goose in Silhouettes. Pictures cut by Katharine G. Buffum. Houghton.

> A few familiar rhymes in a small book with pleasing scissors cuts.

Jack Horner's Pie. A Book of Nursery Rhymes. Selected and illustrated by Lois Lenski. Harper.

> An ample collection, well selected. Pictures and decorations are quite original. Older children will enjoy the unusual page arrangement.

The Chinese Mother Goose Rhymes. Translated by Isaac Taylor Headland. Revell.

> Contains a number of rhymes which any young child might enjoy, and others which older children interested in Chinese life will appreciate.

CHAPTER III

FAIRY FOLK AND FAIRY WAYS

Though none that breatheth livinge aier doth knowe,
Where is that happie land of Faerie.

SPENSER

THE question is often asked, "What is the difference between folk tales and fairy tales?" And when the answer is given that the term "folk tale" is the more general one and includes all traditional "fairy tales," another puzzle presents itself: why are so many nursery tales called fairy tales, although they contain no characters which embody the common conception of fairies?

The explanation of this confusing point lies partly in the gradual change in meaning of the term "fairy" as used both in nursery tales and in English literature. It was borrowed from the French language in which the word *faërie* or *féerie* was used to designate the mysterious abode or country of supernatural creatures called *fées*. Keightley offers the following translation from an old French romance *Lancelot du Lac*: "... all those [women] were called Fays (*fées*) who had to do with enchantments and charms, and knew the power and the virtue of words, stories, and of herbs; by which they were kept in youth and in beauty, and in great riches." [1] In England both the common people and writers soon began to apply the name "fairy" not only to the kingdom of the fairies, but to the mysterious inhabitants themselves. Chaucer uses the term in this double sense, and at a later time it became attached to a great variety of stories of happenings in the world of Faërie. Most modern collectors and translators of old

---

[1] Keightley, Thomas, *Tales and Popular Fiction*, Appendix. London, 1834.

tales of wonder and enchantment have continued to use the term in this loose and inclusive fashion, applying it to many stories in which there are no fairies.

Medieval romances furnished the beautiful fairy maidens and fairy queens, partly human but endowed with supernatural divination and power. They were fit brides for the true knights of chivalry and such tales are full of adventure and mystery. Greek mythology furnished another stream of magic and the nymphs and dryads of Homer and Ovid became fairies in English. They, too, were human in proportion and at times played a seemingly human part in the daily affairs of man.

Since the English belong to the great Northern or Teutonic family, their traditions are largely derived from the same original source as those of Scandinavia and Germany — that is, from Norse Mythology.

Scotland and Ireland have a still deeper vein of ancient Celtic lore which Jacobs [1] believes offers the oldest written record of pagan mystery and wonder. This vein yields conceptions of rich poetic quality as well as much that is dark and sinister. In these countries and in northern England, there persisted in the minds of the people the conviction that there actually was a race of dwarfish people who lived near-by in caves and hills, and who issued forth at night bent upon all kinds of mischief and plunder. They were greatly feared and in an attempt to placate them and to appear friendly to these impish marauders, the superstitious called them "good neighbors," or "the gentry," and spoke them well upon chance encounters.

R. B. Anderson [2] gives an illuminating analysis of the descent of elves, trolls, pixies, mermaids, giants, and other fairy creatures as the offspring of that great company of gods and near-gods which filled the stage of Norse myth.

---

[1] Jacobs, Joseph, Preface and notes of *Celtic Fairy Tales.*
[2] Anderson, R. B., *Norse Mythology*, chapter III.

When the Christian religion superseded that of Norsemen, the native supernatural figures became dwarfed, obscured, transformed, and to some extent humanized, until at last all that persisted were the stories of fairy creatures which inhabit woods, glens, caves, hills, streams and sea, and mingle more or less intimately with human beings. Anderson gives rather a minute description of different types of fairy folk according to the popular conception as regards their nature, dress, and special proclivities. It is interesting to trace these types in the folklore of Teutonic peoples and to find similar ones in Celtic tales.

It is clear that "the complex group of ideas identified with the little people is of more origins than one; in other words, that it is drawn partly from history and fact, and partly from the world of imagination and myth." [1]

While England is indebted to France, Germany, and Scandinavian countries for many of the complete and organized tales which have been long in circulation, no country is richer in brief picturesque tradition and clear-cut conception of the fairy world. Truly England was once "Al fulfiled of fayerye." This is revealed, not so much in prose literature, as in poetry from Chaucer to the present day — a period of nearly six centuries. Here one can find vivid, detailed, and beautiful descriptions of fairy realms, complete characterization of individual creatures of that world, and accounts of fairy traits, customs, and relations to human beings. All the whimsies, ways, and wiles of the "little folk" seem to be well known and understood by untutored people of all lands, but it is exceptional to have these fragments of belief incorporated at an early date in living verse of the highest order. For this reason, and because native prose folk tales are rare in England, an examination of records of folk belief as they appear in poetry is desirable.

[1] Rhys, John, *Celtic Folklore*, Preface, vol. I, p. xi. Oxford Press, 1901.

FAIRIES IN POETRY FROM CHAUCER TO HERRICK

In our search for the land of Faerie and for views of ancient fairy folk we find the first native literary reference in Chaucer (1340–1400), and we notice that even at that time the poet bewailed the departure of fairy folk from England. *The Tale of the Wife of Bath* [1] is really a fairy story, and after the prologue, the story begins with the following lines:

> In th' olde dayes of the King Arthour,
> Of which the Britons speken greet honour,
> Al was this land fulfiled of fayerye.
> The elf-queen, with hir joly companye,
> Daunced ful ofte in many a grene mede;
> This was the olde opinion, as I rede,
> I speak of many hundred yeres ago;
> But now can no man see none elves mo.

Continuing this passage, Chaucer explains why "we see none elves mo." It is because the holy brothers and begging friars have searched every land and every stream, and by their prayers and blessings have driven them out of halls, chambers, kitchens, dairies, and "this maketh that ther been no fayeryes."

Edmund Spenser (1552–1599) mingles classical mythology and native lore with a strong current of allegorical meaning, and it is difficult to extract the more local folk beliefs. There are witches, giants, dragons, poisonous serpents, elfin knights, and enchanted maidens in *The Faërie Queene*, but we find little of the simple, homely tradition which marks later fairy poetry. In two of his less important poems we find reference to popular conceptions regarding fairy folk. He tells us in his Introduction to "Mother Hubbard's Tale" that the poem was "long sithens composed in the raw conceipt of my youth." At the opening of this poem a sick man is being entertained

[1] Chaucer, Geoffrey, *The Canterbury Tales.*

by sympathetic friends who, to help him pass some weary hours, tell tales of various kinds. The assortment is thus described by the patient:

> Some of brave knights and their renowned squires;
> Some of faeries and their strange attires;
> And some of giaunts hard to be beleeved,
> That the delight thereof me much releeved.

The story recorded in the poem is told by Mother Hubbard, "a good old woman," and is neither about "giaunts" nor fairies. It is a fable or allegory concerning the evil conduct of two unscrupulous men disguised as a Fox and an Ape.

Spenser's hospitality to fairy creatures of all sorts and periods is seen in these lines from his poem called "Virgil's Gnat":

> Here also playing on the grassy grene,
> Wod gods, and satyres, and swift dryades
> With many fairies oft were dauncing seene.

But it was Shakespeare who caught, before it ebbed, the full tide of rich poetry, colorful superstition, playful imagination and serious belief which enveloped the simple folk, and which left not untouched the more educated of his day. Chaucer to the contrary, fairies were still abroad in the land. Shakespeare seemed to know to the last detail these fragments of popular tradition, and he wove them into the exquisite pictures and songs which have given the creatures of the land of Faërie the immortality which it is said they crave.

What were some of the most persistent fragments of belief which were current in Shakespeare's day?

The People of the Hills helped or hindered in every kind of work in house, farm and market; they were skilled in all the practical arts such as spinning, weaving and working in metals; the fairy shoemaker or leprechaun in particular is a picturesque and important figure, for shoes and boots seem to have been especially fraught with magic. They teased or prospered lovers, attended weddings and were to be taken account of at births; they helped govern the weather and brought storm or calm at sea; birds and animals were subject to them, and from plants, flowers, and trees they distilled essences of enchantment.

The elves appear to live in communities far underground, for, in several more or less fragmentary tales, the human visitor is taken down, down, hundreds of steps and through winding passages before reaching their sumptuous dwellings. Other fairy bands are supposed to live on highest mountain-tops, on promontories and on remote islands, while, of course, the depths of the ocean as well as caves of lakes and rivers are populated with nymphs and water sprites. From all such places of enchantment the little people come to touch the fringes of human life and sometimes to participate in important affairs. They seem, in these old traditions, to be always hovering around, ready to step forth at nightfall to indulge in their own frolic, to assist favored human beings, or to harass, frustrate and punish those who have offended. All sorts of fairies appear to frequent the forests and open meadows after dark and the idea was prevalent that all their sports and many of their merry pranks took place in these haunts.

Certain propensities of the fairy folk have a bearing on their relations to people. Lovely infants must be carefully guarded lest they be stolen from their cradles and carried away to fairyland or an exchange be made by which an elfin babe is left instead. Elves attempt, also, to secure beautiful human brides, and having succeeded, the victim can only be released through arduous endeavor on the part of husband and friends, often aided by her own patient effort and clever device. To be sure, flesh-and-blood swains show a like predilection for lovely and beguiling fairy maidens. Matings of the latter sort are apt to be temporary, are fraught with many dangers, and are usually terminated (to the sorrow of one party or both) by ignoring or defying some taboo.

Sometimes human beings yield to the importunity of a fairy messenger and go with him to fairyland to perform some urgent service. Sometimes it is a housewife who is moved by entreaty to attend a sick wife or prospective mother among the elves, and again, it is the goodman of the house who is prevailed upon to make the visit and to heal by laying-on of hands. Usually the route is obscure, the night dark, and the movement under escort through air or on horseback, so swift that the mortal visitor is never able to find the way again.

Fairies are possessed of untold wealth in the form of pure gold and coin of the realm, precious stones, gorgeous furnishings, fleet horses and other domestic animals. In Teutonic folklore they deal honestly, as a rule, in all matters except the one just mentioned, of stolen children and brides, but they are often made the victims of dishonest and avaricious human beings. They "doe lend money to any poore man or woman that hath need," but they expect to be repaid at the proper time and any borrower who attempts to defraud will be made to suffer severely in property loss. Quite commonly they employ some clever and innocent trick to detect the true spirit and intent of human neighbors. In paying, as they always do, for service rendered, they like to disguise the reward by filling apron or bag with what appears to mortal senses to be of little or no value; lumps of coal, bits of leather, trash, etc., which, if cast away, is discovered later to have been pure gold, but which, if kept even in part, shows its true quality and multiplies indefinitely. There are many whimsical tricks of this kind by which the lively invention of the fairies misleads the duller wit of ordinary human-kind. The dull-witted in fairyland are usually dwarfs, ogres, giants, and trolls, who rather readily fall prey to the wiles of scheming men or clever animals.

Taboos regarding fairy folk became established in oral tradition among all races and have a prominent place in story and poetry. Among these are the forbidden fairy ring within which mortal foot may not tread; the imposition of silence on a human guest in fairyland; prohibition against calling fairies by name; the requirement that food shall be placed at hand for the little elves who assist in housework and the equally important stipulation that clothing shall not be offered them; the danger incurred in slovenly housekeeping, slighting remarks aimed at fairies, and broken promises. While fairies may partake of human food, human beings must not eat fairy food upon pain of having to remain always in fairyland. Their behavior toward people is consistent and predictable in only a few particulars, however, and at different times the same fairy types may be beneficent, malevolent, or merely tricksy elves having their fun and frolic, sometimes to the advantage of human beings and sometimes to their discomfiture, just as whimsy dictates or some higher fairy power commands. Scholars in this field agree quite generally that the more sinister traits, those which link these figures to the powers of darkness, were much more common and persistent in Scotland, Ireland, and Wales than in southern England.

There are many treatises on folklore which discuss very fully common native beliefs regarding fairy creatures and their behavior, but for our purposes these are revealed in a more interesting way in the poetry, drama, and masques of the sixteenth and seventeenth centuries, and in the fireside tales which have come down to us.

Observe how Shakespeare weaves many of the popular conceits into the magic of *A Midsummer Night's Dream*, and *The Tempest*, and how he employs current superstition in the hilarious buffoonery of *The Merry Wives of Windsor*.

According to popular belief the visits of fairy folk to the homes and haunts of man were either casual and brief or with a deeper purpose and design. They were ruled by a king and queen and the royal pair were accompanied by a train of fairy subjects who entered into helpful schemes or annoying plots concerning human beings. They were supposed to appear between sunset and dawn although some were known to dare the light of day. Oberon, King of the Fairies in *A Midsummer Night's Dream*, shows that he did not fear the approach of day. Puck, who is a night spirit, warns him that dawn is near and Oberon replies:

> But we are spirits of another sort,
> I with the morning's love have oft made sport;
> And, like a forester, the groves may tread,
> Even till the eastern gate, all fiery-red,
> Opening on Neptune with fair blessed beams,
> Turns into yellow gold his salt-green streams.[1]

In the next scene, Puck again warns Oberon of approaching day:

> Fairy King, attend and mark;
> I do hear the morning lark.

And Oberon, submissive to the custom of his own fairy world, replies:

> Then, my queen, in silence sad
> Trip we after the night's shade;
> We the globe can compass soon,
> Swifter than the wandering moon.

The Tempest gives us Ariel, the most ethereal creature of the fairy world. Compared to him, even Oberon and Titania seem quite substantial. Ariel performs many

[1] *A Midsummer Night's Dream*, Act III, Scene 2.

typical fairy acts, but he seems a bodiless spirit. He is invisible to all except Prospero whom he is bound to serve, and the only tangible evidence of his presence (exclusive of the wonders he works) is a voice, or the eerie music he draws from pipe and tabor. Addressing him, Prospero uses the phrase, "thou, which art but air."

Summoned by Prospero, Ariel cries:

> I come
> To answer thy best pleasure, be't to fly,
> To swim, to dive into the fire, to ride
> On the curl'd clouds.

His master calls him "my dainty Ariel"; "my delicate Ariel"; "my tricksy spirit." In one place Ariel says, "I will... do my spriting gently," but as a tricksy spirit, he plays at times a part much like that of Puck or Hobgoblin and employs some very "Puckish" measures which are far from gentle, against his master's enemies. They are pinched, stung, made to stumble upon hedgehogs, frightened "with urchin shows," led "through tooth'd briers, sharp furzes, pricking goss," and, at last, fooled by a will-o'-the-wisp, are plunged into foul pools and sunk in mire.

Prospero, about to abjure all magic and return to his rightful place as Duke of Milan, apostrophizes the friendly spirits of his island in the familiar and beautiful lines which serve better than any definition to convey some of the most significant of the current notions about fairies.

> Ye elves of hills, brooks, standing lakes, and groves:
> And ye, that on the sands with printless foot
> Do chase the ebbing Neptune, and do fly him,
> When he comes back; you demi-puppets, that
> By moonshine do the green-sour ringlets make,
> Whereof the ewe not bites; and you, whose pastime
> Is to make midnight mushrooms; that rejoice
> To hear the solemn curfew; by whose aid
> (Weak masters though ye be) I have bedimm'd

> The noontide sun, call'd forth the mutinous winds,
> And 'twixt the green sea and azur'd vault
> Set roaring war: [1]

Because of the bold delineation and the exaggeration used in the tricking of Falstaff by mock-fairies in *Merry Wives of Windsor*, we get an excellent idea of notions which prevailed in rural England in the sixteenth century. There are certain evil traits in human beings which fairies are supposed to despise and to punish. Chief among these are lewdness, wantonness, and sluttery. Falstaff therefore "corrupt, corrupt, and tainted in desire" is a fit subject for fairy discipline. The plotters devise a hoax by which the "unclean knight" is to be mocked and exposed by a troop of "fairies" represented by Mistress Page's daughter Anne as fairy queen, her young son, and other children. They are to be masked and dressed,

> Like urchins, ouphes, and fairies, green and white,
> With rounds of waxen tapers on their heads,
> And rattles in their hands. [2]

The typical mode of punishment for errant human-kind is to pinch them black and blue and sometimes to burn them. The children are coached accordingly. Out of the darkness of Windsor Forest they are to rush "with some diffused song," encircle Falstaff, and "pinch him sound, and burn him with tapers." All of which is very thoroughly carried out by the masquerading boys and girls, aided by the Welsh parson, Sir Hugh Evans, as Jack-a-napes or Hobgoblin.

Even in this bold comedy, however, there is something more than rough sport, for there occur some lovely passages in which Anne Page as Fairy Queen pretends to instruct her little troop on the eve of action:

[1] *The Tempest*, Act V, Scene 1.
[2] *The Merry Wives of Windsor*, Act IV, Scene 4.

And nightly, meadow fairies, look, you sing,
Like to the Garter's Compass, in a ring:
The expressure that it bears, green let it be,
More fertile fresh than all the field to see.[1]

Other writers of the period employ the prevalent notion that fairies help mortals in household tasks where their aid is deserved, but under very rigid terms. According to Ben Jonson, even the fairy queen acted in this capacity.

QUEEN MAB

This is Mab, the mistress Fairy,
That doth nightly rob the dairy,
And can hurt or help the churning
(as she please) without discerning.
She that pinches country wenches,
If they do not clean their benches,
And with sharper nails remembers
When they rake not up the embers,
But, if so they chance to feast her
In a shoe she drops a tester.[2]

THE FAIRIES

If ye will with Mab find grace,
Set each platter in his place;
Rake the fire up, and get
Water in, ere sun be set.
Wash your pails, and cleanse your dairies;
Sluts are loathsome to the fairies;
Sweep your house, who doth not so,
Mab shall pinch her by the toe.[3]

Some of the supernatural creatures of English tradition, were of a rough, sturdy type such as peasant minds might create out of notions of evil spirits mixed with prevalent legends regarding a dwarfish neighbor race reputed to live in caves and hills. Robin Goodfellow (later called Puck) and Hobgoblin belong to this class. Robin is one of the most prominent characters in early English tradition and

[1] Act V, Scene 5.   [2] Sixpence.   [3] Robert Herrick, *Hesperides*.

plays his rôle in many tales found in literary antiquities. Shakespeare was, of course, familiar with these old tales and fragments, and we find a striking correspondence between his delineation of "that shrewd and knavish sprite" and the accounts in prose and verse which appear in old songs and romances.

Hazlitt gives in full a reprint of a black-letter tract of great rarity called *Robin Goodfellow; his mad pranks, and merry jests, full of honest mirth, and is a fit medicine for melancholy.*[1] It was published in London in 1628, but Hazlitt is of the opinion that it was a much older production and was probably known to Shakespeare. It is in prose interspersed with Robin's songs in which the braggart tells of his wanton tricks and his prowess in many encounters. Robin's musician is Tom Thumb "for hee had an excellent bag-pipe made of a wren's quill and the skin of a Greenland mouse."

> This little fellow, called Tom Thumb,
> That is no bigger than a plumb,
> He is the porter of our gate,
> For he doth let all in thereat.

Puck gives a merry account of himself as a "madcap sprite" in an old ballad, "The Pranks of Puck."[2]

> From Oberon, in fairy land,
>   The King of ghosts and shadows there,
> Mad Robin I, at his command,
>   Am sent to view the night-sports here.
>   What revel rout
>   Is kept about,
>   In every corner where I go,
>   I will o'ersee,
>   And merry be,
>   And make good sport, with ho, ho, ho!

---

[1] Hazlitt, William Carew, *Fairy Tales, Legends and Romances illustrating Shakespeare and Other Early English Writers*, pp. 173–206. London 1875.

[2] Hazlitt, *op. cit.*, p. 418. *The Percy Reliques*, Everyman's edition, volume 2, p. 313.

He tells of his power to transform himself in order to mislead "wanderers... that from their night sport do trudge home:"

> Sometimes I meet them like a man,
>   Sometimes, an ox, sometimes, a hound;
> And to a horse I turn me can,
>   To trip and trot about them round;
>   But if, to ride,
>   My back they stride,
> More swift than wind away I go;
>   O'er hedge and lands,
>   Through pools and ponds,
> I whinny laughing, ho, ho, ho!

Shakespeare, too, makes very vivid Puck's power of instant and complete transformation.

> *Puck.* I'll follow you, I'll lead you about a round,
> Through bog, through bush, through brake, through brier:
> Sometime a horse I'll be, — sometime a hound,
> A hog, a headless bear, sometime a fire,
> And neigh, and bark, and grunt, and roar, and burn,
> Like horse, hound, hog, bear, fire, at every turn. [1]

Puck acknowledges his more malignant nature when he says, "I am feared in field and town," and his mischievous, elfish proclivities in the lines,

> And those things do best please me,
> That befall preposterously.

The many-sided Robin resembles in some ways such household spirits as Lob-Lye-by-the-Fire, Lar, and the ugly, pathetic Aiken-drum in the Scotch ballad "The Brownie of Blednoch." [2] The "drudging goblin" of Milton's "L'Allegro" also belongs to this group of voluntary servants who appear at night, do all kinds of menial work in house and field and ask no pay except a little food,

---

[1] *A Midsummer Night's Dream*, Act III, Scene 1.
[2] Nicholson, William, in *The Book of Fairy Poetry*, Dora Owen, p. 35. Longmans.

white bread and cream, cheese, or porridge. Taboos were mentioned above and they come out strongly in tales of the household drudge. Such spirits are deeply offended if clothing is offered them. They seem to accept the articles but leave the house never to return, displaying anger or distress at the gift.

Robin Goodfellow is thus offended:

> Because thou lay'st me himpen, hampen,
> I will neither bolt nor stampen:
> 'Tis not your garments, new or old,
> That Robin loves: I feel no cold,
> Had you left me milk or cream,
> You should have had a pleasing dream:
> Because you left no drop or crumb,
> Robin never more will come. [1]

Aiken-drum is the true boggart or rough, uncouth house servant of north England and Scotland. In the ballad mentioned above, he presents himself, a fearsome sight, at a farmhouse and asks to be allowed to work. He accounts for himself thus:

> I lived in a lan' where we saw nae sky,
> I dwelt in a spot where a burn rins na by;
> But I'se dwall now wi' you if ye like to try
> Hae ye wark for Aiken-drum?

He states his modest terms:

> I'se seek nae guids, gear, bond, nor mark;
> I use nae beddin', shoon, nor sark;
> But a cogfu' o' brose [2] 'tween the light an' the dark,
> Is the wage o' Aiken-drum.

Help is greatly needed in house and field so the "canny auld wife" engages him. All goes well and he accomplishes wonders until a tidy young wife discarding cast-off garments

---

[1] Hazlitt, *op. cit.*, p. 186.   [2] Porridge.

> Laid a mouldy pair o' her ain man's breeks
> By the brose o' Aiken-drum.

Her act runs counter to the universal requirement of such spirits and the mysterious drudge departs never to return.

> For frae that day forth he was nae mair seen,
> An' sair missed was Aiken-drum.

The house-spirit, Lob-Lye-by-the-Fire, or Lar, could enter a house through the keyhole and then become full size again, for it is said that he liked to stretch his shaggy length across the hearth. There were traditional ways of propitiating such spirits. For some reason, offerings of parsley, garlic, and onions were thought to be particularly acceptable. The poem "To Lar" by Robert Herrick (1591–1674) refers no doubt to his departure from the vicarage of Dean Prior, Devonshire. He was suspected of being disloyal to the Government and in 1648 he was forced to give up the Dean Prior living.

To Lar

> No more shall I, since I am driven hence,
> Devote to thee my grains of frankincense;
> No more shall I from mantle-trees hang down,
> To honour thee, my parsley crown;
> No more shall I (I fear me) to thee bring
> My chives of garlic for an offering;
> No more shall I from henceforth hear a choir
> Of merry crickets by my country fire.
> Go where I will, thou lucky Lar stay here,
> Warm by a glitt'ring chimney all the year.[1]

NOTIONS REGARDING THE SIZE OF FAIRIES

We have seen that the fairy ladies of medieval romance were thought of as enchantresses of normal human proportions, but some of the old tales suggest that the fairies

- *Hesperides*, volume I.

had the appearance of very small human beings. Hazlitt gives extracts from a French romance [1] in which Oberon, the Fairy King, is described as three feet tall, crooked-shouldered, and beautiful of countenance. A company of knights passing through his kingdom have reason to fear him, but one of them says, "I never saw in my life so faire a creature in the visage.... I think hee be not past the age of five yeares." Farther on in the story Oberon accounts for his small stature, saying that a spiteful fairy "when I was borne gave me a gift, the which was, that when I should passe three years of age, I should grow no more, but thus as you see mee nowe." Diminutive stature is not typical of the fairies of common tradition nor of literature up to the time of Shakespeare. Those spirits which could slip at will through cracks and keyholes did so as a feat of magic and not by reason of small proportions.

Extensive research by various scholars has established the fact that until the production of Shakespeare's *A Midsummer Night's Dream*, fairies had not been popularly conceived of as "airy toys," diminutive winged creatures, engaged in dainty, delicate occupations. The most recent study of this question and a very exhaustive one is Latham's *The Elizabethan Fairies*.[2] This book is fully documented and gives a very complete record of ancient beliefs sharply revolutionized, so far as literature was concerned, by the instant and widespread popularity of Shakespeare's imaginative conception of fairies and the fairy world.

Like a wizard himself, Shakespeare with his own magic created the little "atomies" who were soon to supersede

[1] Hazlitt, *op. cit.*, p. 139. *Huon of Bordeaux.* Translated into English about 1540.

[2] Latham, Minor White, *The Elizabethan Fairies.* Columbia University Press, New York, 1930.

all their older, coarser kindred. Titania calls them by name, — "Peaseblossom! Cobweb! Moth! and Mustardseed!" They are the very essence of moonlit meadows and gardens. And what are they to do?

> *Titania.* Come, now a roundel and a fairy song;
> Then for the third part of a minute, hence;
> Some to kill cankers in the musk-rose buds;
> Some war with rear-mice for their leathern wings,
> To make my small elves coats; and some keep back
> The clamorous owl, that nightly hoots and wonders
> At our quaint spirits. Sing me now asleep;
> Then to your offices, and let me rest.

Titania (to Bottom):

> I'll give thee fairies to attend on thee,
> And they shall fetch thee jewels from the deep,
> And sing while thou on pressed flowers dost sleep.

Light as thistledown, they sing and dance and play. No coarse labor or impish pranks, no dark intrigue for these dainty apparitions.

Oberon (to the fairy train):

> Though the house give glimmering light,
>   By the dead and drowsy fire;
> Every elf, and fairy sprite,
>   Hop as light as bird from brier;
> And this ditty, after me
> Sing, and dance it trippingly.

Still more delicately, if possible, Shakespeare etches his picture of Queen Mab, the dream-maker and the fairies' midwife. In her royal equipage she appears as if viewed in one of those incredibly small engravings which can be seen clearly only with a reading-glass or microscope.

> She is the fairies' midwife; and she comes
> In shape no bigger than an agate-stone
> On the forefinger of an alderman,
> Drawn with a team of little atomies
> Athwart men's noses as they lie asleep: [1]

---

[1] *Romeo and Juliet*, Act I, Scene 4.

Her chariot is an empty hazel-nut, her waggoner a small, gray-coated gnat, the harness is made of spider's web and moonbeams.

Other poets of the period give us charming pictures of fairies and their occupations. In Percy's *Reliques* we find that lovely poem "The Fairy Queen." It sometimes bears the title "Queen Mab's Invitation." The exact date of the first printing is not known, but both Percy and Hazlitt assign it to the seventeenth century. There are eight stanzas of which the first and last especially are in the key of Shakespeare's fairy songs.

> Come, follow, follow me,
> Ye fairy elves that be
> Light-tripping o'er the green,
> Come follow Mab, your queen:
> Hand in hand, we dance around,
> For this place is fairy ground.
>
> O'er tops of dewy grass
> So nimbly do we pass,
> The young and tender stalk
> Ne'er bends as we do walk;
> Yet in the morning may be seen
> Where we the night before have been.[1]

Because such a large group of poets and playwrights within a comparatively short period exhibited a remarkable preoccupation with fairy subjects, a brief chronological table may be of use to a student of the subject:

Edmund Spenser	1552?–1599
John Lyly	1554?–1606
Michael Drayton	1563 –1631
William Shakespeare	1564 –1616
Ben Jonson	1573?–1637
Robert Herrick	1591 –1674

All these writers except Spenser appear to have followed the line so happily begun by Shakespeare. The great

[1] *The Percy Reliques*, volume II, p. 317. Hazlitt, *op. cit.*, p. 318.

popularity of Masques at the Court of Elizabeth and James I and under other princely patronage augmented this interest, for the poetic and beautiful aspects of fairies formed a fitting subject for pageantry. Guests of high rank often participated in these Masques and sometimes young boys and girls played suitable parts. Dancing and singing were conspicuous features and some of our loveliest fairy songs were written for such entertainments. Jonson and Lyly in particular produced many such plays. Other poets of the period who did not produce masques in full, wrote in a vein which would have fitted perfectly into such performances.

Was it Shakespeare's verbal portrait of Queen Mab in its charming completeness which let loose such a crowd of wee folk all described with the greatest minuteness and outfitted to the last tiny article of clothing, equipage, and table service? Drayton and Herrick carry this fine-spun, descriptive verse further than any of the others. The former was Shakespeare's neighbor in Warwickshire and his friend. They were born, as noted above, only one year apart. A short selection from Drayton's long poem "Nymphidia" [1] will give some idea of his elaborate, sophisticated, but pleasing style. Henry Morley calls this poem "a delightful fairy mock-heroic." It tells of the Lilliputian struggle between Pigwiggan, a fairy knight devoted to Queen Mab, and the jealous husband, Oberon. The fairy palace is described:

> This palace standeth in the air,
> By necromancy placed there,
> That it no tempests need to fear,
>   Which way soe'er it blow it:
> And somewhat southward tow'rd the noon,
> Whence lies a way up to the moon,
> And thence the Faëry can as soon
>   Pass to the earth below it.

---

[1] Drayton, Michael, *The Barons' Wars, Nymphidia, and Other Poems.* London, 1887.

Mab rides forth to meet her knight:

> Four nimble gnats the horses were,
> Their harnesses of gossamer,
> Fly Cranion, her charioteer
>   Upon the coach-box getting.
> Her chariot of a snail's fine shell,
> Which for the colors did excell;
> The fair queen Mab becoming well
>   So lively was the limning:
> The seat, the soft wool of the bee,
> The cover (gallantly to see)
> The wing of a py'd butterfly:
>   I trow 'twas simple trimming.

At last Oberon and Pigwiggan meet in single combat. There is a delightful description of the knight's accouterment which runs through four stanzas in which we learn that his shield is a cockle shell; his spear, a bent (blade of grass) "well near of two inches long"; his coat of mail of a fish's scale; his rapier, a hornet's sting; his helmet, "a beetle's head, most horrible and full of dread"; his mount, a mettlesome ear-wig.

Thus we get an idea of the irreducible size of these wee manikins from their actions rather than from attempted measurement. A group of Mab's attendants hide in the shell of a hazel nut and are assured that there is ample space — "For room ye need not wrestle."

Herrick's fairy poetry follows a similar vein. With amazing ingenuity of invention amounting at times to a sheer *tour de force*, he spreads before us a pygmy world with its palace, feast, and temple, and all the while he is laughing at his own wee puppets and their pretensions.

The fairies created by these poets are very far removed from the old ones of kitchen, barn, and byre. A sophisticated fay in a masque by Ben Jonson refers disparagingly to

> the coarse and country Faërie,
> that doth haunt the hearth or dairy.

And Pigwiggan has advanced so far in command of human arts that he is able to write a letter to his love.

> And to the queen a letter writes,
> Which he most curiously indites.

FAIRY FOLK IN TRADITIONAL TALES

We have seen that fairy-folk have played a prominent part in early English poetry, and that they are ubiquitous in the small incidents and anecdotes gathered by antiquarians — bits of narrative about the service of human midwives to fairies, stolen brides and babes, mysterious noises in empty houses, disordered rooms showing revelry and mad pranks of elfin visitors, misguided travelers, the sound of elfin horns and glimpses of dancing figures. But when it comes to the fully developed tale with a good plot and coherent action, we are surprised and puzzled to find that these interesting figures play an important part in relatively few of them.

The rarity of real fairy tales in England where imagination had created so many vivid and charming figures is difficult to explain. A reason often assigned is that imported tales, especially from France, crowded the native stories out. This does not seem an adequate and satisfactory explanation. French fairy tales were but little known before 1729, the date of the first publication of Perrault's tales in English. While it appears that certain of these tales became more popular than similar ones of English origin, they could scarcely have choked out any strong growth of native literature of the same sort so close upon the time when publishers began to produce many small books for children. Miss Barry's [1] explanation seems more satisfactory. While she believes that imported stories did supersede similar native ones, she offers an additional reason for the apparent neglect which may be

[1] Barry, Florence V., *A Century of Children's Books*, chapter I.

summarized as follows: Something in the English temper caused a leaning toward certain "Histories" which were really Romances and fanciful tales of high adventure; extravagant accounts of travel became popular; such tales greatly condensed were soon available to young and old in the form of chap-books; the stories "touched the imagination like ballads and fairy tales"; "these romances are, indeed, full of the common stuff of folklore." Into these age-old romances which really know no race or nationality, the English infused much of their own tradition regarding supernatural forces, creatures, and events.

The orderly collecting and printing of folk tales began relatively late in England and proceeded after many alien streams had obscured the native one. Critics are agreed, however, that there are very few genuine English folk tales as distinguished from those of Scotland and Ireland. A large part of the more popular stories now available in the English language are from France, Germany, and Scandinavian countries. Today, through slow infiltration from various races and peoples as well as from extensive introduction of published translations, the Western European world possesses in common a large body of stories. After a story has been accepted and gradually adopted into a national literature, its exact origin and evolution is of interest chiefly to students of literary antiquities or anthropology. In our search, therefore, for fairies and elves, we shall use, when it suits our purpose, any popular folk tale long current in the English language and harmonious with that culture.

Six stories will be sketched which show characters of this kind in leading or important parts and involve typical incidents of fairy lore.

THE ELVES AND THE SHOEMAKER

Sources:
> Grimm: *Household Stories.* Translated by Lucy Crane.
> *Household Tales.* Everyman's Edition.
> *Tales of Laughter.* Edited by Kate Douglas Wiggin and
> Nora Archibald Smith.

This well-known story shows the elves as beneficent spirits of house and countryside, performing acts very similar to those so often mentioned in fragmentary folk-lore, homely services for humble people toward whom they have a kindly feeling. They slip into the poor shoemaker's house at night and accomplish the task of making shoes, unseen and unheard. They have the skill and the amiable disposition of leprechauns or fairy shoemakers. They are discovered at last by the man and his wife. The grateful couple decide the little naked men should have a complete outfit of clothes including wee shoes, and accordingly these outfits are furnished. The reputed attitude of elves to the act of supplying them with clothes is one of active resentment. In this story, however, as it appears in favorite versions, they accept the little garments with delight, put them on, caper about, and depart never to return. They bear a strong family likeness to Robin Goodfellow with his

> Hemton, hamten,
> Here will I never more tread nor stampen!

THE BOGEY-BEAST

Source: English Fairy Tales. Retold by Flora Annie Steel.

Primitive peoples believed in bogies and hobgoblins and all sorts of fearsome creatures. Knowing this, one might expect the bogey of this story to be a terrifying creature. Instead, the tale is one of good-humor and startling but amusing surprise. An old woman finds what she thinks is a pot of gold, and as she toils along it changes its form repeatedly and always to a poorer or meaner object. At last it changes into a huge bogey-beast and goes cavorting off and out of sight. No child would fear this strange creature. The old woman is quite elated at having seen a bogey beast "all to myself," and exclaims, "My goodness! I do feel that uplifted — that GRAND."

THE HILLMAN AND THE HOUSEWIFE

Sources:
   Old-Fashioned Fairy Tales. Juliana Horatio Ewing.
   The Atlantic Treasury of Childhood Stories. Selected and edited by Mary Hutchinson Hodgkins.

On the occasion of a wedding, the little Hill People need an extra saucepan and one of their number goes to a certain housewife to borrow one. She knows that she must show herself friendly, but being rather "close" directs her maid to give the visitor a leaky pan, for she expects the skillful tinkers will mend it free of cost. In due time the saucepan is returned neatly mended, but when they attempt to heat the children's milk for supper, it burns and is ruined. "*And that's twopence,*" a voice cries from the chimney. Each time they try to cook in this pan, the food burns and the wee voice calls out, "*And that's fourpence,*" "*And that's sixpence.*" This last penalty seems to satisfy their sense of justice, for the little fellow calls out as he shows himself and goes laughing through the door, "You did not save the tinkering after all, Mother!" But from that time on the saucepan was all right.

CHILDE ROWLAND

Source: English Fairy Tales. Joseph Jacobs.

There are several facts and features concerning the story of Childe Rowland which indicate that it is a very old English tale. It has the tone of mystery, heroism, and earnestness which seems to characterize the native belief, and there are numerous references to it in later literature as we shall see.

Burd Ellen offends the elfin folk by running around a church "widershins" — the opposite way to the sun. For breaking this taboo, she is seized and carried away to elf-land; her three brothers one after another solemnly undertake to find and rescue her; the two eldest in turn seek counsel of the magician Merlin, and learn that she has been carried away by the Elf King to his Dark Tower; they are given exact directions regarding her release, but each in turn fails in some particular to observe them; the youngest brother then sets forth and succeeds in rescuing his sister. The story embodies many familiar traditions. Elfland is in a round green hill the sides of which are terraced rings; the interior presents a magnificent appearance; no mortal must touch food while in this fairy abode; the two older brothers are unable to resist the tempting food offered, are bewitched, and are found by the youngest in a deep sleep; Rowland fights the Elf King using "his father's good brand that never struck in vain," and conquers; the Elf King is forced to release Burd Ellen and restore the brothers and break the spell by methods of enchantment.

Jacobs points out that the story was current in England in Shakespeare's time. It is clearly referred to in *King Lear* (Act III, Scene 4), where Edgar in the mad scene suddenly burst forth with

> Childe Rowland to the Dark Tower came,
> His words were still "Fie, fah, and fum,
> I smell the blood of a British man."

In this story the King of Elfland rushes into the hall of the Dark Tower where Rowland has discovered his sister and tries to frighten the hero with his cry of "Fee, fi, fo, fum."

Milton bases his *Masque of Comus* on this tale, and Jacobs is of the opinion that he was familiar with a very old form which was doubtless a combination of verse and prose narrative.

There is both nobility and beauty in this story.

CINDERELLA

Sources of the Perrault version:
The Blue Fairy Book. Edited by Andrew Lang.
The Book of Elves and Fairies. Compiled and edited by Frances Jenkins Olcott.
Old-Time Stories. Charles Perrault. Translated from the French by A. E. Johnson.

Charles Perrault is the creator, in permanent literature, of the fairy godmother. In this old French tale she steps forth in full character — competent, in command of the situation, having dominion over the lower creatures, possessing the magic wand and able to produce, by its touch, gilded coach, prancing horses, coachman, footmen in gorgeous livery, and lovely ball costumes including rich jewels and "the prettiest glass slippers in the world." She makes two or three other appearances in the story, once when she listens to Cinderella's eager account of the first ball (a very sympathetic touch) and again after the girl has successfully tried on the slipper. ("Thereupon, in came her godmother.") Presumably, she had appeared previously to prepare Cinderella for the second ball. Her entrances are timely, but they seem almost as casual as if she were a member of the family. This quality makes her seem "real" and almost human. A less tangible, supernatural aspect, is her pervasive influence as seen in her injunction regarding the midnight hour and the mysterious and immediate result of the girl's forgetfulness.

Artists have portrayed this first fairy godmother according to a great many different conceptions of her illusive nature. Sometimes she is made to appear like a little old-fashioned chimney-corner grandmother; sometimes as a dwarfed, wrinkled, but kindly old lady in a high pointed cap; and, again, she is seen as a young fairy queen, tall and beautiful.

The fairy godmother appears much less frequently in old tales than one might expect. She is not easy to find.

THE HERD BOY

Sources:
> *In the Reign of King Oberon.* Everyman's Library. Edited by Ernest Rhys.
> *Magic Casements.* Edited by Kate Douglas Wiggin and Nora Archibald Smith.

This delightful story should be better known than it is. It covers a period of hardship and loneliness in the life of a sturdy and engaging young cowherd and relates how three good fairies helped the boy to render knightly service and to win the princess. Typical elfin treasures play a prominent part in the plot. While tending his cows, the lad finds in turn on three consecutive days "a pair of very, very small shoes of the whitest and clearest glass"; "a very, very little red cap set round with small golden bells"; and, "a little bell... which gave forth so sweet a sound that all the cattle came running together." Each of these fascinating objects is found on a shady hillside at some point where the grass is beaten down in a ring which he rightly judges to be an elfin ring. Each article is, in turn, yielded by the boy to its owner who comes in anxious search and entreats the finder to restore possession. The shoes are claimed by an elfin boy, the cap by an elf maiden, and the remarkable bell by the elf king. Giving up the objects is an act of sacrifice on the part of the unhappy lad, for he has reason to think that they would make his hard life a little easier. His relations with the fairies are of that straightforward sort which the old fragments of tradition seem to dictate and reward.

The remainder of the story tells in not too extended fashion how he escaped from his hard lot, and with what clever ruse and magic instrument the fairies furnished, at just the right moment, the help which he needed in order to rescue and win the captive princess.

THE FAIRIES' BANISHMENT AND VOLUNTARY EXILE

At intervals down the centuries, literary writers tell us that there are no more fairies in England and explain in picturesque and humorous fashion why they vanished. They seem to hold opposing views. Chaucer, as we have seen, declared the fact in the fourteenth century and attributed the loss to overzealous and annoying friars. Bishop Corbet (Richard Corbet, 1582–1635) expresses a contrary view in his charming poem, "The Fairies' Farewell," [1] indicating that they did not like the sober, repressive ways of the Protestants. This poem sometimes appears under the title "Farewell, Rewards and Fairies." We give here two stanzas:

> "Farewell, rewards and fairies!"
>   Good housewives now may say,
> For now foul sluts in dairies
>   Do fare as well as they.
> And though they sweep their hearths no less
>   Than maids were wont to do,
> Yet who of late, for cleanliness,
>   Finds sixpence in her shoe?
>
> Witness those rings and roundelays
>   Of theirs, which yet remain
> Were footed in Queen Mary's days
>   On many a grassy plain;
> But since of late, Elizabeth
>   And later, James came in,
> They never danced on any heath
>   As when the time hath been.

---

[1] Percy, *op. cit.*, vol. II, p. 319. Owen, Dora, *op. cit.*, p. 145. Stevenson, Burton E., compiler, *Home Book of Verse*, p. 244.

Out of the dilemma in which the little creatures find themselves, due to warring factions, Herrick invents an ingenious and amusing way of escape. In "The Temple," he turns them into saints, gives them individual names of fairy sainthood, builds a temple with remarkable ecclesiastical furnishings and adornment, and discovers for them comfortable niches in a mixed religion. And who could better do this than the bachelor clergyman and the fairies' poet-laureate?

> Now, this the fairies would have known,
> Theirs is a mixed religion;
> And some have heard the elves it call
> Part pagan, part papistical.
> If unto me all tongues were granted,
> I could not speak the saints here painted.
> Saint Tit, Saint Nit, Saint Is, Saint Itis,
> Who 'gainst Mab's state placed here right is;
> Saint Will o' th' Wisp, of no great bigness,
> But *alias* called here *Fatuus ignis*;
> Saint Frip, Saint Trip, Saint Fill, Saint Fillie,
> Neither those other saint-ships will I
> Here go about for to recite
> Their number, almost infinite.[1]

The latest historian of the exodus of the Little Folk is Rudyard Kipling. Mr. Kipling allows Puck to be spokesman and he rehearses the tale of the flight of his fellows into France. In *Puck of Pook's Hill* [2] two children, Dan and Una, are acting part of *A Midsummer Night's Dream* on Midsummer Eve when the bushes part and Puck appears — Puck, "the oldest Old Thing in England." He tells them who he is and says that all the other People of the Hill have disappeared, dropping off "one by one through the centuries" — pixies, nixies, giants, trolls, wood-spirits, leprechauns — driven out, as we learn in the

---

[1] Herrick, Robert, *Hesperides*, volume I. Hazlitt, *op. cit.*, p. 305.
[2] Kipling, Rudyard, *Puck of Pook's Hill*, chapters I and IX.

chapter called "Dymchurch Flit," because they could not
endure the disturbances in the country, the hatred and the
cruel practices between opposing parties during the Re-
formation. All the fairies except Puck gathered at last in
the marshland near Canterbury, and in a boat provided
by an old marsh woman, they set sail for France where
the "Images" had not been torn down, and away from
the sound of Canterbury bells. But Puck, or Robin, is a
hardier type and remains behind when the others crowd into
the boat. He professes quite a contempt for the modern
conception of fairies; in fact, he does not like the name
"fairy" at all. He calls them "little buzzflies with butterfly
wings and gauze petticoats" and declares that the original
People of the Hills were not of the "painty-winged, wand-
waving" sort.

A whimsical, melodious, and charming treatment of this
theme is found in "The Fairies' Passage," [1] by an Irish
poet, James C. Mangan (1803–1849). The native fairies
complain that civilization with its noise and din is encroach-
ing upon them, no mysteries remain among the people, and
so two hundred of the wee creatures with babies, bags and
baggage, implore a ferryman to ferry them over the River
Lee — which he does, with amazing results. In their plea,
a spokesman says:

> Oh, we have dwelt over-long in this land;
> The people get cross, and are growing so knowing, too!
>   Nothing at all but they now understand;
>
> We are daily vanishing under the thunder
>   Of some huge engine or iron wonder;
> That iron, oh! — it has entered our souls!

And at last, school teachers are accused of causing the
fairies' departure. Lang in the Preface to *The Yellow
Fairy Book* says, "and in England they have been frightened away by smoke and schoolmasters."

[1] Olcott, Frances Jenkins, *The Book of Elves and Fairies*, p. 413.

Later chapters will attempt to show how modern writers are re-creating much of the beauty, mystery, and inherent truth of fairy-lore in story and poetry.

SUGGESTED PROBLEMS AND TOPICS FOR FURTHER STUDY

1. Make a compilation of passages from folk tales descriptive of appearance and abode of fairies and elves.

2. Make a compilation of passages from folk tales showing under what situations and in what manner fairies and elves presented themselves to human beings.

   Note: The materials of 1 and 2 could be combined under the title "Fairy creatures in old tales, as they appeared to human beings."

3. Construct a verbal picture of the appearance and life of the fairy creatures portrayed by Ben Jonson, John Lyly, Michael Drayton, and Robert Herrick.

4. Fairies in relation to flowers in old tales, poems, and masques.

5. Tabulate current superstitions and beliefs in Shakespeare's England and relate each one very briefly to some poem or folk tale.

6. Compare the traditional fairies of country folk in the sixteenth century with the fairies depicted in stories and poems written since 1850.

7. Which of the old conceptions about fairy creatures and their habits do you think are especially pleasing to children? Which do you find often used by the best modern writers? Which of the old conceptions seldom appear in their stories?

   Note: Probably Topics 6 and 7 can be treated more satisfactorily after the material in Chapters IV, X and XI has been considered.

REFERENCES

Anderson, R. B.   *Norse Mythology*.
    Chapter III names and describes the principal types of
    fairy creatures and shows their probable descent from
    Norse mythology.

Delattre, Floris.   *English Fairy Poetry from the Origins to the
    Seventeenth Century*.   London, Frowde, 1912.
    Rare examples are given through which one can trace the
    English traditions about fairies.

Drayton, Michael.   *The Barons' Wars, Nymphidia and Other
    Poems*.   London, 1887.

Grierson, H.   "Fairies from Shakespeare to Yeats in English
    Poetry."   *The Living Age*.   June, 1911.

Hartland, Edwin S.   *The Science of Fairy Tales*.   Stokes.

Hazlitt, W. C.   *Fairy Tales, Legends and Romances Illustrating
    Shakespeare and Other Early English Writers*.   London, 1875.

Herrick, Robert.   *The Hesperides and Noble Numbers*.   Edited
    by Alfred Pollard, 2 volumes.   Scribner, 1898.
    Volume I contains "The Fairy Temple," "Oberon's
    Feast," and "Oberon's Palace."

Keightley, Thomas.   *The Fairy Mythology*.   London, 1889.
    A very valuable reference on all questions concerning
    fairy-lore.

Latham, Minor W.   *The Elizabethan Fairies*.   Columbia Uni-
    versity Press, 1930.
    This study presents traditional concepts of fairies and
    the body of beliefs commonly held in the 16th and 17th
    centuries concerning them.   It traces also the influence of
    Shakespeare in a changed conception.

Raleigh, Walter, and Onions, Charles Talbut, editor.   *Shake-
    speare's England*.   2 vols.   Oxford, 1916–1926.
    Chapter 16, volume I, treats of folklore and superstition,
    ghosts and fairies of the period.

Shakespeare, William.   *A Midsummer Night's Dream*.   Warwick
    Edition.   Edited by E. K. Chambers.   London, 1911.

The following collections for older children contain many of the examples mentioned in this chapter:

De La Mare, Walter, compiler and editor. *Come Hither.* Knopf, 1928.

> This choice collection of poetry for children contains many fairy poems of the period discussed in this chapter and a wealth of illuminating notes and comments.

Olcott, Frances J., compiler. *A Book of Elves and Fairies.* Houghton, 1918.

> This is an excellent source book for traditional tales. It contains also a good representation of old fairy poems.

Owen, Dora, editor. *The Book of Fairy Poetry.* Illustrated by Warwick Goble. Longmans, 1920.

> A large and well-chosen collection consisting entirely of fairy poetry.

Rhys, Ernest, compiler and editor. *Fairy Gold. A Book of Old English Tales.* Illustrated by Herbert Cole. Dutton, 1906.

> Contains tales, songs, legends, and ballads about fairy folk.

CHAPTER IV

FOLK TALES

Old Grandmother: "I heard it from my mother's mother and she from the mother of her mother."

CHARLES FINGER, *Tales from Silver Lands*

IN THE preceding chapter we sought traces of fairies in folk belief as recorded in fragmentary tales of unlettered people and saw how the creative imagination of poets refined and transformed these crude concepts. We also noted the part played by fairies and elves in a few well-rounded old tales. Our purpose now is to become better acquainted with a variety of folk tales in order to discover diverse features as well as certain qualities which many of them hold in common. Such a study ought to deepen our appreciation of these remarkable old stories and aid in the recognition of certain factors which enter into the achievement of artistic and delightful effects.

Preliminary to examining the stories themselves, it seems necessary to assemble in brief review a few basic facts and opinions regarding their origin and dissemination. Their history has been told at great length by eminent scholars in this field and is readily accessible, but for purposes of immediate orientation a brief sketch is presented.

THEORIES REGARDING ORIGIN

We are struck first with the enormous number of these traditional tales. Their creation bit by bit must have been one of the chief avenues of expression for the emotions and beliefs of our remote ancestors. There has been a good deal of controversy as to the extent to which they are rooted in explanatory myths, that is, in the attempt of primitive peoples to explain mysterious and awe-inspiring natural phenomena such as day and night, summer and winter, sunset glow, thunder, lightning, trembling of the earth, phases of the moon, meteors, strange behavior of animals, and a thousand other manifestations which puzzled and defied our forebears in a world which knew no science. In their blind groping for causes of danger and for ways of escape, gigantic and terrifying forces as well as benign influences were personified and became all-powerful beings to be worshiped, placated, or if possible tricked. Gradually, according to some authorities, the religious element in myth was lost sight of, but the mythical creatures themselves remained in degraded or minimized form and subject to more familiar human contact.

There is quite general acceptance of the theory that some folk tales are in substance shrunken remnants of myths. According to Ruskin, Thor, the awe-compelling thunder god of the Norse, has become a stupid giant and the easy prey of the redoubtable Jack. Extremists believe that Red Riding-Hood devoured by the wolf originated in the daily mystery of a glowing sun drawn into the maw of relentless night.

Andrew Lang, among others, grants only a limited validity to the above accounting and presses vigorously the theory that many folk tales have their basis in actual events of daily life; in historic characters, social customs, and deep-lying human experiences and relations such as birth, death, marriage, the chase, warfare, conquest, bondage, and all the rites and ceremonies that attended these exciting and profound events. This line of thought provides also for the sheer inventiveness of the mind of man in evolving vivid stories out of the strenuous and often dramatic features of a rude life.

STRIKING SIMILARITIES IN FOLK TALES

A slight acquaintance with traditional tales of different races and civilizations is sufficient to impress one with the striking similarity of many of them. What is the explanation of this phenomenon?

The least complicated theory is that all the stories stemmed from a common root in the East, before the dispersal of the Aryan race westward. Migrating groups carried with them the nucleus of a tale, or its main features, which later took shape and color according to various developing civilizations while retaining some of its original characteristics. Those holding this view believe also that all folk tales are the débris of myths. These two ideas are phases of a theory which is now generally discredited or held to be inadequate.

Dissenters grant that dispersal from an Aryan center was one strong factor in the multiplication of tales having the same basic pattern, but they offer more liberal and less simple explanations of such duplication. On various occasions Andrew Lang has expressed an eclectic and well-reasoned opinion which satisfies the less dogmatic. Two references containing a statement of Lang's viewpoint are given in the bibliography for this chapter. His main contention may be briefly explained here. He argues that it is perfectly possible for alien races with no common ancestral root to evolve independently, out of fundamental human experiences, the same crude elements of plot. The persecuted and friendless who win out, the neglected youngest child who obtains unexpected ascendency, abandoned children miraculously preserved, the real service of animals to man, the abduction of wives, curious laws and customs which repeat themselves at the lower levels of civilization — such common experiences as these, Lang believes, form the matrix of fairy tales. He argues that widely separated races might very well happen to compound stories having a general family resemblance from such indigenous and spontaneous ingredients. The best-reasoned opinion holds that in the ancient past any or all of these influences may have operated to produce similar story patterns among different races.

ENDURING QUALITIES

More remarkable than their somewhat uncertain history, and of deeper interest to most students, are their endless variety, lasting quality, and universality of appeal. The perfection of style and form which marks some of them is a feature which arouses wonder and is worthy of study. The modern writer, critic, or compiler of stories for children, and anyone responsible for their selection will do well to make a careful study of the unconscious art exhibited in many of the old tales. They are inimitable, but because of their simplicity and directness they furnish many hints regarding potent elements of appeal to children.

The age of these popular tales no one can reckon. It is reasonable to suppose that up to the time of their first appearance in written form, their development was contemporaneous with other crude art expression — primitive drawing and decoration, symbolic dancing, rude musical instruments, and vocal song. Long before Charles Perrault wrote his *Contes de ma Mère l'Oye*, or the Grimm brothers collected and edited their *Kinder- und Hausmärchen*, there were current among the peasants of Europe many tales which had attained imperishable qualities of strength and beauty. Literary talent and zealous and timely scientific research have made them more widely known to the educated, but their popularity among all classes is due to their origin in, and appeal to, certain primary human attitudes and emotions. We must remember that, while the tales were anonymous, they were nevertheless the product of a true art impulse and attained genuine art forms very early.

The following estimate by one great authority has been echoed or anticipated by scores of others.

We are amazed as an investigation of their contents reveals to us, that such marvelous invention and execution, such tender and moving situations, such a world of romance, should have been the work of men and ages so remote from us, so backward and barbarous, as we suppose. But so it is. The shuttle of fancy shot across the loom of thought, and wrought rich fabrics of imaginative art out of the things of every-day life. And if these tales contain, as was inevitable, wild passions, rough combats, brutal lusts, there exists side by side with them much that is tender and beautiful — rainbow-hued romance, love and heroism, sunshine and sparkling seas, and birds and flowers.[1]

It is our part to seek the finer tales and better versions for children, and one means to this end is to become acquainted with the work of leading collectors and editors of taste and judgment.

THE CONTRIBUTION OF CHARLES PERRAULT

The first collection of folk tales to appear in English was a translation from the French of Charles Perrault (1628–1703). The original edition published in Paris in 1697 was cited in Chapter I as the probable source of the name *Mother Goose* used as a title. The collection was called *Histoires ou Contes du Temps Passé; avec des Moralités*. The frontispiece bore a supplementary title, *Contes de ma Mère l'Oye*.

The first English translation was published about 1729, and it furnished a rich addition to the slender store of native tales in print at that time. Perrault's stories have appeared under several different titles in English, sometimes as *Stories of Passed Times*, and again as *Mother Goose's Tales*. As the latter title is misleading, it is now seldom used, and the collection is commonly called Perrault's *Popular Tales*, or *Fairy Tales*. There were eight prose

[1] MacCulloch, John A., *The Childhood of Fiction; a Study of Folk Tales and Primitive Thought*, pp. 482–483. London, 1905.

stories in the collection: *La Belle au Bois Dormant* ("Sleeping Beauty"); *Le Petit Chaperon Rouge* ("Red Riding-Hood"); *La Barbe Bleu* ("Bluebeard"); *Le Maistre Chat, ou le Chat Botté* ("The Master Cat, or Puss in Boots"); *Les Fées* ("Diamonds and Toads"); *Cendrillon, ou la Petite Pantoufle de Verre* ("Cinderella, or the Little Glass Slipper"); *Riquet à la Houppe* ("Riquet of the Tuft"); and *Le Petit Poucet* ("Little Thumb," sometimes called "Hop o' My Thumb").

It is nearly two and a half centuries since this small collection was published, and it has been reprinted countless times and in many languages. Single stories have appeared in almost every general collection in English during all these years. The importance of the book is to be measured, not only by its lasting popularity, but by its wide influence upon other collectors and editors. The stories themselves were not new in 1695 nor were they the peculiar heritage of France. Every one of them has been identified in other ancient literatures. We know that they had been told in the Perrault household by the children's nurse before any attempt was made to put them into permanent form for other children. An account has been pieced together for us by various literary historians which tells how the father, Charles Perrault, and a young son, P. Darmancour, took down these familiar and loved nursery tales and with a touch like that of their own Fairy Godmother imparted to them immortal beauty and charm. Andrew Lang [1] has assembled important data which give substantial support to an interesting theory regarding their production. Discerning comment on this subject is offered by Miss Barry [2] also, who has her own delightful manner of interpreting significant facts. From these and other sources, as well as from the internal evidence of the tales themselves, the following brief account is drawn.

---

[1] Perrault, Charles, *Popular Tales*. Edited by Andrew Lang.
[2] Barry, Florence V., *op. cit.*, chapter II.

Charles Perrault was a man of many gifts and he received during his life high honors as a writer, critic, and public official. He was a member of the Royal Academy, an independent and virile thinker, and a prominent figure in a group of famous men.[1] Public duties and literary activities brought him frequently into close association with the brilliant court circle of Louis XIV, but he seems to have cared little for the highly artificial life of the period. He had several children, and becoming dissatisfied with the training they were receiving in various schools, he decided to direct their education at home, and in this situation we get the setting for the production of the fairy tales.

Previous to the publication of the prose tales, three stories in verse form had appeared anonymously in a miscellany published at The Hague. This was in 1694. They are familiar in English prose as "The Three Wishes," "The Ass's Skin," and "Patient Griselda." In putting these old tales into verse, Perrault was imitating La Fontaine whose last book of fables was published the same year, and the imitation was not very successful. Critics attacked both the subject and the manner of telling. The Preface to one of the stories shows that Perrault was aware that many thought he was dealing with frivolous and negligible things, beneath the dignity of an Academician. He had signed his stories "Par M. Perrault, de L'Academie Francoise." In defense, he claimed that these "bagatelles" were not mere bagatelles, but that the pleasing story was intended to convey a moral and thus to instruct and, at the same time, to entertain.

And then, two years later, came the famous eight stories in prose, but the name of Charles Perrault did not appear anywhere in the book. The "Privilege of the King" to publish was officially accorded to P. Darmancour; and the

[1] Barry, Florence V., *op. cit.*, chapter IV.

rather florid dedication to a young royal princess,[1] bore the same signature. The opening sentence of this address points to a boy as the author:

> On ne trouvera pas étrange qu'un Enfant ait pris plaisir à composer les Contes de ce Recueil, mais on s'étonnera qu'il ait eu la hardiesse de vous les presenter.
>
> It will not be thought strange that a child has taken pleasure in composing the stories of this collection, but it may seem astonishing that he has had the daring to present them to you.

Apparently few of his contemporaries believed that Perrault's son, a boy of perhaps nine or ten years, was really the author. It was thought that the uncertain reception of his stories in verse had made him willing to hide his authorship of similar tales in prose, behind the boy. Informed critics of the day believed that father and son had shared in the production. Mlle. L'Héritier, a relative of Perrault's, and herself a writer of fairy tales, remarked some time before the *Contes* were published that a child in the family had written some stories in a naïve and charming manner.

The best opinion today is that an old nurse recounted the tales; that all the family knew them well; that a child or children wrote them out, partly for entertainment and partly as a school exercise; and that the scholarly father had a considerable hand in polishing them off for publication. Observant readers point out numerous passages in the stories which show the simple, direct, and naïve touch of a child, and others marked by sophistication and a more elaborate literary style. But a child's manner of telling might be largely a repetition of the simple, dramatic language of the nurse, and it would take a clairvoyant to identify the different contributions. There are places which show uncertainty in handling, as though there had been an attempt to satisfy different standards. "Little

[1] Princess Charlotte of Orléans, born 1676.

Thumb" has two endings: the first, of the crude folk tale type in which the tiny hero obtains all the giant's gold and silver by means of trickery; and an alternative one which is a plain invention compounded of modern elements and intended to account for Thumb's wealth in a more ethical but quite preposterous way.

Very early the ethical soundness of the stories came into question. Perrault believed them to be inherently moral and defended them on that ground. Each story ended with a statement of the moral in verse, the "lesson" frequently seeming rather forced. Five of them were furnished with *two* morals and these are not always in agreement. Usually one of them seems more worldly-wise than the other.

There are other obvious discrepancies in subject and style which a careful examination of a French edition or a good translation will reveal and which arouse interesting conjectures as to authorship.

The peculiar value of Perrault's work is that he eliminated the horrible features from several otherwise charming old tales, added modern touches discreetly, and still preserved and intensified their dramatic quality. On the whole, they are childlike in character, differing in this respect from their crude originals as well as from the extravagant and tiresome inventions greatly in vogue in France at that time. Our interest in this old book is not that of the antiquarian; it is rather to discover some of the inherent qualities which have made these stories so loved by generations of children.

Walter Pater discusses the part that ancient lineage may legitimately play in our appreciation of literature. He is writing of a simple and lovely old French romance, *Aucassin and Nicolette*. He says:

Antiquarianism, by the purely historical effort, by putting its object in perspective, and setting the reader in a certain point of view, from which what gave pleasure to the past is pleasurable for him also, may often add greatly to the charm we receive from ancient literature. But the first condition of such aid must be real, direct, æsthetic charm in the thing itself. Unless it has that charm, unless some purely artistic quality went to its original making, no merely antiquarian effort can ever give it æsthetic value, or make it a proper subject of æsthetic criticism.[1]

Questions will be found at the end of this chapter intended to direct a further study of Perrault's stories.

THE CONTRIBUTION OF THE GRIMM BROTHERS

The work of Jacob Ludwig Carl Grimm (1785–1863) and Wilhelm Carl Grimm (1786–1859) came more than a century later than that of Perrault, but in form and to some extent in content, their stories are much more primitive than his. That is because the entire background of these German scholars and their purposes and methods in preparing their collections were quite different from those of the French author.

The two brothers studied, worked, and lived together in the closest possible way almost all their lives, and their life-spans differed by only a few years. Both developed early a deep interest in historical and antiquarian investigations, both had some years of library experience, both were university professors, and together they produced several works of monumental scope concerning the language and literature of the Germanic races. Outside of the scientific aspects of philology, their chief interest seems to have been in mythology and in German national poetry of all kinds from the earliest times, ballads, epics, and popular tales. In their many different enterprises they, of course, unearthed a quantity of stories familiar to us now as German *Märchen*, and in 1812–1815 they brought out their first collection of the *Kinder-und Hausmärchen*.

[1] Pater, Walter, *The Renaissance*. By permission of The Macmillan Company.

The Grimms had no thought at first of producing collections of stories for the entertainment of either adults or children.   They were concerned with the preservation of the native literature of their country, and their main purpose was to discover and faithfully record this rich heritage (much of it unwritten) before it was too late.   They went into remote country districts, sought out story-tellers of local reputation, and listened to their homely rendering. The stories were taken down as nearly as possible in the style in which they were narrated, and every care was used to reproduce these oral effects in preparing the material for publication.   No such search had been made in any other European country at this time, and consequently we owe to the Grimms many of our most popular nursery tales. Indeed the name Grimm is to many people almost synonymous with fairy tale.

In examining a full collection of Grimm's stories, one should bear in mind that they were not written primarily for children.   The authors stated, however, that they had planned it as an educational book as well as one for scholars, and they had eliminated everything which they deemed unsuitable for children.   But the taste of today is different from that of German scientific investigators of more than a hundred years ago, and they included a good deal which modern judges of children's needs would omit. If the fact is overlooked that the Grimms had in mind both antiquarians and children when they prepared their collection, one is likely to fall into the error of condemning an entire class of stories because of the objectionable features peculiar to some of them.   While a full collection will contain many incidents and scenes marked by the coarseness and cruelty of primitive society, many of the German Märchen are quite free from such features and are indeed models of childlike simplicity and charm.   They are as admirable as any that have been produced by a more conscious artistry which strives to avoid ugliness and to obtain beauty.

The English language does not offer an exact equivalent for the word *Märchen*. The titles most commonly used are *Household Tales*, *Nursery Tales*, and *Fairy Tales*. The stories have been subjected to the critical judgment of many able writers and critics whose object was to select for children of various ages the finest and most appropriate. The younger children in particular have profited greatly by such editorial work, not only as regards the German stories, but in the case of other national folklore as well.

A few of the most popular stories which we owe to the Grimm brothers are: "The Frog Prince"; "The Fisherman and His Wife"; "Hansel and Grethel"; "The Elves and the Shoemaker"; "The Bremen Town Musicians"; "Snow-White"; "Briar-Rose"; "The Golden Goose"; "Snow-White and Rose-Red"; "The Little House in the Wood"; "The Wolf and the Seven Kids"; "Rumpelstiltskin"; "One-Eye, Two-Eyes, and Three-Eyes."

ENGLISH FOLK TALES

As stated above, the systematic and extensive gathering of folk tales in England came much later than in Germany, and by the time Halliwell, S. Baring-Gould, Andrew Lang, and Joseph Jacobs began their search, England's native stock of stories had been quite thoroughly mixed with imported versions or variants. Jacobs tells quite frankly about his method. He makes no claim to exhaustive research among country folk, but says he obtained some of his tales in printed form from chap-books, from Halliwell's collection, and from reports in the *Folk-Lore Journal*. Some of his stories were told to him from memory by both educated and uneducated people. He believed that it was useless as well as unsound to attempt to separate the lore of southern Scotland from that of northern England; therefore his *English Fairy Tales* [1] are not limited to strict geo-graphical boundaries, and he included stories from such published works as Chambers's *Popular Rhymes of Scotland*.

Jacobs further declares that all collectors, including the Grimms, made certain changes in individual stories to render them more acceptable, and that, since his stories were definitely intended for children and not for archives of a scientific body, it was necessary and proper to omit some incidents and to modify others.

Information contained in his *Notes* proves that the stock of old English tales is considerably larger than is usually thought. In retelling them, Jacobs seems to have been very successful in preserving or imitating the familiar idiomatic style of unlettered people. On this point he says, "Generally speaking, it has been my ambition to write as a good old nurse will speak when she tells Fairy Tales." Commenting on style, this author says that English tales are essentially colloquial and rarely rise into romance; instead, humor is the outstanding trait. They do not show great variety as to plot and in his opinion they give very little evidence of constructive plot-ability among the folk who originated them.

Perhaps the most noticeable feature of these stories is the unusual number of extremely simple ones suited to the younger children. Here we find such old nursery favorites as "The Old Woman and Her Pig"; "Teeny-Tiny"; "Three Little Pigs"; "Henny-Penny"; "Tom Thumb"; "Johnny-Cake"; "The Wee Bannock"; "Jack and the Beanstalk"; and "The Three Bears" (not strictly a folk tale).

The *Notes* which Jacobs furnishes in his *English Fairy Tales* throw much light on the ultimate sources and con-spicuous parallels of a number of the stories.

[1] Jacobs, Joseph, *English Fairy Tales*, Preface and Notes. Putnam, 1898.

NORSE FOLK TALES

There are two names which are always linked together in any discussion of Norwegian folklore, and with good reason; for Peter Christian Asbjörnsen (1812–1885) and Jörgen E. Moe (1813–1882) were almost as closely united in their work as were the Grimm brothers. They were close friends from boyhood, and by the time they reached early manhood had developed similar literary tastes. They were keenly interested in discovering and preserving their national folklore, and after some independent work the friends decided to collaborate. Asbjörnsen was a zoölogist, and in his university travels in Norway he combined literary research with his scientific investigations. Moe was a poet and a theologian, and he spent many of his holidays in remote country districts gathering legends and fairy lore.

Their first collection, *Norwegian Popular Tales*, appeared in 1842, and *Tales from the Fjeld* a little later. No one has succeeded better than these two writers in catching the vigorous and homely style of the untutored story-teller, and the language is unusually picturesque and colorful. We owe many delightful stories to the industry and ability of Asbjörnsen and Moe.

Fortunately an English scholar of unusual gifts, Sir George Webbe Dasent, became acquainted with the Norwegian tales and translated many of them into English. His work is highly praised by competent judges who know both languages. Asbjörnsen, himself, referring to Dasent's work, is quoted as saying:

> ... our tales have been not only correctly and faultlessly translated, but even rendered with exemplary truth and care — nay, with thorough mastery.

The following passage from "Osborn's Pipe," a story in Dasent's *Tales from the Fjeld*, shows the translator's command of homely idiom:

The man to keep the King's hares must not dawdle about like a lazy-bones with leaden soles to his stockings, or like a fly in a tar-pot; for when they fell to frisking and skipping on the sunny slopes, it would be quite another dance to catching fleas with gloves on. No; he that would get rid of that work with a whole back had need to be more than lithe and lissom, and he must fly about faster than a bladder or a bird's wing.

Some of the most popular and childlike of the Norwegian stories are: "The Death of Chanticleer"; "The Greedy Cat"; "The Pancake"; "How They Got Hairlock Home"; "The Sheep and the Pig Set up House"; "The Princess on the Glass Hill"; "The Three Billy Goats Gruff"; "The Doll in the Grass"; "The Boy Who Went to the North Wind"; and "Boots and His Brothers."

AMERICAN INDIAN TALES

The children of America probably know the native tales of distant countries far better than they do those of our own aboriginals. There are good reasons for this, but the fact remains that there has been an inexcusable neglect of fine Amerind stories which should have for us and for our children a peculiar charm and interest. Many children go through our elementary schools with little or no knowledge of this literature except the doubtful content of *Hiawatha* with its separate myths and legends. The Hiawatha stories have sometimes been retold in prose, but whether in verse or prose they are very far removed from the rhythmic beauty, characteristic idiom, and unique imagery of the native tales when translated and edited by a faithful and competent writer. The growing interest in social studies, a quickened desire to understand the spirit and life of other races and peoples, and a better knowledge of distinctive differences in the various types of American Indians and in their literary records promise to be helpful influences in bringing about a better appreciation of this literature and its background.

As in all true folklore we find a large number of tales of the explanatory type, the product of groping minds seeking an explanation of the curious, mysterious, and sometimes startling phenomena which surround a people wholly lacking in scientific knowledge. One is struck with the great quantity of such tales in Amerind literature. Certainly no other body of material is richer in mythical creations of this type. Their stories display a truly marvelous acquaintance with natural phenomena and an accuracy of observation which would do credit to a trained expert. Since they lacked the method of science, they turned their observations into poetry and romance. Theirs is a mythology of creation — creation of all things, from the tiniest flower or insect to the most stupendous manifestation of nature. We find, therefore, not only countless small stories giving ingenious and often quite poetic accounts of origins, but similar explanations are frequently woven into the longer tales adding color and entertaining incident to them. The imagery employed in portrayal is peculiarly apt and revealing. We learn how into red-pepper pods flowed color and fire from the scolding tongue of an old woman; why the descendants of a presumptuous centipede are shrunken in size and "appear like a well-toasted bit of buckskin, fringed at the edges"; why the tracks of wild turkeys and other figures are graven on certain rocks near the top of Cañon Mesa; and a thousand other fascinating disclosures.

A theme easily discerned quite commonly gives direction to the movement of Amerind tales; plot is usually well-knit and clear; they abound in interesting incident; and personal encounters carry terse, vivid, and sharply direct dialogue. Animal characters play a large part in all folk literature, but where can one find so many wild creatures, great and small, participating in the affairs of men in such important and altogether delightful ways as in our Indian stories? Yet in this mingling with human beings, the wild creatures retain in a striking way their dominant traits. They are saucy, self-confident, skulking, daring, cowardly, stupid, or clever, according to their kind, and through these entertaining tales one may pick up authentic information about them. The more admirable animal characters are so competent and friendly that the reader, either child or adult, must be left with a warm fellow-feeling for them.

These stories abound also in references to customs domestic and ceremonial, to food, clothing, habitations, and handicraft — all as integral and essential parts of the narrative and not, as in so many modern stories, introduced in order to impart information.

All these points are particularly well illustrated in Mr. Cushing's collection *Zuñi Folk Tales*. In this collection, the best stories for younger children are, "The Poor Little Turkey Girl"; "How the Summer Birds Came"; "How the Coyote Danced with the Blackbirds"; and "The Coyote and the Locust." The first-named is a lovely tale told with great charm. It reminds one of "Cinderella," but it has not the typical happy ending. "The Coyote and the Locust" is gay, amusing, and a model in story form.

Another reliable collection is *The Red Indian Fairy-Book* of which Frances Jenkins Olcott is the collector and editor. In the Introduction, she refers to her stories as "Red Indian Nature Myths," and most of them are of the explanatory type, poetic fancies about conspicuous and beautiful things in the physical world.

A characteristic bit of philosophy is found at the close of one of the stories in *The New World Fairy Book*. A little white boy says to the Indian story-teller — "So they lived happily ever afterwards, didn't they, Ossawippi?" "Indian stories don't go like that," said Ossawippi; "they finish at the end, and 'ever afterwards' is the other side of the end." [1]

OTHER SOURCES OF EUROPEAN TALES

Other European cultures furnish just as choice stories as the four discussed above; Italy and Russia in particular having contributed many interesting ones to the common store now available in English. In the numerous general collections now provided, we find examples of unique beauty and worth from all nations.

The zeal and industry of the folklorist have sometimes been exercised without due regard to the artistic, cultural, and pleasure-giving qualities which we have a right to expect in books addressed to a child audience. So far as the needs of children are concerned, the task in recent years has been, not to search the corners of the earth and the annals of folklore societies for more tales, but to sift and choose generously but with discrimination from the very large offering now at hand. This need is being well met in the excellent general collections of stories selected and edited by people who know both literature and children. Many of the best collections wisely disregard national and linguistic lines and choose wholly for the peculiar merit of the stories and their fitness for certain age levels.

CHARACTERISTIC FEATURES OF FOLK TALES

It is not only the specialist in children's literature who dwells upon the excellencies of the old fairy and folk tales. They are constantly used by other literary critics as striking examples of story construction, dramatic quality, pervading tone, character delineation, clarity of theme,

[1] Kennedy, Howard Angus, *The New World Fairy Book.*

intensity of action, effective dialogue, and other significant traits. Authorities on the drama, the novel, the short story, have drawn extensively upon folk tales to illustrate their points, because the best of these tales exhibit certain striking qualities free from the complexities of a more sophisticated literature. The student of children's literature should be no less aware of the factors which contribute to the excellence of stories which long since became the especial property of the young.

DRAMATIC QUALITY

Everyone knows that the finest of these tales are intensely dramatic. What makes them so? The same fundamental factors which determine more serious drama are found in these simple stories. The following points culled from leading authorities on the structure of the drama have direct application to stories of a' dramatic order:

1. The introduction is brief and sets forth the scene of action, relates a few necessary antecedent events, and introduces the leading characters. The true natures of these characters are revealed, our sympathies are directed regarding them, and causes and motives of future action begin to appear.

2. Drama presents a struggle. Brander Matthews says the chief character must desire something: "The hero knows what he wants and wants it with all his might." Conflict results from opposing wills and the development of the tale shows these warring claims. The hero or heroine struggles against active enemies and difficulties of all kinds and we see that "plot is the result of laws of human nature." Often there is a series of alternate successes and failures in a scale which maintains suspense.

3. Then comes the major climax making a point of high

suspense where "almost the last stand of the conflicting parties occurs." In most traditional tales this point comes near the close of the story and then we see the solution of all difficulties rapidly unfolding. Obstacles are removed, enemies are defeated and often punished, the desires of hero and heroine are fulfilled, and all ends happily for them and their friends.

The objection may be raised that the method of these old tales is not that of drama, since there is no true conflict, the leading character always having assured success through the support of some supernatural power. The answer to this is that the evil forces also are more than human, and seem for a time to outweigh the good. Moreover, even classic Greek drama had its interposing *deus ex machina*.

It will be an exaggeration to attempt to force all these simple tales into the mold set by principles of dramatic construction. It can be shown, however, that a great many of them do conform to the general outline given above. The most satisfactory way to study the question is to test out afresh several stories judged to possess dramatic quality, such as "The Frog Prince"; "Snow-White and the Seven Dwarfs"; "Rumpelstiltskin"; "The Boy Who Went to the North Wind"; "The Twelve Wild Ducks" (similar to "The Six Wild Swans"); "Hansel and Grethel"; and "The Poor Little Turkey Girl."

BEGINNINGS AND ENDINGS

Folk tales are noted for the directness of their beginnings, the finality of their endings, and the brevity and vigor of both. Children do not like to wait long for action to begin, neither do they like anything inconclusive at the end; and no one, child or man, likes a succession of unimportant events to follow the last situation of high suspense. Artistry in these features has been perfected by a long line of story-tellers, as a brief examination will show. Notice the following examples:

There was a poor, good little girl, who lived alone with her mother, and they had nothing more to eat. So the child went into the forest, and an Old Woman met her, who knew her sorrow, and gave her a Little Pot, which, when she said: "Boil, Little Pot, boil!" would cook good sweet Porridge.

In the days when wishing was having, a King's Son was enchanted by an old Witch, and shut up in an Iron Stove in a forest. There he passed many years, and no one could deliver him.
Then a King's Daughter came into the forest....

There was an old mother pig with three little pigs, and as she had not enough to keep them, she sent them out to seek their fortunes. The first that went off met a man with a bundle of straw, and said to him....

And so Ashiepattle was married to the doll in the grass; and afterward they lived happy and comfortable for a long, long while; and if they are not dead, they must still be alive.

"Ouf, ouf," said the pig, and swallowed the pancake at one gulp; and then, as the poor pancake could go no farther, why — this story can go no farther either.

Oh! if one only knew where the trap door was, I'll be bound there's a whole heap of gold and silver down there still!

So the wedding took place, and the feasting lasted for eight days. And as I did not stay any longer with the squire and his queen, I cannot tell you any more about them.

DOMINANT STORY PATTERNS

There are certain patterns, or formulæ, which govern the great majority of native European tales. In spite of their kaleidoscopic variety as regards setting and incident, a few easily recognized plot schemes are repeated over and over again. Some of the most important are:

1. The simple chain of contingent events followed by a reverse movement, as in "The Old Woman and Her Pig,"

and "Titty Mouse and Tatty Mouse." These represent two accumulative patterns of which there are many
variations. As a rule, such stories are quite humorous,
even those which, like "Titty Mouse," end in a regular
cataclysm.

2. The adventures of *three* characters, and the triumph of
one, who may be the youngest, the wisest, the most
foolish, the fairest, the bravest, or several of these super-
latives together.

3. The rescue of lost or banished children, sometimes
by their own endeavors, and sometimes by the sacrificing
effort of another person.

4. The false bride or bridegroom, who must be pursued,
detected, and deposed by the true mate. Usually the
false one is induced to barter the chance for a private
interview with the beloved, for a series of fascinating
objects proffered by the seeking mate.

5. Because of a prophecy that a princess is to marry
someone unacceptable to her parents, she is shut up in a
high tower and is rescued through the prodigious efforts
of Prince Charming.

6. A rash promise is made — lightly, or under terrible
duress. The pledge is fulfilled, as in "The Frog Prince,"
or narrowly escaped as in "Tom, Tit, Tot," and in
"Rumpelstiltskin."

THEMES

Not every good fairy story has an easily discoverable
theme, but many of them do have. Brian Hooker deals
with this point in an article which is unsurpassed as a discerning appreciation of fairy tales. He uses the term
"idea" to express the soul of a story. The following is a
small part of his discussion:

Each of the more familiar fairy tales sets forth emphatically
a single idea of immediate human interest. This is in nowise

to be confused with the plot or narrative outline of the story: the idea is what a story is about, and the plot is what is told about it; the idea is that impression which the artist pretends to convey truly and movingly to his audience, and the plot is the means of its conveyance. But the two are constantly confused: nine out of ten would say that the story of Washington and the hatchet is about cutting down a cherry tree; whereas it is really about telling the truth. Thus *Jack the Giant-Killer*, as one critic and philosopher has already pointed out, is the story of the battle of the weak against the strong; the idea of Cinderella is the idea of the Magnificat, *exaltavit humiles*; and the idea of *Beauty and the Beast* is that love makes unlovely things lovable.... The idea is the soul of the narrative and the plot its body. Now the story which has evidently an idea behind it will always have the advantage over that story, otherwise of equal merit, which exists only to reflect the personality of the writer or intangibly to suggest some lyric emotion... the idea of a story need not by any means be a statement of truth, such as can be formulated in a sentence.... And finally, it is worth considering that none of these ideas is treated as a moral. Most of the stories have not a shred of explicit morality about them; and although *Cinderella* and *Beauty and the Beast* are built around moral ideas, they treat these ideas as truths rather than as precepts.[1]

Other themes or ideas variously developed are, "Kindness comes to the kind"; "Vaulting ambition o'erleaps itself"; "He who would have friends must show himself friendly"; "Love will find a way"; "Choose the worst and get the best" — referring to a modest, unselfish choice; "Scorn no living thing."

CHARACTER PORTRAYAL

The focus of interest in a good story is in the living creatures who move and have their being within it. How are these figures made real, and by what means are they rendered attractive or hateful? Do they reveal themselves through their actions as in the skillfully written

[1] Hooker, Brian, "Narrative and the Fairy Tale," *The Bookman*, June, 1911.

modern novel or short story? Do we see them largely
through the eyes of other characters in the tale? Or does
the narrator simply label them as good, bad, beautiful,
ugly, clever or stupid?

Examination shows that the latter method is quite
often employed in introducing a character. Black is
black and white is white, with little or no shading in these
stories. Simple minds like to know just what to expect
from story or stage characters and prefer to have them
plainly tagged. But once clearly identified, the popular
tales almost always give a real personality to the central
figures by depicting typical attitudes and actions. Their
inner nature does not appear to change through experience;
we discover, rather, a progressive revelation of character.

We are told that Cinderella "was of an exceptionally
sweet and gentle nature"; the "superb beauty of the unknown guest" at the ball is mentioned; and later we are
told that she was "as good as she was beautiful." But
we really know this young girl through her behavior.
She is by no means a passive creature whose changed
fortune results wholly from a kind fairy's intervention,
but is herself, active at every point in the story. We see
in her a very human young girl who, among many other
good qualities, has a sense of humor.

There are only a few very passive heroines. "Sleeping
Beauty" (Briar-Rose) is of this type. She is scarcely more
than a beautiful, romantic ideal with features and traits
miraculously assigned at birth. According to Perrault,
the fairies' gifts to Sleeping Beauty were — that she should
be the most beautiful person in the world, have the temper
of an angel, do everything with wonderful grace, dance to
perfection, sing like a nightingale, and play every kind of
music with the utmost skill. The only act attributed to
her is her fateful wandering about the palace one day, and
the idle and inept experiment with weaving in which she

pricks her finger. Sympathy for her is aroused by her helpless innocence and impending fate. She does not need to *do* anything; we pity and love the beautiful helpless child and wait for the blow which is certain to fall.

The princess who sits upon the "glass hill" is almost as passive as Briar-Rose, but much less lovable. Inaccessibility appears to be her chief charm, to which we may add beauty and mystery. These make her a suitable object for the peculiar and very arduous labors demanded of successive suitors. Only a silent, remote figure would fit the glittering pinnacle on which she sits. She maintains an aloof attitude toward even the dauntless youngest brother, and as he carries her down from her lofty "Siege-Perilous," the mature reader might wonder if she is worth his pains. But in this story the youngest son is the central figure of a plot in which he is to be proved first by the way he faces mysterious terrors by night and then by repeated trials of prowess and endurance. The glamorous princess is merely a desired and seemingly unattainable object well calculated to call forth a display of valor.

Fairy tale heroes appear to be rather more vulnerable as regards character than the heroines. If they display courage, daring, resourcefulness, quick wit, and devotion to some worthy cause or person, that is usually all that is required. The use of deceit to attain these ends and indifference to those who fall by the way are common features. The typical hero is built to force his way through all kinds of difficulties to rescue the princess in distress or to obtain a kingdom and a bride. He is not expected to accomplish these ends by the self-effacing behavior which is usually required of the "perfect" heroine.

Several appreciative critics have pointed out the basically sound and true human qualities which many of the popular fairy tale characters possess. Boys and girls, youths and maidens, are moved by natural desires and impulses even in the midst of supernatural events. We see this illustrated in Red Riding-Hood's confiding nature and the ease with which she is diverted from her errand; Cinderella's girlish longing for pretty clothes and the pleasures she sees others enjoying; Snow-White's susceptibility to the wiles of the witch-queen whose enticements are such as might appeal to any little girl — also the child's charming assumption of domestic duties in the dwarfs' cottage; the lonely little Herd-Boy's longing for the fairy treasures he finds — and all his youthful ardors; the heedless promise of the princess in "The Frog Prince" and her subsequent reluctance to fulfill it; and the charming details of the brother-sister relation of Hansel and Grethel.

ANIMAL STORIES

Out of the numerous attempts which have been made to ascertain children's tastes and choices in literature by means of scientific investigation, relatively few clearly established facts have emerged. Among these, one of the most certain is that children have a strong liking for animal stories. This springs, of course, from their delight in real animals, manifested as it is at a very early age.

Folk tales are particularly rich in animal subjects. The life of man has been so bound up in that of animals that most of his early records show the lower creatures in some relation to himself. They were dreaded enemies, objects of worship, re-embodied spirits of the dead, and at last, friendly neighbors — the givers of life's necessities and, as such, adopted into the family. No wonder the early stories of all races abound in animal characters. Their mysterious and startling likeness to man in many ways, together with the widespread belief in transmigration of souls, caused primitive peoples to attribute to animals the feelings and intelligence of human beings. This accounts in part for the very intimate relation between man and the lower creatures so universal in fairy tales, and for their active participation in his affairs on terms of equality.

As these tales have come down to us, most of the animals have been stripped of their terrifying traits and they are pictured as wise, friendly and beneficent. Sometimes they possess real personalities and play leading rôles as in "Puss-in-Boots," "The White Cat," and "Beauty and the Beast." In the last two, the animals are human beings under a magic spell, restored to their true form at the close of the story. Of this type, there are many interesting examples. In other stories, animals are represented *as* animals with little elaboration of human qualities, and they remain animals to the end. Their power to talk and to reason while retaining their natural appearance and many of their native traits, makes them particularly interesting to children. "Chicken-Little"; "The Three Billy Goats Gruff"; "The Little Red Hen"; "The Bremen Town Musicians"; and "Wee Robin's Christmas Song" (to mention only a few), belong to this class.

The Uncle Remus stories are ancient animal tales retold in Negro dialect and are unique in the sense of reality which they impart to characters and situations. Joel Chandler Harris's Brer Rabbit and Brer Fox are just as "real" as any figures in the realm of serious fiction, and the child who misses these stories misses something preeminent in a field which should be his very own.

HUMOR

Previous experience is always a potent factor in one's response to a given situation and nowhere does it count for more than in the sense of humor. Children may view with solemnity certain scenes and incidents which to their elders appear very funny, because they lack the normal experience which throws into relief the incongruous and absurd. For this reason some folk tales usually classed as humorous arouse no answering laugh from the younger children. This is apt to be true of the type called "Sillies" or "Noodles," such as "Klüge Elsa" and "What the Old Man Does is Always Right." The eminent common-sense of some children sees nothing funny in stupid behavior and they often assume a superior attitude toward such stupidity. When the acts described fit a child's world, however, they may appear laughably absurd instead of merely silly. "Epaminondas and His Auntie" usually brings shouts of laughter from seven-year-olds who would be cold to the apprehensive and weeping Elsa.

A good part of the fun is found in the animal stories where the humor is of a simple and rather obvious sort depending upon surprise, relief, awkward situations, and the discomfiture of unpopular characters. In these there is often a culminating scene of high comedy, such as occurs in "The Bremen Musicians," "The Tar Baby," and "The Coyote and the Locust" (Zuñi). Tales causing merry laughter are not so numerous as those which call forth chuckles of delight and smiles of quiet amusement. Many funny situations are rendered more laughable because the participants are animals possessing a certain individuality. In the language of children some animals are "cute," "cunning," and "smart." They take amused delight in Puss the audacious; clever little third Pig who outwits the wolf; Lambikin, gay and debonair; and in Drakestail (Drakesbill), the undaunted seeker after simple justice.

We have none too many humorous stories of literary worth for children, and traditional literature furnishes some of the best

CERTAIN ELEMENTS OF CHARM AND BEAUTY

The best of these stories are full of romance and poetry. There are scenes of simple rural beauty as well as those of princely splendor. Description is usually brief as befits a short, dramatic tale, but it is often highly pictorial with touches of poetic imagery which children can grasp. Evidence of this is so abundant that it seems useless to quote even short passages.

Among other things dear to a child's heart are the little houses which are so often encountered — not play-houses, but tiny and quaint abodes for all sorts of creatures. One thinks first of the tidy little house of the Three Bears, and the Dwarfs' house which sheltered Snow-White, but there are others just as charming. The Toads' house in Grimm's "The Iron Stove" [1] is a quaint and lively place.

Rare and beautiful objects have an important place in many stories, and one feels inclined to impute to some of them the enhancing effect which Walter Pater claims for two exquisite cups which appear again and again in the French medieval tale, "Amis and Amile":

> ... serving the two heroes almost like living things, and with that well-known effect of a beautiful object, kept constantly before the eye in a story or poem, of keeping sensation well awake, and giving a certain air of refinement to all the scenes into which it enters.[2]

In this connection we think of the lovely tree with leaves of silver and fruit of gold which comforted and sustained Little Two-Eyes, thwarted her enemies, and magically followed her to her new home; of Cinderella's little glass slipper; and of all the mystically beautiful elfin horns, magic harps, caps-of-roses, carved caskets, and prophetic mirrors which serve to enhance the beauty and interest of so many of these tales.

SONGS AND REFRAINS

The admixture of prose and verse in traditional tales is a striking feature and one which contributes much to

[1] Lang, Andrew, *The Yellow Fairy Book.*
[2] Pater, Walter, *The Renaissance.*

their charm. It is believed that the *cante-fable*, or tale in which verse is thus interspersed, owes its form to the ballad as sung in ancient times by troubadours and minstrels. Professional story-tellers of the Orient and among American Indians fall into song at intervals, verses are embedded in *Arabian Nights* tales, and the oldest Norse and Icelandic literature shows the same feature.

In the true *cante-fable*, the verse is something more than a refrain, it helps to develop the tale by narrating certain incidents or deepening certain impressions. Walter Pater defines it as "a tale told in prose, but with its incidents and sentiment helped forward by songs, inserted at irregular intervals." [1]

"Childe Rowland" is a perfect example of this type of story:

> Childe Rowland and his brothers twain
>   Were playing at the ball,
> And there was their sister Burd Ellen
>   In the midst among them all.

> Childe Rowland kicked it with his foot
>   And caught it with his knee;
> At last he plunged among them all,
>   O'er the church he made it flee. [2]

Burd Ellen goes to seek the ball and does not return. As told by Jacobs, all events up to the quest for his sister by the eldest brother are told in verse. From that point on, four-line stanzas are interspersed with fine effect:

> But long they waited, and longer still,
>   With doubt and muckle pain,
> But woe were the hearts of his brethren,
>   For he came not back again.

"The Black Bull of Norroway" [3] is another excellent

[1] Pater, Walter, *The Renaissance*.
[2] Jacobs, Joseph, *English Fairy Tales*. Steel, Flora A., *English Fairy Tales*.
[3] Steel, Flora A., *English Fairy Tales*. Rhys, Ernest, *Fairy Gold*.

example of *cante-fable*. The version referred to introduces three four-line stanzas which tell a part of the story. The first stanza contains definite reference to the minstrel:

> To wilder measures now they turn
> The black, black Bull of Norroway,
> Sudden the tapers cease to burn,
> The minstrels cease to play.

There is a plaintive refrain also which occurs at crucial points and which may have been part of a recurrent song:

> Far have I sought thee,
> Long have I wrought for thee,
> Near am I brought to thee,
> Dear Duke o' Norroway
> Wilt thou say naught to me?

MacCulloch [1] does not attribute all rhymed refrains to a ballad origin. He thinks that some of them were inserted for emphasis, for dramatic effect, or are the remains of incantations and magical spells. The following refrains seem to be of this kind:

> Shiver and shake, dear little tree
> Gold and silver shower on me. [2]

> Flounder, Flounder in the sea,
> Prythee hearken unto me. [3]

> Take not the green!
> Take not the red!
> But take the blue!
> On which you'll see
> The crosses three! [4]

After suggesting several slightly different views regarding the *cante-fable* feature in folk tales, MacCulloch says,

We cannot assert dogmatically... that *all* folk tales once were poems or ballads, though some no doubt were.... There

---

[1] MacCulloch, *op. cit.*, p. 480.
[2] From *Ashenpüttel*, the German *Cinderella*.
[3] From *The Fisherman and His Wife*.
[4] From the Norse Tale, *The Two Sisters*.

may have been some primitive rhythmic narrative, neither verse nor prose, out of which ballads on the one hand and folk tales on the other, were evolved.

With this point of view Joseph Jacobs appears to agree. He says:

> ... there seems to be great probability that originally all folk tales of a serious character were interspersed with rhyme, and took therefore the form of the *cante-fable*. It is indeed unlikely that the ballad itself began as continuous verse, and the *cante-fable* is probably the protoplasm out of which both ballad and folk tale have been differentiated, the ballad by omitting the narrative prose, the folk tale by expanding it.[1]

Children respond with delight to rhymed refrains, and like an audience among primitive peoples, they often join in unison in familiar rhymed and cadenced parts. It is this inimitable quality more perhaps than any other, which enraptures young children with such stories as "The Old Woman and Her Pig," "Henny-Penny," "Drakestail," "Lambikin," and many other favorites. This rhythmic, lyric quality is more pronounced in some languages than in others, but native English and Celtic tales possess much of this charm.

MORAL QUALITY

There has been constant discussion of the moral qualities of these old tales almost from the beginning of their publication, and opposing views were perhaps never more extreme than at present. They range from the earnest advocacy of a few specified tales to be used as a means of developing in children certain catalogued character traits to the sweeping condemnation of all of them during the entire period of childhood. Happily these extreme views are espoused by a relatively small number of theorists and the great mass of educated parents, as well as teachers, librarians, and critics view the question in a much more

[1] Jacobs, Joseph, *English Fairy Tales*, Notes. G. P. Putnam's Sons.

balanced way. They are skeptical of obtaining any marked effect in conduct either good or bad from a specific bit of literature except as it serves in some measure to accent more potent habit-forming influences; and they believe it to be entirely unsound to view the great mass of folk tales as being all of a kind and subject to the same praise or blame. They would like to see traditional literature treated like any other literature or like music and pictures, and judged largely by its probable effect in adding to the recipient's capacity to enjoy fine things. If such a response is spontaneous and genuine, there is basis for hope that literature will not only yield present enjoyment, but that certain ideals and admirations regarding human conduct will be strengthened.

Preoccupation with the idea of making literature teach ethical lessons has always resulted in absurd inconsistencies. "Beauty and the Beast" or "Cinderella" may be cited as exemplifying six or eight specified virtues while other equally good stories are passed over altogether. Or such a story as "Faithful John" may be found over and over again in lists selected for their ethical worth, the sponsors apparently overlooking the fact that this tale employs as an essential step in the plot an act of primitive and hideous slaughter of the innocents.

The only answer to the critics who object to the illogic of these old tales and who see in this trait a species of untruth is that they are using a false measuring-rod. Of course, these tales are illogical, just as a great deal of poetry and other imaginative literature is. The greatest injury that can be done to such stories is to attempt to make them reasonable, to try to explain events in terms of a rational world. Their peculiar charm lies in their freedom from everyday logic, and their richness is derived from the free flight of imagination. Brian Hooker [1] in one of his

[1] Hooker, Brian, "Fairy Tales," *The Forum*, volume 40 (1908).

delightful articles argues that the best fairy tales are truer in an idealistic way than life itself with its chaos and conflict.

Another fallacy has been to judge all of these old stories from their possible effect upon children from three to six years of age, forgetting that a few years are apt to make a vast difference in a child's mental furnishing and emotional reactions. The many choice collections now available, admirably planned to give pleasure at different stages of maturity, render it a comparatively simple matter to make appropriate selections for home and school use without being tempted to resort to inartistic "reformed" and anæmic versions.

SUGGESTIONS FOR FURTHER STUDY

1. Look for passages in Perrault's fairy tales which show: (*a*) simple, direct, childlike ideas and language; (*b*) more sophisticated behavior, or apparent striving for literary effect.

2. Look for evidences of wavering or inconsistency as regards the inclusion or exclusion of primitive and unpleasant folklore features in Perrault's stories.

3. Which of the stories contain fairies, and how are they depicted? What other forms or modes of magic does Perrault employ?

4. Read two or three stories by Madame d'Aulnoy (1650–1705) and compare with Perrault's style, noting conspicuous differences as to simplicity, sincerity of tone, and economy of incident.

5. Starting with Perrault's version of "Little Red Riding-Hood" read five or six other versions or adaptations. Few old tales have suffered so many changes. How do you account for this?

6. Analyze several stories to show their dramatic-narrative qualities. The following questions might be used as guides: Has the story a theme? Do the leading characters greatly desire something? Does the action seem to be the result of laws of human nature? Do causes and motives of action lie in the introduction? What are the incidents in the compli-

cation or entanglement? What are the steps in untangling the threads? Where is the main crisis or climax? Does the end seem final and satisfying?

7. Find several good examples of each of the story patterns mentioned on pages 98 and 99. Try to invent visual schematic representations of a few of the most obvious and striking patterns.

8. The display of human traits:
    The better side of human nature.
    Gross exaggerations of human traits.

9. Character delineation. How is it accomplished?

10. Is it generally true that leading characters obtain their desires with little or no effort on their part? Give extensive evidence.

11. Supernatural agencies which operate. Wonder-working devices, magic articles and labors, their part and power.

12. Unheroic heroes and heroines.

13. Scenes of domestic life.

14. Evidences that folk tales are "close to the soil."

15. Animal characters and their relation to people. (Fables should not be included.)

16. A quantitative study of animal characters in folk tales. Examine eight or ten general collections of European tales (exclusive of fables) and ascertain approximately the percentage in which animals appear.

17. Examine collections of any five or six different national folk tales and make a list of all the fairy creatures which appear — fairies, elves, mermaids, giants, trolls, etc.

18. Truthful representation of animal life in American Indian tales.

19. Poetic imagery in American Indian tales.

20. Study the work of leading illustrators of fairy tales and note how they have conceived of all the fairy creatures they have portrayed.

21. Varieties of humor. Try to make a rough scale from farce to delicate humor, using story titles as steps. This will have to be from the adult standpoint.

22. Extend the discussion in this chapter regarding the mixture of prose and rhyme and seek additional examples, showing

verse used, (*a*) in the development of the narrative, (*b*) for emphasis or pleasing effect.

23. Compose word pictures showing your conception of six child characters in folk tales.

In addition to the above topics omitting all duplicates, the following titles for papers were proposed and used by a class in Children's Literature:

Enchanted Princes in Fairy Tales
Clothes and the Woman
The Glass of Fashion
Fairyland's Social Register
Journeys in Fairyland
Prince Charming
Cinder-Maid and Cinder-Lad
Poetic Justice in Fairy Tales
Witches and Witchcraft
The Child's World in Fairy Tales
Fairy Banquets
Pageantry in Fairy Tales
Magic Numbers
Strenuous Heroines
The Charm of Tiny Objects
Remarkable Frogs
Remarkable Cats

REFERENCES

I

HISTORY AND CRITICISM

Buchan, John. *Novel and the Fairy Tale*. Pamphlet 79. The English Association. Oxford University Press, 1931.
    Traces interesting correspondences.

Cox, Marian R. *Cinderella*; 345 Variants... with notes by Marian R. Cox. Introduction by Andrew Lang. (Folk-Lore Society) London, 1893.

Esenwein, J. B.; and Stockard, Marietta. *Children's Stories*. Home Correspondence School, Springfield, Mass., 1917.
    Discusses typical features of folk tales.

Grabo, Carl H. *The Art of the Short Story*. Scribner, 1913.
    Contains a suggestive analysis of "Cinderella" as a typical fairy tale, pp. 9–18.

Hartland, E. S. *Science of Fairy Tales*, an inquiry into fairy mythology. London, 1891.

Hill, May. "The Place of the Folk Tale Today," *Childhood Education*, November, 1931.

Hooker, Brian. "Fairy Tales," *The Forum*, volume 40, 1908.

Hooker, Brian. "Narrative and the Fairy Tale," *Bookman*, June and July, 1911.
>   The latter article is unsurpassed in its field.

Kready, Laura F. *A Study of Fairy Tales*. Houghton, 1916.

Lang, Andrew. *Custom and Myth*. Longmans, 1884, 1910.
>   Lang here presents his theory regarding the origin and dissemination of folk tales, pp. 10–28.

MacCulloch, J. A. *The Childhood of Fiction;* a study of folk tales and primitive thought. London, 1905.
>   Chapter XVII, "The Origin and Transmission of Folk Tales."

Moore, Annie E. "Shall We Banish the Fairies?" *The Parents' Magazine,* volume 6, no. VIII, August, 1931.

Repplier, Agnes. "Battle of the Babies," *Essays in Miniature*. Houghton, 1895, 1923.
>   A gallant defense of the old fairy tales.

II

The following list is designed to meet the needs of students seeking an acquaintance with some of the strongest streams of national and racial folk literature. Most of these books are intended for children, and have a place above third grade, as a rule. Almost all of them contain some stories which may be read or told to younger children.

AMERICAN INDIAN

Taytay's Tales. Collected and retold by Elizabeth De Huff. Harcourt, 1922.
>   The Preface states that the stories were collected from Pueblo Indians and illustrated by a seventeen-year-old Hopi boy, Fred Kabotie, assisted by another Hopi boy, Otis Polelonema.

Skunny Wundy and Other Indian Tales. Arthur C. Parker. Illustrated by Will Crawford. Doran, 1926.
>   The author is a native Seneca Indian and his stories are

of the explanatory type telling about certain peculiar characteristics of animals. Some of them are very clever and
amusing.

Indian Why Stories. Frank B. Linderman. Scribner.
"I propose to tell what I know of these legends, keeping
as near as possible to the Indian's style of story-telling, and
using only tales told me by the older men of the Blackfeet,
Chippewa, and Cree tribes." (Preface.)

The Red Indian Fairy Book. Collected and edited by Frances
Jenkins Olcott. Illustrated by Frederick Richardson.
Houghton, 1917.
An excellent collection from various tribes, of stories
which Miss Olcott refers to as "Red Indian nature myths....
The character and spirit of the original stories have been
carefully preserved." (Introduction.)

The New World Fairy Book. Howard Angus Kennedy. Illustrated by H. R. Millar. Dutton.
The author does not indicate the tribes from which his
tales were secured nor does he claim that all of them are
pure Indian folk-lore.

Zuñi Folk Tales. Frank Hamilton Cushing, Collector and
Translator. Foreword by J. W. Powell. Introduction by
Mary Austin. First edition, 1901. Knopf, 1931.
Mary Austin says this "collection of Zuñi Folk Tales is
the first... and best sustained translation of aboriginal
American literature." "He [Cushing] remains uniquely
the only man not of their blood who understood completely
the soul of such lore among the Americans of the West."

East Indian

Tales of the Punjab. Compiled by Flora Annie Steel. Macmillan, 1894.
Here may be found the early forms of a number of the
best known accumulative stories together with important
comments.

English

Jacobs, Joseph.
English Fairy Tales. Putnam, 1904.
More English Fairy Tales. Putnam, 1911.
In his Preface to the second book Jacobs as collector and
editor states his position in regard to making certain changes

in the old tales, and defends in vigorous terms such changes as he has made.

FRENCH

Perrault, Charles.

> *Popular Tales*. Edited by Andrew Lang. Clarendon Press, London, 1888.
>
>> The stories are in French and are an exact reproduction of the original. The introduction and Notes by Lang, in English, constitute an invaluable reference.
>
> *The Tales of Mother Goose*. Translated by Charles Welsh. Introduction by M. V. O'Shea. Heath, 1901.
>
>> The stories are told in simpler English, but are in general true to the original.
>
> *Old-Time Stories*. Translated by A. E. Johnson. Illustrated by W. Heath Robinson. Dodd, 1921.
>
>> Contains eight stories by Perrault and several by other early French writers, including Madame d'Aulnoy.

Aulnoy, Marie Catherine, Comtesse d'.

> *The Fairy Tales of Madame d'Aulnoy*. Introduction by Anne Thackeray Ritchie. Illustrated by Clinton Peters. London, 1892.
>
>> A very interesting and enlightening Introduction.
>
> *The White Cat and Other Old French Fairy Tales*. Arranged by Rachel Field. Pictures by Elizabeth MacKinstry. Macmillan, 1928.
>
>> Contains "The White Cat"; "Graciosa and Percinet"; "A Pot of Carnations"; "Prince Sprite" [Prince Elfin]; and "The Good Little Mouse." A notably beautiful book.

GERMAN

Grimm, Jacob L. K., and Grimm, William K.

> *Household and Fairy Tales:* with the authors' notes. Translated by Margaret Hunt. Introduction by Andrew Lang. 2 volumes. London, Bell, 1901.
>
>> The Introduction offers a very full statement of Lang's theory regarding the origin and dispersal of folk tales.
>
> *Household Stories*. Translated by Lucy Crane. Pictures by Walter Crane. Macmillan, 1882.
>
>> Contains 53 stories, several of which if judged from children's needs might well have been omitted. Walter Crane's

pictures in black and white are exquisite in conception and execution.

Same. Macmillan, 1930.

    Contains only 32 stories better chosen for children than the larger book.

Grimm's Fairy Tales. Edited by Frances J. Olcott. Illustrated by Rie Cramer. Penn., 1922.

    Miss Olcott says her edition is based on the Hunt version, which "is considered a most accurate English translation." Selections are well chosen.

NORSE

Asbjörnsen, Peter Christian.

Tales from the Fjeld. A series of popular tales from the Norse of P. C. Asbjörnsen by Sir George Webb Dasent. First published in 1874. Putnam, 1896.

    Many of these stories are of a humorous type. They should be known in a style close to the original before having been modified by later editors.

East of the Sun and West of the Moon: Old Tales from the North. Translated by Sir George Webb Dasent. Illustrated by Kay Neilsen. Doubleday.

East of the Sun and West of the Moon. Illustrated by Hedwig Collin. Macmillan, 1928.

    Contains twelve of the most popular of Asbjörnsen's tales with pictures by an accomplished Danish artist.

III

Collections especially designed for children nine years of age and under, arranged in approximate order of simplicity. Interests of the five-to-seven-year-olds are well met in the first thirteen titles.

Nursery Tales from Many Lands. Eleanor Skinner and Ada M. Skinner. Illustrated by Blanche Fisher Wright. Scribner.

    Nineteen stories well suited to kindergarten–first grade.

Told Under the Green Umbrella. Selected by the Literature Committee of the International Kindergarten Union. Pictures by Grace Gilkison. Macmillan.

    Twenty-six stories of which all but two or three are folk tales. Chosen with taste and judgment, for young children.

My Book House, volume II.   *Up One Pair of Stairs*.   The Book-house for Children.   Chicago.

> This volume contains quite a number of the best old tales in simple form.

Old, Old Tales Retold.   Frederick Richardson.   Volland.

> Eight favorite nursery tales with full page pictures in color.

Chimney Corner Stories.   Edited by Veronica S. Hutchinson. Illustrated by Lois Lenski.   Minton.

> Sixteen favorite nursery tales.   An excellent collection for young children.   Large type.

Fireside Stories.   Collected and retold by Veronica S. Hutchinson. Drawings by Lois Lenski.   Minton.

> Fifteen stories forming another excellent collection. Large type.

East o' the Sun and West o' the Moon.   Gudrun Thorne Thomsen. Row.

> Popular tales from the Norse told in simple but vivid style.

The House in the Wood.   With drawings by Leslie Brooke. Warne.

> This charming picture book contains a number of stories well suited to younger children.

The Book of Fables and Folk Stories.   Horace E. Scudder. Illustrated by Maurice Day.   Houghton.

> A fine and varied collection of old tales.

Picture Tales from the Russian.   Valery Carrick.   Stokes.

More Picture Tales from the Russian.   Valery Carrick.   Stokes.

> Both these books contain delightful old tales told in a simple and vivid style.

The Fairy Ring.   Kate Douglas Wiggin and Nora Archibald Smith.   Doubleday.

> A large collection of tales from many countries.

Tales of Laughter.   Kate Douglas Wiggin and Nora Archibald Smith.   Illustrated by Elizabeth MacKinstry.   Doubleday.

> A superior collection which justifies its title.

Pepper and Salt, or Seasoning for Young Folk.   Howard Pyle. Harper.

> The expanded form of these stories and Howard Pyle's exquisite drawings and decorations make this a choice book for children of nine or ten years.

The Reign of King Oberon. Edited by Walter Jerrold. Drawings by Charles Robinson. Dutton.

    Stories told at the fairy court by "native" fairy creatures from different countries.

The Blue Fairy Book. Andrew Lang. Longmans.

    Authentic version of many old favorites from many nations.

Fillmore Folk Tales. Selected for Young Folks, by Wilhelmina Harper. Illustrated by Jay Van Everen. Harcourt.

    The best tales for children from two of Parker Fillmore's collections. The freshness and variety of these stories from Finland and Jugoslavia make them very acceptable to children who have outgrown the old nursery favorites.

The Atlantic Treasury of Childhood Stories. Selected and edited by Mary D. Hutchinson Hodgkins. Atlantic Monthly Press.

    An excellent general collection which includes several less well known English and Irish tales.

CHAPTER V

FABLES

So the tales were told before Æsop; and asses under lions' manes roared in Hebrew; and sly foxes flattered in Etruscan; and wolves in sheep's clothing gnashed their teeth in Sanskrit, no doubt.

THACKERAY, *The Newcomes*

THE term "fable" has come to be applied rather specifically to the short moralistic stories commonly attributed to Æsop. Such tales are in fact more ancient than the period in which Æsop is supposed to have lived (620–560 B.C.). They have come down to us through a tortuous and complicated route difficult to decipher, but certain dim paths extend back to India. In his *History of Æsop's Fables*,[1] Joseph Jacobs has shown very clearly their origin and descent. This book is now difficult to obtain, but fortunately Jacobs has given elsewhere [2] a condensed account, together with ample notes on sources and a graph showing the "Pedigree of Æsop," which serves every ordinary purpose of the student. One thing is clear — that many tributaries have poured into the main stream since the time of Æsop.

As to Æsop himself, one may choose between the not improbable theory that such a person never really lived and the highly detailed and picturesque biography written by the monk, Planudes (1260–1330). Scholars who have gone deeply into the question are convinced that Planudes had little or no evidence on which to base the characterization of Æsop which has proved so persistent. He pictured

---

[1] *The Fables of Æsop, as first printed by William Caxton, 1484.* Edited and introduced by Joseph Jacobs. Nutt, London, 1889.
[2] *The Fables of Æsop. Selected, Told Anew, and Their History Traced.* By Joseph Jacobs. Macmillan, 1894.

the fabulist as ugly, sadly deformed, and having the appearance of an idiot. His account is given in full in some editions of *La Fontaine's Fables*.[1]

The eminent English scholar and critic, Richard Bentley, considers this story wholly unreliable if not a pure fabrication. Of Planudes he says:

> That Idiot of a Monk has given us a Book, which he calls *The Life of Œsop*, that, perhaps, cannot be matched in any Language, for Ignorance and Nonsense.... But of all his injuries to *Æsop*, that which can least be forgiven him, is, the making such a Monster of him for Ugliness: an abuse, that has found credit so universally; that all modern Painters, since the time of *Planudes*, have drawn him in the worst Shapes and Features, that Fancy could invent.[2]

It does not matter so much where these stories came from or what the status and appearance of their supposed author. Many of them bear very little trace of the downtrodden and subject people to whom some of them were undoubtedly addressed. They constitute a part of our literary inheritance and as such should be examined in various collections for the purpose of judging their fitness for particular ages and purposes. They constitute one of the most changeless types of traditional literature. Folk tales have been transformed through the centuries both unconsciously and deliberately, myths have been drastically edited, but fables as seen in their earliest known written form have undergone few changes in essential features. The appended moral, however, has been tacked on, abbreviated, expanded to sermon dimensions, distorted, or omitted altogether, according to the taste and intentions of various editors.

[1] See, *Fables de La Fontaine*. Nouvelle Édition par M. Charles Aubertin. Paris, Bélin Frères, n.d., pp. 53–72.

[2] *Reflections upon Ancient and Modern Learning*. William Wotton. With a Dissertation upon the Epistles of Phalaris, Themistocles, Socrates, Euripides, and Æsop's Fables. By Dr. Bentley. London. Printed by S. Leake, 1697.

MORAL QUALITIES

Whether the moral is specifically stated or not it is evident that fables have generally been intended to convey a particular lesson concerning human behavior. The preface or prologue of the Caxton [1] edition states that purpose in plain terms.

> ... Esope man of grece/subtyll and Ingenyous/techeth in his fables how men ought to kepe and rewle them well/and to the ende that he shold shewe the lyf and customes of al maner of men/he induceth the byrdes/the trees and the beestes spekynge to the ende that the men may knowe wherefore the fables were found/In the whiche he hath wreton the malyce of the evylle people and the argument of the Improbes/He techeth also to be humble and for to use wordes/And many other fayr Ensamples reherced and declared hereafter/the whiche I Romulus have translated oute of grekes tongue in to latyn tongue/the whiche yf thou rede them/they shalle aguyse [2] and sharpe they wytte and shalle gyve to the cause of Joye/

In some early editions, the moral lesson is stated at the beginning and is then repeated in slightly different form at the end. An example of this is found in Caxton's "The Lyon and the Rat," [3] commonly known today as "The Lion and the Mouse." It begins:

> The mighty and puissant must pardon and forgive to the little and feeble and ought to keep him from all evil. For ofttime the little may well give aid and help to the great. Whereof Esope rehearseth to us such a fable.

The moral statement at the close is:

> Therefore this fable teacheth us how that a man mighty and puissant ought not to dispraise the little. For sometimes he that can do no body hurt nor let, may at a need give help and aid to the great.

---

[1] *The Fables of Æsop, as first Printed by William Caxton, 1484.* Edited and introduced by Joseph Jacobs. Nutt, London, 1889.
[2] Make acute.   [3] *The Fables of Æsop*, p. 26.

Modern collections for children tend to give a very brief statement of the moral at the end, or they omit it entirely.

Although fables more than any other type of literature have been long and widely used for definite moral instruction, their defects in this connection have been pointed out many times. Rousseau's [1] direct attack will be recalled. He says:

> Fables may instruct men, but children must be told the bare truth; for the moment we cover truth with a veil, they no longer give themselves the trouble to lift it.

He believed that fables were misleading and greatly lacking in the clarity that is claimed for them. He cites "The Ant and the Cricket" as an example of a fable which is not unequivocal in meaning; a child, he believes, would be just as likely to admire and imitate the cold justice and contempt of the ant as to take warning from the *insouciance* of the cricket. Felix Adler [2] has enlarged very greatly along a similar vein, though he by no means condemns fables altogether. He believes, as do many others who are greatly concerned with the possible effect of literature on behavior, that many fables are distinctly unethical in their import and that others are quite misleading and calculated to call forth misplaced approval and admiration.

The question of the influence of literature over attitudes, ideals, and behavior patterns is discussed more fully in Chapter IV. Here it is in place to remark that if we believe at all in the effect of vicarious experience we should select all literature, including fables, with some regard to the models portrayed and the kind of responses most likely to be called forth. Will approval, disapproval, consent, admiration, recoil, probably be so directed as to militate in favor of desirable standards of conduct?

[1] Rousseau, Jean Jacques, *Émile.* Book Second.
[2] Adler, Felix, *The Moral Instruction of Children.*

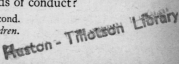

It must be admitted that there are many more fables which show cold selfishness and wanton cruelty as moving forces than there are of those which exhibit kind or generous motives. There are some in which desired ends are obtained, not by force or deceit, but simply by the exercise of discretion and good sense, and a few in which a character gains something for himself by his keen wit, but without taking advantage of another. In a still smaller number motives of kindness and a spirit of magnanimity are dominant. A fable of the latter type (though it is not called a fable) is included in *Merry Tales*.[1] It bears the title "True Friendship" and relates how victorious soldiers bring to the ant their king, four prisoners, a spider, a bee, a grasshopper, and a cricket. The first two save their lives by pleading their usefulness. The last two are about to be executed when they plead the value of their profession as entertainers of weary people. They sing and dance and win favor and freedom for the four. It may not be out of place to mention here a charming modern story on this same theme — *Grasshopper Green and the Meadow Mice*, by John Rae. (Volland.)

FABLES AND NURSERY TALES COMPARED

The implacable quality so often noted in fables is seldom found in popular folk tales or *Märchen*. The situations are sometimes quite similar, but the fable seldom admits a happy outcome. There is a resemblance in situation between the fable "The Fisher and the Little Fish,"[2] and the household tale "The Three Billy Goats Gruff." The little fish begs the fisherman to let him go, pleading that he is too small to eat, but that if put back and allowed to grow he will make the man a fine meal later on. "Nay, nay, my little Fish," says the man, "I have you now.

---

[1] Skinner, E. L. and A. M., *Merry Tales*.
[2] Jacobs, *op. cit.*, p. 124. Macmillan.

I may not catch you hereafter." And that is the end of the little fish.

In the nursery tale mentioned, Little Billy Goat and Middle-Size Billy Goat make a similar appeal to the troll who is about to devour them. Their plea is that they will make him a very small dinner whereas Big Billy Goat who will be coming along soon will furnish a much larger meal. Impelled by greed, the troll lets the two smaller ones go and awaits the third goat, who makes short work of the enemy.

There are several popular household tales in which the central character wins his way through great difficulties by the successive aid of a number of friends whom he has attached to himself by previous acts of kindness. "Drakestail" is of this pattern and so is "Peasie and Beansie." In both of these tales, friends are quickly responsive at a time of need and help to bring matters to a happy issue. The fable called "The Hare With Many Friends" [1] employs a similar situation, but the spirit is quite different. The hare about to be overtaken by hounds appeals for aid to one professed friend after another — horse, bull, goat, ram, calf; but each in turn makes excuse and leaves her to her fate. At last, seeing herself deserted, she "took to her heels and luckily escaped." In this case the character in distress escapes, but not by the help of her friends. In the nursery tale, one expects that the innocent in distress will obtain help from some quarter; in the fable one is surprised if such help arrives. The stated moral of the fable just mentioned is, "He that has many friends has no friends." This is quite the reverse of the dominant idea in nursery tales.

The personality of characters in fables is so meagerly defined that such stories are not calculated to arouse in children the keen emotional response which is called forth

[1] Jacobs, *op. cit.*, p. 168. Macmillan.

by the best nursery tales. The fate of the innocent and wronged in a fable can scarcely enlist the deep sympathy which is felt for an engaging human character or a well-delineated animal character. The laconic account of a lamb, a kid, or a frog in danger or distress will hardly bring the emotional response, the ardent championship, which may be aroused by the pitiful or tragic situation of a Cinderella, a Prince Charming, or a Peter Rabbit. For this reason, if for no other, the possible moral effect of fables has probably been greatly exaggerated.

HUMAN BEINGS IN FABLES

G. K. Chesterton [1] regards as very inferior all fables which employ human beings as leading characters. He says, "There can be no good fairy tale without them." He then proceeds to offer some very interesting and forceful arguments to sustain his position. Of course the key word in Chesterton's stricture is the term "good" and his own taste is the criterion. He argues that animals may be used in an "austere and arbitrary style as they are used on the shields of heraldry," but that human beings cannot, with success, be made to serve as mere symbols. In this, Chesterton is simply enlarging in his own trenchant manner on a principle stated by Aristotle.

La Fontaine [2] cites the same classic authority, but refuses to accept the principle as essential. He says:

Aristotle admits only animal characters in the fable; he excludes human beings and plants. This rule is not so much obligatory as it is a matter of taste (*bienséance*) since neither Æsop, nor Phædrus, nor any of the fabulists observes it.

A hasty count of both ancient and modern collections displays this rule in its breach rather than in its observance. The first sixty in Jacob's collection are from one

---

[1] Chesterton, G. K., Introduction to *Æsop's Fables*. Doubleday.
[2] Free translation, Preface to *La Fontaine's Fables*. Edited 1668, included in Nouvelle édition par M. Charles Aubertin. Librairie Classique, Eugene Bélin, Paris, n.d.

of the most ancient sources, and one third of these have
human beings playing leading parts. In *An Argosy of
Fables* [1] there are 220 attributed to Æsop. Of these 35
per cent contain human beings in important parts and 14
per cent have human characters only. If plants, common
objects, and natural elements were included in the estimate,
the percentage of fables employing animal characters would,
of course, be still further reduced.

No matter how one may regard this rather academic
question, it seems to be true that the most popular, and
universally familiar fables tend to be those in which animals
play the sole or the leading parts. Some of the best known
outside this category are: "The Oak and the Reed";
"The Shepherd-Boy and the Wolf"; "The Wind and the
Sun"; "The Bundle of Sticks"; "The Milkmaid and Her
Pail of Milk"; "Hercules and the Waggoner"; "The Boy
Bathing"; "The Miser."

As a slight clue to the most popular or best-known fables,
the same procedure was followed with certain groups of
students in children's literature as that described on
page 19. The following table shows the frequency with
which certain titles occurred in the returns from these
particular people. Most of them had taught in kindergarten or primary grades. This partial report gives only
those titles which appeared on 25 per cent, or more, of
the papers. Notice how far "The Fox and the Grapes"
exceeds in frequency any other fable named.

Total Number of Lists, 100	Frequency	Rank
The Fox and the Grapes	68	1
The Fox and the Crow	44	2
The Dog and His Shadow	39	3
The Crow and the Pitcher	36	4
The Lion and the Mouse	30	5
The Hare and the Tortoise	28	6
The Dog in the Manger	27	7
The Boy Who Cried Wolf	27	

[1] Cooper, Frederic Faber, collector, *An Argosy of Fables*. Stokes, 1921.

ÆSOP AS AN ANIMAL PICTURE BOOK

Beginning with the very earliest editions, collections of fables have been copiously illustrated, usually at least one picture for every story. Jacobs in his *Fables of Bidpai* [1] shows that illustrations were in very ancient copies, one dating as early as A.D. 750. He says, "There seems every reason to believe that illustrations were regarded as an integral part of the text and were translated, if one may say so, along with it." The Caxton edition of Æsop and others somewhat later had many crude wood-cuts like a child's drawings, which adults today find very amusing. Then came the exquisite wood engravings of Thomas Bewick (1753–1828) and John Bewick (1760–1795) with their delightful conception of incident and character, depicted in small dimensions with clear and beautiful detail.

An account of modern illustrators and their work in this field would fill a volume of some size. We wish merely to call attention to the fact that a well-illustrated copy of Æsop forms a very fine animal picture book greatly enjoyed by children long before they can appreciate the stories themselves.

The following are titles of stories judged to be well suited to the younger children. The list is roughly graded. The first five or six are often included in selections for first grade.

> The Lion and the Mouse
> The Dove and the Ant
> City Mouse and Country Mouse
> The Hare and the Tortoise
> The Wind and the Sun
> The Lark and Her Young
> The Dog in the Manger

---

[1] *Fables of Bidpai.* Edited by Joseph Jacobs. Nutt, London, 1888. Contains early illustrations.

The Dog and His Shadow
The Crow and the Pitcher
The Boys and the Frogs
The Boy Who Cried Wolf
Androcles and the Lion
Hercules and the Cart Driver
The Fox and the Crow (Crow and Cheese)
Belling the Cat
The Milkmaid and Her Pail
The Miller, His Son, and Their Ass
The Fox and the Stork
The Fox and the Grapes

LA FONTAINE'S FABLES

Jean de la Fontaine (1621–1695) was born at the little town of Château-Thierry in the province of Champagne, where his father was King's Councillor and Commissioner of Waters and Forests. As a boy he wandered idly along the streams and among the wooded hills of this beautiful country which was to witness such terrible scenes of devastation in our time. He spent many carefree hours watching intently the animals, birds, and plant life which were protected and abundant. He was a nature-lover, and the keen observations of his youth survived the hectic and artificial life of the court circle of Louis XIV where he later became a prominent figure.

La Fontaine was a poet of high reputation, a member of the Royal Academy, and numbered among his close associates the greatest writers of that golden age of French literature — Molière, Corneille, Racine, and Boileau. It is interesting to note that Charles Perrault, also an Academician, was a contemporary, although the personal relations of the two men were not very close. While Perrault was writing his immortal fairy tales in the midst of a happy domestic circle, La Fontaine was composing his fables in verse for a gay and highly intellectual public. He was living apart from his wife and children in the *entourage* of successive patrons or "protectors" of rank and wealth.

By certain dedications he associated several of his books of fables with three children in turn, but it is quite probable that he had young people very little in mind in most of his compositions.

The first collection (1668) was dedicated to the Dauphin of France, then about six and a half years old. In his address to the child he said:

> You are now of an age at which amusement and play are permitted to princes; but at the same time you should give more thought to serious things. Such reflections you will encounter in the fables which we owe to Æsop. Their appearance is puerile, I confess, but underneath their trivialities are important truths.

He dedicated his twelfth and last book (1694) to another royal child, Le Duc de Burgogne, grandson of Louis XIV. In the dedication he says that he is presenting a work the model of which (Æsop) has been the admiration of great thinkers of all the ages. La Fontaine wrote several original fables at the suggestion of this boy on themes which his teacher Fénelon had probably given him. On one occasion [1] at least La Fontaine gave the fable back to the young prince without a stated moral, advising him in a few clever lines to amuse himself by discovering the meaning.

A single fable, the second in Book XI, was dedicated to another little boy, the Duc du Maine, son of Louis XIV and Mme. de Montespan, a precocious child of seven or eight years at the time. It is an allegory rather than a true fable. The child is called "the son of Jupiter" and is represented in the allegory as having been the recipient at birth of gifts from the Olympian gods.

[1] Fable 2, Book XII. Aubertin. *Le Chat et les Deux Moineaux.* English translation, *Argosy of Fables*, p. 346, "The Cat and the Two Sparrows," omits the closing lines.

La Fontaine's chief sources were Æsop's fables in Latin, Phædrus, and an incomplete collection of East Indian fables of Bidpai, though he drew extensively from many other writers, classic and medieval. Since Æsop and Bidpai are the main sources of English collections, the greater part of La Fontaine's fables are familiar to us in their main features, but most of them have been much elaborated and embellished by description and classical allusion. In the Preface mentioned above, the author declares that he does not hope to attain the brevity or *simplicité magnifique* of the ancients, but to compensate he has dared to enliven the fable more than they have done and to add novelty and gaiety to the narrative. "I do not mean by gaiety that which excites laughter, but a certain charm, a pleasing air which may be given to all kinds of subjects, even the most serious."

French children know their La Fontaine almost as early as our children know Mother Goose and they acquire during elementary school years a very thorough knowledge of the fables as told in verse by this great writer. For English-speaking children, however, there are many difficulties even in the best translations. Poetry always suffers in translations and the fables are no exception. Lines which are simple and direct in the original often become involved or confused in the English rhymed stanza. Of necessity, meter is changed, rhythm is sacrificed, and keen thrusts of wit are often dulled.

Several of La Fontaine's contributions which have excellent story quality have been turned into English prose, and now quite commonly appear in collections attributed to Æsop. So we are sometimes reading his stories without knowing it. "The Milkmaid and Her Pail of Milk"; "Belling the Cat"; "The Man, the Boy, and the Donkey", are from La Fontaine.

Except for such indirect acquaintance with a few stories,

our children will get their chief pleasure from the pictures in illustrated editions published in France. One of the most delightful is illustrated by Boutet de Monvel [1] and has long been popular as an animal picture book.

THE JATAKAS

The Jatakas are believed to constitute the oldest, as they do the largest, body of fables in existence. They formed a part of ancient Buddhist sacred literature and were written in Pàli, a dialect of Sanskrit. Carvings on architectural remains in India illustrate some of the Jatakas and bear inscriptions which further identify the subject. These remains are known to belong to a period as early as the third century before Christ.

These old beast tales tell of the rebirth of the Buddha as elephant, lion, monkey, camel, deer, bull, eagle, wild duck, and numerous other incarnations. Because these fables constituted a part of their sacred literature, they were widely used by wandering Buddhist teachers and at an early time they attained a relatively permanent written form.

The origin of these stories explains other interesting features. In his various forms, Buddha remembers previous existences; therefore he is able to give the "catchword" at the beginning of a tale which identifies him with one of the characters, and also to point out at the close the meaning of the whole. Buddha is, of course, a worthy character, so there is always one figure in the story who satisfies the conscience of the religionists of that cult and time. Since one-time human beings were believed to inhabit the bodies of animals, the sacredness of all life was a dominant tenet strictly observed. In consequence of this, kindliness between human beings and animals,

[1] *Fables de la Fontaine*. Illustrated by Boutet de Monvel. Paris. Plon.

and to some extent among the animals themselves, is a marked feature of this literature.

COMPARISONS

Critics have often compared the Jatakas with other fables, frequently to the disparagement of those which go under the name of Æsop. It has been said that the East Indian stories are on a higher moral plane than the others, that they depict magnanimous and friendly behavior where the Æsopic fables display cruelty, malice, and trickery. Felix Adler [1] says that the Jatakas "are nobly conceived, and lofty in meaning," and that they "are calculated to impress lessons of great moral beauty."

We get a much more comprehensive statement of opinion from E. B. Cowell who edited the five-volume Cambridge edition of the Jatakas. [2] In the Preface to volume I this great authority says,

> Like all collections of early popular tales they are full of violence and craft, and betray a low opinion of woman; but outbursts of nobler feeling are not wanting to relieve the darker colours.

Anyone interested in finding story material for children who turns to this great collection expecting to discover a rich mine of stories of special fitness and great moral beauty will be disappointed. There are 550 of these tales and only a small percentage are likely to suit the taste of Western civilization, while a still smaller number are suitable for children in either theme or incident. The high praise commonly accorded the Jatakas by critics of children's literature has evidently been elicited by the nature of contents of three small collections especially

---

[1] Adler, Felix, *Moral Instruction of Children.*
[2] *The Jataka, or Stories of the Buddha's Former Births.* Translated from the Pali by Various Hands. Editor, Professor E. B. Cowell. In 5 volumes. Cambridge University Press, 1895–1907.

selected for children and edited for their use. Both Miss Shedlock [1] and Miss Babbitt [2] have shown excellent discrimination in selection and their adaptations do not distort the original. Deducting eight duplicates, Miss Shedlock's one volume and Miss Babbitt's two contain in all thirty-one stories. Examination of the complete Cambridge edition shows that a thorough sifting was necessary to discover even this small number suitable for children. As chosen and presented in the books mentioned, the stories deserve all the praise that has been bestowed upon them.

Miss Shedlock's versions are for the most part better suited to the older children. The language is more in the key of the original and she has retained the catchword or briefly stated lesson at the beginning which shows their connection with Buddha. Miss Babbitt has frankly discarded this link and has told the tales in a manner well suited to primary grades.

Most of the Jatakas are considerably longer and are told with richer detail than the typical Æsopic fable. The stark outline of the latter is clothed by means of a more extended plot and the characters have a larger stage upon which to reveal themselves in action. These features furnish more of the story quality necessary to attract young readers. In fact, with no adaptation at all, quite a number of them appear as familiar folk tales which have found their way down the centuries into other literatures or have spontaneously arisen among different races, and no one but a specialist in folklore would think of classifying them as fables. Not only are there talking beasts and birds, but the supernatural is often introduced in the form of giants, ogres, dwarfs, and even fairies. They are

[1] Shedlock, Marie L., *Eastern Stories and Legends*. Dutton.
[2] *The Jatakas, Tales of India*. Retold by Ellen C. Babbitt. Century, 1912. *More Jataka Tales*. Same, 1922.

very close to the soil of Eastern primitive rural and village life and because human beings are so prominent much more of the customs and habits of the people are shown.

It is very interesting to discover in this legacy from the distant past the beginnings of certain treasured gems of story. Clever Brer Rabbit and his dramatic escape by way of the briar patch is recognized in "How the Turtle Saved His Life,"[1] and Henny-Penny, the timid little hen who started a panic by announcing that the sky was falling, is matched by the equally timid and nervous rabbit who conceived the same terrifying idea, as told in Miss Shedlock's first story.

Since the presentation of the Jatakas to children has been comparatively recent, they have not yet appeared in a variety of beautiful illustrated editions such as have added so greatly to the appeal and enjoyment of the fables of Æsop.

SUGGESTIONS FOR FURTHER STUDY

Find among Æsop's Fables examples which illustrate:
  1. Traits often found in children
  2. Traits more commonly found in adults
  3. Worthy behavior on part of dominant character
  4. Successful outcome of trickery
  5. Unsuccessful outcome of trickery
  6. "The Beguiler beguiled" or "one beaten with his own stick"
  7. Cleverness without malice

Discuss and illustrate:
  1. Obscure or equivocal meaning in fables
  2. The quality of humor in specific fables
  3. Proverbs and pithy sayings found in fables or associated with them
  4. Comparison of several of Æsop's fables with La Fontaine's versions of the same.
  5. Illustrators of fables

---

[1] Babbitt, *The Jatakas.*

Write an original fable on a familiar theme.

Which fables are used in the Binet-Simon Intelligence tests? At what age levels?

REFERENCES

The Fables of Æsop, told anew and their history traced by Joseph Jacobs; illustrated by Richard Heighway. Macmillan.
> An indispensable collection.

Æsop's Fables. Edited by V. S. V. Jones. Introduction by G. K. Chesterton. Illustrated by Arthur Rackham. Doubleday.
> The introduction offers an unusual viewpoint and an enlightening appreciation.

Æsop's Fables, an Anthology of the Fabulists of all Countries. Introduction by Ernest Rhys. (Everyman's Library) Dutton.

An Argosy of Fables. A Representative Selection from the Fable Literature of Every Age and Land. Selected and Edited by Frederick Taber Cooper. Illustrated by Paul Bransom. Stokes.

A Hundred Fables from Æsop; from the English Version of Roger l'Estrange. Illustrated by Percy Billinghurst. Lane.
> The archaic language and form of narrative give some notion of early forms.

A Hundred Fables of La Fontaine. Illustrated by Percy Billinghurst. Dodd.
> A prose translation.

Masterpieces of La Fontaine. Translated by Paul Hookham. Illustrated by M. L. Hodgson. Blackwell.
> One of the most satisfactory translations in verse form.

Jean de la Fontaine. Frank Hamel. London, Stanley Paul, 1911.
> Standard biography of the French fabulist, in English.

Most of the collections mentioned above contain material suitable for reading to children, but the following books are especially well designed for the use of children nine years of age and under. Not all the stories are fables in strict definition. Titles are arranged in approximate order of simplicity.

Æsop for Children. Illustrated by Milo Winter. Rand.
> Large picture-book style, double-column text. The fables are a good deal elaborated, thus giving them more of a story quality. Pleasing pictures.

The Fables of Æsop. Told anew by Joseph Jacobs. Illustrated by Richard Heighway. Macmillan.

A book which children like to handle and from which they get the true flavor of the original both in stories and pictures.

The Book of Fable and Folk-Stories. Edited by Horace Scudder. Houghton.

A favorite collection by a scholar well-versed in children's needs and tastes.

Tales of Wise and Foolish Animals. Valery Carrick. Stokes.

Fine animal characterization in stories and pictures.

The Animal's Own Story Book. Ellen C. Babbitt. Century.

A small book with interesting silhouettes.

The Tortoise and the Geese and Other Fables from Bidpai. Retold by Maude B. Dutton. Illustrated by E. Boyd Smith. Houghton.

Good selections from these ancient tales, well told for children.

The Little Wise One. Frank Worthington. Illustrated by the author. Houghton.

The African originals for some of the "Uncle Remus" stories. "Little Wise One" is the Hare who has many of the "Brer Rabbit" traits.

Uncle Remus: His Songs and His Sayings. Joel Chandler Harris. Appleton.

Jataka Tales. Retold by Ellen C. Babbitt. Century.

More Jataka Tales. Retold by Ellen C. Babbitt. Century.

Miss Babbitt gives excellent versions of the Jatakas for the younger children. They are true to the original, but told in simple style.

A Collection of Eastern Stories and Legends. Edited by Marie L. Shedlock. Foreword by Rhys Davids. Dutton.

One of the earliest collections of Jataka tales for children, by a famous English story-teller.

The Talking Beasts. A Book of Fable Wisdom. Selected and edited by Kate Douglas Wiggin and Nora Archibald Smith. Doubleday.

Excellent selections from twelve different fabulists, from Æsop to Gay.

Fables Choises pour Les Enfants. La Fontaine. Illustrated by L. M. Boutet de Monvel. Paris. Plon.

There can be no true age placement for this book in which a great artist speaks a language understood by all races and ages.

CHAPTER VI

MYTHS

GREEK, ROMAN, AND NORSE

... the goodly sandals, golden, that wax never old.
Odyssey, V, 45

Time dissipates to shining ether the solid angularity of facts.
EMERSON

THE essential nature of myth was discussed briefly in relation to the origin of folk tales.[1] In its final analysis all myth is either explanatory of natural phenomena or vaguely reminiscent of historical or legendary events, or a blend of the two. Back of the surrounding mysteries, primitive man sought for beings greater, more powerful than himself, who could subdue the forces inimical to him and distribute benefits beyond his unaided power to attain. While struggling to get control over wild nature, man was endeavoring also to achieve order in his thought-world, to make events fit together, to find something upon which he could rest and escape the sense of being buffeted by irrational forces beyond his control. Slowly the religious element entered and with childlike simplicity he personified the mighty forces of Nature, worshiped the beneficent ones, and feared and tried to escape the terrifying. The gods were persons, but endowed with supernatural power and wisdom.

As man rose to higher levels in thought and feeling, his conceptions of the divinities he worshiped became purer and nobler, and their relations to each other and to him became more complex. Ruskin states this well when he says:

[1] Chapter IV, pp. 78, 79.

In all the most beautiful and enduring myths, we shall find, not only a literal story of a real person — not only a parallel imagery of moral principle — but an underlying worship of natural phenomena, out of which both have sprung, and in which both forever remain rooted....

Now, therefore, in nearly every myth of importance... you have to discern these three structural parts — the root, and the two branches: the root, in physical existence, sun, or sky, or cloud, or sea; then the personal incarnation of that, becoming a trusted and companionable deity, with whom you may walk hand in hand, as a child with its brother or sister; and, lastly, the moral significance of the image, which is in all the great myths eternally and beneficently true.[1]

George E. Woodberry in *The Torch* links together the elements of nature experience and history as the roots from which all mythology springs. He says, "In mythology, mankind preserved from his primitive experience of nature and his own heroic past therein, all that had lasting significance."

These statements refer to Greek tradition, but they are true also of the other two racial mythologies which have played a part in Western civilization. The Roman is so completely drawn from the Greek that one can scarcely be treated apart from the other except from a linguistic standpoint. The names of the heavenly beings are different in the two literatures, and the names of people and places are often changed to suit another locality and a later period, but the central myths, the genealogies, and most of the stories are essentially the same.

While Norse mythology sprang from entirely different roots, it too is anthropomorphic. The Norse gods, like the Greek, are personifications of cosmic forces, human traits and experiences are attributed to them, and they mix intimately in the affairs of men. Gods, giants, and

[1] Ruskin, John, *The Queen of the Air: Being a Study of the Greek Myths of Cloud and Storm.*

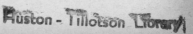

other mythical creatures make swift and easy changes from their usual forms into a new embodiment, but we meet with such transformations less frequently than in Greek myth.

GREEK MYTH

The Greek religion was polytheistic and among this people there seems to have been no limit to the fecundity of imagination by which they personified the forces of nature, gave them corporeal form, and elevated them to the level of divine beings. This same richness of imagination linked almost every flower, tree, bird, stream, and fountain to some incident in the lives of gods or demigods; and it peopled forest, river, and ocean with half-human creatures — dryades, oreades, naiades, and satyrs.

A still further enrichment of Greek mythology came from the belief of the ancients that human beings and the divinities themselves could be changed miraculously into other living forms and into inanimate objects. This exuberance of fancy often attached a very special significance to otherwise commonplace objects and lowly creatures such as stones, trees, reeds, ants, and grasshoppers, because they came to be regarded as a new embodiment of some being which had once lived a freer, happier life. Such changes or metamorphoses might be a resort of the gods to save some lovely and unwilling nymph from being carried off by an impetuous lover, as in the case of Daphne, changed into a laurel tree; or it might be conferred as a reward, as in the case of the old couple Baucis and Philemon who were changed to trees; or decreed as punishment for an impious act, as in the case of Arachne, changed to a spider; or it might occur as a sort of natural outcome of some hopeless longing, such as Narcissus' when he fell in love with his own beautiful image reflected in a pool and became rooted to the spot as a flower.

We find the term "myth" applied to stories which are vastly different in subject, scope, and depth of meaning. They range all the way from the account of small and unimportant episodes in the earthly experiences of the lesser divinities up to a rehearsal in noble language of stupendous events involving the fate of men and the very gods themselves.

After literal belief in miraculous events had passed over into an acceptance of the allegorical and emblematic meaning, Greek and Latin poets told in rich and glowing words of the doings of the gods — in the high heavens and as they walked and talked with mortals inspiring and aiding great heroes of earth, protecting the weak and innocent, and sometimes stooping to petty and ignoble acts themselves. The following passage is descriptive of Greek myth as it emerged from the period of primitive simplicity into a more conscious art expression through the medium of poetry, drama, and sculpture.

The gods in a polytheistic religion like the Greek, are imagined as immortal and endowed with superhuman powers, but in other respects are exactly like human beings. They have their loves and hates, their personal interests and rivalries. They live in a society as men and women do, and are described as related to each other by family ties. Greek imagination invested the gods so vividly with personal characters and was so active, that countless stories were told by priests and poets about them and their doings. The whole collection of these stories is Greek mythology: mythology being a term we also owe to the Greeks. "Mythos" just means in Greek a story, and from its use by the Greeks has come to mean specially a story imagined by people in early times concerning the divine beings of their worship. These Greek myths do not always agree with each other, nor do they make a consistent whole; the stories were differently told in different places and at different times. But they are lively and interesting beyond the similar stories of other races, and sometimes exceedingly beautiful. They are broadly in character with the god as popularly conceived and worshipped, but with a wide margin of free invention. So long as the distinctive characteristics of the deity were maintained, the poets held themselves at liberty to invent details and episodes as their fancy led them.[1]

STORIES FROM GREEK MYTHOLOGY

Opinion concerning the suitability of myth for children, especially at the primary school level, is varied and wavering. Uncertainty often takes the form of a specific question, "Shall myth be included in the literary offering to children in primary grades?" Opposing views seem to be due to different conceptions of what is included under the term myth, and different estimates of children's ability to appreciate and enjoy good literature. Since sharp differences of opinion relate chiefly to the lower elementary school (children ten years of age and under), we will confine our discussion to that period and will take up these two main points of difference:

1. *As literature for children, what is meant by "myth"?* The wide range covered by the term as commonly used was noted above, but those who take the position that Greek myths are unsuitable as story material for the immature, seem to exclude from the classification everything except great epic poems such as the *Iliad* and the *Odyssey* and other cycles of hero tales, and narratives derived from the tragedies of Æschylus, Sophocles, and Euripides and other classic sources. They point out that Greek mythology is weighted with philosophy in the form of allegory, that it is the expression of profound religious experience, and that the subjects treat of mortal agony and immortal glory. It is argued that one must either plunge children into a literature which will prove thoroughly confusing to them or

---

[1] James, H. R., *Our Hellenic Heritage*, p. 59. Macmillan, 1921. By permission of the publishers.

cheapen and ruin a beautiful thing in order to adapt it to immature minds.

But these great works represent myth after it had reached its highest and most perfect expression. What about the great mass of stories from mythology which arose at a lower stage of racial and artistic development and which therefore are more simple and childlike? There are many such stories which are true Greek folk tales having only the slightest relation to religion and philosophy, and in which the allegorical meaning is so little apparent that many high-school students do not perceive it without suggestion from others. These stories are no less truly "Greek myth" and they may serve to introduce children to a great literature without in any way jeopardizing or marring a later enjoyment of its finest examples.

2. *Have the briefer and relatively unrelated myths real literary worth and can primary children appreciate and enjoy them?* This question is involved in the first, where it was implied that if myth is presented to the younger children at all, stories should in general be drawn from sources outside the great classics. For there is a good deal of material, especially in Latin, which tells a brief, straightforward story and in which neither romantic love nor religion nor black crime is portrayed. There is one type of story which seems particularly well suited to children who are outgrowing the simple fairy tale taste and who have acquired some knowledge of natural science — that is the explanatory type of myth which tells how some being or object was miraculously changed in form. For children, the best stories of this type are the most obvious, those which account in a clever and entertaining way for striking traits in familiar creatures or objects.

The literature of all races is full of such stories and we owe to the Greeks and Romans many pleasing ones: How Juno scattered over the peacock's tail the hundred eyes of

Argus slain; how the tears of Phaëton's sisters were turned into amber; why the sunflower seems always to gaze at the sun; why the nymph Echo pined away and became only a disembodied voice; how frogs came to be; why Arachne was changed into a spider; how the first musical instruments, lyre and syrinx, were made; and why a certain river in Lydia has golden sands and pebbles. It seems hardly necessary to remark that children old enough to enjoy such stories should have had enough simple science, or other first-hand experience with nature, to recognize them as a sort of ingenious fairy tale or fable.

Having caught the fanciful and poetic spirit of such "Why and How" stories, many children enjoy inventing short original ones of the same kind. These may purport to explain, for example: why the turtle carries his house everywhere he goes; why the snail leaves a silvery track; why pansies have faces; where the balloon vine got all its little balloons; what "Katy did" that all her tribe still gossip about — and a dozen other natural phenomena in accordance with the children's observation and creative ability.

Most of the leading critics and compilers believe also in giving children in upper primary grades some of the tales of exciting contest and bold adventure which are not too deeply embedded in a larger whole, such as "Atalanta's Race," "Phaëton," "Dædalus and Icarus," and "Bellerophon and Pegasus."

To many, it seems like sheer pedantry to refuse to tell children suitable parts of the longer cycles centering in Perseus, Theseus, and Odysseus, on the ground that it is a kind of sacrilege to break into a fine whole which may be introduced in its entirety a little later. After all, the unity of even the *Odyssey* consists in a skillful combination of many separate mythical and legendary tales held together by a majestic theme, by a few dominating figures, and perhaps by the supreme art of one writer.   Many good judges are unwilling to accept the dictum that none of these dramatic scenes and incidents should be presented to children apart from the vast panorama in which it has been set.

Skepticism regarding the literary worth of myths for children before they become fluent readers is due partly to the attempts which have been made to adapt them to the reading ability of the youngest pupils.   In consequence, the great tragic figure Prometheus and his Titan brother Epimetheus, in the story of "Pandora," are represented as small boys or ineffectual youths, and Pandora is made a silly, stubborn little girl who is excessively curious.   Persephone appears as a little child who, while gathering flowers with her playmates, is suddenly kidnaped by a dark man and carried off through a hole in the ground to be his little girl six months in the year; the gloom is sometimes alleviated by the generous use of gold and jewels in the decoration of the cave!   Hercules, in words of one syllable, becomes a "Tom Hick-a-Thrift"; and Jupiter himself is described in large primer type as a quite unreasonable and implacable old man who inflicts strange and terrible punishment for minor offenses.

Of course no fine tale should be so misused, and mythology is unsuited in every way to early steps in reading. If the stories are told or read to children below fourth grade, and if their own reading at a later period is well selected, there is nothing to prevent the use of excellent versions of all stories which are in themselves appropriate. The best opinion seems to be that no myths should be told in first grade and that only a few of the explanatory type are at all well adapted to second grade.

SELECTING AND ADAPTING

Since this body of myth is in a foreign language, most of us must approach it through translations, and since even the simplest of the stories were intended for adults, the translations must in most cases be rewritten. Also, the same story may have been told in several different ways by the ancients, and so modern writers usually select the most suitable features from equally good authorities and try to combine them into an artistic whole. Then other writers may take the story in this form and readapt it to children of another age. Thus, several times removed from the original, as most of these tales for children are, the thoughtful student of the subject will not be satisfied until she has acquainted herself with some source as near as possible to the Greek or Latin. After one has done this with a number of stories and has found that certain modern writers tend to preserve the spirit of the original and much of its peculiar charm, confidence in those writers and editions is established and one may reasonably rely upon them for authentic and artistic versions. Even then there is a certain pleasure and satisfaction in comparing a modern version with good translations from the original, for one often finds choice phrases, lively word-pictures, and small incidents which are worth restoring.

Greek myth has come to us largely through the Latin, and the Roman poet Ovid (43 B.C. to A.D. 17) in his *Metamorphoses* has given us a more complete record of mythical and legendary lore than any other writer. As the title indicates, Ovid takes as his subject the mysterious transformations found everywhere in mythology. The opening line in Riley's prose translation is, "My design leads me to speak of forms changed into new bodies." Or, in English verse by Brookes More, "My soul is wrought to sing of forms transformed to bodies new and strange!"

The narrative begins with the universe in a state of chaos, "a rude and undigested mass," and with many a skillful turn and twist the poet weaves a resplendent and colorful fabric out of intervening events in the celestial regions, in

the dark underworld, and on the earth, down to the time of
Augustus Cæsar. He ends with a prediction of his own
immortality:

> and wherever the Roman power is extended throughout the
> vanquished earth, I shall be read by the lips of nations, and
> (if the presages of Poets have aught of truth) throughout all
> ages shall I survive in fame.[1]

While in certain portions there is some degree of continuity, the poem really consists of a great number of separate stories somewhat loosely joined together. For this
reason almost any of them can be separated from the whole
without doing violence to either part. Greek and Roman
myth in literary form may be obtained from many other
sources, especially for older children, but the most widely
used stories for primary grades can be traced to the *Metamorphoses*. For various reasons, no story can be told or
read to children exactly as it there appears, but a good
translation constitutes a norm for comparison of plot,
character, tone, and quality of speech, though not necessarily of form.

Few adapters of myths for the younger children have
utilized fully Ovid's rich detail and vivid word painting.
In their attempt to employ a simple style and to tone down
his exuberant fancy, many well qualified writers strip off
too much of the embellishment of the original. They reduce to a few descriptive terms the dazzling picture of
Apollo's palace in the story of Phaëton; or omit details concerning Arachne's home and girlhood which give reality and
personality to her character; or they fail to convey the
sweet simplicity and generous hospitality of Baucis and
Philemon. Less able writers go further and reduce a
charming story to a mere outline. They "simplify" by
omitting most of the colorful details, thus producing an
arid sketch. Students who know these stories chiefly

[1] Prose translation by Riley.

through faint memories of high-school Latin, through
textbooks on mythology, and inferior versions for children,
experience a pleasant and stimulating surprise when they
dip again, or for the first time, into Ovid.

RELATIVE MERITS OF CLASSIC AND MODERN FORM

Just as literature for children benefits sooner or later by
every new and desirable movement in adult literature, so it
is responsive to the major currents of doubt and controversy. It was to be expected therefore that in this field the
age-old debate concerning the "Ancients and the Moderns"
(or, stated differently, the Classic and the Gothic, or the
Classic and the Romantic) should intrude its bristling
form. Naturally it culminated in connection with Greek
tales, since in them was to be seen the perfect example of
classic beauty subjected to the rude touch of the innovator.
In this connection, attention was focused upon Nathaniel
Hawthorne as soon as he published *A Wonder-Book* and
Tanglewood Tales, and he is still considered by some the
arch offender in forcing classic grace and purity of form into
what seems to them a sort of harlequin garb.

This is largely a matter of personal taste and opinion
which refuses to be reduced to the limits of an abstract and
academic question. Hawthorne puts up a very good defense for himself as against the classicists of his day, and
every decade since 1851 when the *Wonder-Book* was published has furnished an army of young readers who unconsciously applaud his point of view seen in the concrete.
Likewise a host of more mature judges refuse to listen to
the carping critics who would like to banish Hawthorne's
tales. In spite of severe criticism there seems to be no
tangible evidence of waning popularity. The question as it
reaches out beyond Hawthorne's genius and bears upon the
work of less talented writers who have attempted a similar
vein, is not unimportant. Some proposals for further

study of it are offered under "Problems" at the close of this section.

ANALYSIS AND CRITICISMS

A number of stories have been mentioned specifically, and for the convenience of those who may not have readily at hand the complete text of each story, a brief outline is furnished of some which are considered best suited to upper primary grades. The selection is limited also to those which are to be found in several collections and which students may have the satisfaction of reading in easily obtainable English translations.

Before taking up the separate myths a few points which enhance or mar a story for children should be considered. They are applicable to other kinds of stories, but because myths lack a definitive form these qualitative features seem to be of special importance.

1. *Is this version of the myth free from distortion and exaggeration and is it true to the spirit of the original?*

2. *Which characters call out the sympathy of listeners and why?* At the childhood level of moral sense and literary appreciation, it is important that sympathy be clearly directed toward those characters who most merit approval. Since myths contain some characters who are supposed to be superior beings, perhaps stories should be avoided which portray the less noble traits of divinities.

3. *Is the theme a simple one which lies within the range of children's comprehension?* By theme is meant the moral essence of the story. Ruskin says the most beautiful myths are "didactic in their essence as all good art is."

4. *Is the portion selected complete in itself, with a beginning free from long explanation, and has it a clear-cut satisfactory ending?* Since these stories are in many cases part of a larger whole, this question is particularly pertinent.

5. *Does this version bring out the childlike traits in certain characters?* It is absurd to turn adult figures into children, but Ovid pictures certain young people as very childlike. He describes Persephone in "the innocence of her childish years" as grieving (in the midst of her terror) for the scattered flowers which "with childlike eagerness" she had gathered. Dædalus toys with the feathers and wax with which his father Icarus is making the wings for their fatal flight — "and by his playfulness, he retards the wondrous work of his father." And Hermes is at one stage an incorrigible infant.

Latona and the Frogs.   Original source: Ovid; *Metamorphoses*, Book VI, lines 339–382.   Modern texts: Tatlock, 61; Guerber, 82 ff.

Juno, jealous of Latona (Leto), has banished her from Olympus and has warned all countries not to give her shelter. She wanders everywhere with her twin babes, Apollo and Diana, but no one will receive her. Weary and famished, she comes to a lake of pure water and stooping is about to drink when some rustics who are gathering osiers threaten and torment her. The goddess pleads with them for the sake of the children not to deny her a drink and reminds them that "Nature has made neither sun, nor air, nor the running stream the property of any one." But spitefully they jump up and down and stir up the mud so that the water is unfit to drink. The outraged goddess ceases to plead and calls down the judgment of heaven upon the cruel rustics, saying, "Forever may you live in that pool." Her cry is answered and the men are changed into croaking frogs. Ovid gives a very telling picture of this transformation and of the appearance of the new-made frogs.

Some authorities place this incident before the birth of Apollo and Diana, but according to Ovid, Latona is carrying the children in her arms. This makes the situation more acute and adds to the dramatic quality of the story.

Phaëton. Original source: Ovid; *Metamorphoses*, Book I, lines 751–786, and Book II, lines 1–368. Modern collections: Peabody, 24 ff.; Pyle, 97 ff.

Phaëton, young son of Apollo and the nymph Clymene, lives with his mother on earth. He boasts to his friends of his father until a boy of his own age, Epaphus, taunts him and says he talks of "an imaginary father." He appeals to his mother for some token, she swears that he is the son of Apollo and suggests that he go to the palace of the Sun with his question. The boy, overjoyed, eagerly sets out and soon accomplishes the journey. The gorgeous palace is explicitly described by Ovid, and so is the throne scene where his father welcomes him affectionately and acknowledges him. The boy begs a token, and Apollo promises to bestow any gift he may ask. Phaëton's choice is to drive for one day his father's chariot drawn by his four "wing-footed horses." In dismay and deploring his rash promise, Apollo implores his son to choose another favor, but the boy will not yield to persuasion or warning. The chariot, the horses, the preparations for the hazardous trip, the father's anxious care and the boy's exultant start, are all vividly pictured, and so is the mad course itself and the dire consequences. At last the scorched and burning Earth prays to Jupiter for help. Seeing no other way, he hurls a thunderbolt, and "Phaëton, the flames consuming his yellow hair, is hurled headlong, and is borne in a long track through the air; as sometimes a star from the serene sky may appear to fall."

This seems a good place to end the story. Some modern versions continue further and tell of the finding of the body by the Hesperian Naiades, the grief of Phaëton's mother and sisters, how the latter with their continued weeping

were changed into poplar trees, and how their tears flowing
from the trees harden into amber.

There is vastly too much detail in some parts of Ovid's
account for a child's story, but modern versions often fail
to make sufficient use of the dramatic effects and glorious
descriptions.

Atalanta's Race.   Original source: Ovid; *Metamorphoses*, Book
    X, lines 566–683.   Modern collections: Peabody, 46 ff.;
    Pyle, 138 ff.

Atalanta, a beautiful huntress, swift of foot and a lover of
the chase, does not wish to marry, but at last agrees that
she will accept the man who can outstrip her in a race.
The penalty of failure is death and numerous suitors have
lost, when Hippomenes appears and serves as judge for a
time.   At first indifferent to Atalanta, he is soon overcome
by her beauty of face, figure, and movement, and challenges her.   The maiden is touched by his appearance of
extreme youth coupled with courage and daring, and hesitates for a moment to engage with him.   Quickly, however, firmness returns and the race is on.   Hippomenes has
implored the aid of Venus and she, having plucked golden
apples from a golden tree, gives them secretly to the youth
and counsels how to use them.   The race is close and exciting.   Atalanta is really the better runner, but Hippomenes drops the golden apples one by one and as she
pauses to pick up the tempting fruit he passes her.   She re-
gains her position, but the third time, very near the goal, he
throws the apple more to one side and she, after a moment's hesitation, speeds after it.   Hippomenes reache
the goal first and so wins a bride who had really been fa
vorably inclined toward him.

For children, should not the story end here?   Peabody
makes this the end.   The complete account tells of thei
union, Hippomenes' ingratitude to Venus, their profana

tion of her temple, and her punishment of the pair. She turns them into lions forced forever to draw the car of the great goddess Cybele (Rhea).

Arachne.   Original source: Ovid; *Metamorphoses*, Book VI, lines 1–145.   Modern: Peabody, 49 ff.; Pyle, 120 ff.

Arachne was of a humble family, but she was such a skillful weaver and designer that her fame had spread throughout Lydia.   Her mother was dead and her father dyed the wool which Arachne used in her weaving.   Nymphs from vineyards and streams loved to watch her at work, for her skill showed at every stage of the process.   In praise of her they said that she must have learned from Minerva, but the arrogant girl denied that anyone had instructed her and her boastful talk amounted to a challenge to the goddess who presides over handicrafts.   Minerva appears, disguised as an old woman, and offers Arachne a chance to recede from her position and to beg pardon, but the girl becomes more angry and insulting until at last the outraged goddess reveals herself and takes up the challenge to a contest.   Then follows an interesting description of threading the looms and other steps incident to the work of the two skillful weavers.   Minerva weaves a marvelous web displaying the great and noble deeds of the gods and also the fate of those who contended against them.   Arachne works under the impulse of pride, resentment and defiance, and depicts with great skill every unworthy act of the gods. Her portraiture is so clear that each is easily recognized and held up to scorn.   Ovid makes clear that the goddess did not excel the maiden in technical skill; her wrath was called out by Arachne's insolent and impious design.   She tore her web across, struck her three times on the forehead with her boxwood shuttle, and pronounced her doom, which was that she and all her posterity were to labor as weavers, but not in human form.   As Minerva turns to go, she sprinkles Arachne with the juices of aconite, and quickly her shrinking figure turns into the size and form of a spider. Her body "gives forth a thread and as a spider she works at a web as formerly."

The story has been many times rewritten for children. It offers several difficulties which some authors have either evaded or interpreted in a false way. Attempts to bring this story down to very immature minds usually result in making Minerva seem unjust and vindictive, since what started out as a simple contest of skill is suddenly turned into a battle in the realm of the spirit and Arachne's real offense is not made clear. The modern versions mentioned above are clear and unambiguous. The Homeric Hymn to Aphrodite says that Athene (Minerva) "teaches tender maidens in the house, and puts knowledge of goodly arts in each one's mind."

Dædalus and Icarus. Original source: Ovid; *Metamorphoses*, Book VIII, lines 183–256. Modern: Peabody, 21 ff.; Pyle, 108 ff.

In Athens there was a famous architect, engineer, and inventor, by the name of Dædalus. Exiled from home, he went to the island of Crete where he built for King Minos the wonderful labyrinth in which the terrible Minotaur was confined. Later he fell under the displeasure of the king and with his son Icarus was imprisoned. He escaped, but finding no way to return to Athens he decided to attempt flight. The two gather feathers from birds and Dædalus arranges them in graduated order and fastens them together with thread and wax. Icarus watches the process with boyish delight and interferes somewhat in the work. The wings are tested and fastened on, Dædalus gives careful and tender instructions and the start is made. The father leads, with anxious glances backward — "just as a bird which has led forth her tender young from the lofty nest into the air." He had previously warned Icarus not to fly too near the sun lest the heat melt the wax, but the boy exulting in the new power mounts up and up until "the fragrant wax" is melted, the wings drop off, and with naked arms beating the air, and calling on his father, he falls into the sea. Dædalus sees the wings floating in the water, rescues the body, and buries it on an island which is then given the name *Icaria*.

Features which may well be emphasized are the home-sickness of Dædalus, his high hopes in making the wings, the boyishness of Icarus displayed in several ways, the tender anxiety of the father, and the heedlessness of the youth. Notice the beauty of Peabody's closing paragraphs.

Arion and the Dolphins. Guerber: 82 ff. Modern: Baker, 108 ff.

Arion was a great musician who had won many prizes for his skill in playing the lyre. Returning from Sicily where he had won a large sum of gold as victor in a contest, he embarked in a vessel which had a crew of pirates. These men plotted to seize his money, bind him, and throw him overboard. He begged to be allowed to have his lyre and to play once more upon it. The pirates consented and the magical strains of his music drew a school of dolphins who swam close about the ship in a listening attitude. The pirates, alarmed at this display, seized Arion and threw him and his instrument into the sea. A friendly dolphin caught him on his back and carried him safely to the shore. When he died the gods placed him and his lyre and the dolphin in the heavens as a constellation.

Syrinx. Original source: Ovid; *Metamorphoses*, Book I, lines 689–714. Modern: Baker, 184.

Syrinx was one of the loveliest of the nymphs who hunted with Diana and danced and played in the mountains of Arcadia. As a huntress she might have been mistaken for Diana herself except for the fact that she had "a bow of cornel wood, the other, a bow of gold." Pan often danced and played with the nymphs and made sweet music on his flute. The nymphs half-feared him with his pointed ears, and horns, and goat legs. One day he tried to bear Syrinx off to be his own, but she in fright fled from him. He was about to overtake her when she came to the edge of a river. Unable to cross, she called to the river nymphs and they changed her into a clump of reeds. Pan tried to put his arms about her, but clasped instead the swaying reeds through which the wind was making a murmuring like the voice of Syrinx. Charmed with the sweetness of the sound and realizing that the lovely nymph was lost to him, Pan thought that he might speak to her and she to him in a new way. He cut the reeds in unequal lengths, fastened them together with wax, and made a kind of shepherd's pipe which he called the syrinx. This became Pan's special instrument and on it he made music that was soft and plaintive.

The last two stories are not often included in collections for children. Mrs. Baker tells them well, but for younger children they could be made somewhat more pictorial and dramatic. They may have a special interest today, since children are now contriving simple musical instruments in school. There are several other myths which tell of the origin of certain instruments.

Among other stories which, with slight adaptation, are considered suited to upper primary grades are the following:

King Midas. Original source: Ovid, *Metamorphoses*, Book XI, 85 ff. Modern: Baker, 179 ff.; Hawthorne, *A Wonder-Book*, story title, "The Golden Touch."

There are several stories about Midas. This one tells of the gift of the golden touch which made him "both rich and wretched."

Æolus and the Bag of Winds. Original source: *The Odyssey*, Book X. Modern collections and texts: Baker, 200–203; Guerber, 213–215 and 346–347.

Echo and Narcissus. Original source: Ovid, *Metamorphoses*, Book III, lines 354–510. Modern collections: Baker, 93 ff.; Pyle, 103 ff.

Baucis and Philemon. Original source: Ovid, *Metamorphoses*, Book VIII, lines 622–733. Modern collections and texts: Baker, 70 ff.; Tatlock, 28 ff.; Hawthorne, *A Wonder-Book*, story title, "The Miraculous Pitcher."

Bellerophon and Pegasus. Modern collections and texts: Pyle, 240 ff.; Hawthorne, *A Wonder-Book*, story title, "The Chimæra"; Guerber, 291 ff.; Tatlock, 237 ff.

Persephone. Original source: *Homeric Hymns*, "To Demeter"; [1] Ovid, *Metamorphoses*, Book V, lines 385–417 and 461–574. Modern collections and texts: Guerber, 183–195; Tatlock, 154–158; Hawthorne, *Tanglewood Tales*, story title, "The Pomegranate Seeds."

SUGGESTED PROBLEMS AND TOPICS FOR FURTHER STUDY

1. The relation of myth to affairs of today. At one time, under the influence of the principle of "correlation," literature (and myth in particular) was often forced out of its natural uses and applied to the teaching of some other subject in the curriculum — nature study, geography, etc. Disclaiming any such intention, the question may still be asked, "Might not some of these stories have an added meaning and be more enjoyed if told in connection with certain arts, or other experiences which the children are having?" With this in mind, it might be worthwhile to make a collection of stories which concern musicians and musical instruments; or pastoral life; or spinning and weaving; or well-known flowers; or getting acquainted with a few constellations.

2. Examine into the basis of criticism of Hawthorne's versions of Greek stories. Piece together his own defense as expressed in the introductions and interludes of *A Wonder-Book* and *Tangle-*

[1] Hesiod, *The Homeric Hymns, and Homerica*, translated by Hugh G. Evelyn-White, pp. 289–325. Putnam, 1926, New York.

wood Tales. Read Chapter VII in MacClintock's *Literature in the Elementary School*. Is this critic too severe? Does Hawthorne actually invent certain incidents and characters? Do some of his stories seem more flippant, more discursive and moralizing than others? If so, try to find a reason.

Make a comparison of Hawthorne's "Circe's Palace" and the account of this adventure as told in the *Odyssey*, Book X. Notice the behavior of the men and their relation to Odysseus; the dominant tone of the narrative; proportion; language; humor or wit.

Make a similar comparison of Hawthorne's "The Miraculous Pitcher" with the story as told by Ovid. (See reference above.)

3. Adapt the story of "Echo" for children eight or nine years of age. Since the real ground of Juno's jealousy cannot and should not be understood by children, how will you make the punishment of the nymph seem suitable and somewhat deserved? Should the whole of the Narcissus story be merged with this story? Considering your audience, what feature of "Echo" is probably the most interesting? Be careful not to distort or exaggerate incidents, and avoid a sentimental tone.

4. Adapt the story of "Æolus and the Bag of Winds," for children seven or eight years of age.

5. Look for examples of myths brought down to the level of beginning reading and judge them as literature.

6. Select passages of unusual beauty from some of the stories mentioned in this chapter as told in the *Homeric Hymns*, the *Odyssey*, *Metamorphoses*, or other classic sources.

7. Invent five or six explanatory "myths" regarding such phenomena as were mentioned on page 144, using outline form. Propose other promising phenomena. If you desire, write one story in full.

8. Using any available translation of the *Homeric Hymns*, prepare in rather full outline the story of the infant Hermes told in the hymn "To Hermes," omitting such parts as seem to break the thread of the story. Give exact pages of the edition used.

In this section on Greek and Roman myths the Latin names of divinities and heroes have generally been used, for the reason that Ovid is the great source to which modern writers have turned. The Latin names, therefore, with a few exceptions, are more familiar than the Greek, especially in adaptations intended for children.

Roman	Greek
Jupiter	Jove, Zeus
Juno	Hera
Minerva	Pallas, Athene
	Apollo, Phœbus
Diana	Artemis
Venus	Aphrodite, Cytherea
Mercury	Hermes
Cupid	Eros
Vulcan	Hephæstus
Neptune	Poseidon
Dis	Pluto, Hades
Ceres	Demeter
Proserpina	Persephone
Latona	Leto
Ulysses	Odysseus

NORSE MYTH

Another rich mine of story material is found in Norse mythology. This old Northern lore has not permeated Western art and literature as Greek and Roman myth has done, but it is important to us as a part of our own cultural background and as possessing in itself intrinsic literary worth and beauty. Norse myth has been but little known to the English-speaking world until comparatively recently because there have been few satisfactory English translations of either the *Poetic Edda* or the *Prose Edda* — the two great collections of Northern myth in the form of dramatic poems, ballads, lays, proverbs, charms, and prose narratives. Some of the mythological poems are believed to have taken form through oral rehearsal in the Icelandic tongue about a thousand years ago, and the date of their first appearance in written form is placed as not later than the middle of the twelfth century. Some of the same themes and characters appear in other Germanic legendary lore, the *Nibelungenlied* giving proof that there was an early transplanting in one direction or the other of the roots of a great hero-cycle; and in England, Scotland and the islands of the North Atlantic there are traces of Northern myth clearly due to Scandinavian settlements following Viking invasions. The subject-matter of Norse mythology was widely diffused, but the weight of opinion points to Iceland as the center where the Eddic poems as we now know them were composed and most successfully preserved.

Emigrants from Norway settled in Iceland in the ninth century when driven from their native land by the tyrannical oppression of Harold Fairhair. Many leading chieftains with families and clans emigrated at this time, taking with them their religion, arts, and literary lore. Life in that forbidding and barren land was a stern and bitter struggle, but the conditions of partial isolation were favorable to the development of an independent culture, and education and literary activity were greatly stimulated there.

No literature ever expressed more clearly the dominant racial characteristics of a people, the surrounding physical conditions of life, their thought patterns and elemental religious beliefs. Most Americans have some line of ancestry which leads back into related origins and this may seem an added reason for a keen interest in the ancient lore of Scandinavia.

This mythology is very different from that of the Greeks and it was also caught and fixed in the *Edda* at a cruder stage of development than that of the earliest Greek literature. A much younger, ruder civilization is displayed, and a system of belief which seems in parts inconceivably chaotic but which is in the main noble and majestic.

By the time the *Elder Edda* was put into written form the native pagan belief had been quite thoroughly shattered, for Christianity was forced upon Iceland about the year 1000. Barbarous practices were at first forbidden, and gradually pagan conceptions were overlaid and transformed by the new faith. By the time the *Younger*, or *Prose Edda* was compiled, its author looked upon his work as that of an antiquary whose main purpose was to preserve and render available the mythological background of his people which in the Christian age might be lost or disregarded. The *Eddas* then represent the highest level of Norse mythological literature scrupulously gathered and recorded by scholarly men who did not believe the myths, but who had a great respect for them and for all that they represented of racial tradition and culture. Fortunately, this oral literature was recorded before an alien civilization had had time and opportunity to destroy its magic and its power or to modify it to any great extent.

THE POETIC EDDA

The *Poetic Edda*, also called the *Elder Edda*, or Saemund's *Edda*, is the oldest known collection of Norse mythological poems, the separate poems being of uncertain date and unknown origin. When Snorri Sturluson (1178-1241) compiled the *Prose Edda*, he quoted copiously from extant poems which told the same tales. He also cited many separate stanzas in illustration of certain features of Norse verse. About this time and for some centuries later there was current the tradition that Saemund the Wise (1056-1133) had made such a collection. When, in the seventeenth century, a manuscript was discovered which contained twenty-nine poems of this type, some of them in the exact form quoted by Snorri, the work was very soon attributed to Saemund.

Not much is known of Saemund the Wise, but the few assured facts give evidence of his fitness for such a task. He had studied at Paris, was reputed to be very learned, and was the founder of a school at Oddi in western Iceland. In the next century Snorri Sturluson lived at Oddi and was as a youth under the tutelage of Saemund's grandson. Perhaps Snorri's keen interest in the tales themselves and in the established forms of versification began here. It is thought probable that he became acquainted while at Oddi with a collection of poems made by Saemund or some other scholar.

These heroic poems constitute a great storehouse of Norse mythology and here we can get at the roots of stories which have been made more or less familiar to us through modern prose adaptations. We have lacked until recently adequate translations in English, but there is now available the complete collection in metrical form, with an illuminating Introduction and copious notes. Mr. Bellows, the translator of this edition of the *Poetic Edda*, says:

> It is a collection including some of the most remarkable poems which have been preserved to us from the period before the pen and the printing-press replaced the poet-singer and oral tradition.... It is evident that the *Poetic Edda*, as we now know it, is no definite and plainly limited work, but rather a more or less haphazard collection of separate poems, dealing either with Norse mythology or with hero-cycles unrelated to the traditional history of greater Scandinavia or Iceland. How many other similar poems, now lost, may have existed in such collections as were current in Iceland in the later twelfth and thirteenth centuries we cannot know, though it is evident that some poems of this type are missing. We can say only that thirty-four poems have been preserved, twenty-nine of them in a single manuscript collection, which differ considerably in subject matter and style from all the rest of extant Old Norse poetry, and these we group together as the *Poetic Edda*.[1]

The Eddic poems give every evidence of having been sung or recited by skalds. They do not tell a straight narrative, but consist chiefly of dialogue and description, the necessary narrative parts being in prose. Evidently each

---

[1] *The Poetic Edda.* Translated by Henry Adams Bellows. American-Scandinavian Foundation, 1926.

reciter interpolated these prose links to give continuity to a
succession of dialogue stanzas.   It is believed that the sequence of ideas in the stories was well known to most of the
hearers and that the reciter judged how much supplementary narrative was needed.   These prose passages enable
the reader of today to piece the story together and Mr.
Bellows's notes in the edition mentioned are of still further
assistance in this.

VERSE FORM

Before the time of Saemund, Scandinavian poetry had
taken on very definite and rather rigid forms of versification which regulated the use of meter, initial rhyme, and
the cæsural pause, and controlled the choice of metaphors.
This early fixation of form must have contributed also to
the permanence of content during the long period of oral
transmission; for sudden and capricious changes could not
easily have been made by the skalds, and the people themselves must have had the repeated initial sounds of words
and the beat of accented syllables deeply embedded in
memory.

Translators have found it very difficult to attain in the
English language more than an approximation of this versification.   The following stanzas are the first three from
Voluspo, or "The Wise Woman's Prophecy," one of the
most famous of the Eddic poems.   They illustrate line division, alliteration, and accent, as they appear in English.
This poem tells of the creation of the world and of man, and
prophesies the destruction of all creation and of the very
gods themselves.   In these stanzas, a "Volva" or wise-wo-
man is replying to Odin who has gone to her seeking knowledge of the future.

> Hearing I ask   from the holy races,
> From Heimdall's sons, both high and low;
> Thou wilt, Valfather, that well I relate
> Old tales I remember, of men long ago.

I remember yet   giants of yore,
Who gave me bread   in the days gone by;
Nine worlds I knew   the nine in the tree
With mighty roots   beneath the mold.

Of old was the age   when Ymir lived;
Sea nor cool waves   nor sand there were;
Earth had not been,   nor heaven above,
But a yawning gap,   and grass nowhere.[1]

The following stanzas show the ballad in dialogue form. Notice the cæsura in the first and third lines and the use of initial rhymes. Othin (Odin) who is ever seeking wisdom wishes to visit the giant Vafthruthnir and he discusses the matter with his wife in the opening stanzas of the poem *Vafthruthnismol*, or "The Ballad of Vafthruthnir."

Othin spake:

1   "Counsel me, Frigg,   for I long to fare,
    And Vafthruthnir fain would find;
    In wisdom old   with the giant wise
    Myself would I seek to match."

Frigg spake:

2.   "Heerfather here   at home would I keep,
    Where the gods together dwell;
    Amid all the giants   an equal in might
    Of Vafthruthnir know I none."

Othin spake:

3.   "Much have I fared,   much have I found,
    Much have I got from the gods;
    And fain would I know   how Vafthruthnir now
    Lives in his lofty hall." [2]

Fortunately, the student seeking story material for young people does not have to depend on the rather difficult text of the *Poetic Edda*, but anyone who is truly interested in the beginnings of things will wish to read one or

[1] *The Poetic Edda*, translated by Henry Adams Bellows, pp. 3–4.
[2] *Ibid.*, p. 69.

more of these ancient poems, the substance of which is constantly encountered in modern literature, music, and art.
We get here a tone and spirit which should form a part of
our basis for judging the many adaptations of Norse myth
for children. From this standpoint, the selections which
will perhaps best repay study are:

Voluspo and *Vafthruthnismol*, which have already been
mentioned. These two are cosmic in scope and grandeur
and tell of all the great events in the vast cycle from original chaos to the final destruction of the very gods themselves, and on to a new heaven and a new earth.

Skirnismol, or "The Ballad of Skirnir," is quite different,
telling in dramatic dialogue how Skirnir, Frey's foot-page,
acting for his gentle master, woos Gerth (Gerda), a giant's
daughter, using measures that are by no means gentle.

Thrymskvitha, or "The Lay of Thrym," is one of the oldest poems in the collection. In his Introductory Note, Bellows says that it is "one of the most vivid short narrative
poems ever composed" and that the unknown author
must have been "a poet of extraordinary ability." In narrative verse so plain that prose links were not needed, the
skald told the lively story of how Thor found his mighty
hammer Mjollnir which Thrym, a frost giant, had stolen
and hidden eight miles deep in the earth.

THE PROSE EDDA

As already indicated, Snorri Sturluson lived about a century later than Saemund. The *Prose Edda* was com-
pleted about 1222. Pagan beliefs and practices had been
quite thoroughly stamped out by this time and Snorri was
a Christian (though hardly a model one). In the Prologue
the author gives a rationalized account of pagan belief
which is a strange compound of the Biblical account of the
creation and flood, and a summary of the Norse cosmology.
But he permits Christian doctrine and enlightened intel-

lect to touch the body of the text in only a few places.
Snorri was a prominent man in Iceland and Norway — a
statesman, historian, poet, and an authority in all aspects
of versification. The *Prose Edda* is really a commentary
on the *Poetic Edda*, and as compiler and editor he addressed himself to the skalds of his day and advised them
in these words:

> But now one thing must be said to young skalds, to such as
> yearn to attain to the craft of poesy.... One is not so to forget
> or discredit these traditions as to remove from poesy those an-
> cient metaphors with which it has pleased Chief Skalds to be
> content; nor, on the other hand, ought Christian men to be-
> lieve in heathen gods, nor in the truth of these tales otherwise
> than precisely as one may find here in the beginning of the
> book (referring to the Prologue).[1]

To illustrate his points Snorri uses so much poetry that a
first glance at the book makes one wonder why it is called
Prose. Further examination, however, shows that the author has told in prose narrative the principal stories in
Norse mythology. This book is the chief source for all modern renderings in poetry and prose for old and young.
Most of the tales which have commonly been selected for
children of elementary school age, are given briefly in the
first section called *Gylfaginning*, or "The Beguiling of
Gylfi." This is really a contest in matters of deep wisdom
between Gylfi, a reputed King of Sweden skilled in magic,
and Odin, seated on his throne in Valhall. Gylfi is able to
propound deep questions and Odin answers out of his profound wisdom.

Here are a few of the questions, the answers to which
often expand into a story and reveal the whole of Norse
mythology and much of its inner meanings:

Who is foremost or oldest of the gods? Where is this

[1] Snorri, Sturluson, *The Prose Edda*, translated from the Icelandic by
Arthur Gilchrist Brodeur, p. 97. American-Scandinavian Foundation,
1929.

god? What power hath he? How were things wrought before man? Whence come the men that people the earth? How is the course of the sun and the moon governed? What is the way to heaven from earth? Whence comes the wind? What tidings are to be told concerning the Weird of the Gods (the Dusk of the Gods)?

NORSE MYTHS FOR CHILDREN

Something of the background outlined above is important for those who are expecting to help direct the literary experience of children, but what stories shall be presented to the children themselves, and in what form?

Considering the vastness of the subject-matter, the somber character of many of the incidents, and the tragic culmination of the whole, judicious selection and skillful adaptation are called for to meet the needs of children and at the same time to preserve in a fair measure the spirit of the original. In this line some excellent work has been done and there are available several collections from which a few stories may be chosen for telling, as low as third grade. Versions possessing good literary quality can scarcely be read below the fourth grade level, and specialists tend to place this material at about that stage. When used in the third grade, it is usually as a part of some larger experience such as a study of the life of the Vikings.

With groups of children at any level in the elementary school, it is usually desirable for some older person who appreciates this literature to help the children over the confused beginnings which concern the making of the world and the relations of the gods to each other and to man. After that, there are many single stories which fall naturally and easily into place. A few which seem best suited to the younger children may be mentioned. They appear under different titles in certain editions and these will be indicated by symbols as follows:

M — *Norse Stories*.   Hamilton Wright Mabie
Br — *In the Days of Giants*.   Abbie Farwell Brown
Ba — *Out of the Northland*.   Emilie Kip Baker
C — *The Children of Odin*.   Padraic Colum

M.   Odin's Search for Wisdom
Br.   How Odin Lost His Eye
Ba.   Odin

This story presents Odin in his majesty and shows his
nobility of soul.   The giants too are seen to be very different from the cruel stupid kind which "Jack" slew.

M.   The Wooing of Gerd
Br.   The Giantess Who Would Not
C.   How Frey Won Gerda, the Giant Maiden

A story of bold adventure in which Frey woos by proxy
the beautiful daughter of a giant who proves to be a suitable bride for one of the gentlest of the gods.

M.   The Making of the Hammer
Br.   The Dwarf's Gifts
Ba.   Sif's Golden Hair
C.   Sif's Golden Hair.   Also,
         How Brock Brought Judgment on Loki

One of the most delightful of the Norse stories.   Loki's
cruel mischief sets going an interesting chain of events including a contest between some very skillful dwarfs.   They
produce six magic articles, several of which play important
parts in other stories.

M.   How Thor Found His Hammer
Br.   The Quest of the Hammer
Ba.   The Hammer of Thor
C.   How Thor and Loki Befooled Thrym, the Giant

One of the few real comedies in this literature.   The
gods shake with laughter at Thor's appearance when required to masquerade as a timid bride, and they rejoice at
the giant's discomfiture.   For once Loki performs a helpful act, but one which suits his impish nature.

M. The Apples of Idun
Br. The Magic Apples
Ba. Iduna's Apples
C. Iduna and Her Apples

Idun guards the golden apples which are the pledge and source of eternal youth to the gods. Loki betrays her into the hands of the giant Thjasse and she is carried off bearing the precious apples. There is a dramatic rescue which involves a very exciting race. Younger children enjoy the unusual plot and action, and the older ones may get a glimpse of a deeper meaning.

M. Thor's Wonderful Journey
Br. Thor's Visit to the Giants
C. Thor and Loki in the Giants' City

This story has many folk tale features. Thor puts on his belt of strength, takes his mighty hammer and he and Loki go to Jotunheim to seek adventure among the giants. They do not acquit themselves very creditably and the story is marked by what Carlyle calls "a broad Brobdingnag grin of true humor."

M. The Death of Balder
Br. Balder and the Mistletoe
Ba. Balder

Unless one believes that children should be spared all sadness in literature, there seems no reason why this beautiful story should not be given to them. Perhaps Miss Brown judged well in closing it with the majestic and solemn launching of the funeral ship; the attempt to restore Balder from the kingdom of death she includes in a separate story.

Original sources of the above stories:

The Wooing of Gerd: *Poetic Edda*, "The Ballad of Skirnir." *Prose Edda*, "The Beguiling of Gylfi," chapter XXXVII.

The Making of the Hammer: *Prose Edda*, "The Poesy of the Skalds," chapter XXXV.

How Thor Found His Hammer: *Poetic Edda,* "The Lay of Thrym."

The Apples of Idun: *Prose Edda,* "The Poesy of the Skalds," chapter I; same, in verse, chapter XXII.

Thor's Wonderful Journey: *Prose Edda,* "The Beguiling of Gylfi," chapters XLV–XLVII.

The Death of Balder: *Poetic Edda,* "Balder's Dream."

SUGGESTED PROBLEMS AND TOPICS FOR FURTHER STUDY

1. Make a comparative study of style in rendering, using editions prepared by Mabie, Brown, Baker, Colum, or any others available. Mabie makes very few changes in the substance of the tales and these are of a minor kind; so, if the *Eddas* in English are not available, Mabie might well be used as a check on this point. Consider clarity of organization, truth of characterization, pictorial effects, dramatic quality, expansion of interesting details, and fitness for particular age levels.

2. Draw together the most important and interesting facts about the giants. Compare them with the giants of folk tales. Read Carlyle on this. (See Bibliography.)

3. Find out all you can about the "runes" so often mentioned in Norse literature.

4. Select passages in the stories which portray the physical features of the far north, or modes of life among the people. Give exact references.

5. What do these stories reveal regarding the peaceful arts of the Norse at this period?

6. Pick out scenes and incidents which seem to have a true folk tale quality; for example, parts of Thor's Wonderful Journey." Try to read "The Lay of Grotti" in the *Prose Edda.* It is evidently the source of a well-known tale.

7. Make a list of all the magic articles which you discover in these stories, identify the owner, and indicate very briefly the wonderful attributes of each object.

8. Select a number of very brief passages which characterize each of the following figures: Odin, Thor, Loki, Frey, Brage, Balder, Njord, Frigg, Sif, Idun, Freyja, Skadi, Gerda. Consult

if possible "The Beguiling of Gylfi" in the *Prose Edda*. Give exact references.

9. In the Introduction to the *Prose Edda*, Brodeur says these myths are "half grotesque and half sublime." Find examples of both qualities.

BIBLIOGRAPHY

HISTORY AND GENERAL CRITICISM

Fiske, John. *Myths and Myth Makers*. Houghton, 1900.

Gray, L. H., and Moore, G. F., ed. *The Mythology of All Races*. 13 volumes. Marshall Jones, 1916–1932. Volume I, Greek and Roman; volume II, Eddic.

Lang, Andrew. *Custom and Myth*. Longmans, 1885.

MacClintock, Porter Lander. *Literature in the Elementary School*. University of Chicago Press, 1907. Chapter VII, "Myth as Literature."

Rawlinson, Eleanor. *Introduction to Literature for Children*. Norton, 1931.
> Contains a brief discussion of myth, and a number of stories both Greek and Norse, retold.

Woodberry, George E. *The Torch*. Harcourt, 1920. Chapter II, "The Language of All the World."

GREEK AND ROMAN MYTHS
Original Sources, Criticism, and Collections for Adults

Gayley, Charles M. *Classic Myths in English Literature and in Art*. Ginn, 1893–1911.

Guerber, Helene A. *Myths of Greece and Rome*. American Book Company, 1893–1921.

Hesiod. *The Homeric Hymns, and Homerica*. Tr. by Hugh G. Evelyn-White. (Loeb Classical Library.) Putnam, 1914.
> Note especially II, "To Demeter," and IV, "To Hermes."

Homer. *The Odyssey*. Translated into rhythmic prose by George H. Palmer. Houghton, 1891.
> Same. Illustrated by N. C. Wyeth. Houghton, 1929.
> This beautiful book is much enjoyed by children in upper grades.

James, H. R. *Our Hellenic Heritage*. Macmillan, 1921.

Ovid. *Metamorphoses*. Literally translated into English prose by Henry T. Riley. In 2 volumes. First published 1851. McKay, 1899.

    Same. The Translation Publishing Company, New York, 1925.

Pater, Walter. *Greek Studies*. Macmillan, 1895-1925.

Pater, Walter. *Marius the Epicurean*. The Modern Library, New York. Chapter V, "The Golden Book," contains a beautiful translation of Cupid and Psyche.

Sabin, Frances E. *Classical Myths That Live Today*. Silver, 1927.

    This book is designed for older children but adult students find it interesting and useful.

Tatlock, Jessie M. *Greek and Roman Mythology*. Century, 1917.

    Although intended for older children, this book has proved a convenient handbook for adult students.

NORSE MYTHS
Original Sources, Criticism, and Collections for Adults

Anderson, R. B. *Norse Mythology; or The Religion of Our Fore-fathers*. Containing all the Myths of the *Eddas*. Chicago, Griggs, 1891. Part II quotes extensively from the *Poetic Edda*.

Carlyle, Thomas. *Heroes, Hero Worship, and the Heroic in History*. Ed. by Archibald MacMechan. Boston, 1901. Lecture I, "The Hero as Divinity." An interpretation of Norse myth in terms of natural phenomena of the far north.

Carpenter, William H. "The Eddas," Warner's *Library of the World's Best Literature*, volume 9, pp. 5113-5194. New York, Knickerbocker Press, 1917.

    Gives a condensed but clear account of all that is really known about the origin, and includes extensive selections from the *Poetic Edda*.

Guerber, Helene A. *Myths of Northern Lands*. American Book Company, 1895-1923.

    Contains a brief sketch of the Icelandic background of the *Eddas*, as well as outlines of many myths.

Munch, Peter A. *Norse Mythology*, *Legends of Gods and Heroes*. Revised by Magnus Olsen. Tr. by Sigurd B. Hustvedt. American-Scandinavian Foundation, 1926.

The Poetic Edda. Translated from the Icelandic by Henry Adams Bellows. The American-Scandinavian Foundation, 1923.

Snorri, Sturluson. *The Prose Edda.* Translated from the Icelandic by Arthur Gilchrist Brodeur. The American-Scandinavian Foundation, 1916.

Books for Children

Most of these books should be regarded as collections of stories for reading or telling to children, although the first two or three in each group can be read with pleasure by children in fourth grade.

Greek and Roman

Tales from Greek Mythology. Katharine Pyle. Illustrated by the author. Lippincott.

Old Greek Stories. James Baldwin. American Book Company.

Stories of Old Greece and Rome. Emilie Kip Baker. Macmillan.

Stories of Long Ago. Grace H. Kupfer. Heath.

Old Greek Folk Stories Told Anew. Josephine Preston Peabody. Houghton.

A Wonder-Book for Girls and Boys. Nathaniel Hawthorne. First published, 1851. (Riverside Literature Series.) Houghton.

Same. With sixty designs by Walter Crane. Houghton.

A Wonder-Book. Nathaniel Hawthorne. Illustrated by Arthur Rackham. Doubleday.

Tanglewood Tales. Nathaniel Hawthorne. First published, 1853. (Riverside Literature Series.) Houghton.

A Wonder-Book and Tanglewood Tales. Nathaniel Hawthorne. Illustrated by Maxfield Parrish. Duffield.

The Adventures of Odysseus and the Tale of Troy. Padraic Colum. Illustrated by Willy Pogany. Macmillan.

Norse

In the Days of Giants. Abbie Farwell Brown. Houghton.
Well-selected stories told in a vivid style.

Out of the Northland. Stories from the Northern Myths. Emilie Kip Baker. Macmillan.
A small book intended for younger children, a large part being devoted to the Siegfried legends.

The Children of Odin.   Padraic Colum.   Illustrated by Willy
   Pogany.   Macmillan.
          The stories are told with interesting detail and in a style
      calculated to appeal to children.
Norse Stories Retold from the Eddas.   Hamilton Wright Mabie.
   Rand.
          Authentic versions in which the spirit of the original is
      well preserved.

GENERAL COLLECTIONS

The Book of Nature Myths.   Florence Holbrook.   Houghton.
          Short, simple stories of the explanatory or *pourquoi* type.
The Curious Book of Birds.   Abbie Farwell Brown.   Illustrated
   by E. Boyd Smith.   Houghton.
          Interesting explanatory myths or legends.
Myths from Many Lands.   Selected and arranged by Eva March
   Tappan.   The Children's Hour, volume II.   Houghton.
          A representative collection from Hawthorne, Peabody,
      Brown and others.
Myths Every Child Should Know.   Hamilton Wright Mabie.
   Doubleday.
          Familiar myths, Greek, Roman and Norse, as told by
      various writers.

CHAPTER VII

EARLY BOOKS FOR CHILDREN

> He knows the policies of foreign lands;
> Can string you names of districts, cities, towns,
> The whole world over, tight as beads of dew
> Upon a gossamer thread; he sifts, he weighs;
> All things are put to question;....
>
> WORDSWORTH, *The Prelude*

NONE of the literature discussed in the preceding chapters was originally created for the express pleasure and entertainment of children. Until the latter half of the eighteenth century very few books other than textbooks and books on courtesy had been written especially for the young. For entertainment, they shared in much of the literature designed for their elders — ballads, legends, lives of the Saints, Æsop's Fables, Reynard the Fox, translations from Latin classics, tales of King Arthur, and various unauthentic and highly colored stories of history and travel. Many of these appeared in whole or in part in the shape of broadsides and chap-books, and in the same ephemeral form old and young read such tales as "Jack the Giant-Killer," "Tom Hick-a-Thrift," "The Babes in the Wood," "Guy of Warwick," "The History of Fortunatus," and "Fair Rosamond's Bower."

The Chap-man or peddler must have been a welcome visitor in those days, especially in village and country homes. He carried in his pack all kinds of trinkets, toys, and small objects of utility, as well as songs, ballads, stories, and the latest printed news. We see in Autolycus a perfect picture of the peddler, his methods and his wares.

Servant. He hath songs for man or woman, of all sizes: no milliner can so fit his customers with gloves. He has the prettiest love-songs for maids;...

Clown. Pr'ythee bring him in, and let him approach singing.

Enter Autolycus, singing
Lawn as white as driven snow;
Cyprus black as e'er was crow;
Gloves as sweet as damask roses;
Masks for faces and for noses;...
Come buy of me, come; come buy, come buy;
Buy, lads, or else your lasses cry:
Come, buy.

Clown. What hast here? ballads?

Mopsa. 'Pray now, buy some: I love a ballad in print, o' life, for then we are sure they are true.[1]

No doubt children spent their pennies freely for chapbooks as well as for toys, or waited eagerly for their elders to pass the little books on to them. Many of the stories were coarse, ribald jokes were not uncommon, the English was generally very bad, and the pictures were crude little woodcuts. According to Darton,[2] chap-books were published before 1700, but they appeared in the greatest profusion during the reign of the Georges. Until late in this period the books were for the most part anonymous and undated. The approximate date of publication has often been determined by the subject-matter, by advertisements, and other internal evidence. Original copies are today very rare. They were flimsily made in the beginning and they must have received very hard usage at the hands of successive owners. Miss Barry[3] treats of chapbooks very fully and also furnishes a chronological list of some of them and of early books for children, which is of great assistance to the student. From copies in museums

---

[1] *The Winter's Tale*, Act IV, Scene 3.
[2] Darton, F. J. Harvey, *The Cambridge History of English Literature*, volume XI, chapter 16, "Children's Books."
[3] Barry, F. V., *A Century of Children's Books*.

and private collections, facsimile editions have been produced and reprints of specimen pages have been made showing covers, text, and illustrations, so that one is able to get a fairly good idea of the content and appearance of some of the earliest editions. Several sources for such reproductions are indicated in the bibliography of this chapter.

In the first half of the eighteenth century there appeared a number of compilations which professed to be for the pleasure and profit of children. The titles were designed to attract young readers but the contents must often have proved disappointing and depressing. Darton says that Thomas White's *A Little Book for Little Children* (1720) was a volume of brief moral addresses based on the lives of "tortured saints — young ones, for choice."

James Janeway's *Token for Children* is said to have been the most widely read, but Darton calls it "a supreme example of morbid and gloating piety." Most of the "Miscellanies" he sums up under the phrase, "these oppressive compilations" and declares that none of them meets his conception of true children's literature which he defines as "books read or meant to be read by children for pleasure or profit, or for both, in their leisure hours."

But this ideal was shortly to be realized, for with the establishment of John Newbery as a publisher in London in 1744, the era of real children's books began. Before long he had succeeded in enlisting the help of leading literary men in his undertaking, Doctor Samuel Johnson offering counsel and criticism if nothing more, and Oliver Goldsmith actively co-operating as editor, compiler and, quite probably, as contributor. It took another seventy-five years, however, to complete the transformation in children's books — to shake off the incubus of literal-mindedness, dogmatism and sermonizing, and to establish firmly the ideal that literature is an art which should yield satisfaction, pleasure and delight to the reader.

JOHN NEWBERY

Into the No-Man's-Land of children's books John Newbery entered with original and liberal ideas, boundless enthusiasm and energy, a real respect for children, and standards of work which included beauty. Order began to emerge out of the chaos of random, disconnected and trivial little booklets in slovenly dress, and the Newbery juveniles quickly attained their well deserved popularity. Parents and children soon became familiar with the gayly covered little books which issued in rapid succession from the shop, "corner of St. Paul's Churchyard at the sign of the Bible and Sun."

Several features made the Newbery books outwardly attractive to children. For covers, he used the now famous Dutch paper — "flowery and gilt" which he imported from Holland in a great variety of beautiful colors and designs touched up with gold. Then the juvenile books were almost all quite small, many of them not more than four inches tall and sometimes even smaller — a feature which the American collector, Mr. Stone, calls "a definite and shrewd appeal to the small hands which were to hold them." [1] Good workmanship went into the printing and sewing, and many of the books attained the dignity of board covers instead of the paper covers commonly used. The character of the contents did not change all at once, as we shall see, but Newbery put into pleasing form many of the popular traditional tales, thus helping to pass them on to later generations; he published several very notable books, to be mentioned later; substituted pure childish fun and humor for the vulgarly comic; and was responsive to new currents of thought, social, educational and literary, as they manifested themselves. For the first time, leading minds and a publisher with imagination and vision com-

[1] Stone, Wilbur Macy, "Flowery and Gilt," *Saturday Review of Literature*, March 23, 1929.

bined to produce attractive books for quite young readers, and these books continued to give pleasure to several generations.

As a fitting tribute there has been awarded annually in this country since 1921 the Newbery medal to the author of the most notable children's book of the year.

When John Newbery died in 1767, his son Francis and his nephew (another Francis Newbery) headed separate branches of the business and both carried on its fine traditions. An eloquent but smiling panegyric was addressed to Francis Newbery in the Introduction to a collection of fairy stories [1] published in this country nearly a hundred years ago. It conveys something of the enthusiasm felt by those in a position to know well the work of this family of publishers, and seems to fit Mr. John Newbery quite as well as his successor.

> I cannot very well tell why it is, that the good histories and tales, which used to be given to young people for their amusement and instruction, as soon as they could read, have, of late years, gone quite out of fashion in this country. In former days, there was a worthy English bookseller, one Mr. Newbery, who used to print thousands of nice little volumes of such stories, which, as he solemnly declared in print, in the books themselves, he gave away to all good little boys and girls, charging them only sixpence apiece for the gilt covers; these of course no one could be so unreasonable as to ask him to furnish at his own expense. I well recollect the lively impression this marvellous generosity made upon my youthful imagination. The good man, lived in London, near St. Paul's churchyard, as his books informed us; and for above half a century, he supplied a great part of the civilized world with excellent little editions of "Jack, the Giant-Killer," "Goody Two-Shoes," "Tom Thumb," "Whittington and his Cat," "Giles-Gingerbread," and the "Children in the Woods."...
> Good, wise, generous, public-spirited Mr. Francis Newbery! Gratitude and honour be unto your memory. Then what a

---

[1] *The Fairy Book.* Harper and Brothers, New York, 1836.

delicate, what an exquisite taste hadst thou! What covers were those wherein thou didst enclose thy stories — covers worthy of the charming contents, for they glittered in fairy-like magnificence of red, green, and yellow gold! What choice cuts — *cuts!* It is thine own word, honoured Newbery — what choice cuts embellished thy delicious pages! How many a stammering tongue has screamed with joy at the sight of the heroic Jack clambering up his bean-stalk! How many a sparkling young eye has been dimmed with thick tears at the sight of the expiring "Cock Robin"; or more touching still, at the view of the good father and mother of the two hapless children in the wood, breathing their last, side by side in the same bed, with their night-caps on? .... They are all gone; the glittering covers and their more brilliant contents, the tales of wonder and enchantment, the father's best reward for early merit, the good grandmother's most prized presents. They are gone — the cheap delight of childhood, the unbought grace of boyhood, the dearest, freshest, most unfading recollections of maturer life. They are gone — and in their stead have succeeded a swarm of geological catechisms, entomological primers, and tales of political economy — dismal trash, all of them; something halfway between stupid story-books and bad schoolbooks; being so ingeniously written as to be unfit for any useful purpose in school, and too dull for any entertainment out of it.

A kindred spirit, that, to the Newberys themselves and to all lovers of children and true literature! We wish we knew more of the writer than is told by the signature "John Smith," a name which is given to the editor of this good little collection of fairy tales. The eclipse of imaginative writing under the shadow of "things as they are" which he so hotly resents was neither the first nor the last of its kind to darken the world of children's books.

The custom of anonymous writing for children continued under John Newbery and he wrote many of the unsigned books himself. Oliver Goldsmith contributed to the publications between 1762 and 1767 but there is no single piece of work which authorities attribute to him with absolute certainty. Two of the most notable Newbery books were published during this period, *Mother Goose's Melody*, and *Goody Two-Shoes*. Goldsmith's reputed collaboration on the first of these was mentioned in Chapter II, and the best authorities express little doubt that he is the author of *Goody Two-Shoes*, which was published in 1765. Goody, the little itinerant school mistress, self-appointed "trotting Tutoress" going from door to door with her basket of "Rattle-traps" or devices for teaching children younger than herself to read and spell, is a living character vividly drawn. This book is regarded as the first real child's novel — the first story of simple realism in which a consistent child character reveals herself through her actions in relation to other people. It is easy to find the little girl's pedagogical sanctions in Locke's theory and methods, but Goody herself is an original fictional creation. The author discards all the padding so common in children's books of the period — extraneous information, interlarded stories and anecdotes, disjointed moralizing, improbable travel sketches, and develops his theme around the central figure of a quaint and over-serious little girl engaged in practical everyday affairs. Goody Two-Shoes is a gallant little figure worthy of "a very great Writer of very little Books." If her creator could have foreseen her great popularity and lasting fame, he certainly would have acknowledged her.

We repeat, the evolution of children's books did not follow a straight and unencumbered course. Parents, teachers, and theorists clung to the idea that children were simply miniature adults and they were much concerned with the direct inculcation of morals and religious beliefs. The Newbery firm and other publishers of the day continued through the latter half of the century to print a good deal of solemn, heavy stuff, along with their offering of more childlike material. But on the whole such books were better done than their earlier counterparts, and the gloom was brightened in various ways.

At least a small beginning of almost every type of literature known to children of today can be found in eighteenth century publications. There were some contributions in poetry which will be noted in Chapter X; books of games and indoor amusement, and dramas for school and home appeared; and the heightened interest of adults in science and mechanical invention was soon reflected in tiny volumes of an encyclopedic character which often wore a thin disguise of playfulness. Newbery himself reduced the "Newtonian System of Philosophy" to the dimensions of a *Philosophy of Tops and Balls*.

Newbery was a shrewd business man and he and his successors employed ingenious and original publicity measures which would do credit to a modern advertising agency. Frequently, right in the heart of a story, would appear a casual reference to certain cherished books (giving titles), published at the sign of the "Bible and Sun." Other publishers copied this device, announcing with words of praise alluring titles of their own publications to be had at the sign of "Great A and Bouncing B" or some other bookshop — perhaps "The Toy and Marble Warehouse." The very shop names declare a new spirit, that of fun and pleasant humor. But these currents were still rather weak as compared to certain others which converged at this time, took possession of the field, and moved with great vigor well over into the nineteenth century.

MORAL TALES AND EDUCATION

All of the prominent writers of this period in England and several of the minor ones were more or less directly concerned with education, and the phrase which we meet so often today — "education for a changing civilization" — fitted admirably the needs of the whole civilized world in the late eighteenth century. The upheaval in France started by Rousseau's doctrines, and the less explosive reactions elsewhere, brought about the need of adjustment in every direction and, as at other times of rapid change in social ideals, educational theory and practice came prominently to the front.

One would have to turn to certain periods in adult literature to find another such example of response to current problems and movements, as is seen in children's books in France and England during the approximate period, 1760–1825. There were vast stirrings in the social structure, as well as in industry, science, invention, religion, philosophy, and education, and all of these can be seen reflected in some measure in children's books of the day. No one of the writers named exhibits all of these features, and sometimes the cherished tenets themselves seem to suffer a sea-change as they cross the channel from France to Georgian England, or move on to turbulent rural Ireland. Still the purpose is always clear — to mold children from infancy or to reform them later, according to certain prevalent theories and models. A brief reminder of some of these theories may help in understanding the English stories which were written as an aid to their realization.

Rousseau's theories of childhood education as elaborated in *Émile* (1762) found ready acceptance in England where the way had been prepared about seventy years earlier by Locke's *Some Thoughts Concerning Education* (1693). There was agreement in certain important features as well as marked dissimilarity in the two philosophies, but after a time, English common-sense worked out an amalgamation which suited the temper of her people. The writers of "moral stories" contributed to this synthesis and taken singly they show their individual predilections and antipathies.

The main points in which Locke and Rousseau agreed were: — their respect for young children and belief in their capacities, their rejection of empty abstractions, the importance they attached to the *useful*, and their distrust of the fanciful and romantic. Rousseau would dispense with books altogether in childhood and Locke would avoid all "useless Trumpery," meaning by that, stories of fancy and imagination. Both wished children to be happy in their expanding lives and Locke would transform their learning of symbols into a kind of sport — they were to be "cozined into a knowledge of the Letters." Rousseau's "Child of Nature" was to educate himself in and through his experience with realities. He was to enjoy the inherent reward or suffer the inevitable pain resulting from his free acts.

All of these theories as well as the intellectual hunger of the age, the fervor for freedom and democracy, and a quickened human sympathy, are readily traceable in children's literature. Perhaps the most noticeable features are, the emphasis on reason as guide, the exaltation of the useful, a recognition of the humble, a challenge to pride and hypocrisy, and the cultivation of a premature self-consciousness regarding "inner states" and moral issues, major and minor.

For the first time in England (and only slightly earlier in France) a group of writers of some literary standing concentrated on children's books, produced a quantity of stories similar in character, published under their own names as a rule, and became known chiefly as the authors of these books. At last it was considered quite respectable to write simple stories for children. The group can truly be called a "school" of writers — writers of didactic stories. Poets are found among them, but in this chapter we are considering only the writers of prose.

Theirs was a literature created largely for teaching purposes and the most dominant principle of construction was that of contrast. Fact and fancy, utility and beauty, luxury and simplicity, the real and the imaginary, reason and feeling, were viewed as opposed to each other and there was an insistent demand in the stories for choice and decision on the part of children. Realism was in the saddle, truth was always literal, and things of the imagination were taboo.

Some of these same thought-currents are easily discernible today among parents and educators, and writers are always responsive to such stirrings. For this reason if for no other, students can well afford to give some attention to the exaggerations which asserted themselves a century and a half ago.

REPRESENTATIVE WRITERS OF DIDACTIC STORIES

The most prominent members of this group of writers are Lætitia Aikin Barbauld (1743–1825); Thomas Day (1748–1789); Maria Edgeworth (1767–1849); and Martha M. Sherwood (1775–1851). They will be considered in chronological order though that does not indicate stages of approach toward a more modern spirit, since Mrs. Sherwood is in some respects the most remote of all. A few of the most characteristic traits in the work of each of these four writers will be presented, together with some facts in their lives which will partly explain their point of view and methods.

LÆTITIA AIKIN BARBAULD

Mrs. Barbauld belonged to a literary family and had attained some distinction as a poet before she began to write for children. The Barbaulds had no children but they adopted a nephew, Charles Aikin, when he was a small boy, and *Easy Lessons*, Mrs. Barbauld's first child's book, was written especially for him. She was in a school atmosphere most of her life; first, that of her father's school, and later as an active associate of her husband's in their own school for boys. She had just as definite ideas about education as the Edgeworths propounded a little later, but she did not elaborate her theories so fully.

Easy Lessons (1780) is not unlike some of the poorest of our modern primers which present the familiar things of life in an utterly commonplace way, to children who already know more about them than the author conveys. The book is a text for teaching the child to read and little more.

Mrs. Barbauld's best-known and most popular book is *Evenings at Home* which was written in collaboration with her brother, Dr. John Aikin. It was published in six small volumes appearing from 1792 to 1796. It is probably the best example of a juvenile miscellany of this period. It is definitely intended for instruction and is partly in the form of dialogue between parents and children, or tutor and child. These dialogues quite commonly deal with deportment, character traits, geography, natural science, and manufactures. The handling of the last-named topic is quite as good for that day as much of our modern social studies material. At the time of publication, the introduction of such matters as industry and the processes of manufacture into children's books must have been a very modern note indeed, since the steam engine was adapted to drive mills in 1785, and was introduced at Manchester in 1789.

This Miscellany contains stories of real life, more often concerning adult characters than children, and some fables or parables which appear to be original. Conversations with humble people occur at intervals — the lowly usually imparting some admirable philosophy of life or expressing some attitude which calls forth the approval of friendly neighbors of the upper class. There are a few fairly good poems, and one of Mrs. Barbauld's *Hymns in Prose for Children* — a collection to which critics of that day accorded high praise. The minute observation of nature, regardless of specific purpose, is set up as an ideal and is made concrete in the story "Eyes and No Eyes." This tale had a great vogue, was repeatedly imitated by other writers, and has survived until today. It was based on the old psychology which held that one could develop a general power such as keen observation, by a determined attention to everything in sight. Mrs. Barbauld went a step further, carried the matter into the moral realm, and tried to show the folly and loss attendant upon failure to develop the all-seeing eye.

There is not a real fairy story in the book. The author frankly discards them, but she devises a sort of allegory which she calls "Order and Disorder: A Fairy Tale." With the aid of the good fairy Order, a little girl is enabled to repair much mischief caused by the bad fairy Disorder, whom she has been harboring. Did this story let loose upon the world the troop of pestiferous pseudo-fairies which still try to usurp the real fairies in children's books?

Mrs. Barbauld displays an occasional flash of mild humor, but there is little in her books which can be called really childlike. On the other hand, her adults do not assume the judicial aloofness that is quite common in didactic stories.

THOMAS DAY

Thomas Day's *Sandford and Merton* is the most perfect example of a book written for children and designed to disseminate and exemplify a particular philosophy of education. One can find in this story almost every one of the major doctrines advocated in Rousseau's *Émile* — doctrines which Day ardently espoused, practiced quite consistently, and endeavored to promote among parents and teachers.

He was a man of marked eccentricity and one is tempted to enlarge upon his idiosyncrasies as they affected his personal relations and his writing. But this has been done quite fully by others and our main purpose should be to show his part in the widening stream of realistic stories. He was a warm personal friend of the Edgeworths, and like them, he believed that interesting and instructive reading should play a large part in the education of children — differing in this respect from Rousseau. He had no children of his own, but he took a keen interest in the training of the Edgeworth children, and *Sandford and Merton* was in the beginning expressly intended for home education in that family.

It was published in three parts from 1783 to 1789, proved very popular, and continued to be read through three generations. The student examines the book with interest in an effort to discover the means used to render abstract principles concrete and attractive to young readers.

To get the point of view of children with whom one is in close and sympathetic relation is difficult enough, and of course it is quite impossible for us to read at all clearly the minds and hearts of eighteenth-century children. But the best records we have show that children in all ages have been interested in other children, in animal life, in growing things, in adventure (especially under romantic conditions and in strange lands), and in deeds of courage and prowess; and Day appeals to all of these interests which we may call "universal." He does this by the simple process of turning a rather dull story about two little boys into another Miscellany. The affairs of the children occupy a comparatively small space. Mr. Barlow, the "Infallible Tutor" has, in addition to other superior qualifications, an inexhaustible supply of tales

to fit all occasions. Some of these are meant to be inform-
ing and others are especially suited to warning and re-
proof. There are numerous other actors whose entrance
on the scene is for the obvious purpose of spinning a yarn;
in fact, almost every character pours forth anecdotes and
stories on all occasions, opportune and inopportune. No
doubt the interest in the book was largely due to these
separate stories which are held together quite loosely and
clumsily by events which concern the boys. The book
itself is quite forgotten by the public at large but some of
the separate stories are found occasionally in anthologies.
Since it cannot always be easily obtained, Day's creed
will be stated and a few corresponding incidents from the
story will be cited.

Although a rich man, he despised luxury and display
and gave away a large part of his fortune; he was truly
democratic and deplored sharp class distinctions; he
advocated a "Return to Nature," as represented in a
simple rural life, and also lauded the supposed ideals
and customs of primitive peoples; he preached and practiced humanitarian principles as related to both man and
animals; he advocated useful labor for everyone; he was
a student of philosophy and a trained lawyer; perhaps
this last fact served to accentuate his espousal of "Reason
as Guide" and the tiresome arguments which he imposed
on his friends and on his fiction-children; and finally, he
believed in the Rousseauistic "natural method" of reward
and punishment.

In *Sandford and Merton*, Day endeavored to present his
theories in a concrete way by contrasting the characters,
abilities and general attainments of two boys — aged
about eight years; Tommy Merton (gentleman), an awful
example of the effects of a soft, effeminate policy, and
Harry Sandford, the sturdy little rustic reared according
to modified Rousseauistic principles.

Tommy was "so delicately brought up that he was perpetually ill. He was taught to sit still for fear of spoiling his clothes and to stay in the house for fear of injuring his complexion."

Harry was the son of "a plain, honest farmer" who lived near Mr. Merton's country seat. "As he had been always accustomed to run about in the fields, to follow the labourers while they were ploughing and to drive the sheep to their pasture, he was active, strong, hardy and fresh-colored." On the occasion of his first visit to the Mertons, the farm lad proceeds to discourse at length on the subject of the foolish and pernicious practice of using a silver service, drinking wine, eating delicate food, being served by a retinue of servants and wearing fine clothes.

Mr. Merton is so impressed with Harry's spirit and attainments that he covets for his spoiled offspring the same training, and the result is that his son is sent to join Harry under the tuition of the clerical pedagogue, Mr. Barlow. In this plan we see put into effect three of Rousseau's tenets — life close to Nature, separation of the child from home and family, and a tutor who will not accept money for his services. Rousseau's "natural" method of discipline or the spur of necessity is observed. Mr. Barlow and Harry cultivate the ground and when weary from their labors sit down in an arbor to partake of ripe cherries. Tommy, who has scorned to "slave like a plough-boy," is ignored and goes hungry. The next day he takes a hoe and works with the others and with them partakes of ripe cherries. Tommy cannot read and is for some time entertained by hearing the country boy read aloud. At last Harry goes home for a week, and Tommy mopes around deprived of his usual pleasure. Whereupon he decides to learn to read and soon accomplishes the task. He is scornful of a poor ragged boy, and attempts to domineer over him, asserting the prerogatives of a gentleman's son. Unpleasant consequences ensue as he lands in a ditch and has to be fished out by the despised urchin.

In everything, Harry's superiority is demonstrated and Tommy is directly or indirectly counseled to imitate him. In season and out of season, the excellent Mr. Barlow labors to open up to the unregenerate Tommy the satisfaction that is to be found in a life of simplicity and industry, and to arouse in him a contempt for a life of indolence and elegant ease. He tries to demonstrate the utter uselessness of the unproductive rich and to show the meanness of being supported by the labor of the poor. Harry, the model boy-companion, joins in this worthy effort giving utterance from time to time of precocious counsel.

In the main current of the story, which is concerned with the lives of these boys, their families and associates, the author extols not so much the life of "the noble savage" as that of the sturdy, intelligent, and cheerful laboring class in rural England. But in the numerous tales which are interlarded there is much that savors of a belief that the life of the barbarian is better and happier than that of more highly civilized peoples. The favorite plot of these interspersed tales is that of crossed threads in the lives of two people of supposedly widely different opportunities, with the final fortune always turning in favor of the one whose life was closest to nature and whose dependence was not at all on polish, social gifts, gentle birth, money or other worldly acquisitions.

Tales are told of the mode of life of Laplanders, Greenlanders, Scythians, Arabians, American Indians, and Spartans; and in each, the virtues of independence and courage, of prowess in war and of cheerful industry in peace are extolled. In many of these we see displayed a fine disregard for fact. We learn many interesting and surprising things about the North American Indian and note that Mr. Barlow is a warm admirer of our aboriginal tribes. This is his comment on the story told by the Highlander who wandered for months in the wilds of America. "Nor can I consider without a certain degree of admiration the savage grandeur of man in his most simple state.... I see many around me that are disgraced by the vices of uncivilized Americans, without a claim to their virtues."

The conclusion of such stories is summed up in Tommy's remark, "In all these stories which I have heard, it seems as though those nations which have little or nothing are more well-disposed and better and braver than those that have a great deal." And Mr. Barlow agrees that "This is indeed sometimes the case."

Day's humanitarian principles are reflected in the "good" boy Harry, who was "so careful and considerate that he would step out of the way for fear of hurting a worm and employed himself in doing kind offices to all animals in the neighborhood.... In the winter time, when the ground was covered with frost and snow, and the poor little birds could get no food, he would often go supperless to bed that he might feed the robin redbreasts."

He seems to have been a sort of knight-errant to all the hunted rabbits, wounded chickens, abused donkeys and other hapless creatures.

Conversing with Mr. Barlow about crocodiles one day, Tommy says, "Pray, sir, is this dreadful creature capable of being tamed?" "Yes," answers Mr. Barlow, "I believe, as I have before told you, there is no animal that may not be rendered mild and inoffensive by good usage."

We are introduced incidentally to a remarkable boy and a no less remarkable snake. Harry asserts, "I knew a little boy who took a great fancy to a snake that lived in his father's garden, and when he had his milk for breakfast, he used to... whistle and the snake would come to him, and eat out of his bowl."

It may be some satisfaction to know that Tommy responds to the efforts of the worthy and erudite Mr. Barlow and his other friends. The experiences which he undergoes and the stories to which he listens seem to work to his edification, and as *Sandford and Merton* draws to a close, we see young Merton transformed into just such a boy as Thomas Day would approve. Indeed the last glimpse of the regenerate Tommy suggests Day himself, as he returned from France on one occasion and renounced the follies and fripperies which he had half-heartedly attempted to acquire. So Tommy, aged about nine, appears at last shorn of his curls, his clothes "divested of every appearance of finery, every article of his attire plain and simple" and announces to his astonished mother, "I am now only what I ought always to have been.... From this time I shall apply myself to the study of nothing but reason and philosophy; and therefore I have bidden adieu to dress and finery forever."

In "The History of Little Jack," [1] Mr. Day grants to the foundling baby the barest means of a primitive existence, at the hands of an impoverished but kind and intelligent old man aided by a quite essential Nanny Goat. The boy develops great resourcefulness and strength of character, puts to rout several weakling aristocrats, champions a number of causes dear to the heart of Mr. Day, and incidentally encounters numerous exciting adventures. A study of this story will reveal all of the author's most cherished beliefs, and his full bag of tricks for getting a hearing from children.

MARIA EDGEWORTH

No writer of children's stories ever had a better oppor-

[1] Included in *Old-Fashioned Tales*, edited by E. V. Lucas.

tunity to know children and to judge the reaction of her prospective audience than Maria Edgeworth. She was next to the oldest of the twenty-one or twenty-two children of Richard Lovell Edgeworth, who was married four times. She lived harmoniously with each of her three step-mothers, never married, and became a sort of second mother to the fifteen brothers and sisters born after she reached the age of about sixteen. Miss Edgeworth and her father were the continuing members of this changing group, though unity was perhaps made easier by the fact that the wives of the second and third marriage were sisters — the Misses Honora and Elizabeth Sneyd.

Very early, Miss Edgeworth began to share in the development of a scheme of education which her father was attempting to bring into practical operation in the home, and the two did a large part of the teaching of the younger children. It became a custom in the family to give one of the older children special charge of some younger one; and when Maria was sixteen, Henry, the first child of the third marriage, became her particular care. She was a fond, devoted, and apparently very wise elder sister who saw the charm and beauty as well as the weaknesses of childhood, and had a keen perception of individual traits.

Mr. Edgeworth and Mr. Day were lifelong friends and they held many views in common, but the former arrived at a much more balanced and workable philosophy than his friend ever accepted, and escaped the disappointment and chagrin which followed most of Mr. Day's ventures. In their early enthusiasm for Rousseau, however, they had one rather disastrous failure in common, and that was in their combined efforts to rear the eldest Edgeworth child, Richard, in accordance with Rousseau's doctrines and methods.

Later, Mr. Edgeworth had quite an extensive laboratory for his social theories in the management of the large estate in Ireland which he inherited, and an equally stimulating situation for educational experiment in the home training of his remarkable family. As there was a period of more than forty-five years between the birth of his first child and that of his last, there was ample time in which to revise theories and create materials of instruction. Having rejected pure theory as rigid and artificial, father and daughter proceeded to evolve their own schemes of "practical education" appropriate to normal family life in a home of ample means and wide opportunities for culture. There were contributions from the maternal side of the house also, and Mr. Day continued to co-operate in various ways.

The Edgeworths were less obsessed with the desire to instruct than Mrs. Barbauld was; they did not follow Mr. Day's example as preacher of political and social reform; and Mrs. Sherwood's consuming desire to save souls had no place in their purposes. They were intent upon discovering and promoting the best ways of developing a particular group of young people and helping other parents and teachers in a like endeavor. Ideally, children were to become reasonable, responsible, industrious, generous, upright, and resourceful. They were to be well informed, especially in matters of practical importance, and acquire some manual skill. Young children were to be carefully protected from all evil influences, one avenue of great danger being the literature to which they were exposed. It was to furnish this wholly harmless and definitely moral literature for children and young people that Miss Edgeworth set her hand, and in so doing entered a field in which she was to become famous.

If opportunity offers, the student of this period should examine *Practical Education*, a treatise setting forth the Edgeworth ideas and methods, written by father and daughter and published in 1798. A first reading offers many surprises to those who think "progressive" education is a new movement. A few features which seem most closely related to the spirit and form of Miss Edgeworth's stories will be mentioned briefly here. Notice that the authors hold the very modern view which regards education as both an art and an experimental science. The Preface says:

> To make any progress in the art of education, it must be patiently reduced to an experimental science; we are fully sensible of the extent and difficulty of this undertaking, and we have not the arrogance to imagine, that we have made any considerable progress in a work, which the labours of many generations may, perhaps, be insufficient to complete.

There is an excellent chapter on toys which clearly sets forth the superiority of those toys and materials which permit a child the maximum of creative and constructive activity.

The authors advocate first-hand experience with simple science:

> We have found from experience, that an early knowledge of the first principles of science may be given in conversation, *and may be insensibly acquired from the usual incidents of life.*
> [Italics not in the original.]

There is an excellent discussion of "real history" as distinguished from prejudiced and over-romantic treatment.

Specific recommendations are made and practical suggestions offered for such activities as gardening, carpentry, home dramatics, making scenery and costumes, dyeing, and constructing simple scientific apparatus. There is ample evidence that the Edgeworth children engaged happily and with a good deal of independence in all these attractive occupations, and we see Miss Edgeworth's story-book children enjoying similar activities.

In *Practical Education* we find a clue to the complete

absence of the element of imagination and romance in Miss Edgeworth's stories which strikes everyone who reads them today. Her father disapproved strongly of stories of an imaginative type and Maria was his unquestioning disciple. Elsewhere she states that she has no talent for that kind of writing, but almost all critics have felt that her creative power suffered under the too close supervision and minute criticism of a dominating personality.

Fairy tales are dismissed as not worthy of comment and most travel-tales are put under the ban:

> There is a class of books which amuse the imagination of children without acting upon their feelings. *We do not allude to fairy tales, for we apprehend that these are not now much read*, but we mean voyages and travel; these interest young people universally. [Italics not in original.]

Such tales, they say, are very popular and there is great danger that boys especially will be diverted from steady pursuits or ordinary callings. The passage continues:

> The history of realities written in an entertaining manner appears not only better suited to the purposes of education, but also more agreeable to young people than improbable fictions.

Mr. Edgeworth wrote the Preface to *The Parent's Assistant, or Stories for Children*,[1] Miss Edgeworth's first collection, published in 1796. There again he sets forth their objections to fairy tales. He has been much disturbed by Dr. Samuel Johnson's championship of such tales and takes occasion to express disagreement, being impelled to this "from a fear that his (Dr. Johnson's) authority should establish errors." He quotes Dr. Johnson to the effect that "Babies do not like to hear stories of babies

---

[1] Unless otherwise stated, all of Miss Edgeworth's stories mentioned in this chapter are in this book.

like themselves; they require to have their imaginations raised by tales of giants, and fairies, and castles, and enchantments." Mr. Edgeworth challenges this statement as unproved but offers no real argument against it. He simply propounds a series of questions: "But why should the mind be filled with fantastic visions, instead of useful knowledge? Why should so much valuable time be lost? Why should we vitiate their taste and spoil their appetite by suffering them to feed upon sweetmeats? It is to be hoped that the magic of Dr. Johnson's name will not have power to restore the reign of fairies."

From the beginning, then, Miss Edgeworth set her face against "improbable fictions," committed herself to writing realistic stories with a purpose, and (in the words of the Preface) "attempted... to provide antidotes against ill-humor, the epidemic rage for dissipation, and the fatal propensity to admire and imitate whatever the fashion of the moment may distinguish." She was careful "to avoid inflaming the imagination, or exciting a restless spirit of adventure, by exhibiting false views of life, and creating hopes which, in the ordinary course of things, cannot be realized."

Though fairies and magic were banished, Miss Edgeworth frequently contrived plots which involved a combination of events so remarkable as to far transcend "the ordinary course of things" and to verge upon the miraculous. On this point Mrs. Ritchie [1] says her stories "open like fairy tales, recounting in simple diction the histories of widows living in flowery cottages, with assiduous devoted little sons, who work in the garden and earn money to make up the rent. There are also village children busily employed, and good little orphans whose parents generally die in the opening pages. Fairies were not

[1] Edgeworth, Maria, *The Parent's Assistant, or Stories for Children*. With an Introduction by Anne Thackeray Ritchie. Macmillan, 1897.

much in Miss Edgeworth's line, but philanthropic manu-
facturers, liberal noblemen, and benevolent ladies in
traveling carriages, do as well and appear in the nick of
time to distribute rewards or to point a moral."

Miss Edgeworth wrote in the common living-room sur-
rounded by a large family group who engaged without
hindrance in conversation and all other ordinary activities.
Numerous little brothers and sisters served in some measure as her models. They also suggested themes for stories
and criticized the tales as they developed and were read
aloud. One would like to know more about the children's
contributions; as to the father's, it is generally believed
that the moral philosopher and theorist in his rôle of self-
confident literary judge and critic, had a deadening effect
upon the story-teller's natural spontaneity.

As landowners, the Edgeworths held and practiced
advanced democratic ideas, but they were not radicals
and believed it useless and unwise to ignore class distinctions. The logical outcome of this view was to write
stories addressed specifically to children of the upper and
lower ranks of society, and Miss Edgeworth's leading
characters and scenes of action are divided about equally
between the two classes. She was very active in the
management of the estate and was familiar with the life
of peasants, small farmers, simple villagers, and trades-
people. Walter Scott, who was her friend and admirer,
paid a very high tribute to her ability to impart convinc-
ing reality to her characters.

Not all of her child characters are entirely convinc-
ing, however. Several are incredibly hateful, possessing
not a single pleasing trait of childhood — Bell in "The
Birthday Present," and Barbara Case in "Simple Susan,"
for example. Others are without a flaw either in motive,
judgment, or action — Laura in "The Birthday Present,"
and Ben in "Waste Not, Want Not," being of this type.

More interesting and natural than these are the children
who display the small faults and errors of judgment common to childhood and who get into difficulties because
they have these human imperfections. Rosamond, who
is acknowledged to be drawn in part at least from Maria
herself as a child, is of this type. She appears, aged seven,
in "The Purple Jar," [1] in *Early Lessons*, and again, at
nine years of age in "The Birthday Present." In the
first-named story in particular, she is a winsome little
girl, and our sympathy is turned to her because we see
her trapped by a mother who makes no allowance for her
inexperience and who is fundamentally insincere with the
child, although Miss Edgeworth intends her as a shining
example of the "Superior Parent."

Miss Edgeworth inherited the method of accenting
character traits by sharply drawn contrasts as employed
by Thomas Day and other writers of the period. Like
them she often uses one child as a foil for another of opposite character but she does this in a less mechanical
way than the others. Her narrowest use of this device
is seen in "Little Dog Trusty" in *Early Lessons*, and in
"Waste Not, Want Not." She is the first novelist of
childhood and most of her characters are much more
living than those of any of her predecessors. There is
great variety in both her good and bad children and their
behavior is seldom exactly predictable. Most of the
really bad children repent and reform — only one, Lazy
Lawrence, has to be sent to jail! And the heedless,
naughty ones set about their own improvement after a
series of unhappy experiences in which they see the folly
of their behavior.

Miss Edgeworth occasionally deals with the baser types
of conduct — stealing, lying, cruelty, and gross disloyalty;
but her chief preoccupation is with refinements of ethical

[1] In *Old-Fashioned Tales*. Edited by E. V. Lucas.

social behavior such as the subordination of passion and sensibility to reason, freedom from false pride and pretense, "well-regulated sympathy," "benevolent affections," frankness, good-temper, industry, self-reliance, and loyalty to family and friends. All of these, seen in action, are held up for admiration in various stories, and their lack in an individual always results in final disappointment or distress.

This author knows how to secure dramatic effects and does so in almost every tale. She introduces checks, reverses, and various obstacles to bring temporary defeat to her hero and thus maintain suspense; and there are mysteries calling for quite a bit of detective work, with surprising outcomes. Who stole Jem's hard-earned money in "Lazy Lawrence" and how was the thief discovered? Who stole the apples and tried to poison the dog in "Tarlton" and how was young Hardy cleared of the false accusation? Who gave the gold piece to the children in "The Basket Woman" and how was the owner identified? How were Cecilia's mixed motives and inconsistent behavior exposed in "The Bracelets"? Who was responsible for ruining Rosamond's precious filigree basket in "The Birthday Present"? How would "The Orphans" extricate themselves from difficulties arising out of finding the buried gold? Doubtless children enjoy mystery that is not too profound and detective work that is not too intricate just as their elders do, and they certainly like to see an unpopular culprit brought to justice and suffering innocence relieved.

Mr. Edgeworth was the author of an extensive study of familiar proverbs and maxims, and it is a safe surmise that he was not slow to apply them in his family. Some of the stories use such formulations to express both theme and title as in "Waste Not, Want Not"; or "Two Strings to Your Bow"; and the adage "Forgive and Forget" sounds a refrain through the story of that title. Other maxims often declaimed by children and adults are: "A warm friend and a bitter enemy"; "Better live in spite than in pity"; "A soft word turneth away wrath"; "Like father like son"; "The mother of mischief is no bigger than a midge's wing"; "Evil communications corrupt good manners"; "A good beginning makes a good ending"; "Honesty is the best policy"; "More haste, worse speed."

Another earmark of the didactic story extensively used by all of that school is the allegorical name so often assigned to a character. Miss Edgeworth makes some use of this device, but does not carry it to an extreme. We meet Mrs. Theresa Tattle, Attorney Case, Mrs. Bustle, Justice Headstrong, Dr. Carbuncle, Miss Croker (a singer), Colonel Epaulette, Lady Sweepstakes (a lady of fashion), Farmer Truck, Corkscrew (a butler), and Sir Charles Slang. These are all either minor or farcical characters; child characters as a rule bear good old English names — Rosamond, Peggy, Nancy, Lucy, Sophie, Louisa, Helen, Susan, Frank, Harry, Arthur, Philip, Robert, William, Paul. In the delineation of these children there are certain exaggerations of type for the purpose of emphasis, and of course their language and deportment often appear quaint and stilted, but most of them are as normal as their names.

No parents ever took their responsibility more seriously than those in Miss Edgeworth's stories. The children would have been less badgered if her fiction families had been more like her father's in size. Instead, the families are small and the concentrated attention of the mother, and sometimes the father, can be bent upon every spoken thought and every act of one helpless child; for if there are two children, one of them is usually so wise and correct that he is not subjected to analytical inquiry. The inquisitor is gentle but unrelenting, and the matter in question is more likely to concern the child's reasons and motives than actual misbehavior. The principle of "Reason as Guide" has full sway, and children seven or eight years old are expected to explain and justify every opinion, every spontaneous emotion, every proposed action. By the time Rosamond in "The Birthday Present" has struggled to meet the cool logic of both parents regarding the unimportance of birthday celebrations in general and of her Cousin Bell's in particular, the doubtful nature of her motives and the flimsiness of the gift she has made, the child's anticipation of pleasure has vanished and she is ready to call herself a fool. Children were expected to examine into inner states of thought and feeling, to inhibit all actions until they could offer sound reasons for their course, and to check spontaneous and trustful response toward a new acquaintance until they could produce ample evidence of the person's true worth. The method if successful would turn out a calculating and cold-blooded generation.

Perhaps the most interesting stories as regards individuality of characters and plot construction are those which concern very humble people. In "Lazy Lawrence," "The Basket Woman," "Simple Susan," and "The Orphans," the parents are either ill, or dead, or so driven by hard work that they cannot be always "educating" their offspring, so the children develop marvelous initiative and efficiency. Sweetness and nobility of character and a confiding nature seem already to have been formed by some unrevealed process.

To sum up Miss Edgeworth's contribution: she set the example of a gifted writer who dignified the art of creating children's stories; broke away from most of the old traditions and made her stories stand on their own merits rather than on extraneous material; largely discarded set patterns for stories and invented interesting plots; drew a large number of fairly well-rounded child characters and developed a few unforgettable ones; wrote more fully for entertainment than any previous or contemporary writer and in so doing furnished at least two generations with good stories well suited to the time. There is some evidence that the best of her stories are still read and enjoyed by children.

On the negative side this author displays the unfortunate effect that writing for some ulterior purpose, such as conveying information or imparting moral lessons, has upon literature. This fault is not peculiar to eighteenth-century writers, it is one which asserts itself continually and with special force at any time of stress and strain such as war, social unrest, or anxiety about the religious and ethical training of the young. It behooves us to watch this tendency today.

Stories most likely to prove interesting to children today, beginning at a mental age of about eight years, are:

> The Purple Jar
> The Cherry Orchard
> The Basket Woman
> Waste Not, Want Not
> Simple Susan
> The Orphans

Others in which students may find additional illustration of Miss Edgeworth's traits and methods are "The Bracelets"; "The Birthday Present"; and "Mademoiselle Panache."

Since the original collections are not easy to obtain, several different sources for a number of these stories are given in the bibliography.

MARTHA MARY SHERWOOD

Mrs. Sherwood is a far less important figure in the development of children's literature than Miss Edgeworth, and except for two or three considerations she might be passed over with the briefest mention. Compared with her immediate predecessors she is a reactionary and there is no doubt that she exerted a powerful influence in the wrong direction as judged by literary standards and the emotional health of children.

After a happy girlhood in England as the daughter of a country rector, Martha Mary Butt married an army officer, Captain Henry Sherwood, whose post was in India, and she lived there for about twenty years. She was deeply religious and her faith developed into a very rigorous evangelical type. The pitiful condition of the native children led her into active missionary work and this resulted in a still deeper immersion in the doctrines and prescriptions of her faith. We have in Mrs. Sherwood another author of children's books who is also a teacher, for the children of officers and others of the English colony had to have a school, and she conducted one in her home for several years. It appears that she was greatly concerned with the children's spiritual and religious growth and with this purpose uppermost she developed numerous teaching procedures concerned with the Scriptures, hymns, prayers, and exhortations, for use with mere infants as well as older children.

Mrs. Sherwood's preoccupation with death and the future life must have been greatly increased by the tragic loss of one lovely baby after another. In that climate she could not rear beyond infancy or early childhood her own little ones, though she gave them tender and devoted care. One pities the desolation and marvels at the religious fervor which carried her through this sorrow, leaving no trace of bitterness. She adopted or became guardian to several children whose need was great, one at least being a native. Mrs. Sherwood's literary background, her unusual experiences, her love for children and watchful study of them, and her genuine ability, might have made her a really notable writer of children's books if her concern for their soul's salvation here and in eternity had not swallowed up almost every other consideration. As it was, she set the model for Sunday-School books for more than fifty years in England and America, and probably more than any other author is responsible for the vast crop of trivial and melancholy little books about childish saints and sinners which were so long accounted the only kind suitable for a Sunday-School library.

Mrs. Sherwood wrote a prodigious number of little stories many of them unsigned and issued as chap-books or tracts. Where identification was possible they were gathered together and published in 1817 in ten volumes under the title *The Works of Mrs. Sherwood*.

The Fairchild Family is her best-known book and it displays all of her dominant traits — the best and the worst. Some critics still comment favorably on this book. Students should not judge it by the modern edition, which is greatly modified. By the time all of the highly objectionable and sometimes quite shocking parts have been eliminated there is not much left, but what remains does show Mrs. Sherwood's ability to picture children in natural, happy play when freed for a time from customary restraint. As a whole, however, the book lives up to its sub-title. The title in full reads:

The History of the Fairchild Family; being a collection of stories calculated to show the importance and effects of a religious education.

The children in the family are Lucy, aged about nine, and Emily "next in age" (younger), and Henry between six and seven. They have a pleasant home in the country, lead a simple life and do not go to school. Mrs. Fairchild teaches the little girls and Mr. Fairchild teaches and disciplines Henry. Each chapter has as its theme a Bible text, one of the Commandments, or some other very serious subject. Some of these are:

"*The General Depravity of Mankind in all Countries after the Fall.*"

After this "story" the following conversation occurs: "Papa," said Lucy, "may we say some verses about mankind's having bad hearts?" Ready consent is given and little Henry's verse is, "For I know that in me, that is, in my flesh, dwelleth no good thing."

"*On the Formation of Sin in the Heart.*"

Henry takes an apple from a very special tree and denies it. He is severely punished for the deceit. His father says, "It is better that he should be punished in this world, while he is a little boy, than grow up to be a liar and a thief, and go to hell when he dies."

"*Thou Shalt Not Kill.*"

The children had quarreled, anger was displayed, and Mr. Fairchild thinks a warning is needed. So he takes them for what promises to be a pleasant walk but which he directs toward a crossroad gibbet on which the body of a murderer hangs. Henry is so young that he has to be carried part of the way.

"*A Story on the Constant Bent of Man's Heart Toward Sin.*"

This story is quite jolly in spite of the title. The parents go away for a day leaving the children in the care of the faithful servant, John. They are very naughty, indulge in various exciting escapades, and show themselves real children and unregenerate young sinners. When the time of reckoning comes and they have done proper penance, Mrs. Fairchild presents Lucy with a blank book and says, "Take this book and write in it every day the naughty things which pass in your heart." Then follows on Lucy's part such a self-examination as might have turned her into an "introvert" if the term had been known in that day. The child tries to record every thought or mood that is not lofty.

"*A Happy Death.*"

The children are taken to call on a little farmer boy who is dying. He talks like a voluble saint and tells of his preparations for death, including a visit to the cemetery and inspection of a vault.

Mrs. Sherwood reverts to some extent to the old trick of including extraneous stories in her book. John goes to the Fair and is commissioned by the children to bring them each a book. They give him their pennies — Henry one, Emily two, and Lucy three. They run gaily to meet him on his return and receive their books with every evidence of delight.

Henry. "Here are many beautiful pictures in mine. It is about a covetous woman — *The History of a Covetous Woman.*"

Emily. "Mine is *The History of the Orphan Boy*, and there are a great many pictures in it. The first is a picture of a funeral."

Lucy reads her title, *The History of the Good Child who was made the instrument of turning his father and mother to the ways of holiness.*

Mr. Fairchild says, "They appear to be very nice books: I see they are written in the fear of God; and the pictures in them are very pretty."

Six-year-old Henry reads *all* the stories aloud, so we get the three in full. They are quite in harmony with the Fairchild method of child training.

Mrs. Sherwood is conscientiously opposed to fairy tales. Her point of view is voiced by Mrs. Teachum in *The Governess*. Mrs. Teachum rebuked the oldest girl in her boarding-school, Miss Jenny Peace, for reading a fairy story to the younger ones when left in charge one day. She relents somewhat when she reads the story herself and decides that it is relatively harmless. The story is in reality a very weak invention, but by this device it finds a place in *The Governess* along with the schoolgirl affairs of Miss Dolly Friendly, Miss Lucy Sly, Miss Henny Fret, Miss Polly Suckling (aged five years), et al.

One of Mrs. Sherwood's short stories, "Little Robert and the Owl," is often included in modern anthologies. It is wholly free from sermonizing, and the little boy's adventures when lost in a snowstorm in an effort to aid his grandmother, his good sense and calm philosophy, are made to appear quite plausible. This story shows what she might have done if her intensely religious purposes had not overtopped all others.

OPINIONS OF A FEW CONTEMPORARIES

Several leading literary men of the day disagreed violently with the point of view, purposes, and product of the didactic writers and assailed them in vigorous terms. Charles Lamb, Wordsworth, Coleridge, and Dr. Samuel Johnson were outspoken, each in his own characteristic way. Charles Lamb exploded in a letter to Samuel Taylor Coleridge dated October 23, 1802.

I am glad the snuff and Pi-pos's [1] books please. "Goody Two-Shoes" is almost out of print. Mrs. Barbauld's stuff has banished all the old classics of the nursery; and the shopman at Newbery's hardly deigned to reach them off an old exploded corner of a shelf, when Mary asked for them. Mrs.

---

[1] "Pipos" was a pet name for Coleridge's little son.

Barbauld's and Mrs. Trimmer's nonsense lay in piles about. Knowledge insignificant and vapid as Mrs. Barbauld's books convey, it seems, must come to a child in the *shape of knowledge;* and his empty noddle must be turned with conceit of his own powers when he has learnt that a horse is an animal, and Billy is better than a horse, and such like; instead of that beautiful interest in wild tales, which made the child a man, while all the time he suspected himself to be no bigger than a child.   Science has succeeded to poetry no less in the little walks of children than with men. Is there no possibility of averting this sore evil? Think what you would have been now, if instead of being fed with tales and old wives' fables in childhood, you had been crammed with geography and natural history!

Hang them!   I mean the cursed Barbauld crew, those blights and blasts of all that is human in man and child.[1]

Wordsworth began *The Prelude* [2] in 1799 and finished it in 1805 which covered a period of high popularity for moralistic stories.   In this poem Wordsworth describes the little paragon of virtue and learning who figures in these tales and, like Lamb, sighs for the banished fairy tales of his childhood days.   The entire passage well repays reading.   Here are a few lines:

> Full early trained to worship seemliness,
> This model child is never known
> To mix in quarrels; that were far beneath
> Its dignity; with gifts he bubbles o'er
> As generous as a fountain; selfishness
> May not come near him, nor the little throng
> Of flitting pleasures tempt him from his path;
> .   .   .   .
> Meanwhile old grandame earth is grieved to find
> The playthings, which her love designed for him,
> Unthought of; in their woodland beds the flowers
> Weep, and the river sides are all forlorn,
> Oh! give us once again the wishing-cap
> Of Fortunatus, and the invisible coat
> Of Jack the Giant-killer, Robin Hood,
> And Sabra in the forest with St. George!

---

[1] Lamb, Charles, *Letters*, volume I, Letter XCIV.

[2] Wordsworth, William, *The Prelude*, Book V.

TOPICS AND PROBLEMS

1. Arrange in tabular form, significant dates during the eighteenth and early nineteenth centuries, indicating a known or probable relationship to the development of certain types of children's literature.

2. Construct a composite picture of English child-life of the eighteenth century, drawn largely from available stories. Poetry may be included if desired. See Chapter X for poetry of the period.

3. Present very briefly about twenty short passages or scenes from at least seven stories of the period, which seem to you to picture the most genuine child behavior.

4. Contrast *Mrs. Leicester's School*, by Charles and Mary Lamb, with Mrs. Sherwood's *The Governess*. The latter is a complete rewriting of Sara Fielding's story of the same title published about 1750.

5. Nemesis: The miraculous chain of events by which a child is brought to the consequences of his error. Miss Barry uses the telling phrase "cumulative fatality."
   Draw your material almost entirely from the stories. Do not overlook Thomas Day.

6. Irrational parents of rational children. Or, The "Infallible Parent" on trial.

7. The "Perfect Tutor" judged by modern psychology.

8. Crises in the lives of child characters revealing moral fiber.

9. A list of moral issues discovered in these stories and how children met them. (Similar to Number 8.)

10. Reward and punishment — kinds and effects. If possible read the chapter in *Practical Education* on this subject.

11. Play life and happy occupations in these stories.

12. A Study of plot in Miss Edgeworth's stories.

13. Relationship of upper and lower classes.

14. The child philanthropist, his attitude and his acts.

15. If possible, read a few stories from such books as the E. V. Lucas collections, to children eight to ten years of age, and try to discover whether they really enjoy them.

BIBLIOGRAPHY

History, Criticism, and Biography

Ashton, John. *Chap-Books of the Eighteenth Century*. With facsimiles, notes and introduction. London, 1882.
> Numerous old folk tales are listed and illustrated.

Barry, Florence V. *A Century of Children's Books*. Doran, 1922.
> The history of books for children (chiefly in England) from early eighteenth to early nineteenth century. Contains a wealth of historical data and clear-sighted criticism presented in an original and delightful style.

Barry, Florence V. *Maria Edgeworth; Chosen Letters*. With an introduction by Florence V. Barry. Houghton, 1932.
> A part of these letters have not been published before and Miss Barry has had access to other unpublished family records.

Butler, Harriet J., and Butler, Harold Edgeworth. *The Black Book of Edgeworthstown and Other Edgeworth Memories*. London, Faber, 1927.
> A granddaughter and great-grandson of Richard Lovell Edgeworth write entertainingly of many phases of family history and literary work.

Darton, F. J. Harvey. "Children's Books" in *Cambridge History of English Literature*, volume XI, chapter 16. Cambridge University, 1914.

Darton, F. J. Harvey. *Children's Books in England*. Five Centuries of Social Life. Macmillan, 1932.
> A very full and authoritative survey and appraisal by an English scholar and a specialist in the field.

Field, Mrs. E. M. *The Child and His Book*. Wells, Gardner, 1895.
> An excellent reference when supplemented by later books.

Gignilliat, George Warren. *The Author of Sandford and Merton. A Life of Thomas Day*. Columbia University, 1932.
> A full-length portrait of Thomas Day, and in the background, the Edgeworths and other contemporary writers are given an important place.

Godfrey, Elizabeth. *English Children in the Olden Time*. London, 1907.
> Chapter XVII, "The Superior Parent." A pointed analysis of a marked characteristic of the didactic story.

Halsey, Rosalie V. *Forgotten Books of the American Nursery*.
Boston, Goodspeed, 1911.
> The author shows the further development of the English
> tradition in America as well as the more distinctly native
> product. Especially good in tracing the parallel between
> types of books for adults and those for children.

Hare, Augustus J. C., ed. *The Life and Letters of Maria Edgeworth*. 2 volumes. Houghton, 1895.
> A very interesting and complete picture of family and
> social life and literary activities.

Moses, Montrose. *Children's Books and Reading*. Kennerley,
1923.
> Treats of the historical development and offers excellent
> criticism of early writers.

Tuer, Andrew W. *Forgotten Children's Books*. London, 1898.
> Gives pages of text and pictures from old books, chiefly
> early nineteenth century. Note especially "Cautionary
> Stories in Verse," pp. 138–144.

Welsh, Charles. *A Bookseller of the Last Century*. London,
1885.
> Valuable not only for the interesting account of John New-
> bery and his successors, but for exact data on Newbery
> publications.

Welsh, Charles. *On Some of the Books for Children of the Last
Century*. Privately printed. London, 1886.
> Very interesting and useful regarding original sources.
> Note that "last century" means the eighteenth century.

DIDACTIC STORIES: OLD EDITIONS, REPRINTS, AND MODERN COLLECTIONS FOR CHILDREN

Early Editions

Often old editions and reprints of eighteenth- and early nineteenth-century children's books may be found in libraries. It is a
satisfaction to examine some of them in full. The order of publication is followed here. Strictly speaking *Goody Two-Shoes* is
not of the didactic type, but is a forerunner of that school.

Goody Two-Shoes. Attributed to Oliver Goldsmith. Published
by Newbery, 1765.
> A facsimile reproduction of the edition of 1766. Intro-

duction by Charles Welsh.   London, Griffith and Farren,
1882.

The History of Sandford and Merton.   Thomas Day. volume I,
1783; volume II, 1786.   Sometimes published in one volume.

Evenings at Home.   Dr. John Aikin and Anna Letitia Barbauld.
6 volumes, 1792–1796.
> Has been many times reprinted.

The Parent's Assistant, or Stories for Children.   Maria Edgeworth.   First published 1796–1800.
> Reprinted many times.   See below for more recent editions.

Early Lessons.   Maria Edgeworth.   In 4 volumes.   Volumes I
and II, 1801; volumes III and IV, 1815.

The History of the Fairchild Family.   Mrs. Martha M. Sherwood.
> First published, 1818.   It is in volume 2 of Mrs. Sher-
> wood's *Works* (10 volumes).   *The Governess* is in volume 6.
> A full set of Mrs. Sherwood's *Works* was published in America
> by Harper and Brothers in 1834.

Modern Editions Intended for Children

There is evidence that many children in upper grades enjoy
some of these stories and a few of them are satisfactory for reading aloud to children of eight to ten years.   Many of these old
tales have excellent plot, good characterization and interesting
incident.

The History of Little Goody Two-Shoes.   Illustrated by Alice
Woodward.   (The Little Library.)   Macmillan.

Simple Susan and Other Tales.   Maria Edgeworth.   Illustrated
by Clara M. Burd.   Macmillan.
> The stories in this book are selected from *The Parent's
> Assistant* and *Early Lessons*.   Miss Edgeworth wrote the
> latter book for young children.

Tales.   Maria Edgeworth.   Introduction by Austin Dobson.
Illustrated by Hugh Thomson.   Stokes.
> Stories are selected from *The Parent's Assistant*.

The Parent's Assistant, or Stories for Children.   Maria Edge-
worth.   With an introduction by Anne Thackeray Ritchie.
Macmillan.
> According to the editor all but one or two of the stories in
> this edition were in the first edition.   [Verified also by Miss
> Barry's list, p. 244. *A Century of Children's Books*.]
Same.   (The Children's Classics.)   Macmillan.

The Fairchild Family. Mrs. Martha M. Sherwood. Illustrated by Florence Rudland. Stokes.

A modern edition greatly abridged. Students should not judge Mrs. Sherwood by this "expurgated" edition only.

General Collections Intended for Children

Old-Fashioned Tales. Edited by E. V. Lucas. Illustrated by Francis D. Bedford. Stokes, 1905.

Contains nineteen stories. The Preface by Mr. Lucas will interest adults. Among the authors represented are Barbauld, Day, Edgeworth and Sherwood.

Forgotten Tales of Long Ago. Same.

Contains twenty stories, ten of them from anonymous authors.

The Children's Hour. Volume VI. Edited by Eva March Tappan. Houghton.

Contains many old-fashioned stories and poems from Edgeworth, Barbauld, Day, Watts, and the Taylor sisters.

CHAPTER VIII

HANS CHRISTIAN ANDERSEN

The fairies dance no more. Some say it was the hum of the schools —
some think it was the din of factories that frightened them; but nobody
has been known to have seen them for many a year, except, it is said, one
Hans Christian Andersen, in Denmark.

FRANCES BROWN, *Granny's Wonderful Chair* (1857)

HANS CHRISTIAN ANDERSEN'S stories mark
clearly the transition from pure folk tales to the
modern, imaginatively conceived fairy story or
fanciful tale; and a study of his stories throws light both
forward and backward on the development of literature
for children. Collections of his tales contain many which
are pure folk tales, easily recognized as such by any one
who knows the field at all. Others are original in plot,
character and form, but are shot through with the legendary lore of his country, and it is sometimes difficult to
distinguish the traditional elements from those of the
author's own creation. Many of his stories are wholly
original and these show great variety, including such
different types as the anecdotal account of minor episodes
of everyday life; fine-spun tales of inanimate objects and
humble creatures of the animal world given a real personality; short realistic stories; tales of pure fancy; and the
longer tale or novelette carrying the flavor of romance.

Thus Andersen's work embraces that of collector and
interpreter of folk tales, and writer of original stories both
realistic and fanciful. On one side he is kin to all those
known and nameless writers who have helped preserve in
true form, native literary treasures; and on the other side
he is one of the first of a long line of writers who have
devoted much of their time and talent to creating stories

for children. His work has survived, and as we near the close of the century which has elapsed since the publication of his first collection (1835), we find many of his tales still popular with children and still taking front rank in contemporary library lists and lists for the story-teller.

To the student of literature, the life of an author should be interesting chiefly as an aid to a clearer understanding of his work and a truer appreciation of his unique contribution. In these respects, Andersen's life is peculiarly revealing. Seldom can one see literature so clearly as a leaf out of the book of life. Starting with only a few known facts, a keen reader and student could construct a fairly accurate picture of the author's life (or at least, a sympathetic conception of his personality), by means of bits of evidence embedded in his stories. We are often warned by expert critics against the fallacy of seeing an author himself portrayed in the characters of his productions, and the events of his own life woven into a particular literary fabric. No doubt such seeming correspondence is often baseless or exaggerated. But in the case of Andersen such relations are so evident as to be inescapable, especially as he quite frequently points out the actual scenes or events which are incorporated in particular stories and sketches. Gosse [1] says, "In his writings we can trace every change of temperament every turn and whim of this guileless and transparent mind." He reminds us, however, that we would need to read the travel books to get the full revelation.

It is not our intention to repeat here the story of Andersen's life. Writers well fitted for the task have made easily available both brief and extensive accounts of his unusual career. It seems in place, however, to direct attention to some of the dominant facts and circumstances

[1] Gosse, Edmund W., *Studies in the Literature of Northern Europe.* London, 1879.

of his life and his characteristic responses thereto, especially such as are strikingly reflected in his stories. Further on in this chapter we shall seek in certain tales the precipitation of emotional and intellectual responses to experience in forms of beauty, terror, mystery, sage wisdom, humor, and whimsical conceit.

There are numerous sources of information regarding Andersen's life and we have a fuller account of his childhood and youth than of most writers of his day. The most interesting account is found in his Autobiography written and published after he had attained substantial success and wide recognition. This was published in 1846 under the title *Mit Livs Eventyr* and was soon translated into English with the title *The True Story of My Life.*[1] Perhaps a closer approximation in English to the original title is found in the form sometimes used, "The Fairy Story of My Life." Gosse offers as the English equivalent, "The Romance of My Life." Andersen was not very reticent and at various times and places he has enlarged upon events in his life and given his own interpretation of them. Allowing for a certain tendency to see his own career through rose-colored glasses and himself as a child of fortune especially favored and blessed by benign powers, the "ups and downs" of his life in sequence do constitute a sort of wonder tale — a tale told without disguise in "The Ugly Duckling."

Hans Christian Andersen was born at Odense, Denmark, April 2, 1805, of very poor and humble parents. His father was a shoemaker who, like many men of that contemplative trade, had some education, a spirit of independence, and the ability to see further than bench and last. He seems to have achieved for himself a better education than was common among craftsmen. The boy's

[1] Andersen, Hans Christian, *The True Story of My Life.* Translated by Mary Howitt. The American Scandinavian Society, New York, 1926.

mother was ignorant, deeply superstitious, with little understanding of her eccentric son, but affectionate and indulgent. She is said to have kept the poor little home neat and clean and she also hired out at all kinds of coarse work including washing.

There was a shelf of precious books over the father's work bench, and through his father, Hans was early introduced to much of the best in Danish literature. The eager child also drank in tales of the *Arabian Nights*, Bible stories, and some colorful history. They took long walks together through forest and field and on these holiday trips the father read aloud classic drama and legendary tales.

There were other means at hand by which the boy became acquainted with traditional tales as well as current superstition and countryside gossip. His paternal grandmother and grandfather lived in poverty not far away. The grandmother took care of the gardens of the lunatic asylum and Hans often accompanied her there. At times he visited the harmless patients and was both attracted and repelled by them. He listened to their stories, fascinated, but often terrified as well. Of these weird experiences Andersen says in his Autobiography,[1]

> The stories told by these old ladies, and the insane figures which I saw around me in the asylum, operated in the meantime so powerfully upon me, that when it grew dark I scarcely dared go out of the house.

A goodly number of tales from this source must have been more happily received, however, since he remarks, "and thus a world as rich as that of the thousand and one nights was revealed to me."

The grandmother was almost a daily visitor at her son's home. She brought flowers from the garden she tended, and these were a source of great pleasure to the beauty-

[1] Autobiography, p. 9.

loving, imaginative child. In later years Andersen spoke tenderly of her and said, "she loved me with her whole soul." In idealized form she appears in several of his stories. The old lady seems to have been a bit of a romancer herself, for some of the things she told the lad regarding his ancestors she either invented outright or painted in colors much too rosy.

The boy was afraid of his feeble-minded grandfather, avoided him so far as possible, and suffered deep humiliation when confronted with the relationship. The simple old man cut out strange wooden figures — half beast, half man — and carried them about the countryside giving them away to peasant children. But his grandson fled from the sight of him in fear and shame.

With his mother, the boy gleaned in the fields after the reapers. With her he went also among the hop-pickers. These contacts with peasants and itinerant seasonal workers yielded still more current gossip, legendary lore and rank superstition.

Thus, in spite of some schooling and regular religious training, the boy grew up, as he says himself, "pious and superstitious," and these two traits display themselves very strongly in his writing. He was a solitary, dreamy, introspective lad. We see him — tall, lank, awkward, with large hands and feet and homely countenance, a shock of yellow curly hair worn long, and eyes habitually half-closed. He says he was thought to have poor eyesight, whereas in fact he was an unusually keen observer. The half-closed eyes meant that he was carrying on some inward vision or drama and was at the time more or less oblivious to his immediate surroundings. That he carried through life indelible impressions, minute and circumstantial, of scenes and sensations experienced in childhood and youth, is abundantly evidenced in his writings.

His hard-working mother kept him clothed in neat but

made-over garments. Bareheaded, yellow locks flying, in the wooden shoes and bare feet of the peasant, he wandered about footloose and irresponsible, in school very irregularly, and wholly undisciplined. His timorous nature, his tendency to withdraw and indulge in day-dreams, his lack of virile masculine traits and his love of quiet, imaginative play, caused him to find his greatest satisfaction in a very limited kind of play-life. His father cut out for the boy puppet figures to represent certain plays they had read together or seen. The boy developed great skill in dressing these dolls in character, arranging a puppet theater, composing dialogue, and enacting plays. It was a type of activity exactly suited to him, for he had certain technical skills, a love of stories, a keen interest in dramatic action, a very lively imagination and a growing talent for verbal expression. He composed poems, stories and dramatic plays, at an early age. In his Autobiography, Andersen comments in an amused way on these early efforts, but it is clear that immature creative genius was finding crude expression at this time.

The boy had a beautiful soprano voice, clear and high, which often attracted the attention of passersby. At times it seemed as if this voice might prove an open sesame to some of the opportunities for which he longed, but during the boyhood years at Odense this was never realized. Instead his "girl's" voice brought upon him coarse, offensive teasing from rough associates in a cloth factory where Hans worked for a brief time. His fondness for books, his passion for reciting poetry, and his unusual voice at last attracted the attention of some of the gentry and occasional visits to the homes of cultivated people introduced him to a wider range of literature and did something to supplement his very meager education. He seized eagerly upon Shakespeare's plays. Their effect upon this boy of twelve or thirteen years he later describes as follows: [1]

> The bold descriptions, the heroic incidents, witches and ghosts were exactly to my taste. I immediately acted Shakespeare's plays on my little puppet theater. I saw Hamlet's ghost, and lived upon the heath with Lear. The more persons died in a play, the more interesting I thought it.

When Hans was eleven years old his father died and for the next few years with his mother alone, and then with an indifferent stepfather, the child's life was more at loose ends than ever. During the months of preparation preceding his confirmation, at about fourteen years of age, Hans longed to attend the class in which the boys and girls of the gentry were enrolled instead of the charity class, and by a step which seems a bit disingenuous he succeeded in enrolling in the "superior" group. We get here the full picture of an eager, ambitious, sensitive and vain child standing outside and looking in upon a favored group, received at last by an act of mere tolerance only to encounter coldness, indifference and a still more profound isolation. It is the epitome of his life through childhood and young manhood.

Soon after his confirmation, an astounding resolution forms in the mind of this remarkable boy. Entirely unaided he takes matters into his own hand and decides that he will go to Copenhagen to enter upon a career. Colossal ignorance of what was ahead of him, the urge of thwarted ambition, wounded pride, buoyant faith in himself, the determination to escape from a threatened apprenticeship in tailoring, surging emotions of dawning adolescence, the wanderlust which characterized his whole life — all of these factors must have entered into his decision. The doubts and tears of his poor mother, the pleadings of his feeble old grandmother, had no effect and in a short time

[1] Autobiography, p. 20.

he took his departure with the declared purpose of becoming a famous man. In mature years he writes of himself, "I do not belong to the courageous; I feel fear, especially in little dangers; but in great ones, and when an advantage is to be won, then I have a will, and it has grown firmer with years." [1]

He was a very ignorant boy. Not only had the years in school been few, but he was a lazy, flighty student and gave small heed to subjects which did not interest him. So when he started for Copenhagen with the all-embracing ambition to become an actor, playwright, singer, poet, or dancer, he lacked command of even the rudiments of an elementary education. The next ten years show a record of alternating hopes and fears. He met with grinding poverty, sordid surroundings, humiliating school experience, painful effort in hated tasks and occasional triumphs. The attention of generous and influential people was drawn to the vivacious, erratic yet engaging youth, and in various ways they aided and sustained him while he tried out one after another of his real or supposed talents. He has been called egotistical and vain, but even with the strong friends who stood behind him at various times, probably a spirit less confident of its own destiny and less persistent, would have surrendered to the buffetings of fortune.

This period of his life is worthy of a fuller study than can be presented here. One by one his tentative and rather daring attempts in different lines of artistic expression had to be abandoned. His voice proved inadequate, he was an awkward and probably a comical dancer, he was declared to be impossible as an actor, and he lacked the education necessary for a writer, though latent talent in the latter field was evident.

Convinced at last that he would have to go to school

[1] Autobiography, p. 162.

like anyone else, and under the patronage of influential friends, the temperamental youth of eighteen settled down to commonplace tasks and a severe regimen at the grammar school at Slagelse. He says, "My place in the school was in the lowest class, among little boys: I knew nothing at all." [1]

He calls the years of regular schooling at Slagelse, and later at the grammar school of Helsingör, the bitterest of his life. He describes himself at this stage as "sensitive and childlike." The severe and rigid discipline, the dry belated tasks, and, more than all else, the lack of understanding and sympathy on the part of several of his school masters, certainly made learning a very different experience from that pictured in his story, "The Garden of Paradise." There, a king's son when about to begin his school life is told by his grandmother,

> that every flower in the Garden of Paradise was a delicious cake, and that the pistils were full of wine. In one flower history was written, in another geography or tables, you had only to eat the cake and you knew the lesson. The more you ate, the more history, geography and tables you knew. [2]

But Andersen's school life offered no magic cake. Instead, he ate what was to him the bitter bread of uncongenial toil. Many years later when extensive reading, travel, and serious study had greatly enlarged his conception of education he could say with feeling, "Yet still the volume which afforded me the greatest pleasure was that of nature... [and I acquired] more true wisdom, assuredly, in my solitary rambles, than I ever could have gained from the schools." [3]

During the years when, as a mere boy, Andersen was attempting to make his way, cramped by grinding poverty

[1] Autobiography, p. 67.
[2] Andersen, Hans Christian, *Fairy Tales*, Everyman's edition, p. 155.
[3] Autobiography, pp. 136, 137.

and also under the regimen of boarding-school, he was like an imprisoned bird. In the spring of his third year at Copenhagen, he got out into the open country for the first time and you feel his quick emotional release:

> I stood still suddenly under the first large budding beech tree. The sun made the leaves transparent — there was a fragrance, a freshness — the birds sang. I was overcome by it — I shouted aloud for joy, threw my arms around the tree, kissed it.[1]

He calls Helsingör "one of the loveliest places in Denmark," but this beauty was tantalizing to him since long hours of study prevented him from doing more than "to cast stolen glances at it."

All through life he was subject to sudden alternations of mood. His mercurial spirits rose and fell with physical surroundings as well as with any real or imagined change of attitude toward him on the part of his associates. He longed for beauty, peace, and order in his surroundings and craved affection, appreciation, and admiration from his fellows.

At last the boy's friends decided that he would benefit very little by the continuation of formal school work and he was allowed to return to Copenhagen and to pursue his studies with a private tutor. A small stipend was granted to him and he established himself in a poor little garret room in an humble neighborhood. The room is described in the opening paragraph of "What the Moon Saw":

> I am only a poor lad, and live in one of the narrowest streets; but light is not wanting to me, for I live high up, and I have a fine view over the roof. For the first few days when I came to live in the town, it seemed very cramped and lonely. Instead of green woods and hills, I only had chimney pots on my

---

[1] Autobiography, p. 54.

horizon. I had not a single friend, and there was not even the face of an acquaintance to greet me.[1]

But here he obtained a certain degree of independence and freedom, without which his eager spirit could not expand. Of this period Andersen says:

> My teacher dwelt at a considerable distance from me. I went to him twice a day, and on the way there my thoughts were occupied with my lessons. On my return, however, I breathed more freely, and bright poetical ideas passed through my brain, but they were never committed to paper.[2]

The lessons which Andersen appropriated with zest and eagerness and which he quickly wove into his very being were those obtained through direct association with people of cultivation and refinement, and through the extensive travel which he enjoyed almost as soon as he was through with formal instruction. From boyhood on, one interested friend after another introduced him to people of high rank, social and professional, and gradually he found a welcome in houses which furnished the environment essential to the development of a nature innately refined. There were several homes in particular which became places of refuge where the impact of broad experience was softened and where he felt himself at one with the family and with the friends who gathered there.

He found a staunch and lifelong friend in Councillor Collin whom he had the good fortune to meet during his early struggle to get a footing in Copenhagen. The Collin home was opened to the crude, hypersensitive youth, and there he soon felt himself accepted as another son and brother.

> Even the bird of passage has one fixed spot to which it hastens: mine was and is the house of my friend Collin.

---

[1] *Fairy Tales from Hans Christian Andersen*, Everyman's edition, p. 228.

[2] Autobiography, p. 84.

He pays a beautiful tribute to Mrs. Collin and speaks with
deep appreciation of all that this home and family meant
to him. He found here not only affection and understanding but he benefited also by the cheerful and rational outlook on life which characterized the household.

Patrons of literature in Denmark regularly encouraged
young writers of promise to broaden their experience by
means of travel, and an annual stipend was granted to certain chosen ones for this purpose. Andersen had the good
fortune to win this distinction in 1833, and later events
showed that his country never made a better choice. Regarding his own state of mind just previous to this, he says:

> I felt, what since then has become an acknowledged fact,
> that travelling would be the best school for me.... I felt a com-
> pulsion of soul to be away, that I might, if possible, breathe
> freely.[1]

Before receiving the grant, the young author had seen
very little of the world. He had taken a memorable trip
in his own small beloved country, at which time his nature-
loving soul drank in the beauty and mystery of "immense
woods and hills"; beech woods which "hang like a garland over the white chalk cliffs"; "mountains and quick-
sands"; "infinite expanses of brown heath, with their
wandering gipsies, their wailing birds, and their deep
solitude." He had enjoyed also a brief excursion to North
Germany. But beginning with the special stipend in
1833 Andersen became a great traveller, and in the course
of his life he visited almost every country in Europe, some
of them several times. Germany he came to look upon
as "a second fatherland," and Italy always thrilled and
held him.

Attentions and honors were showered upon him. He
was entertained many times by royalty and was a guest
for long periods in palaces of princes and in princely homes

[1] Autobiography, pp. 105, 106.

of wealth. In manhood he was as susceptible as a child to all such attentions and got from them a pleasure which seems to have been a mixture of gratified pride, naïve self-satisfaction, a heartfelt appreciation of human kindness, and gratitude for a chance to work in surroundings of peace, beauty, and freedom.

Andersen never married and he never had an established home of his own. He lived mostly in lodgings which met the ordinary needs of life, but weeks and months at a time were spent in the homes of wealthy friends to whom he was sincerely attached and who welcomed him always. When in lodgings in Copenhagen, there were certain homes in which he dined regularly. There is abundant evidence that he gave pleasure to these generous friends and to their other guests. He delighted in telling stories to young and old and participated gaily in all kinds of home entertainment. He was a master hand at puppet shows and amateur theatricals and he was clever at free-hand cutting of pictures. He often improvised stories along with this rapid paper-cutting and one can imagine how fascinating this must have been to the children in any company.

It has been said that Andersen did not really like children. That bare statement, one can scarcely credit. As a nervously unstable creative artist, he probably was easily annoyed by restless, noisy and troublesome children. No doubt he wished to play with them in his own way and at his own time and he certainly wanted a quiet, rapt audience when he told stories. He refers quite specifically to certain child friends and to homes where the children were dear to him. We meet such comments as these: "A gentle friendly wife and beautiful children make his... house blessed and pleasant"; "I must away from children and old people who were near, as it were, to my heart"; (at another home) "and when we parted the children wept"; again, "whose charming little son immediately won my heart." One little girl called him her "fairy-tale prince," and on more than one occasion children divided precious toys with him in the same spirit they might have shown to another child who had won their sympathy and affection. Furthermore, Andersen's stories show a very remarkable understanding of children and an intimate knowledge of their play-life down to the most minute details. These portrayals reveal a penetrating eye, quickened and guided in its observations by a tender feeling for the young.

Bachelorhood is not very easy to explain in Andersen's case. Writers on the subject offer a few well-established facts together with a good deal of surmise. However vain and assertive the man may have been in some matters, he seems to have been under no delusions regarding his personal appearance and he seems to have had very little self-assurance where women were concerned. He was easily wounded and a feeling of inferiority often asserted itself when social situations brought him into close comparison with other young men. He was attracted to women of a high type and in several instances was able to win their lasting friendship, but he was unsuccessful when it came to the question of marriage. One love seems to have been deeper and more enduring than the others but doubtless each reacted strongly on his inner life. There is very frequent reference in his stories to youthful lovers, marriage, and domestic life. The disappointed lover outstripped by a rival of higher social position is a familiar figure, and there are fickle sweethearts as well as gentle, devoted girls and women, highly idealized according to a lovely pattern.

LITERARY EFFORTS

Andersen was slow to accept the fairy tale for children as his particular *métier* and reluctant to pursue that form

to the neglect of other cherished literary ambitions. For
years he clung tenaciously to the hope that he would win
recognition as a poet, dramatist and novelist, and he did
achieve a certain success in these lines. He appears to
have made the hardest fight to establish himself as a
dramatist, but most of his plays were accounted failures
or received only moderate praise. Like many another
artist, he achieved a reputation in foreign countries before
he did in his native land. Several novels were warmly
received, and formed in part the basis for his growing
popularity abroad. His avidity for travel and his genius
for seeing and picturing natural scenery, life, and manners,
resulted in two or three travel books of distinction. But
Andersen's unique place in world literature rests upon
his stories for children.

FIRST COLLECTION OF FAIRY STORIES

In 1835 there appeared the first little collection of the
tales which were to make their author famous and beloved.
The title of the book was *Eventyr fortalte for Born*. The
word *Eventyr* has no exact equivalent in English. Miss
Howitt, the first English translator, says the German
Märchen conveys the meaning well. The element of
wonder is implied in *Eventyr*, and lacking a more precise
English term this first collection was called *Fairy Stories
for Children*. A new collection was brought out every year
for several years at Christmas time, and Andersen soon
chose to drop out of the title the designation "told for
children" and each new collection was called *New Stories*.
He made this change because, as he says, "I had myself
related them by word of mouth to the little ones, and I had
arrived at the conviction that people of different ages
were equally amused with them." Unconsciously he had
set himself a very difficult task, but one for which he was
particularly fitted — the sustained production of stories
which young and old would read with equal delight.

The first stories published were largely folk tales which he says he had heard as a child. This collection (1835) contained "The Tinderbox," "Great Claus and Little Claus," "The Princess on the Pea," and "Little Ida's Flowers," the three first-named being true folk tales and the fourth a wholly original dreamlike fantasy of child-play, poetically conceived. The next two volumes each contained one or two stories of his own invention including "Thumbelisa," and "The Little Mermaid." From that time on, purely original work increased rapidly and familiar folk tales appeared infrequently. It must be remembered that even the pure folk tales when told by Andersen were rendered, as he says, "in my own manner," and a comparison of different versions of some of these easily recognized tales reveals how they are enhanced in style and tone by this gifted story-teller.

FEATURES OF STYLE

Every observant student of Andersen notices that his style is that of vivid, dramatic, oral speech. The zest, eagerness, vivacity, piercing keenness of observation and dramatic sense which characterized him as boy and man, all come out in his writing. Particularly do we note the verbal forms of direct oral speech which occur in lively conversation in everyday life, and which a natural and accomplished *raconteur* would be sure to use in telling stories to eager children. All critics refer to his unusually effective use of this feature. Here are a few examples. Others may be found on almost every page.

Over his head flew hundreds of crows screaming, "Caw! Caw! what for? What for?..."

"Ding-dong! ding-dong! now I go to bed!" rang the bell, as he flew into Odense River.

All at once the book under his head went "cribble, crabble! cribble, crabble, bang!" — something plumped down; it was a wooden bird from the Shooting Association in Praestö.

"Tara-ra-ra-ra!" blew the postillion on his horn.

They all [ships] fire a salute when they pass the old castle — "boom," and the castle answers, "boom." That is the way cannons say "how do you do" and "thank you."

"Whew! — whew! Fare away!" roared the wind.

"Attention, please, we're going to begin. When we've got to the end of the story we shall know more than we do now."

"Lady!" said the Collar; "little widow lady, I'm getting quite hot, a change is coming over me!"

An old chair speaks — "Oh, how it cracks inside me! I shall certainly have the gout like the old cupboard. Gout in my back, ugh!"

Georg Brandes writes with a deep understanding of Andersen's many-sided nature and of his peculiar gifts. The following brief passage from a delightful essay of his points out some features of style which Andersen seemed to use almost unconsciously but which in effect represents the highest art in narration.

To replace the accepted written language with the free, unrestrained language of familiar conversation, to exchange the more rigid form of expression of grown people for such as a child uses and understands, becomes the true goal of the author as soon as he embraces the resolution to tell nursery stories for children. He has the bold intention to employ oral speech in a printed work, he will not write, but speak, and he will gladly write as a schoolchild writes, if he can thus avoid speaking as a book speaks.... Whoever, therefore, addresses himself in writing to a child must have at his command the changeful cadence, the sudden pauses, the descriptive gesticulations, the awe-inspiring mien, the smile which betrays the happy turn of affairs, the jest, the caress, and the appeal to rouse the flagging attention — all these he must endeavor to weave into his diction, and as he cannot directly sing, paint, or dance the occurrences to the child, he must imprison within his prose the song, the picture, and the pantomimic movements, that they may lie there like forces in bonds, and rise up in their might as soon as the book is opened. In the first place, no circumlocution; everything must be spoken fresh from the lips of the narrator, aye, more than spoken, growled, buzzed, and blown as from a trumpet: "There came a soldier marching along the high-road — *one, two! one, two!*" "And the carved trumpeters blew, 'Trateratra! there is a little boy! Tra-teratra!'" — "Listen how it is drumming on the burdock-leaves, 'rum-dum-dum! rum-dum-dum!' said the Father Snail."

... In order to be understood by such youthful readers as those to whom he addressed himself, he was obliged to use the simplest possible words, to return to the simplest possible con-ceptions, to avoid everything abstract, to supply the place of indirect with direct language; but in thus seeking simplicity, he finds poetic beauty, and in attaining the childlike he proves that this childlike spirit is essential to true poetry;...[1]

Writing in 1879 Edmund Gosse said:

No modern poet's work has been so widely disseminated throughout the world as these stories of Andersen's... they are equally familiar to children all over the world. It is the simple earnestness, humour, and tenderness that pervades them, their perfect yet not over-subtle dramatic insight, their democratic sympathy with all things in adverse and humble circumstances, and their exquisite freshness of invention that characterize them most, and set them on so lofty a height above the best of other modern stories for children.[2]

STORY TYPES

Stories of infinite variety were produced. They are difficult to classify because the author's untrammeled imagination and his repudiation of classic forms resulted in a mixture of patterns and modes which will prove dis-concerting to the critic who likes to classify and tag. These tales present a mixture of the traditional, realistic, historical, highly imaginative, or delicately fanciful. Sometimes they take the form of allegory, parable, or fable; stories within stories are found, and sometimes the

[1] Brandes, Georg, *Creative Spirits of the Nineteenth Century*. Thomas Y. Crowell Company.

[2] Gosse, Edmund W., *Studies in the Literature of Northern Europe*, London, 1879, pp. 173-184.

inner story is the more beautiful or dominant; folklore and legend may play a large part in a story which appears in the beginning to be realistic. This shifting from reality to dream-life, and from the world of pure imagination to stark realism is one of Andersen's most characteristic traits.

For purposes of convenience in discussion, a rough classification into major groups may be made. Any classifications of stories and story material of such infinite variety must be very elastic, however.

Complete folk tales. Andersen was not a collector of native folk tales in the sense that the Grimm brothers were. The scientific aspects did not interest him at all. He relates in completeness only a few such tales and these are drawn from his childhood store. The clearest examples are: "The Tinder Box"; "Great Claus and Little Claus"; "The Princess on the Pea"; "The Traveling Companion"; "The Wild Swans"; "Hans Clodhopper" (Stupid Jack); and "What the Goodman Does is Always Right."

A careful examination of these stories shows that the narrator's "own manner" has left its imprint. Memory reproduces these old tales, and an imagination like that of a playful child and a poet, decorates them. "The Wild Swans" is a good example. In general outline the story is found in many countries. In Andersen's version the eleven young princes and their little sister Elisa are introduced as usual at the beginning, but the very first paragraph contains childlike details of princely glory not found in other versions. "The eleven brothers, Princes they were, went to school with stars on their breasts and swords at their sides. They wrote on gold slates with diamond pencils and could read backwards as easily as forwards; anybody could see straight off that they were Princes." The jealous queen disposes of all the children, but in a manner which does not alienate the brothers from their innocent sister. Relations of tenderness are at once revived when they meet again in exile. Descriptive passages of great beauty and fresh conception are frequent.

> The trees on either bank stretched out their rich leafy branches towards each other, and where, from their natural growth, they could not reach each other, they had torn their roots out of the ground, and leant over the water so as to interlace their branches....
> If the clouds were red and the wind dropped, the sea looked like a rose-leaf — now white, now green. But however still it was, there was always a little gentle motion just by the shore, the water rose and fell softly like the bosom of a sleeping child.

Piety (not characteristic of pure folk tales) is prominent; and a philosophy of life delicately expressed gives deeper significance to events. Certain brutal primitive features are omitted altogether. The old tale, while intact as to its main features, has been transmuted into a finer form by the poet's alchemy.

Tales of a more robust peasant type such as "Hans Clodhopper," Andersen touches up in a different way. This is the well-known story of the adventures of two brothers who seek to marry a king's daughter, and of the third brother who is supposed to be very stupid and who of course wins the princess. To the rough humor common in such tales, Andersen adds many light, audacious touches of his own. He delights in poking fun at inflated egos and pompous underlings, and in stories of this class he makes good use of his opportunity. He tosses bits of modern life into primitive molds and produces a calculated incongruity which is delightful to readers old enough to appreciate his jibes. Original embellishment of this kind is found in almost all of the familiar traditional tales mentioned above.

Stories with distinct folk tale elements. Andersen constantly weaves legendary lore and superstition into his

tales. He introduces not only a wealth of native Scandinavian tradition, but when appropriate, he draws upon the
lore of other countries. The following stories are rich in
such material: "The Wind's Tale"; "The Marsh King's
Daughter"; "The Mermaid"; "The Flying Trunk";
"The Elf-Hill"; "The Goblin and the Huckster"; "The
Garden of Paradise"; and "The Goloshes of Fortune."
Sometimes as important figures and again as quite minor
ones, we meet witches (good and bad), the Northern *nisse*
or church elf, mermen, mermaids, trolls, magicians,
dryads, will-o'-the-wisps, woodland elves and fairies,
friendly animals and birds with magic power, Fata Mor-
gana in her castle in the air, the mysterious Ice Maiden
(a phantom of ill omen in Andersen's childhood), and enchanted princes and princesses. Bound by no folk tale
patterns, Andersen's creative imagination evolved new
ones, and in so doing made lavish use of the rich store of
fairy tale material which he possessed.

Stories of inanimate objects. His most unique contribution is found in the stories of common objects of everyday
life, treated as if they were human in feeling and action.
We know of no stories of this kind prior to Andersen.
No object is too small or obscure, too humble or mean, to
be elevated to the position of hero by this wizard. One
wonders if he did not sometimes set himself the congenial
task of making something out of nothing. Whatever
his eye chances to light upon may inspire him to construct
in imagination a chain of events supposedly related thereto, the whole forming in miniature a coherent slice of life
for the characters concerned. The neck of a broken
bottle, a worn-out street lamp, a frayed shirt collar, a
discarded darning needle, a bunch of faded flowers, an assortment of kitchen utensils — around such outcasts or
objects of utility are woven tales of romance and adventure. Objects of greater apparent interest also are

invested with human traits and walk the play stage —
a child's toy (top, ball, tin soldier), a pair of china figures,
a fir tree, a child's money-box, a foreign coin — all such
objects come alive at the will of this writer and under his
magic touch.   Their actions are compatible with their
actual place in life, but we see them swayed by human
emotions, noble or petty or blind, according to the mood
of their interpreter.   These characters may take the blows
of life with jaunty self-assurance, stalwart courage,
stubborn egotism, or pensive submission, but most of
them have a very good opinion of themselves and are not
timid in asserting it.   Lively conversations occur among
these objects and through such discourse Andersen delights in exposing small human weaknesses as well as portraying the nobler traits of mankind.   He particularly
likes to exalt the humble, and a frequent theme is the
idea that no matter how lowly the office or station in life,
one may with courage, give a good account of one's self.

As already stated, Andersen seems to have invented
this type of story — certainly he has no rival in its production.   His genius is shown in the fact that after nearly
a hundred years, a certain little rusty tin soldier, two little
mantel ornaments (a china shepherdess and chimney
sweep) and a thawing snow-man are living creatures.
They inhabit the thought-world just as truly as do many
more elaborated characters of fiction.   Probably they are
as immortal as Robinson Crusoe and Alice in Wonderland.

Since Andersen's day we have had a huge crop of attempted imitations of this kind of story, mostly of the
utilitarian sort which purport to teach something, such
as the history of a drop of water or a lump of coal.   Acquaintance with the best of Andersen's stories of commonplace objects should aid one in distinguishing the authentic
and artistic from the spurious and dull wherever found.

There are several accomplished writers today who seem

to be endowed with something of Andersen's genius in the matter of making inanimate objects come alive. Stories of toy animals, dolls and puppets animated by the magic touch of a few contemporary writers, are mentioned in Chapter XII.

Stories of animals, birds, and insects. Creatures of the animal world are very prominent. Just as this author made inanimate objects living, so he humanizes the lower creatures. They may be the only characters or the chief characters in a story, or they may merely move across the stage in minor parts offering wise counsel, making clever comments, joking and philosophizing.

Naturally, storks have a prominent place. The superstitious and affectionate regard in which they are held in all countries which they frequent, their habits of building and nesting, the mystery of their migration, their apparent intelligence — all these characteristics rendered them especially fascinating to a Danish poet and romancer.

Next to storks, creatures of the poultry yard have the most prominent place in these miniature dramas. There are many amusing scenes in which hens, cocks, ducks and drakes deport themselves very much after the manner of human beings and yet they are never forced out of their own poultry-yard behavior. The Ugly Duckling who turns out to be a swan, is the prototype of every genius of noble soul who is misunderstood and flouted and who at last achieves happiness and success.

The Portuguese Duck poses as a tender-hearted benefactor, but shows herself to be blundering, inept, and wholly selfish. In her attempt to improve her protégé, the sparrow, she kills him and then turns chief mourner and declaims an eulogy.

The Nightingale is the true artist, generous, impelled by the spirit of joy in his art and happy only when free and untrammelled in its exercise.

The Beetle demands to be shod with golden shoes after the manner of the Emperor's favorite horse, and when refused, goes off on his travels in high dudgeon. He expects to be taken at his own evaluation and is contemptuous of every other living thing. "I will just see if I can find anyone with whom I can associate. I'm proud, certainly; but I'm also proud of being so." With much amusing detail a portrait is painted of the small and insignificant of this world who assume a pompous and grandiose manner ill-calculated to conceal their petty souls.

Mice, moles, frogs, hares, fish, butterflies, snails, and even earthworms, are frequently brought into the action, and birds in great variety play their part. One marvels at the distinct characterization of the native traits of all such creatures and at the sense of real personality which they convey.

Longer tales of marked originality and beauty. No very satisfactory term suggests itself as descriptive of some of the finest of Andersen's stories. "The Snow Queen" and "The Nightingale," for example, do not belong under any of the heads mentioned above, but they are "Andersen" at his very best. The first-mentioned contains a few small bits of folk belief, but it is really a story of idealized character — Gerda and Kay, and their relations to each other from happy childhood through the stress of early adolescence. Adult readers see the basic psychology involved, enjoy the artistic development, and the delightful display of delicate humor; most child readers probably see it simply as a story of high adventure and of loyal devotion on the part of Gerda. Swiftly changing and sharply contrasted scenes hold the attention, and there are many amusing and exciting situations which young readers enjoy.

The theme of "The Nightingale" is one which Andersen loves and which he often suggests — the measure of true worth and loyalty as contrasted with specious popularity. The theme is developed by showing the faithful devotion of the real nightingale, its banishment in favor of an elaborate mechanical bird, the failure of the latter in the Emperor's time of sorest need, and the return of the real nightingale to cheer and heal. It is a simple theme developed with originality, humor and charming detail.

These two stories are gems of artistic elaboration and they illustrate almost every unique trait of the writer.

Miscellanies. One group of miscellanies stands alone. Andersen called this collection *A Story Book Without Pictures, or What the Moon Saw.* It was published in 1840 and contributed greatly to his growing popularity. The thread of connection between these otherwise unrelated incidents is the nightly travel of the Moon and his report to the poor young student of the scenes upon which he has gazed in all corners of the earth. A soliloquy introduces this group, in which the student says, "What I have given here are only hasty sketches, with my own thoughts occasionally interspersed." The Moon looks upon scenes of real life and the sketches represent sharp contrasts in character, situation, and mood. Of the thirty-three narratives only a few are at all suited to children. There are, however, a number of children in these sketches who are drawn truthfully and with great charm.

There is one other group of stories which must be considered apart from the above classification. The "Olé Luköié," or "Sandman" stories, constitute a delightful little series. Seven stories in all are told by the Sandman to a little boy, Hjalmar — one for each night of the week "Sandman" seems to be the nearest English equivalent for the Danish "Olé Luköié," the literal translation being "Olaf the Eye-Shutter."

There is nobody in all the world who can tell as many stories as Olé Luköié! And such stories as he can tell! When night is drawing on and the children are sitting around the table as good as possible,... in walks Olé Shut-Eyes. He comes so quietly up the stairs without his shoes, and opens the door so softly that nobody hears him; and, puff! he sends a shower of milk into their eyes in such fine spray as to be invisible; but they can't keep their eyes open after it, and so they never see him. He steals behind them and breathes upon their necks, making their heads as heavy as lead; but he never hurts them. ... He only wants them to be quiet, and the best way to make them quiet is to have them in bed; when they are settled there, he can tell them his stories.

And, as Olé says — "such stories!"

Where else can one find such an entrancing medley of childish experience and dreamy wonder! Potted plants become great trees bearing magic fruit; the boy's slate and copy-book do fantastic and amusing things; wall pictures become animated, and Hjalmar is able to walk right into the scene and take part in the action; he attends a mouse wedding conducted with mouse-like propriety, and a doll wedding such as little girls are always contriving; in preparation for Sunday, the stars are all taken down and polished and properly returned. These stories are full of delightful fooling, but imagination does not run riot, for each in its short length, is a model of balance and beauty. Of course Andersen is himself a veritable Olé We see him at every turn of the old story-teller's magic umbrella.

CHARACTER PORTRAYAL

Several critics have pointed out that this writer does not portray children directly — that is, through their own actions and speech; that instead, we see them indirectly through the eyes of other characters, or as described by the story-teller. The children in "What the Moon Saw" are sometimes mentioned as almost the only ones portrayed directly. In general, one feels the truth of the comment, but even where there is not much action on the part of child characters they are made to stand out quite clearly as individuals. Through brief action, Little Tuk shows himself to be a kind-hearted and obliging little boy attempting under great difficulty to do his school tasks. The rest of the story is a dream — just the kind of dream that an anxious school boy might be glad to have as preparation for the next day. In "Little Ida's Flowers" also, immediate experience furnishes the content for a dream fantasy in which the child becomes merely a spectator, but the reader knows very well just what sort of little girl Ida is. This story furnishes an idyllic picture of imaginative play in which a poetic young student and a sensitive child engage together. The little boy in "The Metal Pig" is a dream child although he plays such an important part in the story. He is nameless, although even the pet dog is given a name — Bellissima.

The little boy in "The Old House" is remarkably well defined through a few incidents showing a tender relationship between him and his old neighbor. Again, this child is not given a name, he is "the little boy" all the way through.

A few child characters are portrayed more fully through their own action. Gerda in "The Snow Queen" is one of these and Kay in the first part of the same story gives a direct account of himself through behavior. In the childhood period, Ib and Christina reveal themselves through play and exploit. In this story, it is the boy who is more fully drawn.

At first glance, it may seem strange that the folk tale characters are often more sharply drawn than are the original ones. But second thought presents the fact that virile, and even crude characters are ready to hand in the former, whereas Andersen's introspective mind was certain to create characters of greater complexity and refinement.

No matter what the method of portrayal, his original characters are psychologically "real." Portrayal is flawless so far as imparting a distinct personality is concerned. He seems to like gentle, kind, and dainty little girls on the order of Emily, in "The Porter's Son":

> … how charming she was, how gentle, how light, and how fragile! If she was to be painted, it must be in a soap-bubble. There was a fragrance about her clothes, about her curly, golden hair, as if she was a fresh-blossomed rose-tree.

Several of his little girls prove themselves to be not only gentle and tender-hearted, but capable also of courage and fortitude.

His boys are seldom very daring but they usually take a protective attitude toward their little girl playmates — and there is almost always such a playmate. One is struck with the way he pairs his children, though quite often their paths diverge in later life: Kay and Gerda; Emily and George; Ib and Christina; Marie and Sören; Anthony and Molly (or Maddalina); Knud and Johanna.

CHILD-PLAY

Many of Andersen's stories are not at all suitable for children even though they contain interesting child characters, but almost all of them reveal an amazing acquaintance with the play-life of children, especially that of the lonely child and of little ones whose playthings are mostly improvised. One encounters every small familiar trick known to childhood — heating pennies to make peep holes on a frosted window-pane, gazing through a tiny hole pricked in a leaf, telling fortunes with feathery dandelions, hitching captive beetles to paper boats, making willow whistles, paper cutting, doll weddings and funerals with ceremonial, puppet plays, and innumerable similar bits of amusement. The boy in the following passage is only one of many such ingenious children.

> Childhood has for everyone, its bright points, that gleam and sparkle through the whole after life. And little Jörgen had his fill of play and pleasure; all those miles of coast were strewed with toys for him; it was a mosaic of pebbles, red like coral, yellow like amber, or white and round like birds' eggs; all so bright, so smooth, polished by the sea. Even the hard fish skeleton, the water plants, dried by the wind, the long narrow seaweed, fluttering among the stones; all these even were a delight to eye and to heart.... And so handy was he! he could make little boats with stones and shells, and pictures, such as were quite an ornament to the room; he could cut his thoughts out wonderfully declared his foster-mother, when he was only a little boy, and his voice was so sweet, and caught hold of a melody so quickly.[1]

THE STORY-TELLER

Andersen's own conception of the art of story-writing and story-telling is conveyed in many short passages as voiced by a great many picturesque characters. To assemble such pertinent passages is a profitable study as they afford a lively, graceful and whimsical commentary on the art, by one of its great masters. A few stories which should be read in this connection are "The Elf Hill," "Olé Luköié," "The Flying Trunk," "Will-o'-the-Wisps in Town," and "The Elder-Tree Mother."

LOCAL COLOR

As nature-lover, alert traveler, and sensitive poet, Andersen was at all times keenly aware of his surroundings. His attention was arrested by tiny and obscure objects at his feet as well as by more scenic features. In conse-

[1] "A Story from the Sand-Hills," *More Fairy Tales by Hans Christian Andersen*. Everyman's Library.

quence, his recorded observations are minute yet not wearisome, colorful, vivid, in tune with the scenes, and suffused with its atmosphere. Naturally, he is most completely in harmony with his own beloved Denmark. From his stories alone, one could construct a very good picture of this country and the life there a hundred years ago, for there are countless bits of description delicately etched.

We see the moors, fens, and heather-covered sand dunes; the rich cornfields, the flowery meadows, and (most characteristic of all) the lovely beech woods; lacey elder trees and fragrant limes appear almost as often as beeches, and willows grow along the canals and the slow-moving streams. Snowy swans choose this north country, storks return to their "family roof" in the spring, song-birds in great variety haunt the woods and meadows, and flocks of ravens add a jocular or sinister note according to the mood of the observer.

Poor little fishing villages dot the stormy shore, and comfortable, hospitable farm houses are sheltered behind protecting hills. Wandering gypsies are met on the heath, strolling players and puppet showmen find a ready welcome, troops of soldiers are no uncommon sight, and all the homely trades are carried on in town and village. It is easy to observe the fascinating work of miller, blacksmith, charcoal-burner, shipbuilder, woodcarver, weaver, and other craftsmen. There is life and color in the city streets for there is a remnant still of the Guilds with their picturesque processions and pageantry. Such scenes and figures as these are woven into the rich fabric of his stories, adding interesting detail, influencing action, or creating the desired atmosphere.

THE POET

Andersen's aspirations in the field of poetry had only a meager fulfillment and at last he turned his attention entirely to prose, but a poet at heart he remained. He was a lover of beauty who possessed keen, alert senses to detect it, and the inner illumination necessary to interpret it. We find in his prose, therefore, phrases and passages which are the essence of poetry in thought and diction. Even in the simplest little stories, original and beautiful imagery is constantly employed.

> The sun went out like the last sparks of a bit of burning paper.

> [Referring to swans] They flew in a swaying line, one behind the other, like a ribbon streamer.

> The careful willows had covered their blossoms with woolly gloves.

> [A snowfall] The white bees are swarming, stinging the traveler's face.

> The tree's crown bowed itself, as though it missed and sought something.

There is marked rhythm in Andersen's writing though no doubt this feature has suffered considerably in translation.

HUMOR

Laughter rings out with gusto occasionally, but more frequently the fun is of a delicate or subtle sort calculated to bring an appreciative smile or chuckle. The humor may depend chiefly on character and situation or it may be found in sly comment and mild satire. While some of the laughter-provoking characters are of the robust primitive type such as Silly Hans, Little Claus, the trolls in "The Elf Hill," and the simpleton in "What the Goodman Does is Always Right," many more are a fine compound of the amusing and pathetic. They posture and boast like the arrogant Beetle and the superfine Darning Needle, they make their compromises like the little Goblin, or, like the Snow Man, they "interrogate a puzzling universe." There is constant badinage between characters, clever raillery, amusing thrusts at personal traits, and often a solemn treatment of some lilliputian affair which amuses through its incongruity. The quaint behavior of these actors and their characteristic comment on life delight young and old, but they are made so human that one may feel also a little pity for them equipped as they are with such puny strength.

Some of these little figures are given such dignity and cheerful courage that they arouse admiration rather than pity. Among others, the Tin Soldier, the Ugly Duckling, the Fir Tree, and the Flax are likely to inspire this feeling.

Pitched in a different key, but calculated also to arouse sympathy, is the story of the little china Shepherdess and her Chimneysweep lover with their daring flight, their startled wonder at the bigness of the world and their subdued return to the familiar mantel shelf.

In stories possessing this kind of humor, delicate and sometimes wistful, Andersen has no rival.

PHILOSOPHY IN MINIATURE

At one period in his young manhood Andersen turned cynic and tried to meet life's blows with keen sarcasm. This attitude was short-lived, but out of its bitterness he retained the smiling aloofness of the critic who knows that things are not always just what they seem. His light rapier thrusts are most often aimed at pretense, arrogance, and self-glorification. Toplofty servants and the stupid "great," receive particular attention. On the other hand, he brings to the surface by many a penetrating judgment, the essential triumph in seeming loss or frustration. As a rule, such observations are brief and cleverly stated, but occasionally they seem a bit sentimental or moralizing.

Of course, children do not get the more subtle points   Andersen recognized this himself.   He says,

> The children made themselves merry for the most part over what might be called the actors; older people, on the contrary, were interested in the deeper meaning.[1]

BASES OF SELECTION OF STORIES

A certain validity attaches to the fact that Andersen's stories have long been rated as classic.   This means that they have had a widespread and continued popularity and that the most competent critics consider them to be of universal interest and value.   On this ground alone they should be well represented in the story-teller's repertoire, the curriculum, and the open library shelves. Specific reasons for their inclusion may be found in much of the discussion in this chapter.   To summarize: many of Andersen's stories are superior because:

1. They are full of humor and delightful incident.
2. They are often about interesting characters and these characters are graphically drawn.
3. The language and style of many of them are keyed to the level of simple oral speech.
4. They are full of dramatic action.
5. They have high artistic merit.   Beauty is revealed.   Values are much the same as in poetry.
6. Many of them are inherently ethical.   Loyalty, truth courage, are made attractive and opposite qualities are made to appear shameful.   Bits of wisdom are often clinched by a clever turn of speech.   They furnish a commentary on life out of which children may appropriate what is suited to them.
7. For intermediate grades there are many passages which present vivid pictures of natural scenery in Scandinavia and authentic records of early customs.

---

[1] Autobiography, p. 205.

The examination of any large collection of Andersen's stories quickly reveals the fact that many of them are unsuited to children of primary and intermediate grade level. Some of them will appeal only to mature minds and particular tastes. In the many collections which have been published, different editors have been guided by their own taste and by their judgment as to what will appeal to children. In some cases the number of stories included is quite small and it would appear that their selection has depended largely upon the opportunity they offer to se-cure fine effects in illustration. Whatever collection is used, the story-teller will be obliged to select those tales which seem to fit best the maturity and background of the particular group of children concerned. The following suggestions are offered in the hope that they may prove of general use. More specific choices must always rest with those in close contact with particular children.

1. Few, if any, of Andersen's stories seem well suited to average six-year-old children. Probably they should be placed from second to sixth grade.

2. The folk tales are likely to appeal to second and third grade pupils as it has been reasonably well established that fairy tales are popular at this period.

3. A happy ending, provided it is not out of harmony with preceding events, is preferred by children. However, the critic should be slow to classify as sad, endings like those of *The Snow-Man*, *The Fir Tree*, and *The Brave Tin Soldier*. Such events are in the nature of things and are well within the experience of children in upper primary grades.

4. Stories which contain much description, frequent change of scene, and complex relationship of characters (for ex-ample, "The Snow Queen") probably belong above Third Grade.

5. With due regard to other qualities, the story which contains a well-knit plot is to be preferred. Many of Andersen's stories are lacking in action.

6. Artistically *told*, some of Andersen's stories commonly be-

lieved to be too mature for children are greatly enjoyed by them.   Spell-bound child-audiences who listened to the English story-teller, Miss Shedlock, when she visited this country are proof of this.

The following short list proposes certain representative stories for grades II to V, roughly graded from easy to more difficult:

> The Brave Tin Soldier
> The Dancing Bear (Thirty-First Evening in
>   "*What the Moon Saw*")
> The Fir Tree
> The Candles
> Five Peas in a Pod
> The Snow Man
> Little Ida's Flowers
> The Princess on the Pea
> The Ugly Duckling
> The Money Box
> The Shepherdess and the Chimney-Sweep
> Olé Luköié
> The Adventures of a Beetle
> Thumbelina
> The Flax
> The Wild Swans (omit some unessential parts
>   which seriously retard story)
> The Emperor's New Clothes
> The Tinder Box
> The Flying Trunk
> The Nightingale
> The Snow Queen
> Little Tuk
> The Swineherd
> The Goblin and the Huckster

Different titles for the same story are given by different translators.   Usually the story can be readily identified but a few are likely to prove confusing.   Among these are:

> The Metal Pig
> The Bronze Boar

The Money Pig
The Money Box

Hans Clodhopper
Jack the Dullard
Silly Hans

The Pig Boy
The Swineherd

Daddy Dustman
Olé Luköié

Top and Ball
Sweethearts

There's a Difference
The Conceited Apple Branch

Twelve Travelers by Post
The Mail Coach Passengers

SUGGESTED TOPICS FOR PAPERS, AND PROBLEMS FOR FURTHER STUDY

The following subjects for papers call for an extensive study of Andersen's stories. The student will have to seek internal evidence since there is very little in the way of published opinion or comment on these topics. In a few cases, the paper might be composed almost entirely of passages taken from the stories. When so treated, the text should be given in full, accompanied by page reference. In any case, the particular editions used should be indicated since translations differ greatly in text and even in titles of stories.

1. Features of Andersen's life and character as reflected in his stories.

2. Folk lore and superstitions in Andersen's stories.

3. Andersen's fairy folk and magic.

4. Andersen as humorist.

5. The story-teller and his art.
   There are many story-tellers in Andersen's tales. Who are they? What do they say about themselves and their art? In what ways does Andersen himself seem to be the pattern?

6. Andersen's characterization of children.

7. His characterization of old people.

8. Children and child-play.

9. The relation of children to adults.

10. Andersen as philosopher and gentle cynic.

11. Andersen as poet.

   The main part of this study should deal with his poetic prose. Different translations should be examined. Knowledge of the Danish language would, of course, be a great asset though it is not essential.

12. Local color in Andersen's stories.

13. Andersen's Denmark.

   In a short introduction give main facts of geography, immediately antecedent history, and conditions of contemporary social life. Then develop the subject through content of the author's stories.

14. Frequently recurrent themes and their elaboration.

   For example, his exaltation of the genuine and sincere and his arraignment of the artificial as in "The Nightingale," "The Swineherd," "The Emperor's New Clothes." Another favorite theme is found in the courageous struggle of the poor and humble, especially poor boys. There are many other oft-repeated themes.

15. Plan a series of tableaus or silent "movies" with interludes, such as might be evolved by children from stories deemed suitable. Suggested examples, "Little Ida's Flowers," "The Snow Queen," "Twelve Travelers by Post."

16. A comparative study of several different translations. Knowledge of both English and Danish, especially in the vernacular, is essential here. Notice the claims and the style of M. R. James, W. A. Craigie, and Lucy Crane, among others.

17. Make a comparison of Andersen's version of certain traditional tales with those of other writers. For example: "The Tinder-Box" and Grimm's "The Blue Light"; "Great Claus and Little Claus," and Dasent's "Big Peter and Little Peter," also Grimm's "The Clever Countryman"; "The Wild Swans," and Grimm's "Twelve Brothers," also Asbjörnsen's "Twelve Wild Ducks."

For longer papers, several of the above topics might be combined with entire consistency under a more comprehensive title. For example, the materials appropriate to 8 and 9 might be embraced under such a topic as Child-Life in Andersen's Stories. Similarly, 2 and 3, or 1 and 10, might be combined under a fitting title.

BIBLIOGRAPHY

Biography and Criticism

American-Scandinavian Foundation. "Hans Christian Andersen." A reprint from *American-Scandinavian Review*, April, 1930, published in honor of Hans Christian Andersen's one hundred and twenty-fifth birthday. American-Scandinavian Foundation, New York.
>   Deals in a fresh way with many different aspects of his life.

Andersen, Hans Christian. *The True Story of My Life*. American-Scandinavian Foundation, 1926.
>   The original edition of Andersen's autobiography, in the contemporary translation of Mary Howitt, 1846.

Bain, R. Nisbet. *Hans Christian Andersen: a Biography*. Dodd, 1895.
>   A very full and interesting account of Andersen's life and work.

Boyesen, Hjalmar H. *Essays on Scandinavian Literature*. Scribner, 1895.

Brandes, Georg. *Creative Spirits of the Nineteenth Century*. Translated by R. B. Anderson. Crowell, 1923.
>   Essay on Hans Christian Andersen, a delightful analysis and appreciation of Andersen's stories.

Brandes, Georg. "Hans Christian Andersen and His Tales," *The Bookman*, 36: 404–409, December, 1912.
>   Treatment similar to that in *Creative Spirits*, but briefer.

Gosse, Edmund W. *Studies in the Literature of Northern Europe*. London, 1879.

Scudder, Horace E. *Childhood in Literature and Art*. Houghton, 1894.
>   Chapter VIII, "Hans Christian Andersen."

Wells, Benjamin W. "Hans Christian Andersen." Warner's *Library of the World's Best Literature*, volume I, pp. 500–539. New York, Knickerbocker Press, 1917.

COLLECTIONS AND EDITIONS

Editions Especially Useful to Adult Students

Stories and Tales.   Houghton.

Wonder Stories Told for Children.   Houghton.

These two books are carefully edited and furnish a full and authentic collection.   The introduction to the first volume contains interesting information from Andersen regarding sources and background of certain stories.

Fairy Tales and Other Stories.   Revised and in part newly translated by W. A. and J. K. Craigie.   Oxford.

"The arrangement follows that of the standard Danish edition, in which the tales are printed for the most part in the order in which they were originally written or published." (Preface.)

A very full collection.   Small pictures in black and white add little to the interest of the text.

Danish Fairy Legends and Tales.   Translated from the Danish by Caroline Peachey and H. W. Dulcken.   Macmillan.

Contains a good Memoir of Andersen and a helpful discussion of his use of Scandinavian folklore.

Fairy Tales.   Translated from the Danish original by H. L. Braekstad.   Introduction by Edmund Gosse.   (The Queen's edition.)   London, Heinemann.

Illustrations are after the drawings of the Danish artist Tegner and are true to the life of Andersen's time.   The Introduction offers a penetrating but sympathetic criticism and gives dates and contents of the first published collections.

Fairy Tales.   Translated by Mrs. E. Lucas (Everyman's Library.) Dutton.

More Fairy Tales.   Translated by Mrs. E. Lucas.   (Everyman's Library.)   Dutton.

These two inexpensive books may well form a part of a student's working equipment.   The first contains forty-one stories most of which are well-known and popular. The second contains thirty stories many of which are less well known.   Some of these furnish excellent examples of Andersen's particular traits of style and mood.

Hans Andersen.   Forty Stories Newly Translated from the Danish by M. R. James.   London, Faber, 1930.

The special claim of the editor is that most translations

into English have been made not from the Danish original but from the German, with a considerable loss in the poetic simplicity of the idiom. The majority of the stories included are from Andersen's earlier work which, for the most part, James deems superior. The Preface gives valuable information regarding Andersen's source material. Considering the editor's claims, this edition might profitably be compared with other translations.

A Few Editions Especially Attractive to Children

Fairy Tales. Translated by Mrs. E. Lucas. Illustrated by Maxwell Armfield. Dutton.

Fairy Tales and Stories. Edited by Signe Toksvig. Illustrated by Eric Pape. Macmillan.

Fairy Tales and Wonder Stories. Introduction by W. D. Howells. Illustrations by Louis Rhead. Harper.

Fairy Tales. Illustrated by Kay Neilsen. Doran.

A beautiful gift-book, containing sixteen stories, twelve full-page illustrations, and many others in black and white. The latter are drawn with much interesting detail and are in key with life as depicted by Andersen — especially as regards the peasant type.

Stories from Hans Andersen. Illustrated by Edmund Dulac. Doubleday.

One of the most beautiful editions ever published. There are only seven stories, five of which are long and best suited to older children. There are twenty-eight lovely full-page pictures in color showing fine characterization and in full harmony with the content and spirit of the stories.

Andersen's Fairy Tales. Illustrated by Elizabeth MacKinstry. Coward.

Fifteen well-chosen tales with characteristic MacKinstry drawings and an interesting introduction by Anne Carroll Moore.

School Editions for Younger Children

Fairy Tales. In two volumes. Edited by J. H. Stickney. Ginn. Plain little books containing very good selections on the whole. The adaptation is as restrained as possible to bring the text to about third grade reading ability.

Fairy Tales.   Edited by Edna Lee Turpin.   Merrill.

Selections are especially good for about third grade reading ability, and style is not seriously sacrificed.   There is a good sketch of Andersen's life which will interest children.

The Single Story

Thumbelina.   (The Little Library.)   Macmillan.

A charming little book with pictures by Einar Nerman. This story is especially loved by little children.

Biography

A Child's Story of Hans Christian Andersen.   Paul Harboe. Duffield, 1907.

The Ugly Duckling: Hans Christian Andersen.   Isabel Proudfit. Illustrated by Malthe Hasselriis.   McBride, 1932.

Both these books contain much that will interest children who are fond of Andersen's stories.   The second is particularly pleasing in style and form.

CHAPTER IX
THE NATURAL RESPONSE OF CHILDREN TO POETRY

> The gallant child where'er he came
> Threw to each fact a tuneful name. . .
> Methought like water-haunting birds
> Divers or dippers were his words.
>
> EMERSON, *The Poet*.

THERE is a prevalent notion, sometimes stated as a fact, that children do not like poetry. Such an opinion is not justified by any investigations which have so far been made — and it goes counter to the common experience of a multitude of competent witnesses. The strongest statement which can be backed up by research is that under particular school procedures groups of children at specific age levels did not like certain poems which were read to them as well as they liked certain stories in prose. Genuine æsthetic pleasure is such a subtle thing that it cannot be measured quantitatively and *en masse* by any means as yet devised, for there are potent factors in a child's background and in the immediate situation which seem to defy capture and analysis.

There is a marked correspondence between certain native traits and early inclinations of children, and many of the essential qualities of poetry, which confer upon the latter a potent charm. Whether this attraction is developed beyond a very rudimentary stage, depends upon many factors some of which are easy to define and, in a measure, to control. It is the purpose of this chapter to identify these prepotent traits of childhood which seem to point toward the enjoyment of poetry, and to seek the elements in simple poetry which promise to meet and satisfy these inclinations. The subject will be treated in a general way here with only brief illustrations, the intention being to offer a basis for a fuller appreciation of the rich and varied contributions in poetry for children which will be presented in the next chapter.

The adult who aspires to foster and develop in children a love and appreciation of the finer types of verse must of course be a lover of poetry herself. With this qualification as a basis, the most fundamental steps which such a leader can take toward her own improvement are, first, the continued reading of poetry for pure enjoyment; and second, the careful examination of representative poetry recommended for children for the purpose of discovering the nature of its promised appeal. Happily there is no sharp line between poetry for children and for adults. Poetry speaks a more universal language than prose literature and therefore the area of common enjoyment is greater.

SPECIFIC TRAITS BASIC TO AN EARLY LIKING FOR POETRY

Children possess at least five strong bents which if recognized and encouraged will incline them toward poetry, for each of these finds a very genuine correspondence in the inherent nature of poetry itself.

1. They are responsive to rhythm as shown by the way they are swayed by every measured movement. Metrical verse stimulates this pleasurable response almost as much as music does.

2. They delight in the sounds of words and in all kinds of striking language effects. Such effects are the very essence of all kinds of poetry.

3. Their keen and alert senses are ever busy building up conceptions of a tangible world. Poetry recognizes and ap-

peals to the senses beyond any other kind of literature. It is full of childlike sensory images.

4. The fresh and active imagination of children enables them to see beauty, and to feel wonder and delight, in experiences which are regarded as commonplace by most of their elders. Poetry offers idealized, imaginatively reconstructed experience much of which is harmonious with the naïve responses of the immature.

5. Children are eager participants in nature experience and they exhibit very early a keen interest in living things. Nature in its various forms is the subject of much simple, beautiful poetry.

With such an equipment, if children in considerable numbers appear indifferent to poetry it is highly probable that the selections to which they have been introduced, the manner of presentation, or other features of the total experience, have been mistaken and out of harmony with the kind of enjoyment which should be associated with it. Some small beginnings have been made in learning how to help children in larger numbers to make a happy acquaintance with lovely things in verse which they should, in the deepest sense, possess.

As a step in this direction it may be profitable to consider in some detail the five correspondences mentioned above, between child nature and poetry. In this we shall be merely building up a simple A B C of verse without which we might lack a common language of understanding when we attempt in the next chapter a survey of periods and types of poetry. In connection with the work of particular writers also, we shall have frequent need to refer to these factors.

1. *Rhythm and Meter*. Rhythm pervades the whole of nature as well as most of the acquired arts of man. It is seen, felt and often heard in the movement of water and

air, and is observable in swaying branches, nodding flowers, undulating wheat fields, and the unfettered actions of almost all living creatures. The human organism is predisposed toward rhythm by the beat of the heart and by the very breath of life with its measured motion. The baby gradually gets his random and unco-ordinated movements under control and at last they are built into walking, running, dancing and perhaps swimming. Clapping the hands to a little rhyme or tune is one of the first learned motor reactions, and with this the child has taken his first clear step in a direction toward which his whole organism is strongly inclined — the satisfactions to be found in music and poetry.

Human speech has its rhythms as have the calls of animals and the chirrup and twitter of birds, but ordinarily such waves in spoken language are not sufficiently regular to be noticed. But we have developed certain artificial forms of speech which we call song or verse in which there is a regularity of pulse satisfying to something in human nature which is always seeking harmonious patterns.

There is a magic in certain types of poetry which arrests and holds attention even when the sense is but little understood, and many young children will listen entranced to Poe's "Raven" or Macaulay's "Lays of Ancient Rome," although they are able to get only occasional flashes of intellectual content. They are emotionally responsive to the rhythm and melody of poetry as it rolls and ripples and bounds along. Indeed, there is evidence that young children listen with rapt attention to the fluent and musical reading of poetry in a foreign language, Latin or French, for example.

It is believed that the measured beat in speech which is so prominent in poetry came about from two influences — first, the tendency of every sustained movement such as paddling, pounding, treading, chopping, etc., to become rhythmic, especially if two or more persons are working together; and second, the audible expression of emotion whether of joy or sorrow which in primitive people takes the form of shouts and cries of exultation and the wail of lamentation. Many kinds of manual labor have developed songs in which the meter is consonant with the particular movement which workers naturally employ to secure ease and economy of effort, and we have the tread of the wine press, the stroke of oar or paddle, the hammer blow on the anvil, and the sweep of the scythe, all plainly recorded in certain chants and musical refrains. Likewise, communal joy left its record in tripping dance steps and such gay refrains as "Ha! ha! ha!" and "hey, nonny, nonny"; while communal sorrow found vent in the slow drum beat of the dirge.

The significant thing is that these measured rhythms which grew out of human labor and emotion carry their own reverberations today and arouse in sensitive listeners at least a faint response in kind. There have been an infinite number of refinements of these primitive measures and many elaborations, but there are just a few which are basic and which are easy to detect in all simple poetry having a regular meter. Of all the elements which constitute poetic form, meter and rhyme make the strongest appeal to children for they operate together in a direct appeal to nerve centers, muscles, and emotions. These two features are very prominent in all folk songs, nonsense rhymes, and ballads. Mother Goose alone illustrates every basic meter as well as a great variety of rhyme arrangements. Almost all of Mother Goose incites to clapping, tramping, tripping or swaying, and the inevitable accent in the right tempo may convey a certain mood even when the words carry very slight meaning.

The regular recurrence of accented syllables in a particular relation to the unaccented, divides the larger flowing rhythm of verse into smaller and more regular measures or feet. The three most common types of meter in English verse are the iambic, the trochaic and the dactylic. Examples of these will be given from poetry for adults as well as for children.

The Iambus. In this foot or beat, an unaccented syllable is followed by an accented one. Examples of single words — *mature, impart.* Examples of phrases with this stress — I *much* re*gret*; He *said* he *would.* The iambic is the most common meter in English verse. In mature poetry it tends to impart a serious or even stately effect. In simple child-like verse this measure may merely be slower or less gay than some others:

> My heart leaps up when I behold
> A rainbow in the sky.
>
> WORDSWORTH

> He prayeth best who loveth best,
> All things both great and small.   COLERIDGE

> I saw you toss the kites on high,
> And blow the birds about the sky.
>
> STEVENSON

> They went to sea in a sieve, they did;
> In a sieve they went to sea.
>
> EDWARD LEAR

The Trochee. This foot or beat starts off with an accented syllable followed by an unaccented one. Examples of single words — *poet, enter.* Examples of phrases with this stress — *I* will *find* it; *cheer*ful *sing*ing. The trochaic meter is quite common in English verse. When it predominates in a poem the mood tends to be happy and the movement light.

Now the lusty spring is seen;
  Golden yellow, gaudy blue
Daintily invite the view.   JOHN FLETCHER

By the shores of Gitchee Gumee,
By the shining Big-Sea-Water.

               LONGFELLOW

Twinkle, twinkle, little star,
How I wonder what you are.

             JANE TAYLOR

Bless you, bless you, burney bee
Say, when will your wedding be.

          Nursery rhyme

The Dactyl. This foot or beat contains three syllables
beginning with an accented one. Examples of single
words — *flexible, poetry, intricate.* Examples of phrases
with this stress — *Who* will go; *Beau*tiful *vi*olets. Authorities tell us that this meter is much less common in
English verse than the two first mentioned, but it is a noticeable fact that it occurs with great frequency in poetry
for children. This is quite natural since the predominance
of the dactylic foot suggests a lilting or swaying or gallop-
ing movement. Lullabies and cradle songs are almost all
in this meter, and poems about swings, boats, and the sea,
are apt to use it.

Away in a manger, no crib for a bed,
The little Lord Jesus laid down His sweet head.

      MARTIN LUTHER, "Cradle Hymn"

Twas the/night before Christmas, when all through the house
Not a creature was stirring, not even a mouse.

         CLEMENT C. MOORE

I know the song that the bluebird is singing,
Out in the apple tree where he is swinging.

         EMILY H. MILLER

> How do you like to go up in a swing,
> Up in the air so blue?
>
> STEVENSON

Even Isaac Watts comes out with a cheerful note in dac-tylic measure:

> How/fine has the day been!   How bright was the sun!
> How lovely and joyful the course that he run!

Kipling's "The White Seal's Lullaby" is one of the most perfect examples of the effect produced by this measure carried with absolute regularity through eight lines and aided by other beautiful and harmonious elements.

For the purpose of identifying metrical schemes, it is sometimes necessary to read a poem aloud, exaggerating the stresses but making due allowance for pauses which often take the place of a syllable, just as a rest fills out a measure in music.   Again, by a process of acceleration, ex-tra syllables may have to be crowded into a beat just as in setting words to music.

Rarely does one find in modern verse a really fine poem of any length written throughout in one meter.   Such reg-ularity is apt to become tiresome and it does not provide for variations of mood and shades of meaning.   Clement Moore's "A Visit from St. Nicholas" is an exception. "More rapid than eagles his coursers" go "prancing and pawing" without missing a single small hoof-beat, through twenty-seven rhymed couplets — and to the infinite de-light of all listeners.

2. *Pleasing Language Effects*.   Melodious language, fitting words, and pleasing sound, rank next to meter as primary factors in verse, and children display very early a delight in all such effects.   As mere infants they begin to play with sound and as they grow older they experiment spontaneously with the curious and pleasing syllables and words which they hear or invent.

Rhyme comes first in its universal appeal, for, whatever opinion one may hold regarding the relative merits of rhymed and unrhymed verse for adults, probably no one would claim that cadenced, unrhymed verse is any real rival to rhyme with an audience of children. Rhyme accentuates the metrical effect by marking another regular division larger than that which the meter itself supplies, with the result that expectation is aroused and the regular recurrence of a sound satisfies the waiting ear. Children are very susceptible to such effects and we are all familiar with the way they invent strings of rhyming syllables and nonsense jingles. Rhyme is always found in traditional verse, and modern poets seldom dispense with it when writing for children.

Poetry for children contains many kinds of stanza patterns but in all of them the tendency is to bring the terminal rhymes close together. Continuous rhymed couplets as in "A Visit from St. Nicholas" are often used, especially in narrative poetry, but the three following stanza arrangements are the most common.

At evening when I go to bed   a
I see the stars shine overhead;   a
They are the little daisies white   b
That dot the meadow of the night.   b
           FRANK DEMPSTER SHERMAN

There's no dew left on the daisies and clover   a
   There's no rain left in heaven;   b
I've said my "seven times" over and over,   a
   Seven times one are seven.   b
           JEAN INGELOW

Robins in the tree-top,   a
   Blossoms in the grass,   b
Green things a-growing   c
   Everywhere you pass;   b
           THOMAS BAILEY ALDRICH

Notice that while there are only two rhymed words in the above stanza, they come close together because the lines are short.

The disappointing effect of delayed and very imperfect rhyme is seen in the following eight-line poem by Christina Rossetti:

A motherless soft lambkin	a
Alone upon a hill;	b
No mother's fleece to shelter him	c
And wrap him from the cold:	d
I'll run to him and comfort him,	
I'll fetch him, that I will;	b
I'll care for him and feed him	
Until he's strong and bold.[1]	d

By the end of the fourth line, one expects a rhyme, but the first true rhyme occurs at the end of the sixth line, and there are only two true rhymes in all. Miss Rossetti usually achieves a more tuneful effect.

The internal rhyme helps to produce a happy, light movement.

> Spring, the sweet Spring, is the year's pleasant king;
> Then blooms each thing, then maids dance in a ring,
> Cold doth not sting, the pretty birds do sing;
> *Cuckoo, jug, jug, pu we, to witta woo!*
>
> THOMAS NASH

Great variety in meter and rhyme patterns is found in twentieth century poetry for children as an examination of any standard anthology will show. The tendency seems to be to break up the regularity somewhat but to preserve and perhaps intensify the musical quality.

Alliteration, or a succession of identical initial sounds, gives delight too. The repeated utterance of an explosive consonant as in "Peter, Peter, pumpkin-eater," carries a pleasurable sensation and the less extreme ex-

[1] Rossetti, Christina G., *Sing-Song: A Nursery Rhyme Book*. The Macmillan Co., publishers.

amples which are frequent in true poetry form one of its great charms. This device is very ancient. We noted it in the Norse Edda, Anglo Saxon poetry employed it in much the same way, and it was a favorite poetic form with early English poets. Spenser is noted for his skillful use of the "head rhyme":

> Piers, I have pyped erst so long with payne,
>
> That all mine Oten [oaten] reeds bene rent and wore,
> And my poore Muse hath spent her spared store
> Yet little good hath got, and much less gayne.
> > EDMUND SPENSER, *The Shepherd's Calendar*, 1579

In William Blake's "A Dream" we find the lines:

> Pitying I dropped a tear;
> But I saw a glow-worm near,
> Who replied: "What wailing wight
> Calls the watchman of the night?"

Few poets use alliteration quite so conspicuously but it is constantly employed and helps to define and accentuate mood and tone. Notice the sparing and exquisite use which Shakespeare makes of this feature in the whole of "Puck's Song." Here are the first six lines:

> Over hill, over dale,
> > Thorough bush, thorough brier,
> Over park, over pale,
> > Thorough flood, thorough fire,
> I do wander everywhere
> Swifter than the moon's sphere;

Where white flows the river and bright blows the broom.
> > R. L. STEVENSON

Single words of peculiar or striking sound interest children. They ask to have them repeated, struggle to master them and often say them over and over for no purpose but to enjoy the sound and to *feel* the syllables rippling or flowing and coming together to form the new and delightful word whole.

In many instances the inherent quality of words is due to the fact that echoes from their distant origin in action still resound in them.   There are countless examples of words which originally sprang from attemps to imitate natural sounds.   A long list of such words could be quickly assembled but a few examples will suffice: the *soughing* of the wind; the *cackle* of hens; the *swish* of skirts; the *hum* and *buzz* of bees; the *rumble* of thunder; *crackling* and *hissing* fire; *murmuring* and *gurgling* water; the *tintinnabulation* of the bells; the *shriek* of whistles.   This articulate imitation of inarticulate sounds is called *onomatopœia*, and it is one of the most potent factors in creating a desired literary effect.   All writers are fully aware of this and poets in particular make use of the principle in skillful and delicate choice of words.

Probably children had a share in inventing some of these imitative words, for we see the process still going on today; *choo-choo*, *bow-wow*, and *ding-dong* have already an established place, but babies of this year will recreate the same ancient nursery vocabulary, and they may make additions to it.

Beginning with Mother Goose, every good collection of verse for children furnishes striking examples of sound imitation such as the following:

> Ding, dong, bell,
> Pussy's in the well.

> Hark! the little lambs are bleating,
> And the cawing rooks are meeting.
> > MARY HOWITT

> "Minne-wawa!" said the pine trees,
> "Mudway-aushka," said the water.
> > LONGFELLOW

> Tinkle! tinkle —
> Like a fairy silver bell;
> Like a pebble in a shell;
> Tinkle, tinkle!
> Listen well!
>
> FRANK DEMPSTER SHERMAN, *The Waterfall*

Children and poets find pleasure in beautiful, high-sounding, peculiar, and amusing names of objects, people and places. The simple enumeration of harmonious names constitutes an effective bit of poetic art which is as old as song and story. Even the "begat" chapters of the Bible used to hold a certain fascination when read aloud in solemn and sonorous tone: "And Canaan begat Sidon, his firstborn, and Heth, and the Jebusite, and the Amorite, and the Girgasite, and the Hivite," etc.

Several poets have grouped in rhythmic fashion the lovely and arresting names of stars so that they cling together like new and glorious constellations. Sara Teasdale's "Rhyme of November Stars"[1] is a soul-stirring pageant of "the noiseless marching of the stars" in which she recites their melodious names and attributes; and Walter de la Mare in "Wanderers"[2] achieves a serene marshalling of the planets, those "wanderers amid the stars." Marie Emilie Gilchrist's "A Wreath for Persephone"[3] is a perfect little poem of this kind for children. Unusual beauty resides in the rhythmical enumeration of the names of flowers in sweet accord which Persephone gathered and which the poet weaves together into a glowing and fragrant wreath. And in a somewhat different key, De la Mare in "A Widow's Weeds"[4] tells off the names of the Widow's precious garden flowers and pungent herbs,

[1] In *Stars Tonight*. Macmillan.
[2] In *Peacock Pie*. Henry Holt.
[3] In *Wide Pastures*. Macmillan. Also in Miss Harrington's anthology *Ring-a-Round*.
[4] In *Peacock Pie*.

until he has named fourteen in rhymed couplets; among them,

> Brown bee orchis and Peals of Bells;
> Clover, burnet and thyme she smells.

Other children get in some degree the kind of pleasure from "words in tuneful order" which Wordsworth felt as a young boy:

> Twice five years
> Or less I might have seen, when first my mind
> With conscious pleasure opened to the charm
> Of words in tuneful order, found them sweet
> For their own *sakes*, a passion and a power;
> And phrases pleased me chosen for delight,
> For pomp, or love.[1]

Examples could be multiplied of the compelling and almost hypnotic power of glamorous names. Child psychology is shown in truth and beauty in the poem "Romance," by W. J. Turner. The boy in this poem is spellbound by the names "Chimborazo, Cotopaxi" and the vision of "a golden land" which they evoke.

> I dimly heard the master's voice
> And boys far-off at play,
> Chimborazo, Cotopaxi
> Had stolen me away.[2]

3. *Sensory Images*. Another trait which children and poets seem to possess in common is the avidity with which they welcome and seek sensory experience and the sharpness and clarity of the images which they receive through the gateways of sight, sound, touch, taste and smell. Sensory images are built into the fabric of mental and emotional life in youth, and the poet is one in whom these

---

[1] From *The Prelude*. Book V.
[2] From "Romance," published by E. P. Dutton & Company, Inc., New York, in *The Dark Wind*, by W. J. Turner. Also in De la Mare's anthology, *Come Hither*.

images have not become dulled.   On the contrary his life and the practice of his art have increased his native endowment of sensitiveness to environment and he has learned to make finer and more significant distinctions.

The child's love of sound, color, and movement, his eagerness to handle objects of pleasing form and texture, his gusto for food which suits his palate, and his delight in sweet odors, all help to build up a receptivity to ideal representations in literature, music, and art.   Poetry is full of beautiful, clear, and simple imagery which is often quite childlike in quality.   Color glows in word pictures; language, as we have seen, suggests familiar auditory experience; the right metrical arrangement of well-chosen words conveys a feeling of movement; and occasionally, tactual sensations and flavor are revived and odor is faintly wafted back.

A careful reading of Hilda Conkling's poems written when she was a little girl shows us in magnified form the responses and attitudes of natural, happy, and vibrant childhood.   The little poems composed by this child reveal her as an alert and active observer who could also be quietly receptive to sights and sounds.   She makes frequent use of the phrases *I see, I watch, I think I see, I peep out, I looked, I like to watch, I searched, They love to look, I watched it long and long*.   Her little poems glow with light and color.   An attentive ear is indicated by the phrases, *I hear, I have to listen, I heard a voice, The fields listened —* and with Hilda we hear bees humming, gulls calling, water laughing, the tree toad's silver voice, and the loud "crooked words" of the rooster.   One tiny poem captures the fragrance of pinks and mint and in another we are reminded that balsam trees "smell like a wind out of fairyland."

Children are industrious collectors and hoarders of the stuff from which dreams and poetry are made and it is no exaggeration to say that every normal child is at some time and to some degree a true poet. An elaboration of this thesis would take us into a discussion of the creative powers of children; we are here chiefly concerned with their readiness to participate in the enjoyment of poetry — which after all is only another aspect of the same thing.

4. *Imagination*. Imagination is a wizard whose magic touch transforms the commonplace world about us and gives an added significance to its plain facts, and poetry offers one clear channel through which imagination thus operates upon the jaded and dulled spirits of men and women.

> Poetry lifts the veil from the hidden beauty of the world, and makes familiar objects be as if they were not familiar.[1]

Children with their fresh outlook and unclouded vision do not need this particular service from literature, for to them, nothing is commonplace and outworn. It is the office of poetry to preserve their capacity for wonder and to enlarge and deepen their native interests and sympathies. The power of poetic imagination to illuminate and transcend the literal is well expressed in Sir Philip Sidney's *An Apologie for Poetrie*, written about 1581.

> Nature never set forth the earth in so rich tapistry, as divers Poets have done, neither with pleasant rivers, fruitful trees, sweet smelling flowers; nor whatsoever else may make the too much loved earth more lovely.

Children, adult nature-lovers, and poets pick out some striking feature of an object, see its likeness to something else, name it according to this novel association of the two concepts, and by so doing create what rhetoric chooses to call "figures of speech." Our language has been immeasurably enriched by this creative tendency, and its fruits constitute a good part of the spirit and form of

[1] Shelley, P. B., *A Defence of Poetry*.

poetry by which the latter is able to make the "loved earth more lovely" and give new meaning to experience.   The naïve and playful spirit of simple-minded and imaginative people shows in the common nomenclature of flowers, plants, birds, mountains and streams.   Names such as those below are condensed similes and metaphors and are the very essence of poetry.   They represent the swift and sure discovery of some likeness between two objects and the union of the two in "a happy epithet" which forever endures with its richer meaning.   Loving intimacy and quaint humor dictated these christenings: Lady's-slipper; soldiers-in-the-grass; Jack-in-the-pulpit; pin-cushion flower; heart's-ease; bacherlor's-buttons; bleeding-heart; bridal-wreath; weeping willow; mourning dove; hermit thrush; lady-bird; fiddler crab; spice-bush bugaboo.

Children are quick to catch the meaning of poetic lan-guage provided they have the necessary experience, for generations of boys and girls have in their play life ante-dated most of the nature poets.   They have gathered "rubies and emeralds" from the hedgerows for necklaces and have filled their treasure chests with "dandelion gold"; "fragrant curls" from the carpenter shop and "graybeard" moss from the woods have adorned their heads; the elder flower's "lace umbrella" has shaded royalty, while "sen-tinel trees" and the "corn's serried ranks" have served their liege lords for thousands of years.   Children are thus attuned to much of the imagery of poetry, for to them the poet's conception is often a joyful reality.

5. *The Subjects of Poetry*.   Literary critics have often pointed out that subjects are not in and of themselves "poetical."   Wordsworth gave great impetus to this principle but he did not originate it.   He helped greatly to dignify and exalt the common everyday experiences of life and to show the beauty and the spiritual values inherent in simple and humble things.   This principle, universally ac-

cepted with regard to poetry for adults, is even more forceful when applied to poetry adapted to the needs of the
young. A great many objects and situations which appeal
to adults appeal also to children, but whether a child's
stature permits him to reach and claim certain beautiful
things will depend upon the way the subject is handled.
There is choice poetry intended for children which deals
with the same subjects which have found favor with
adults. Domestic scenes, family affection, the inter-
course of friends, are portrayed, and colorful activities of
city and country are dramatized and sung. Young and old
are attentive to flowers, birds, animals, rain, snow, wind,
the heavenly bodies, and change of seasons, especially as
they relate to human thought and action. For children,
no matter what the subject, the treatment should be short,
objective, melodious and not heavily weighted with mature emotion or philosophy.

While sensuous delight is fundamental to the enjoyment
of poetry, meaning plays its part too, and in the highest
poetic expression we find a perfect and satisfying fusion of
sound and sense. For the fullest enjoyment, the listener
must be not only attuned to the feeling but receptive to
whatever thought is expressed. This responsiveness is in
part spontaneous and intuitive, but it is also the product of
experience. Variety and intensity of experience therefore
have much to do with the enjoyment of true poetry.

Interests peculiar to children occupy a large place in
verse written for them — pets, toys, play, sport, school
life, youthful adventure, vagrant fancy, fairies, small joys
and sorrows find lyric celebration. Often such subjects
inspire very sincere and artistic expression, but when
grown-ups enter childhood's own realm, very fine insight
and understanding are required to save them from seeming
patronizing, sentimental or consciously clever.

There is today no small amount of authentic poetry

which views experience from the level of childhood and en-
shrines it in beautiful and appropriate form. As in all
creative work there are delicate and indefinable beauties
which spring from the artist's sure and often unconcious
touch and which defy the most sympathetic analysis.
Terms of definition are clumsy and inadequate when applied to such work and the only way to arrive at an appreciation of it is to read widely and to think from time to
time, "What is it that makes this poem or those lines so
lovely?" And some people know how to get hints from the
children without resorting to an inquisition which destroys
beauty in the very act of seeking it.

Questions and references for Chapters IX and X cannot
well be separated, so all are placed at the close of Chapter X.

CHAPTER X
MAKERS OF POETRY FOR CHILDREN

A little stream best fits a little Boat,
A little lead best fits a little Float,
As my small Pipe best fits my little note.
ROBERT HERRICK

Here we our slender pypes may safely charme.
EDMUND SPENSER

POETRY for children has paralleled rather closely the development of prose literature addressed to them. At first they had only folk rhymes, singing games, ballads, and other traditional verse originally enjoyed by all ages but which the adult world with its increasing sophistication gradually relegated to the young. And just as children appropriated in whole or in part certain prose classics such as *Robinson Crusoe, Gulliver's Travels*, and *The Pilgrim's Progress*, so they extracted what they could assimilate from the poetry of their elders.

Poetry of the first rank in the seventeenth and eighteenth centuries contained a good deal which must have appealed to the older children as it continues to do today, but except for the anonymous verse already mentioned, there was very little which the younger children could fully enjoy.

It is easy to ascertain what the offering was from the time of Shakespeare to the time of Tennyson by examining that remarkable collection, unsurpassed of its kind, *The Children's Treasury of Lyrical Poetry*, by Francis Turner Palgrave, published in 1875. About ten per cent of the selections are anonymous, chiefly ballads, and the remainder are by poets of high rank. Palgrave made a thorough survey of English poetry and here is the cream of it judged suitable for young people. He recommended the collection for children from nine or ten years of age to about sixteen.

A still more extensive view may be obtained by a careful examination of *Come Hither*, an anthology for young people edited by Walter de la Mare. This book includes some of the very earliest poetry deemed suitable for young readers and the period at which selections were written may be discovered by consulting its "Index of Authors." It is a notable collection in which the editor has gathered together many beautiful things old and new, but it confirms the opinion that English poetry offered very little for the younger children before the time of William Blake, or late in the eighteenth century.

The assertion is often made that poetry written for children seldom rises to a high level, that children care little for poetry written especially for them and find satisfaction chiefly in simple things having a universal appeal. There is just enough truth in the statement to make it misleading unless viewed from several angles. The term "children" is very indefinite. Does it include the six-year-old as well as the sixteen-year-old? Does it refer only to inferior verse written by both minor and great poets? Does it take into account all the choice poems which have appeared at intervals for nearly a century and a half and which were certainly intended much more for children than for adults?

When the true poet tunes his "slender pipes" to childish ears he neither forgets his art nor loses his magic. He composes in a key and a range adapted to immature thought and emotion but he continues to exercise his high creative powers and to employ most of his own particular skills. The word *poet* means *maker*.

The Greekes called him a Poet, which name, hath as the most excellent, gone through other Languages. It commeth of this word *Poiein*, which is, to make:... which name, how high and incomparable a title it is...[1]

A study of the development of poetry for children shows that with each successive period in its history, gifted makers of verse for them display in their work more and more of the veritable substance and essence of true poetry. Development has been irregular but certain, and the brief survey offered in this chapter will include some of the old-fashioned versifiers as well as those poets whose right to the "high and incomparable title" is unquestioned. The chronological order will be followed as far as Walter de la Mare who introduces a large group of living writers. From this point the order of appearance is no longer of importance since all are the inheritors of the past and each in his or her own individual way is trying to sing the songs of childhood in key with the spirit of the eternal child and the spirit of the times.

ISAAC WATTS

There is a perfect correspondence in time, spirit, and style between the Barbauld-Day-Edgeworth school of prose fiction, and writers of informational, moralistic, and cautionary verse; but there was one forerunner of this group who, writing nearly a century earlier, exerted a marked and long-enduring influence which should be taken into account.

As a writer for children, Dr. Isaac Watts, D.D. (1674–1748) is chiefly known today by a few little hymns and songs which school textbooks and anthologies have preserved for two hundred years. The first lines of these will serve to designate them better than their cumbrous and forbidding titles: "How doth the little busy bee"; "Let dogs delight to bark and bite"; "Tis the voice of the sluggard." To these should be added a few selected

[1] Sir Philip Sidney.

stanzas of rare beauty from the original fourteen of "A Cradle Hymn" beginning "Hush, my dear, lie still and slumber."

Dr. Watts was an "Independent" English minister and his *Divine and Moral Songs for Children* (1715) were written for the express purpose of teaching the tenets of faith and duty to which he subscribed. His belief in the efficacy of rhymed verse as a means to this end is set forth in the Introduction where he says that children "take great delight in the very learning of truths and duties this way. There is something so amusing and entertaining in rhyme and in meter that will incline children to make this a part of their business and diversion.... What is learnt in verse is longer retained in memory, and sooner recollected. The like sound and like number of syllables exceedingly assist remembrance." This introduction shows that while the author's principal aim was foreign to the chief purposes of poetry, he had some faint notion of the delight and entertainment which it should afford.

In spite of the somber and often quite terrifying aspects of the religious teaching which Dr. Watts wished to impart, many of his poems display a real tenderness for children. The vengeance of an angry God gives place again and again to a more compassionate attitude, as if the writer were suddenly reminded that his "song might sound too hard" to infant ears. He never doubted for a moment that morals and religion could be directly taught through hymns and songs, and many of his titles serve to catalogue their prescriptive contents — "Against Lying," "Against Evil Company," "Against Scoffing and Calling Names," "Examples of Early Piety." But we find also titles which suggest happy childhood — "Innocent Play," "A Summer Evening," "A Morning Song." In these there are always a few stanzas which fulfill the promise of the title though all too often they trail off into sorrow and darkness. The drift is seen in the first stanza of "The Rose":

> How fair is the Rose! what a beautiful flower!
> The glory of April and May;
> But the leaves are beginning to fade in an hour,
> And they wither and die in a day.

In "A Summer Evening," the course of the sun from sunrise to sunset is made emblematic of life, and it ends on the cheerful and almost light-hearted note sounded in the second stanza:

> But now the fair traveller's come to the west,
> His rays are all gold, and his beauties are best;
> He paints the sky gay as he sinks to his rest,
> And foretells a bright rising again.

Creatures of the imagination have no place in this serious world in which the children's thoughts are constantly directed toward life's duties and uncertainties, but penitent little sinners are vouchsafed the comforting presence of guardian angels:

> I lay my body down to sleep
> Let angels guard my bed:
> And, through the hours of darkness, keep
> Their watch around my bed.

Animal life is introduced only to serve as texts for exhortation; "birds in their little nests" exemplify harmony and peace; bees and ants admonish to industry; lambs and doves are "lovely sweet innocent creatures," models of cleanliness and gentleness; while dogs, bears, and lions offer negative examples of behavior.

A great many of the subjects of *Divine and Moral Songs* were copied again and again by imitators, most of whom lacked the spirit of devotion and the sure metrical skill of Dr. Watts. Ann and Jane Taylor were accomplished followers who took many a leaf out of this old book while developing along original lines; Charles and Mary Lamb's poems for children show unmistakable traces of Watts; and even so inspired a rebel as William Blake owes something to this orthodox pietist and moral instructor who could at times melt into tenderness at childhood's innocence and promise.

WILLIAM BLAKE

The first clear musical note in poetry for children came from William Blake (1757–1827) in his *Songs of Innocence*, written in early manhood. These lyrics represent the first body of poetry produced by a writer of power, speaking from his own pure spirit to the unsullied heart of childhood. Probably these poems were not written especially for the young. Blake was an idealist, and the sweet innocence and confiding nature of children appealed to him just as lambs and all tender young things did. Whatever the poet's underlying plan, it brought into this group of poems a quality which renders them equally well suited to the immature and to a developed taste in poetry. From beginning to end, merry boys and girls fill the pages and sing the songs, smiling babies stretch out their hands, and a few less happy children make their wistful appeal.

William Blake was a mystic, a dreamer of dreams, a visionary in the literal sense of the word — one who saw visions and claimed to talk face to face with heavenly visitants. He believed that he was inspired and guided by some of the prophets of old and that his brother came back from heaven to reveal to him new and effective processes in art. There were indications in childhood of nervous instability, and life's severe buffetings produced in his sensitive nature a condition bordering at times on madness. His most sympathetic friends thought him "a little mad" in his later years, but they agree that the unusual mental state was of a type which served to inspire very original and noble expression in etching, painting, and poetry. He had, too, an insight into human needs which was more than sane — it was prophetic of social reform.

From early childhood, Blake resisted physical restraint and drooped under it. He was the son of a London hosier living in the outskirts of the city, and during his boyhood, field and woodland were not far from his home. He wandered there almost at will, for his parents soon discovered that he could not endure the hard, cold regimen of school. They did not understand the child, but they were alarmed and dismayed at certain manifestations — daydreams, visions which he reported at about eight years of age, but which had begun at four, the "lies" which he continued to tell, the outbursts of passion which greeted punishment or the torment of teasing companions. Freed from school, the child fed on the sights and sounds of the country which constantly filled him with wonder, and he began to write verse at about eleven years of age. Almost incidentally he acquired a liberal education in literature. His art education was more systematic, but in this field also, he refused to be dominated by tradition and his genius expanded along independent and original lines.

This sketch is of necessity far too brief to permit the tracing of Blake's remarkable career as an artist although his peculiar gifts in that field and in poetry are fundamentally inseparable. A knowledge of his many-sided life, private as well as artistic, is necessary to a full understanding of his marked traits of character and disposition, his passions and loyalties, the things that stirred his soul and came out in freshness and beauty in creative expression.

Ardent desire for freedom of body and soul, love of his fellowman and other living creatures, and belief in the inherent goodness and worth of man's original nature, pervade his thought and stir his emotions. He craved freedom not only for his own fulfillment but cried out in fiery aphorism at the sight of caged and suffering animals, and of children cribbed, confined or cruelly treated.

> A robin redbreast in a cage
> Puts all heaven in a rage.

> Each outcry of the hunted hare,
> A fibre from the brain does tear.

> A skylark wounded in the wing,
> A cherubim does cease to sing.

> He who shall hurt the little wren
> Shall never be beloved by men.

The quickened humanitarian spirit of the age flowed in Blake, and he turned his "bow of burning gold" and his "arrows of desire" against hypocrisy, cruelty, cold selfishness, and false standards of life.

Most of these ideas began to take shape in early youth but *Songs of Innocence*, first printed in 1789, expresses the softer, less agitated and denunciatory attitude of that period. In children and in the innocent creatures of field and wood, Blake saw the unspoiled handiwork of Divine love. He anticipated Wordsworth's "Ode on the Intimations of Immortality," for he presents with equal clearness, though in smaller compass, the ideal conception that the newborn come from some purer realm "trailing clouds of glory." To Blake, this was not merely a poetic idea, it was a philosophic conviction. He also felt that oneness and accord between the spirit of man and the face of nature which, a little later, Wordsworth was to express much more fully. He epitomizes this harmony in four memorable lines which remind us of "Flower in the crannied wall":

> To see the world in a grain of sand,
> And a heaven in a wild flower,
> Hold infinity in the palm of your hand
> And eternity in an hour.

And now we come to the pure and melodious *Songs*, a few of which will never be forgotten if the stream of human life offers any continuity in things of the spirit. To Blake, children were not little sinners to be warned and frightened, nor were they wax tablets awaiting the imprint of worn tradition; instead, they were the happy possessors of a joyous inner wisdom out of our lost Eden — a wisdom which might be communicated to a responsive ear. And so the "Introduction," which is the first poem in *Songs of Innocence*, is dictated by a dream-child, a laughing child "on a cloud," who sets the key of sweet rural joy which pervades this group of poems.

> Piping down the valleys wild,
> Piping songs of pleasant glee,
> On a cloud I saw a child,
> And he laughing said to me: —
>
> "Pipe a song about a lamb:"
> So I piped with merry cheer.
> "Piper, pipe that song again:"
> So I piped; he wept to hear.
>
> "Drop thy pipe, thy happy pipe,
> Sing thy songs of happy cheer:"
> So I sung the same again,
> While he wept with joy to hear.
>
> "Piper, sit thee down and write
> In a book that all may read —"
> So he vanish'd from my sight;
> And I plucked a hollow reed,
>
> And I made a rural pen,
> And I stained the water clear,
> And I wrote my happy songs
> Every child may joy to hear.

And in this strain, Blake continued to write of lambs and shepherds, of children dancing on the green, of flowers and spring, of "painted birds" and of

> Sweet dreams of pleasant streams
> By happy, silent, moony beams.

It is hard to resist giving a number of these poems in full. A few must be especially mentioned because of some feature significant in the development of verse for children. "Laughing Song" is one of the merriest, gayest things ever written, with its "sweet chorus of Ha, ha, he!" from "Mary and Susan and Emily." Isn't this the first time that little children have laughed aloud in English poetry?

Blake is noted also for originality of rhythm and stanza pattern and the fitness of these to the spirit of his songs. He discovered and used poetic forms which were inevitably right for a particular mood:

SPRING

Sound the flute!
Now it's mute.
Birds delight
Day and night;
Nightingale
In the dale,
Lark in sky,
Merrily,
Merrily, merrily, to welcome in the year.

Note how in "Infant Joy" the poet catches and frames in miniature the smiling mystery of infancy, and the tender benediction that wells up in its presence.

I have no name,
I am but two days old.
What shall I call thee?
I happy am,
Joy is my name.
Sweet joy befall thee.

Pain and sadness are sometimes hinted in this collection but their sharp portrayal comes in the next group of poems called *Songs of Experience*, printed in 1794. To-day, Blake's fame as a poet rests very largely on these two groups, but it is from *Songs of Innocence* that selections especially designed for children are chiefly drawn. His famous "Tiger, tiger, burning bright," is in *Songs of Experience*, placed there by Blake because it raises a profound and insoluble question of faith and philosophy.

Sympathy for the oppressed and disinherited is beautifully expressed in "The Little Black Boy," "The Chimney-Sweep," and "Holy Thursday."

William Blake made four notable contributions to English poetry and, in particular, to children's poetry:

He added a substantial amount to the world's store of sheer beauty and delight.

He turned his back on everything prosaic, artificial and purely formal.

He found his themes in nature and in the lives of simple people, and created a style in harmony with these.

He gave beautiful and startling expression to a higher social creed which was just beginning to emerge.

There was no immediate successor to make flute-like music for children on a shepherd's pipe, but the strains never died out and have been picked up at intervals by kindred spirits for nearly a century and a half.

ANN AND JANE TAYLOR

Except in point of time, Ann and Jane Taylor have a much closer relation to Isaac Watts than to William Blake. They began to write for little children when they were scarcely more than children themselves, and their first book of simple verses was published only fifteen years later than Blake's strangely beautiful hand-printed *Songs of Innocence* began its very limited circulation. There is nothing to indicate that the Taylor sisters knew Blake's poems at all, but their acquaintance with *Divine and Moral Songs* is evident. To the extent that they contributed to the development of poetry for children, it was along lines quite different from those which Blake had set going.

Biographical material is easy to obtain, therefore only a few leading facts need be mentioned here. Ann Taylor (1782–1866) married a minister — the Reverend Josiah Gilbert, had several children, and lived to an advanced age. Jane Taylor (1783–1824) did not marry, and died in the prime of life. Both wrote throughout their lives, at first in such close collaboration that it is often impossible to discover the authorship of certain early poems. A friend, Adelaide O'Keefe, contributed to the first collection of verses published in 1804, which bore the title *Original Poems for Infant Minds: By Several Young Persons.* Miss O'Keefe's contributions can be identified, for they are signed by the initial *A.* She had no hand at all in *Rhymes for the Nursery,* published in 1806.

The sisters wrote some of their poems when still in their teens, and the origin of the book was quite spontaneous, growing out of a happy but exceedingly busy girlhood, home education in a literary and artistic family, and the early discovery that they, like other near relatives, had a talent for versifying. They had a warm affection for children and many intimate contacts with them, but their conception of the office of poetry was identical with that of contemporary writers of didactic stories — their chief purpose being to develop the morals, refine the manners and impart interesting information to young children. Like Watts, they recognized that rhyme and meter added appreciably to the attractiveness of the materials of instruction.

While narrative poems involving matters of conduct occupy a large place, these writers also expanded greatly the range of subjects for juvenile verse and included many drawn from nature experiences and a few from play. They wrote about flowers, birds, sun, moon, stars, the seasons, the village green, meadows and gardens. Most of these are forced at the close into some application to conduct but children, like squirrels, know how to extract the meat and discard the hull.

The claims which the Taylors made for themselves were modest indeed. When modern critics say that their "poetry" is merely "versified prose" they are only repeating the authors' own estimate contained in the Preface to their second collection, *Rhymes for the Nursery*. There they state that if the book should meet with success, "... the writers must certainly acknowledge themselves indebted rather to the plainness of prose, than to the decorations of poetry." In the Preface to the first collection they had already declared their intention to "abridge every poetic freedom and figure, and to dismiss even such words as, by being less familiar, might give, perhaps, a false idea to their little readers, or at least make a chasm in the chain of conception." The remainder of this passage further elaborates the opinion that all poetic imagery must be avoided even though its use "may tend to excite a taste for natural and poetic beauty." Their purposes and convictions compelled them to regard as "superfluous" everything except literal truth, moral ideas, and metrical form, and they observed these restrictions not only in the verse intended for mere babies but in compositions obviously meant for older children.

As might be expected, one searches almost in vain for tonal effects, adaptation of meter, refrain, poetic imagery, unusual language, and other elements of beauty described in Chapter IX. Emotion is very lightly touched, children are kissed and fondled a good deal, and endearing terms are often used, but in a complete collection of these poems — quite a sizable book — there is not one that *sings* the deep and universal tenderness found in the cradle songs of earlier writers, Luther and Watts, for example. There are references to putting babies to bed, about going to bed, about safety and comfort, but no true lyric on the subject, and not a single real lullaby.

In spite of these obvious defects, a few of their "pieces" possess a quality which offers ample ground for the belief that Ann and Jane Taylor possessed a gift for true poetry. Their wings of song were early clipped to fit the limits set by current educational thought, which involved a low opinion of the capacity of children for enjoyment of finer things. We should remember also that poetry for adults at this period had not moved far in its release from eighteenth-century forms and conventionalities. The fruits of the Romantic movement in English poetry were yet to be reaped.

The Taylors were the first poets to write exclusively for children, and after all, the children are the final and in-exorable judges of literature intended for them. Thou-sands of children for many generations have taken to their hearts a few of their poems; they claim them as their own and love them — and there is the verdict. A short advertisement of one of the quaint original editions which the publisher, Harvey and Darton wrote, no doubt speaks the truth:

> We have not room for extracts or could convince our read-ers, that the writers of these "Rhymes" have better claim to the title of poets, than many who arrogate to themselves that high appellation.

Out of a complete collection, the following titles rank high as regards literary quality and lasting popularity. First lines or couplets are given in addition to titles, as an aid to identification. Since there was no rivalry be-tween the sisters and since they often neglected to sign their work, the same plan is followed here. Adelaide O'Keefe wrote a number of interesting and pleasing narra-tive poems, but nothing of hers attained lasting popularity.

The Cow.
> Thank you, pretty cow, that made
> Pleasant milk to soak my bread.

The Sheep.
> Lazy sheep, pray tell me why
> In the pleasant field you lie.

The Star.
> Twinkle, twinkle, little star.

The Baby's Dance.
> Dance, little baby, dance up high.

Questions and Answers.
> Who showed the little ant the way?

Little Birds and Cruel Boys.
> A little bird built a warm nest in a tree
> And laid some blue eggs in it, one, two, and three.

The Field Daisy.
> I'm a pretty little thing
> Always coming in the spring.

The great popularity of *Original Poems* and *Rhymes for the Nursery* brought forth speedily a crop of imitators who, without a shred of talent or taste, harangued children endlessly in doggerel verse of the "cautionary" type. Today these productions seem a veritable pestilence. Child characters were drowned, crippled, burned to death, poisoned, turned into chimney sweeps, or brought to some other untimely end because, through ignorance or childish waywardness, they made a slight misstep of some kind. But this outburst was almost the last gasp of the didactic school.

When clever writers today utter warnings or point out lessons, it is either in the form of amusing caricatures as in Hilaire Belloc's *The Bad Child's Book of Beasts* or in some passing comment or reflection nicely adjusted to the poem as a whole. Quite commonly they simply draw a vivid picture and leave to the intelligence and perception of children the obvious application. For example, Aline Kilmer's engaging little vandals in "Song Against Children"[1] who eat all the berries from the Christmas greens, do not suffer violent death as some earlier writers would certainly have decreed. The only remonstrance is that implied in the title. But watch the faces of children who listen to this tale as told in three very musical stanzas, and listen to their horrified comments! The most officious and conscientious adult may step aside when culprits are judged by their peers — unless they feel impelled to offer a plea for mercy.

EDWARD LEAR

Edward Lear (1812–1888) had no literary forerunner — he is simply himself. The pure nonsense which he wrote must have sprung from sheer exuberance of spirits which found a ready outlet through his facility in making clever, rapid sketches, and witty rhymes. Add to this the constant stimulation of an audience composed of merry youngsters and appreciative elders, and the situation is perfect for the production of some of the jolliest verses ever written. In Lear's own words:

> There was an Old Derry down Derry,
> Who loved to see little folks merry;
> So he made them a book
> And with laughter they shook
> At the fun of the Derry down Derry.

And children have been shaking with laughter ever since, as one edition after another of the "Nonsense" books has come out.

Edward Lear was a gifted young English artist who at the age of nineteen years was doing important work for

[1] In *Silver Pennies*. Edited by Blanche Thompson.

the Zoölogical Society in making colored drawings of birds. Only a little later, he was employed by the thirteenth Earl of Derby in a similar capacity, and this work required that he take up his residence for a time with the family. He soon became a great favorite with young and old, the family at this time including a number of grandchildren of his patron.

In the Introduction to one of his collections Lear says:

> Long years ago in days when much of my time was passed in a country house where children and mirth abounded, the lines beginning "There was an old man of Tobago," were suggested to me by a valued friend, as a form of verse lending itself to limitless variety for Rhymes and Pictures; and henceforth the greater part of the original drawings and verses of the first *Book of Nonsense* were struck off with a pen, no assistance ever having been given me in any way but that of uproarious delight and welcome at the appearance of every new absurdity.

Sir Edward Strachey, in his Introduction to one edition of *The Book of Nonsense and More Nonsense* (Warne), points out that Lear's type of nonsense is not simply a negative of sense, "not a mere putting forward of incongruities and absurdities," but such a treatment of life's contradictions as can be produced only by the creative imagination of a genius.

The general public could not believe that pure unadulterated nonsense was all that the author intended, and they sought for some hidden significance in these rollicking verses. Lear at last came out with a disclaimer stating that there was no intention to caricature anyone and that "nonsense, pure and absolute" had been his aim throughout.

The first *Book of Nonsense*, published in 1846, consists entirely of limericks, and young children find these much funnier when carried along by the contagious laughter of grown-ups. The unity between the crude, absurd sketches and the ridiculous verses is perfect.

The second volume called *Nonsense Songs* published in 1871 was written at different times and for different sets of children. This collection contained some of the most delightful of his poems. They are just as nonsensical as the limericks, but there is a fine show of coherence and plot which makes their inconsequence the more amusing. Among the most popular of these are "The Owl and the Pussy Cat" who went to sea in a boat; "The Jumblies" who went to sea in a sieve; "The Nutcrackers and Sugar Tongs" who eloped at a mad gallop (in perfect dactylic measure!) and never came back; "Mr. and Mrs. Spikky Sparrow" whose mutual solicitude results in an outfit of clothes which makes the pair feel "quite galloobious and genteel."

In discussing principles of poetry, many writers have made the comment that poetry may be found in a short phrase or even in a single word, and this is equally true regarding fun and nonsense. Lear gets many of his most delightful effects through the words and names which he invents so "sponge-taneously"; they seem so much better — really *are* so much better, than any which the sober English language supplies. The events he describes could only occur in the Torrible Zone, Chankly Bore, Gromboolian Plain, Zemmery Fidd, Jelly-Bo-Lee, or on the Coast of Coromandel; and only Jumblies, Quangle Wangles, Pobbles, and like creatures, could drink "forty bottles of ring-bo-ree," discover a Twangum Tree, or consort with a Runcible Cat; only Mr. and Mrs. Discobbolos have ever heard the cry of the Nupiter Piffkin or the call of the Biscuit Buffalo.

Lear must have had a good time experimenting with Alphabet rhymes. There are five of these, all quite different. Four are well suited to young children and the other would delight any grown person able to invent alliterative lines. It runs like this:

> The Melodious Meritorious Mouse
> who played a merry minuet on the
> Piano-forte.

> The Tumultuous Tom-tommy Tortoise,
> who beat a Drum all day long in the
> middle of the wilderness.

The ability to entertain all ages at one and the same time is one of the most characteristic traits of fine humorous writing, and Lear possessed it to a high degree. Very young children enjoy the "silvery sound" produced by his most jingly jingles and perfect meters. They agree with Mr. Floppy Fly who begs Mr. Daddy Long-Legs to sing;

> For, if you would, the silvery sound
> Would please the shrimps and cockles round,
> And all the crabs would gladly come
> To hear you sing, "Ah, Hum di Hum!"

Older readers having a larger command of the English language find endless delight in the audacious puns and other linguistic contortions which occur on every page of the *Nonsense Books*. Lear's fantastic verses were composed directly for groups of children, with older people applauding on the side lines, and each generation has supplied an enthusiastic circle of all ages.

> Far and few, far and few
> Are the lands where the Jumblies live:

sings Lear; and all the world echoes, "Far and few, far and few, are the makers of such unforgettable rhymes."

CHRISTINA ROSSETTI

In Christina Rossetti we find a poet of great natural gifts and high accomplishment who chose at times to turn her talent toward writing very simple little poems for young children. She possessed much of the spiritual quality which we found in Blake and is his direct successor in all respects except chronological order.

Christina Rossetti (1830–1894) began to write verse when still a child, and in the little collection of poems which her grandfather Polidori privately printed when she was sixteen are several which are remarkably good. The four Rossetti children stimulated each other greatly along artistic lines and Christina blossomed out as a poet while Dante Gabriel won distinction as both poet and artist when the two were quite young. Critics agree that Miss Rossetti had attained her full power by the time she was twenty years old.

She was not strong physically even as a child, and while still a young woman developed a malady which gave her a wan and sad appearance. Her pale delicate face and slender form appear in many of the paintings of Dante Gabriel Rossetti and others of the pre-Raphaelite school, for she often served as a model. She was deeply religious and this, combined with her very modest opinion of herself and devotion to the needs of her family, led her into an almost nun-like seclusion. Her life was one of renunciation and of habitual inhibitions. Twice she refused to marry, though in the second instance she was apparently deeply in love. She became more and more introspective and at last her warm and enthusiastic nature found outlet almost exclusively in poetry, in service to others, and in religious devotion. Her brother William writing of this aspect of her life says, "Impulse and *élan* were checked both in art and writing, but the most extreme spontaneity in poetic performance remained."

Miss Rossetti was a great master of musical language and of all metrical arts. Her *Goblin Market* was a startling and exciting event in English poetry both in its richness and beauty of imaginative conception and in the perfection with which form embodies spirit, and emotion governs movement. One finds in this single poem an amazing variety of metrical schemes nicely adjusted to the shifting scene. Saintsbury [1] says of it, "the air is thick with meters." While not designed for children, nine-year-olds who have had experience with real poetry and fairy lore get a great deal of pleasure from it. The old tale of a bartered lock of golden hair is simple enough, and the enticements offered by the goblins to "sweet-tooth Laura" have a luscious sound. They tempt her with "fruits which that unknown garden bore;... sugar-sweet their sap."

> Morning and evening
> Maids heard the goblins cry:
> "Come buy our orchard fruits,
> Come buy, come buy:
> Apples and quinces,
> Lemons and oranges,
> Plump unpicked cherries,
> Melons and raspberries,
> Bloom-down-cheeked peaches,
> Swart-headed mulberries,
> Wild free-born cranberries,
> Crab-apples, dewberries,
> Pine apples, black berries,
> Apricots, strawberries; —
> All ripe together
> In summer weather —
> Morns that pass by,
> Fair eves that fly;
> Come buy, come buy:" [2]

In going from this poem which represents Miss Rossetti's most inspired and finished work, to the simple

[1] Saintsbury, G. E. B., *History of English Prosody*, volume **III**.
[2] Rossetti, Christina. *Goblin Market and Other Poems*. Macmillan, London, 1862.

little nursery poems published nearly ten years later (1872), one moves from the atmosphere of supernatural events into the fresh air of English meadows and the serene security of home. If one knew nothing more of her work, these extremes would show the wide range of her command over subject and mood, as well as her great flexibility in style.

Sing-Song bore the following dedication — "Rhymes dedicated without permission to the baby who suggested them." This child was the infant son of Professor Arthur Cayley of Cambridge with whose family Miss Rossetti held very close ties of friendship. A few years later there were several small nieces and nephews in her brother William's family. So in spite of a life of seclusion she had intimate contacts with children. She must also have retained vivid impressions from her own ardent childhood when she and her sister and brothers drained all possible joy out of visits at the country home of their maternal grandfather. Other opportunities for nature experience were very limited, being confined to London parks and small city gardens, but the children developed an unusual interest in animals, especially strange, lowly and grotesque little creatures such as frogs, toads, and the "wombat obtuse and furry." The wombat continued to fascinate Christina and her artist brother, for he wrought some of these queer little beasts into the designs which he drew for *Goblin Market*. There are several delightful stanzas in her poem "From House to Home" which assign a place of peace and safety to creatures often considered repulsive:

> Frogs and fat toads were there to hop or plod,
> And propagate in peace, an uncouth crew,
> Where velvet-headed rushes rustling nod
> And spill the morning dew.[1]

---

[1] Rossetti, Christina G., From *House to Home*. By permission of The Macmillan Company, publishers.

There are no wombats or other weird creatures in *Sing-Song*.[1] Cows and lambkins and sitting hens; birds and flowers, wind and sun; cherries, pancakes, and bread and milk; play-time, work time and tender care at bedtime — these are the immortal subjects of the first collection of pure lyrics written especially for young children. And with their gentle voices Miss Rossetti repeats her merciful message to little obscure creatures:

> Hopping frog, hop here and be seen,
> I'll not pelt you with stick and stone
> Your cap is laced and your coat is green;
> Good-bye, we'll let each other alone.

It is not strange that an occasional note of sadness slipped into these poems and we find there a few small graves, sorrowing mothers, and motherless children, but the dominant key is major, not minor. A recent edition with a few judicious omissions and some welcome additions from other collections, brings to children a book of pure happiness. The only tombstone left is one of snow erected with proper ceremonial to "a song-singing thrush." Students will of course try to examine the original and complete collection with the illustrations by Arthur Hughes which the author so much admired.

Like Blake, Miss Rossetti used very few figures of speech in her poems for young children. Both presented an idealization of childish experience with the utmost simplicity of style. The few examples of poetic imagery which do appear in *Sing-Song* are extremely simple — milk, "white as swansdown, smooth as silk"; the moon "within her misty veil"; the daisy which "stands up like a star." But this poet used in these simple and seemingly artless little poems, a great variety of those arts which she so well understood: smooth, flowing dactyls which dip and curve in a swallow's flight,

---

[1] Rossetti, Christina G. *Sing-Song: A Nursery Rhyme Book.* London, Macmillan, 1871.

> Fly away, fly away over the sea,
> Sun-loving swallow, for summer is done;

crisp, monosyllabic trochees,

> Mix a pancake,
> Stir a pancake,
> Pop it in the pan;

iambus, in thoughtful interrogation,

> A diamond or a coal?
> A diamond, if you please:

explosive consonants and liquid combinations of sound chosen with unerring sensitiveness; and melodious catalogues of names,

> Jacob's ladder and Solomon's seal,
> And Love-lies-bleeding beside All-heal
> In the garden.

Simple, direct and childlike sensory images are found on almost every page — color, light, sound, odor, taste, each recalls and amplifies happy experience.

Other interesting features of Miss Rossetti's poems for children are noted under "Topics for Further Study," at the close of this chapter. All in all, *Sing-Song* marks an epoch in poetry for young children. It might well be a matter of regret that Miss Rossetti did not create more for children beyond the nursery level, giving play to that supreme power of enchantment which *Goblin Market* casts upon readers young and old.

CELIA LAIGHTON THAXTER

Celia Laighton Thaxter (1835–1894) was one of the earliest American writers of verse for children. While her work as a whole is not accorded very high rank today, a small sheaf of very charming poems can be gathered from her *Stories and Poems*, first published in 1883. A few of these are found in almost every representative collection of verse for children and one, "The Sandpiper" takes its place in general anthologies as one of the most perfect interpretations of a felt relationship between human beings and little "brothers of the air." It belongs to that comparatively small group of poems which children enjoy and which, in its fuller meaning, is still held dear in later life.

Celia Laighton spent her childhood and much of her later life on the island of Appledore, Isles of Shoals, off the coast of New Hampshire. Her father was keeper of the United States Government lighthouse there, and the life of the seas and of the wind-blown shore entered into her very soul and gave substance and color to almost all of her writings. Her poems are localized to an unusual degree, but that very concentration led to faithful and sensitively drawn pictures. The little maid depicted as the "Spray Sprite" in the story of that title is clearly Celia herself, and in rarely beautiful language she tells of childhood experiences and sensations at her beloved Appledore.

> It was bliss to her to watch that great sea, to hear its sweet or awful voices, to feel the salt wind lift her thick brown hair and kiss her cheek; to wade, barefooted, into the singing, sparkling brine.... Every wave that whitened the face of the vast sea was dear to her; every bird that floated over, every sail that glided across — and all brought her a thrill of joy.... And blissful it was to run with the sandpipers along the edge of the shallow waves on the little beach, and dance in the clear green water; or, at low tide, to hang over the still surface of pools among the rocks, wherein lay treasures untold.[1]

Mrs. Thaxter is especially noted for her many beautiful and truthful pictures of birds and their ways, "The Sandpiper" being only one of a considerable group of this kind. In the same collection are poems called "Wild Geese," "The Sparrows," "The Kittiwakes," "The Great Blue Heron," "The Burgomaster Gull" — to give

[1] Thaxter, Celia, *Stories and Poems for Children*. Houghton, 1885.

only a partial list of the bird poems. "Under the Light-House" tells very tenderly of the pitiful loss of life among birds which beat themselves to death against the gray rocks, drawn "like frail moths" by the dazzling light. She names each one and attaches to each a fitting and often quite unusual epithet:

> Gay soldier blackbirds, wearing on their shoulders
>   Red, gold-edged epaulets,
> And many a homely brown, red-breasted robin,
>   Whose voice no child forgets.

Some children come upon the sorrowful sight and following an impulse universal in childhood they bury the birds:

> And so they laid the sweet, dead shapes together,
>   Smoothing each ruffled wing,
> Perplexed and sorrowful, and pondering deeply
>   The meaning of this thing.

> They bore them from the rough cliffs of granite
>   To where the grass grew green,
> And laid them 'neath the soft turf, all together
>   With many a flower between.

Children are Celia Thaxter's other great love, and she shows herself a close and understanding observer of them. A few of her poems may contain too much of the affectionate demonstration of mother or grandmother, but she succeeded several times in presenting in charming action and with little comment, the living portraits of sweet, natural little girls. Of these, "Little Gustava" is the best known.

This writer was able to catch the true character and tone of homely farm life quite as well as that of seashore and woodland. Young readers recognize and respond happily to the characteristic sounds and sensations of early morning in village or country which "Chanticleer" presents so melodiously:

> I wake! I feel the day is near,
>   I hear the red cock crowing!
> He cries "'Tis dawn!" How sweet and clear
> His cheerful call comes to my ear,
>   While light is slowly growing.

The second line is repeated in each of the five stanzas, and "the red cock crowing" becomes the stirring symbol of dawn.

Another deservedly popular poem is called "Lost." It is a veritable poultry-yard chorus, amusing, and imaginatively realistic — if such a phrase may be permitted — having much in common with folk verse. There are a number of stanzas; this is the first:

> "*Lock the dairy door!*" Oh, hark, the cock is crowing proudly.
> "*Lock the dairy door!*" and all the hens are cackling loudly:
> "*Chickle, chackle, chee,*" they cry; "*we haven't got the key,*" they cry;
> "*Chickle, chackle, chee! Oh, dear, wherever can it be!*" they cry.

Mrs. Thaxter's poetry for children marks a step forward in the pleasing and effective use of sensory images — sight, sound, color and feeling of movement. She has the true poet's vision and at times this is displayed in imagery of great charm and simplicity: A tiny child sees the rainbow as a wreath, "a beautiful water-bloom"; the waning moon is "a thin shell, pearly and pale"; crocuses are "bubbles of amethyst"; the little snow-bound island is "white like a frosted cake"; the eye-brights (small white flowers) are "scattered like pearls all milky fair"; a little owlet is described as "half a handful of feathers and two great eyes"; we find the yellowbird with "golden breast bedropped with amber."

American children should have an opportunity for a fuller acquaintance with this nature-poet than can be obtained from a few poems commonly included in anthologies, well chosen as these usually are.

ROBERT LOUIS STEVENSON

Robert Louis Stevenson (1850–1894) occupies a unique place as a writer for children. In the opinion of many critics, he founded a new school of poetry for the young and became their first true "poet-laureate." Some go so far as to consider him the only one deserving of that popular acclaim, and regard *A Child's Garden of Verses* as not only a classic, but as representing a standard of style and quality for all other writers in this field.

The world was ready for this little book when it came out in 1885, for the nineteenth century had seen a great change in the prevailing attitude toward children. Published nearly a century later than Blake's *Songs of Innocence*, its author found an audience, young and old, from whose lives most of the old strait-laced moralistic notions as well as the stilted society manners had been stripped. Certain ephemeral sentimental products had come and gone, and the time was ripe for a simple, natural, and happy approach through literature to the hearts and minds of children.

Stevenson himself had unconsciously helped to prepare the way for his verses by that penetrating and beautiful essay called "Child's Play"[1] which appeared first in the *Cornhill Magazine* in 1878. Has any psychological treatise ever presented a more truthful picture of the life of the imagination and of its overt expression in the dramatic play of children? This young man, a dreamer all his life, knew that children wandered in "starry solitudes" and groped in terrifying shadows, and he had an understanding sympathy with all romancers "passionate after dreams and unconcerned about realities" who often cannot distinguish with exactitude between fact and fiction. He remembered with marvelous clearness his own daydreams and could recall in words that move us today the

[1] Stevenson, R. L., *Virginibus Puerisque.*

ardors of his youthful pursuits. In "A Penny Plain and Twopence Coloured" [1] one feels the transport of joy with which the boy selected and purchased the little booklets containing dialogue and scenes for a toy theater and hurried home, treading on air, to color and cut out the figures and scenes of adventure and romance. Electrifying names these playlets bore:

> Names of El Dorados that still haunt the ear of memory... *Lodoiska, Silver Palace, Echo of Westminster Bridge.* Names, bare names, are surely more to children than we poor, grown-up, obliterated fools remember.

These two essays give us much of the background out of which grew all those poems of dramatic play, such as "A Good Play," "Pirate Story," "Block City," "The Little Land," and they introduce us to the child quietly happy with his books in "Picture Books in Winter" and "The Land of Story-Books."

In one of his autobiographical sketches,[2] Stevenson tells of how he exercised and trained his own powers as a writer. He escaped scholastic tasks whenever it was possible to do so, but he put himself through an exacting and persistent self-discipline in writing, beginning when a mere boy. He imitated again and again certain writers of distinction whose work he admired and he says that at this stage he "played the sedulous ape" to Hazlitt, Lamb, Wordsworth, Hawthorne, and others. He refers to the "innumerable gouty-footed lyrics" which resulted from this following of many masters. But there was little that he could have aped as a writer of poetry for children even if he had been disposed during his apprenticeship days to attempt such a mastery, and there is nothing lame or gouty about his mature work and no visible crutch. If, as

---

[1] Stevenson, R. L., *Memories and Portraits.*
[2] Stevenson, R. L., "A College Magazine," *Memories and Portraits.*

is said, a book of Kate Greenaway's verses about children suggested to Stevenson the writing of similar ones, it served only as a springboard from which he might dive into his own quiet pool of childish memories. His phenomenal success in this field must have been due to the fact that the child in him survived to a rare degree through years of pain and disappointment, and that by some happy inspiration he turned his mature talents toward the interpretation of that little world which he could still see "by the standard of my childish stature."

The main facts of Stevenson's childhood and youth are well known. He was a very delicate child, an only child, with a mother who was also frail. His father, Thomas Stevenson, was a civil engineer and not the first Stevenson to follow that profession. The boy's grandfather on the mother's side was a minister, the Reverend Lewis Balfour, who lived at Colinton on the Water of Leith, only about five miles from Edinburgh, and it was in the manse garden and the neighborhood that the boy gathered many of those "little sunbright pictures of the past" which he wove into his poems for children. His essay "The Manse" [1] gives many clues to these "marvelous places, though handy to home." There were many cousins of about Louis's age at Colinton, and there the more active play life of his childhood took place. Several of his cousins are mentioned by name in his verses. Here, too, lived that "chief of our aunts," Jane Balfour, whose praises were sung by one nephew, but in the name of all of her "dozen of nurslings." His home in Edinburgh figures largely also: the cold and frosty air, the long summer days and the long winter evenings of that northern latitude, the coziness of his comfortable home, his mother's tender care, the devotion of his beloved nurse, "Cummie," and the many quiet pleasures devised for the sickly child

[1] Stevenson, R. L., *Memories and Portraits.*

and improved upon by him — all these, as a young man he recalls and weaves into his verses.

After early childhood, Louis was able to take long walks in the country about Edinburgh and he writes of himself as "a rambling boy" who haunted the Pentland Hills and tramped the upland sheep-walks with rough shepherds tending their flocks. He frequently made trips with his father to the lighthouses along the rugged Scottish coast which three generations of the family had either built or superintended. But none of this bolder, freer life got into the quiet sheltered "Garden." Having turned back the pages of his picture book to early childhood, the poet was content to call up only the intimate scenes of that period. In so doing, he gave a very unusual unity to this collection of something over sixty poems.

These poems have the true lyrical quality which at once suggests vocal song, and many of them have been set to music. There is not great variety in meter but neither is there tiresome monotony and the meter is almost always well suited to subject and situation. Perhaps the most common is the iambic, with four feet to the line as in, "I saw you toss the kite on high"; "The coach is at the door at last." Crisp trochees are occasionally introduced as in some of the lines of "Marching Song" and "Good and Bad Children." Smooth, flowing dactyls tell of the movement of water and mill-wheel in "Keepsake Mill," carry the listener through the long sweep of "The Swing," and convey the feeling of quiet happiness and mystery in "The Unseen Playmate."

Compared with earlier poetry for children, we find a marked increase in the use of clear, sensory images, poetic imagery or figures of speech, and sensitive emotional response to environment. Metaphor and simile are kept very simple and are drawn from such familiar experiences that they are almost certain to add meaning rather than obscure it. "Grasses run like a green sea"; the river is "the sky's blue looking glass"; the child's bed is "like a little boat"; the sun — "a blood-red orange"; objects in a winter scene are "frosted like a wedding-cake"; the red fire "paints the empty room." Alliteration is never exaggerated, but there are many lines in which the repetition of initial sounds adds to the musical effect:

> Sounds of the village grow stiller and stiller,
> Stiller the note of the birds on the hill;

Another noticeable example is in the last stanza of "Autumn Fires":

> Sing a song of seasons!
> Something bright in all!
> Flowers in the summer,
> Fires in the fall!

W. E. Henley wrote a poem in which he attempted to paint a portrait of Stevenson. One line describes the latter as possessing "A deal of Ariel, just a streak of Puck." There is only a very faint streak of Puck in the poems for children, for the humor when present is delicate and light, but Ariel's voice is often heard.

It has been the vogue in recent years to point out the defects and limitations of Stevenson for children. In brief, the criticism is that there is little that is actively joyous in his poems and nothing of the choral or social type; that the child portrayed is not a normally healthy one, but a lonely little boy with a tendency to introspection; that the poet usually writes in a reminiscent vein and with adult interpretation of childhood experience; and finally, that many children do not care for these poems. These criticisms probably represent a reaction from the undiscriminating and universal praise which established this collection for so many years as almost the only verse for younger children which possessed true literary quality.

In addition to this, some critics seem to have fallen into the very common error of evaluating one type of verse in terms of a totally different type.

Many of these poems are far beyond the range of the nursery period and the mistake has often been made of trying to arouse an interest in them on the part of children who are still at the Mother Goose level of enjoyment.

Probably too much emphasis has been placed upon the individualized nature of the life portrayed. These poems deal with the veritable experiences of children whether alone or in groups, and the artistic portrayal of such simple and universal types of play activity may help children to identify themselves with a larger group of "contemporaries" than their own playmates are likely to provide.

Today, with the greatly increased offering of choice verse for children, Stevenson's work is likely to be viewed in a more balanced way and to take its true place as a source of lasting pleasure to the many minds and many moods of childhood.

LAURA E. RICHARDS

The mantle of Edward Lear seemed to fall upon the shoulders of an American woman, Laura E. Richards. The period between the publication of Lear's last book and Mrs. Richards's first was not long, and her verse, while seldom imitative, has a quality much like that of the earlier humorist. We are reminded strongly of Mother Goose also, some of the rhymes seeming just as unpremeditated and innocent of literary intention as the old dame's ancient jingles. Starting with Mother Goose and adding the name of Lewis Carroll to the list, we have the four chief producers of nonsense verse for children up to the present writing (1933). Mrs. Richards's place in this group is not undistinguished and she has recently proved her enduring spirit of youthful gaiety by producing thirty new poems in the old vein. These are in the new collection, *Tirra Lirra*,[1] and although the author is now over eighty years of age they show her undimmed power and take their place harmoniously among the old favorites which she wrote as a young mother for her small sons and daughters.

Laura Elizabeth Richards, daughter of Julia Ward Howe, was born in 1850. She enjoyed all the benefits of a home of broad culture with fine family and social relations, and in passing these on to her own children thousands of other children have shared her gifts. She contributed extensively to *St. Nicholas*, the leading magazine for children, and published several collections of songs and rhymes as well as numerous stories during the period of greatest productiveness. Measured by quality and quantity, she is more truly the poet of the nursery than any other writer so far discussed and she was, and is, peculiarly fitted to play this rôle. She called her first book of verse, published in 1890, *In My Nursery*.[2] The first poem in the collection bears that title and the first two lines are,

> In my nursery as I sit
> To and fro the children flit.

After naming and characterizing six little boys and girls, the poem continues:

> Flitting, flitting to and fro,
> Light they come and light they go:
> And their presence fair and young
> Still I weave into my song.

---

[1] Richards, Laura E. *Tirra Lirra: Rhymes Old and New.* 1932. Foreword by May Lamberton Becker. Quotations by permission of Little, Brown and Company, publishers.

[2] Richards, Laura E. *In My Nursery: A Book of Verse.* 1919. Quotations by permission of Little, Brown and Company, publishers.

> Here rings out their merry laughter,
> Here their speech comes tripping after:
> Here their pranks, their sportive ways,
> Flash along the lyric maze,
> Till I hardly know in fine,
> What is theirs and what is mine:
> Can but say, through wind and weather,
> They and I have wrought together.

This stanza gives the clue to the greater part of this writer's verse better than any analysis might do, however sympathetic.

The latest appreciation to be written is the Foreword to *Tirra Lirra* by Mrs. May Lamberton Becker. She tells in an entertaining manner the story of events which led up to the publication of this new collection. The story is too long to repeat here, but it relates how the plan grew in response to a persistent chorus of demands from admirers of an earlier generation — perhaps *two* earlier generations. These nonsense verses are seemingly imperishable, for, as Mrs. Becker says, they have "rocked and laughed their way into the memory without conscious effort at memorizing." People brought up on them can recite them endlessly and with fresh delight in their absurdity.

Titles for Mrs. Richards's collections of verses have always been well chosen, at least if one is willing to accept her own modest estimate implied thereby. She called the second collection (1902) *The Hurdy-Gurdy* — a term suggestive of the homely flavor of the verses and the inevitable beat of their rhythm. Perhaps *Tirra Lirra* is the best title of all. It may have been suggested by the song of Autolycus in Shakespeare's *The Winter's Tale:*

> The lark that tirra-lirra chants —
>   With heigh! with heigh! the thrush and the jay.

The title sets the key and marks the step for tripping

songs of laughter, many of which give delight far beyond the nursery years.

The features which charm in childhood are the features which make these verses unforgettable. Prominent among these characteristics are:

1. The haunting chime of euphonious words and names, real or manufactured. Like Lear, this writer blandly makes up a word or modifies one at need, and her poems furnish countless examples of this sort of amusing invention. As —

> Timothy Tiggs and Tomothy Toggs,
> They both went a-fishing for pollothywogs.

The "Legend of Lake Okeefinokee" is full of made-up words which delight children. In the course of the narrative the incredible name (however real) continues to work its charm by being rhymed with *smokee*, *brokee*, *pokee*, etc.

2. The "catchy" melody produced by rhyme and meter, especially in the numerous refrains such as

> The fairest spot to me,
> On the land or on the sea,
> Is the charming little cupboard where the jam-pots grow,
> Where the jelly jolly, jelly jolly jam-pots grow.

The chorus of "Johnny's By-Low Song" is soothing and sleep-producing —

> Where all the flowers go niddlety-nod,
> Nod, nod, niddlety-nod!
> Where all the flowers go niddlety-nod,
> And all the birds sing by-low!
> Lullaby, lullaby, by-low.

3. The colorful and astounding tales that are told. Mrs. Richards with mock candor anticipates the realist who demands facts, when she ends her remarkable pedigree of a kangaroo ("He and his Family") with these lines,

> You may think these things are strange,
> And they *are* a little change
> From the ordinary run, 'tis true.

It is this pretense of seriousness in a topsy-turvy world, much like Lewis Carroll's nonsense verse in the "Alice" books, which is so irresistibly funny.

4. The surprise or joke that quite often comes at the end of a poem. There is no misplaced sentiment, folly brings its due reward, the adventurer does not always come safely home, and the practical joker is paid in his own coin. The elephant inadvertently steps on the silly chicks ("The Three Little Chickens"); five little monkeys taunt the crocodile once too often ("The Monkeys and the Crocodile"); "Belinda Blonde," a doll, is handled severely when the annoyed Jack-in-the-Box yields to her pleading and jumps out.

Good nonsense verse is enjoyed by many children who have not developed a taste for the higher ranges of poetry, and it may serve to stimulate a taste for metrical composition. A considerable number of the poems in *Tirra Lirra* are better adapted to upper primary and elementary grades than to the youngest children, and the new title removes the odium which older readers would attach to *In My Nursery*. Like all the best nonsense literature Mrs. Richards's verse is for the entire family.

FRANK DEMPSTER SHERMAN

> In Nature's open book
> An epic is the sea;
> A lyric is the brook;
> Lyrics for me!
>
> F. D. SHERMAN

In his Introduction to Mr. Sherman's *Poems*,[1] Clinton

---

[1] Sherman, Frank Dempster, *Poems*. Introduction by Clinton Scollare Houghton Mifflin Company, 1917.

Scollard quotes the above stanza, with the following comment: "Early to recognize his limitations, it was thus that he proclaimed his credo." Sherman realized that his gift as a writer lay almost entirely in the field of lyric poetry, and in harmony with this he drew his inspiration and his subjects very largely from nature experience. In this vein he wrote many very melodious and charming poems for both adults and children, for he had the poet's vision which enabled him to see beauty and meaning in the world about him, and an intuitive taste in selecting the right form in which to convey these feelings and impressions. He is never guilty of exaggeration, never uses startling or overdrawn imagery, and yet his lyrics are characterized by remarkable freshness of observation. Some of his small word-pictures are as clear and perfect as the finely executed and artistic drawings for which Mr. Sherman was noted; for he was a graduate from the School of Architecture and was, at the time of his death in 1916, Professor of Graphics at Columbia University.

Frank Dempster Sherman was born at Peekskill, New York, in 1860, the oldest of nine children. His family is an old one on both sides, and he had every opportunity for broad culture and self-development. In spite of ill health, therefore, Mr. Sherman was able fully to realize his ambitions in the two lines of greatest interest to him, literature and architecture.

No other poet writing for children has dwelt so exclusively on nature experience. Celia Thaxter might be thought of in this connection, but she wrote on other subjects more often than Sherman and her nature subjects were much narrower in range. He takes young readers out with him to look up at clouds and stars, to peep into hedgerows and gardens, to listen to birds, and wind, and tinkling brook. He watches the seasons come and go and seizes upon certain aspects of the attendant phenomena which he elaborates in childlike manner; and the processional of the months in their order is celebrated with appropriate incident and symbol.

In a poem introductory to *Little-Folk Lyrics*, the poet pays a tribute to his mother, recalling the bedtime tales of Fairyland which she told him and the interest in all beautiful natural objects which she awakened in his childish mind:

> For me she made the world anew, —
> A jewel of each drop of dew;
> The autumn leaves of golden tint
> Were coins come freshly from the mint;
> The birds were poets all, who sang;
> The flowers were bells the fairies rang;
> And everything I saw became
> Another, with another name.[1]

The first edition of this collection (1892) contained fifty-four short poems of which only three or four could be classed as other than Nature poems. With few exceptions, those in which people appear contain also some pronounced nature reference. Because of this subordination of human activity, it follows that Mr. Sherman's poetry, charming as much of it is, will not be fully enjoyed by all children. Those who are innately sensitive to beauty and wonder, and those who have enjoyed at home or at school the inspiring companionship of a nature-lover such as the poet's mother evidently was, will find an added enjoyment in many of the poems in this collection. Now that nature experience is being made more commonly available to children, with provision for their non-technical participation, poetry such as Sherman's plays an important part as both an awakener of, and an outlet for, thought and feeling.

[1] Sherman, F. D., *Little-Folk Lyrics*. Houghton Mifflin Company, 1892.

Children sometimes express themselves quite spontaneously somewhat as Mr. Sherman does in some of his lines, but, of course, in a much more fragmentary and less polished way. This is just another way of stating that his language and imagery are for the most part extremely simple and childlike:

Cherries are like "lanterns by the pixies hung"; goldenrod's "torches flare like lighted street-lamps"; winter's trees "with branches bare, like beggars shiver in the air"; snow-crystals are "ghosts of the flowers that died"; clusters of white fruit blossoms are "like tufts of snow, that had forgotten when to go"; in the cheerful sound of "the logwood fire, we may hear the wood-elves choir"; and in the reference to the tiny tracks of the snowbird, notice the fresh and charming conception;

> But happiest is he, I know
>   Because no cage with bars
> Keeps him from walking on the snow
>   And printing it with stars.

Almost every page of *Little-Folk Lyrics* offers imagery as lovely and childlike as the examples given, and there is a perfect unity about many of the poems that gives them a gemlike quality. There is no great variety in verse patterns, but subject and mood do not call for great variety. A few additional poems which appear in a later edition (1897) are narrative in character or strike out into the short-line impressionistic style found in "Humming-Bird Song," but the major part of Sherman's contribution to child poetry is found in the first edition of the *Lyrics*, the contents of which were repeated, I believe, in all later editions.

Because nature is relatively changeless, the experiences pictured are familiar in northern and temperate climates and there is little to go out of style. There is one fascinating sight, however, which probably many children living in the dry heated atmosphere of the modern house have never seen, and what a loss to them! It has been years since I saw a really fine display of frost etchings on the window-pane. One of Sherman's most perfect evocations is of "Wizard Frost" and his exquisite pictures

> ... on a space
> Scarcely larger than the hand,
> Of a tiny Switzerland.

Another poem for older children is a perfect example of the type which makes use of scientific facts but clothes them in beauty and refrains from elaboration. It is called "Pebbles." It would be difficult to find another twenty short lines of verse which tell so vast a tale with such complete economy of words and such clarity. The words are beautifully chosen and not one is wasted. This poem in rhymed couplets is one which commits itself to memory on the part of children who have the necessary background. It illustrates also that device used so effectively by poets of today — the enumeration of a succession of colorful and arresting names:

> Ruby red and sapphire blue,
> Emerald and onyx too,
> Diamond and amethyst —
> Not a precious stone I missed:
> Gems I held from every land
> In the hollow of my hand.

We are all thankful for the many excellent anthologies of verse which we now have; but Sherman is usually not adequately represented — few poets are, or can be. The titles most frequently included are "Daisies," "Clouds," "The Four Winds," and "A Dewdrop," all well chosen from among those best suited to the younger children, but some of the selections mentioned above are much enjoyed by children of nine or ten years.

Mr. Sherman's own special vocation is well expressed in his poem for adults called "The Poet":

> Voice of the wind, of singing brook and bird,
> Dawn's message white and midnight's word,
> These secrets all belong
> Unto his song.[1]

In the closing lines of the Introduction cited above, Mr. Scollard makes a prediction with which many other admirers are in accord:

> When more ambitious verse has been forgotten, it would not be surprising if some of Mr. Sherman's exquisite lyrics would hold their place in the thought and memory of our children's children.

WALTER DE LA MARE

With the turn of the century, there entered the most important figure who has so far appeared among writers of poetry for children, for in 1901 Walter de la Mare published *Songs of Childhood*, his first collection of poems in a field in which he has since become so famous. This little book was followed in 1912 with *A Child's Day*. *Peacock Pie*, his best-known collection, came out in 1913; and the last to date bears the inviting title, *Down-a-Down Derry: A Book of Fairy Poems*, published in 1922. These books represent a large amount of poetry of a very high order, of great originality and variety, and written by a poet who occupies an assured position among leading English writers. No other poet of equal rank has created so much beauty and delight for children. Mr. de la Mare seems also to have opened the gateway for a stream of lovely verse by other writers of imagination, so that the twentieth century is witnessing a remarkable richness of production in poetry for young readers, by English and American writers.

[1] *Poems*, p. 217.

Walter de la Mare was born in Kent, England, in 1873. The family name is that of French Huguenot ancestors, Jean Baptiste Delamare being the first of the line in England, according to R. L. Mégroz.[1] On his mother's side he is of English and Scotch extraction. He was educated at Saint Paul's Cathedral School, but when only seventeen years old circumstances required that he leave school and go to work. He accepted a position with the English branch of the Standard Oil Company, where he remained for eighteen years, most of the time in the department of statistics. During these years he wrote many lovely poems for children, made a beginning in prose romance, and produced a collection of poetry for adults, all of which showed either rare promise or a finished art. To those who know Mr. de la Mare only through his delicately imaginative writing, there seems the same incongruity between exacting office work and his literary endeavors that appears in the case of Lewis Carroll in his capacity as teacher of mathematics and creator of the "Alice" books. De la Mare's creative work, however, has gone on to the accompaniment of a normal and many-sided life. His wife was a Miss Ingpen, of a family well represented in English letters, and there were several children growing up during the earlier years of Mr. de la Mare's career as a writer. Since 1908 he has devoted most of his time to writing. Evidently he possessed from the beginning that trait which marks so many of his fictitious characters — the ability to withdraw into the world of the imagination and there become a "listener" to the voices which whisper in old gardens, deserted houses, and other places of mystery.

It is evident that this writer knows children intimately and well. No other poet has shown such insight into the

[1] Mégroz, R. L., *Walter de la Mare: A Biographical and Critical Study.* Doran, 1924.

fleeting moods and deep-lying roots of child nature. He loves and respects them and recognizes both unique and universal traits, elfish, domestic, and those which spring from their unconscious relation to a super-world. Undoubtedly as a young father, Mr. de la Mare wove into his writing, experiences with his own children and made them his audience, but he does not exhibit them. There are two poems which tell very tenderly of events in family life. The first, called "The Birthnight: To F.," is for adults; the second, called "The Christening," in *Songs of Childhood*, is a sweet and moving picture of what might be called a family processional to the church, except that the term fails to express the simplicity of the observance.

Perhaps *A Child's Day* is a composite picture of all the little people who have been attended with affection and humor through the daily rites of bath, and buttons, and drinks at night. The whole is one of the most complete pictures of a small child ever put into verse. There is the greatest variety in this simple rhymed story of Elizabeth Ann which tells

> ... just what she did one long, long day,
> With her own little self to play with only,
> Yet never once felt the least bit lonely.[1]

I do not know of another poem which approaches this one as an example of simple everyday experience told with exquisite grace and beauty and with an entire absence of sentimentality. If it were possible ever to capture the secret of Mr. de la Mare's magic, it might be done by watching him with this little girl. Just *how* does he make such simple everyday things as waking, bathing, brushing the teeth, dressing, and all the rest of the daily round, seem

[1] From Walter de la Mare, *A Child's Day*, 1923. By permission of Henry Holt and Company, publishers.

so interesting and charming? There is no fanciful dis-
guising of these acts, no coaxing, no make-believe. The
adult reader, fascinated by the sheer beauty and delight
of the poem, may at the same time pry a bit into the art
that conceals art.

Quiet humor pervades the poem. Ann's bathing is
compared to that of certain animals —

> Seal and Walrus
> And Polar Bear
> One green icy
> Wash-tub share.

And the drying process —

> As for the plump Hippopotamus
> He steams himself dry to save a fuss.

At intervals the narrative concerning Ann is broken off to
tell how the Queen of Arabia, Uanjinee, is attired; or how
"The King in slumber when he lies down, Hangs up in a
cupboard his golden crown." This kind of fun is sprinkled
all through the book.

The poet's skill in verbal harmony and most of his
metrical arts are employed — musical words and phrases,
varied rhythms, pleasing rhymes close together, poetic
imagery which tends to create atmosphere, and arresting
contrasts. There are several sections of unusual beauty
which could be temporarily taken out of the whole for
special enjoyment. Among these are the "waking"
passage beginning "Softly, drowsily, Out of sleep"; the
distant music which the child hears in the garden —
"Happy, happy it is to be, Where the greenwood hangs
o'er the dark blue sea"; and the dream pictures she sees
before the fire when the Dustman comes. This passage
constitutes one of the loveliest poems for children that
has ever been written, yet it is simple enough for a six-
year-old. In miniature, it is a perfect example of that

fusion of theme, mood, and poetic form which all great poetry achieves.

At the end, poor old Lob-Lie-by-the-Fire gets his just dues at De la Mare's hands, and what more could pook, fairy, or witch desire! Every child should have a chance to know this household drudge with the novel and gracious touch added to his traditional character, for Lob guards Elizabeth Ann as she sleeps:

> Who would think, now, a throat
> So lank and so thin
> Might make birds seem to warble.
> In the dream she is in! [1]

Quite young children who take delight in recognizing themselves and their doings in stories of other children, enjoy many parts of this book, while there are other parts which appeal strongly to the imagination of boys and girls (especially the latter) when they are nine or ten years old.

A Child's Day is by no means the only poem which deals in a more or less idealized way with everyday affairs. Because Mr. de la Mare writes supremely well of fairies, woodland spirits, and wistful little wraiths, his accomplishments in subjects which lie on the hither side of the spirit world have sometimes been overlooked or underestimated. One of his characters, old Susan, is so "rooted in Romance" that she can give only a fleeting "glance into reality," but the poet himself, for all his seeming absorption with a world of dreams and shadows, does much more than glance into the warm and vivid life about him. Just as he produced a number of finely etched portraits in verse for grown-ups, so in his verse for children he has created quite a group of child characters and picturesque adults.

The delineation of children ranges from the strong out .

[1] From Walter de la Mare, *A Child's Day*, 1923. By permission of Henry Holt and Company, publishers.

lines of the rebellious "Dunce," who defies his small world, and the equally rebellious but eager boy in "The Bookworm," to the tiny thumb-nail sketches of three children in "Bunches of Grapes."[1] In the latter, the children have a chance to make several choices and each time Jane is seen planted firmly and sweetly among the plain homely things of life:

> "Chariots of gold," says Timothy;
> "Silvery wings," says Elaine;
> "A bumpity ride in a waggon of hay
> For me," says Jane.

Events dwindle or enlarge in importance according to a child's perspective, and it is from that viewpoint that De la Mare tells of the little girl's naïve appeal for help in finding her lost dog ("The Bandog"); the mild excitement of a visit to the barber ("The Barber's"); the futile resistance of "Poor Henry" to a nauseous dose; the possessive attitude of the child toward the "little cupboard with a teeny, tiny key" ("The Cupboard"); and the fascination of watching Bess feed the chickens — "Dorking, Spaniard, Cochin China, Bantams sleek and small" ("Chicken").

The younger children are fond of these objective poems. De la Mare's greatest gift, however, is displayed in the realm of fairyland or on its mysterious borders, and here there are selections which appeal to a wide range as regards taste and maturity. It is interesting to note that poems of wonder for children are shaped with the same delicate sensitiveness and depend upon the same kind of suggestion as the much-admired groups for mature readers called "The Listeners" and "Motley."[2] For example, the feeling attendant upon the experience of straying into an old deserted garden as presented in the child poem "The Little Old Cupid," and in one called "The Sunken

[1] In *Collected Poems,* volume II, page 11.   [2] *Ibid.,* volume I.

Garden," is the same in quality, though not in intensity; and something of the pervading mystery of "The Listeners" is felt in the child poems "The Old Stone House" and "The Little Green Orchard":

> Someone is always sitting there,
>   In the little green orchard.

But the children in these poems find nothing terrifying in the spirits which brood in orchards and old gardens or peer from the windows of deserted houses. The children brood, too, serene and happy, but they move on tiptoe and with finger on lip —

> Not that I am afraid of being there,
>   In the little green orchard.

Even ghosts, although they are made to seem veritable wraiths of former inhabitants of houses, are not fearsome objects. They may indeed bring comfort. In "The Phantom" a little girl is asked by her grannie to lay down her story-book, take a taper, and go on an errand to the attic of the rambling old house. There she dimly sees another child as solitary as herself, and listens to her sweet song. The errand accomplished, she returns to the firelit room, where

> Seated upon her tapestry stool,
>   Her fairy book laid by,
> She gazes into the fire, knowing
>   She has sweet company.

Quite often characters in these poems find themselves, as in "The Pilgrim," "alone, and yet not solitary."

Fairies as depicted by De la Mare are never little airy sprites wearing ballet skirts and carrying wands. "Berries" shows the plain fairy of the hills who knows all the hedgerows and lanes where berries grow thickest and is generous with kindly human neighbors. This is one of his most delightful poems. "Melmillo" is as melodious as the title and shows a true wood-spirit in possession of the woodland, all her birds folded to rest —

> In the wood — thorn, elder, willow —
> Danced alone — lone danced Melmillo.

There are rustic, puckish spirits too, in this world of imagination, creatures which hark back to ancient country-side tradition; and these are often very amusing and some-times startling in their strange, wanton behavior.

Laughter and fun ripple and sparkle in many poems, often as an accompaniment to magic so daring and so assured that the most fantastic events seem as convinc-ing as attested facts. Did those "three jolly gentlemen" ride their horses up to bed? Assuredly. Otherwise how could they come "clitter-clatter" down again? And that other three, the farmers who entered a dance marathon in "Off the Ground" — they were seen in broad daylight as they passed the schoolroom window, and skipped by "seven fine old churches and five old mills." Testimony in phrases as crisp as the fish himself in "Alas, Alack!" must convince us that he really did speak, especially when Heath Robinson pictures his eloquent posture in the frying-pan, and the little maid's shocked expression.

Animals have only a small place in De la Mare's poems, but there is one which has achieved a real personality, a self so completely realized that the creature must have been evoked out of the poet's own boyhood. "Nicholas Nye," the forlorn old donkey, had "a wonderful gumption under his skin," and between him and the boy there passed "something much better than words."

There are a number of longer poems of magic and romance in *Songs of Childhood* — narratives, ballads, and songs, which are well suited to older children. Several of these are to be found in anthologies, but this book and *Peacock Pie* are in their completeness true literary treasures, and children ought to come as near as possible to personal ownership of them.

ROSE FYLEMAN

In addition to Miss Fyleman's natural gifts, certain phases of her life have contributed to her qualifications as a writer of verse and stories for children. She is a highly trained musician and was for some years a teacher of music. She also directed for a time the work in oral expression and interpretation of literature in her sister's school. This included training the children in natural and pleasing oral reading. In public lectures and published interviews Miss Fyleman has stated that these two lines of work with children (music and literature) not only served to acquaint her with their dispositions and needs but also inspired and helped to shape her own creative work for them. To her knowledge of music, she attributes much of her success as a writer of very melodious verse which moves with varied and satisfying rhythm.

According to published biographical data, Miss Fyleman was born in Nottingham, England, in 1877, and is now living in London. After studying music in Paris, Berlin, and London, followed by a brief career as a public singer, she turned her whole attention to writing. She was a frequent contributor to *Punch*, using the signature R. F., and in 1918 her first book of poems for children, *Fairies and Chimneys*, was published. Three other small volumes of verse followed in rapid succession, *The Fairy Green*, *The Fairy Flute*, and *Fairies and Friends*, the titles showing that fairies are "the burden of her song." This theme has earned for Miss Fyleman the affectionate and appropriate title, "Poet of the Fairies."

Among children of kindergarten and primary school years Miss Fyleman is probably the best-known living poet, not excepting A. A. Milne. As a real person she is better known than he to American children, since hundreds of them saw and heard her during her lecture tour in 1929 and again in 1930. They claimed her as theirs and felt deeply injured if lectures were scheduled for adults and no program was arranged for them. Some of the littlest ones seemed to expect her to be attended by a troop of fairies or at least to be able to summon them like a master of legerdemain.

Only a few of Miss Fyleman's poems possess the eery atmosphere, the sense of mystery and enchantment which De la Mare creates. For the most part her fairies mix rather openly in the affairs of modern life, urban as well as country and often in broad daylight; they slide down steeples, ride along with you on a London motor-bus, perch on roof and chimney pot, go a-marketing and do gymnastics on the foot-rail of a child's bed. This acceptance of the marvelous mixed up with the ordinary, accords with the make-believe play of children, a kind of self-created illusion which is sincere while it lasts but not so gripping as old folk tales or the poetry of deep enchantment. These poems sing and dance their way along in a gay and happy mood admirably adapted to young children.

> There are no wolves in England now, nor any grizzly bears;
> You could not meet them after dark upon the attic stairs.[1]

Besides the many simple and playful poems, Miss Fyleman has written a number of very lovely ones which touch a little more closely the roots of folk tradition. Among these are "Dunsley Glen," beginning, "There is no road to Dunsley Glen"; "Fairies in the Malverns," an old tradition re-created in happier mood; and "The Island," which tells of an enchanted island in a fairy lake. These are all in *The Rose Fyleman Fairy Book* (Doran), a

[1] From *The Fairy Green*, by Rose Fyleman. Copyright, 1923, by Doubleday, Doran and Company, Inc.

very representative collection of her poems. There is ample room within the full range of her verse, for children to make a real advance in the enjoyment and appreciation of poetry.

While Miss Fyleman is best known through her fairy poetry, she has written a good deal of verse which narrates actual child experience very happily and with clear insight. She knows children well, the things they like and the things they do not like, and she has the faculty of expressing these with originality and charm. All her collections include some such subjects.

A. A. MILNE

Mr. Milne's initials "A. A." are so familiar that the full name, Alan Alexander, looks odd in print. Easily accessible biographical notes state that he was born in Scotland in 1882 and was educated at Westminster School and Cambridge University. Like De la Mare and many other prominent authors, he wrote verses, stories, and sketches when just a schoolboy. It is evident that he gave promise along literary lines in early college days, but his later success as dramatist, novelist, and poet was attained only after persistent effort in the face of difficulties.

Journalistic work, begun upon leaving college, soon led to the position of assistant editor of *Punch*, a post he held until 1914. The World War carried Mr. Milne to the Western Front with the Royal Warwickshire regiment, and later, because of impaired health, he became signaling instructor at a military training camp in England. To the extent that he was able to engage in literary work at all during these years, his attention was given to the writing of plays, an art which, as all the world knows, he has continued to exercise with rare success. One does not always find such harmony of tone and spirit between the works of an author addressed to adults and those which he intends for children. Milne, the creator of plays which contain so much of ideality along with a true portrayal of character and motive — *Mr. Pim Passes By*, *The Dover Road*, *The Ivory Door*, and *Michael and Mary* — does not have to undergo any sharp reversal of mental and moral attitude in order to evoke the very spirit of fun and innocence in poems and stories for children. The gentle humor, the fine human feeling, and the faint air of enchantment which pervade most of his plays, find expression also in his portrayal of children in the domestic scene as well as in their own particular play-world.

After the war was over, Mr. Milne decided to devote all his time to independent writing. He had married Miss Dorothy de Sélincourt in 1913. They have one son who was a tiny boy at the time his father began to write the poems published in 1924 under the title *When We Were Very Young*, and he was of course their inspiration and subject. Seldom has a book of verse met with such instant and wide popularity as this first collection for and about children. When the second collection *Now We Are Six* was announced in 1927, it was thought that even so facile a writer as Mr. Milne would be unable to sustain the delightful humor, contagious rhythms, and appealing childish fancies and vagaries which had made the first book so irresistible to all ages. But it was soon seen that he had turned the trick again, and that the engaging Christopher Robin, who at the close of the first book had arrived at the dignity of "shoes with laces" and "knickers and a pair of braces," was only slightly more grown-up at the mature age of six. And "Pooh," his *alter ego* still "wants to do whatever I do" even to learning multiplication tables and "Pounds and ounces."

Never before had such bundles of merriment been dropped into the lap of childhood — merriment which

bubbles up out of the simplest experiences of young children and is kept on that plane, and yet is capable of arous-
ing something deeper than a smile from the more sophisticated.   Investigators desiring to know whether or not
children like Milne's poetry can spare themselves the time
and paraphernalia required for "scientific" testing.   There
are countless proofs that they do.   Christopher Robin, and
Pooh, and Piglet, and the rest of the thoroughly animate
though obviously fabricated menagerie, have been taken to
the hearts of an army of children on both sides of the Atlantic and they demand every line of prose and verse which
gives news of these friends.

It is a rare thing in literature for characters to *live* in the
minds of readers as these do.   This sense of reality results
from the author's acceptance of toys and make-believe,
playful superstition and magic, the tragedy of a lost mouse
or an escaped cricket, the presence of an imaginary playmate, and a hundred other remarkable characters, incidents, and situations, with all the seriousness of a child.
The spell is never broken by skeptical comment or patronizing assent.

There are numerous amusing and sparkling poems in
which Christopher Robin plays no part.   Mr. Milne's inventive genius has produced many delightful absurdities
which have such a way of fastening themselves in memory
that it seems safe to predict a long life for them.   No
writer in lighter vein has succeeded better than he in giving an air of plausibility to the most improbable tale.
The art is beyond analysis which enables him to make
children and grown-ups laugh at the absurd kings in "The
King's Breakfast" (*When We Were Very Young*) and
"King John's Christmas" (*Now We Are Six*), and yet
feel a bit sorry for them.   We should all be disappointed if
the poor neglected king in the first did not get at least "a
little butter for his bread," and if King John's plaintive

plea for "a big, red india-rubber ball" at Christmas were denied. Illusion of this kind is rendered perfect for children and works in at least a shadowy way for older readers.

Part of the delight which grown-ups find in Mr. Milne's verse for children lies in the charming revelation of the personality of one little boy, his ways and words, his quaint imaginings and doings. The child has been permitted to express himself with no intrusive interpretation of his transparent behavior, and the artist, E. H. Shepard, has drawn him with both realism and ideality in all the variety of natural childish movement and posture. In these pictures, graphic and verbal, each of us sees not only Christopher Robin, but some other child near to us who exhibits many of the same amusing and endearing traits.

Like all competent writers of light verse, Milne manufactures "funny" words and takes great liberties with others, especially when he wants to increase rhyme effects. This is the basis for most of the mirth in "The Three Foxes" with their sockses, shopses and copses, prizes and mince-pieses; and "At the Zoo" are to be seen animals more extraordinary than usual, such as "biffalo-buffalo-bisons," "badgers, bidgers and bodgers," as well as "that sort of a something called a wollaboo." Add to these features marked meter, pleasing emphasis by means of repetition, the spice of small jokes and surprises, and we have the bare enumeration of a few of Milne's more visible and audible resources. To speak specifically of his use of meter, it is observed that he uses swinging dactyls a good deal — "Christopher Robin goes hoppity, hoppity"; "What is the matter with Mary Jane?" Notice the same smooth flow of the long lines in "The Dormouse and the Doctor" in which the natural accent of its polysyllables fits perfectly into the dactylic foot — "Del-phin-e-ums (blue) and ge-ra-ni-ums (red)." The light tripping tro-

chee is used appropriately also, "I've got shoes with
grown-up laces"; and trochees and dactyls are happily
combined as in "Summer Afternoon." [1]

The features so far mentioned appear to be most
characteristic of Milne but a little search shows that he
writes some poems for children in a different vein. In the
two books mentioned one can find more than a dozen
which possess beauty of a different kind. These derive
their poetic quality from sources a little more remote from
the young child's everyday world of experience and feeling
and therefore the appeal is to the perceptions of somewhat
older children. We are leaving it to the interested student to identify some of these.

OTHER CONTEMPORARY POETS, AND FEATURES OF THEIR WORK

England and America have at present an unusual number
of writers who are producing poetry of considerable merit
for children. Their best work displays most of the
characteristics that have been found in the twentieth-cen-
tury poetry already discussed, although each offers something that is individual in style or subject. It will be noticed that several of these authors are prose writers of distinction as well as poets, and that women now seem to be
taking the lead in verse for children. The many-sidedness
of childhood is recognized by most of these writers and
their verse offers gateways to both quiet and merry play,
to the pictorial and sensuous side of nature, to an idealized but not sentimental presentation of a great variety of
everyday experiences of the modern world, and also to
scenes of beauty and delight in the realm of dream and
fancy. A few of these features stand out so prominently
that they call for especial notice.

[1] All the poems mentioned in this paragraph are in *When We Were Very
Young.* E. P. Dutton and Company, Inc., publishers.

THE FAIRIES RETURN

Chapter III recorded farewells to the fairies from English poets of the seventeenth century and later, who wrote in terms of regret at their departure from England. Exiled from that country, the fairies did not come to America, for Puritanism and the reign of Reason made them quite unwelcome here also. And now, after more than two hundred years, they have sprung up in the liveliest manner in both countries, transformed somewhat, it is true, but still exhibiting hereditary traits which prove their descent from the fairies of Shakespeare and Ben Jonson, with a faint outcropping here and there of a darker, cruder, and more ancient strain.

One of the most striking developments of children's literature is this return of fairy creatures in force, summoned by poets in the face of a large and vocal public which insists that children must have the Truth, that scientific facts, mechanical constructions, and verifiable human behavior constitute the most important and almost the only suitable subjects for literature designed for the modern child. In spite of this clamor, something within the heart of childhood and dormant in many grown-ups, has sprung up to reject this point of view every time a "practical" world has tried to impose it. Let a Walter de la Mare appear, followed by a Rose Fyleman and numerous other poets who write with equal beauty in a similar vein, and walls crumble and fairy troops trip back again.

Of course, fairy subjects never suffered a total eclipse. Great poets in every age have written about an imaginary world that touches the fringes of the real and have mingled the two in their writing. Christina Rossetti, as we have seen, Coleridge, Keats, and Tennyson created "forms more real than living man." [1] But for children, first-rate

[1] Shelley, Percy B., *Prometheus Unbound.*

poetry dealing with the fairy world was rare until the period of "renaissance" heralded by William Allingham (1824–1889) and fully ushered in by Walter de la Mare. Among other living authors who write for children and who sometimes succeed in capturing the true fairy spirit in their verse are Elizabeth Mackinstry, Rachel Field, Eleanor Farjeon, Winifred Welles, and Nancy Byrd Turner.

Miss Mackinstry's *Puck in Pasture* has the Celtic quality of mystery and magic and is suited to older readers.

Fairy poetry is not Rachel Field's most characteristic vein, but included in *Taxis and Toadstools* is a group called "Fringes of Fairyland" which contains several very pleasing poems dealing with elves and fairies. Two of these, "The Visitor" and "The Green Fiddler," are delightful narrative poems having authentic fairy quality.

Winifred Welles (Mrs. Harold A. Shearer) has written only a few fairy poems and most of these are woven out of a child's fanciful interpretation of experience, but there is one narrative poem in *Skipping Along Alone* called "Minim and the Two Mice" which pictures with delicate humor and poetic charm a surly gnome and his meek, solicitous, soft-spoken attendants — two little field mice.

SUBJECTS FROM EVERYDAY LIFE

Along with this revival of interest in the world of fancy, writers are giving ample attention to the real experiences of life and are drawing their subjects from events and objects which matter-of-fact adults might deem prosaic. Perhaps it is in this idealized portrayal of everyday life that contemporary writers are making their greatest contribution.

Rachel Field has been particularly successful in this *genre* and both of her collections contain numerous poems which present for the younger children brief colorful and sympathetic word pictures about "The Flower-Cart Man," "Taxis," "Skyscrapers," "The Cuckoo-Clock Shop," and many other people and objects belonging to the immediate environment, especially that of the city child.

The name of Dorothy Aldis presents itself in this connection. She has written many short poems for young children choosing quite commonly simple domestic scenes and events which she portrays with humor and charm. Her work is rather uneven as to literary quality but there is much which pleases the nursery group and arouses happy response from kindergarten children. Her two collections are called *Here, There and Everywhere*, and *Everything and Anything*.

Another prominent contributor is Elizabeth Madox Roberts whose collection *Under the Tree* attracted attention first as the work of so eminent a novelist, but which has met with sustained interest because of the unique quality of the poems. Her subjects are drawn as distinctly from very simple country life as Miss Field's are from the city. These poems reveal a writer keenly sensitive to the sights, sounds, odors, and tactual sensations associated with rural experiences. Some of these sensory impressions are very minute and circumstantial as registered in the memory of one very responsive child, but scarcely transferable to any considerable number of children. She employs most commonly a simple narrative form, making frequent use of the rhymed couplet. Among the most objective poems from the standpoint of early childhood are "The Rabbit," "The Hens," "The Woodpecker," and "Milking Time." More mature lovers of poetry find much that is delightful in this collection and are made more aware of nature's fine undertones.

In *Magpie Lane*, Nancy Byrd Turner treats the small

events of everyday life with childlike imagination. A number of her poems lie on the border-line between a world of fancy and one of actuality and the balance is sustained unusually well. In "Adventure," the little men of meadowland help a child to a near view of wild bunnies, and they are real bunnies who eat "lettuce green and crinkly, and munchy, crunchy tidbits." The poem "Magic" conveys a feeling of wonder regarding the garden on the other side of a suddenly revealed door. Light graceful touches and a musical form are given to such subjects as "Sweeping," "Lost Things," "Balloons," and "Wings and Wheels" (roller-skating). Many times Miss Turner achieves real poetic beauty in poems which are kept distinctly on the level of appreciation of children five to seven years of age.

John Drinkwater's *All About Me* is almost wholly concerned with the likes and dislikes, interests and activities of one little girl who is somewhat older than Milne's Christopher Robin and considerably more experienced and worldly wise.

Another English writer, E. V. Lucas, offers a pleasing collection of quite objective poems reflecting English scenes and portraying customs of other lands. This collection is called *Playtime and Company*. An added sense of reality is given to these subjects by Ernest H. Shepard's characteristic sketches.

THE USE OF IMAGERY AND FIGURATIVE LANGUAGE

Some students of the subject believe that figurative language and sensory images constitute a sort of decoration in poetry which interferes with its understanding and enjoyment. Undoubtedly poetry can be so overweighted with symbols as to be incomprehensible; also, the symbols or figures may be drawn from fields so far removed from experience as to be confusing instead of illuminating; or, they may be so exaggerated as to fail to carry a clear impression. How does modern verse for children rank in these respects?

The only way to answer this question without dogmatism is to direct the student to read widely, examine carefully, and try out with children whenever possible the poetry under discussion. I think it will be found that leading writers use figures of speech rather sparingly and that these are seldom exaggerated in character; and that they make a wide use of sensory images of a simple kind which appeal to the unjaded senses of the young and serve to shed a new light on experience. Winifred Welles is exceptional in the discreet use of almost every means to beautiful poetic effects, but every poet mentioned in this section furnishes excellent illustrations of the points discussed.

In two of her poems Nancy Byrd Turner expresses with truth and beauty the thought that children hear the sounds and see the pictures which are really for them. I refer to "The Bagpipe Man" and "Old Man Long Ago," from *Magpie Lane*. In the first, a child asks the strange player, "What do you play so queer, so queer?" And he replies, "What do you hear?" Then different children tell what they hear — a trumpet sweet, the tramp of marching feet, light steps of fairies, the song of a bird, a running river. The poem ends,

> But he never would tell us the name of his tune,
> The funny old bag-pipe man.[1]

In "Old Man Long Ago" a child sees at dusk a quaint old figure, so clearly described by the author that any child-artist could draw his picture. The child telling of the mysterious vision feels she may be doubted, and she adds,

---

[1] From *Magpie Lane*, by Nancy Byrd Turner. By permission of Harcourt, Brace and Company Inc., publishers.

Some see this and some see that,
As soon as shadows fall;
Some see little, and some see much,
And some see nothing at all.[1]

It is one of the offices of poetry, simply and artistically presented, to reduce the number of those "who see nothing at all." ⌐

In addition to the writers who are producing most extensively for children, many of the leading poets in England and America write an occasional poem which appeals to young readers. Every new anthology of merit includes representative selections from Amy Lowell, Sara Teasdale, and Vachel Lindsay of the recent past, and from such living authors as Robert Graves, Humbert Wolfe, Edith Sitwell, Robert Frost, Edna St. Vincent Millay, Christopher Morley, and Lizette Woodworth Reese. It is true now, as always, that choice literature written for no particular class or age often contains something for all but the youngest of the family or school.

SUGGESTED PROBLEMS AND TOPICS FOR FURTHER STUDY

1. Compare motives, attitudes, and actions of children in *Sing-Song* with those in the poems of Watts and of Ann and Jane Taylor, in such matters as: helping the unfortunate; kindness to animals; fun, play, work; relation to each other and to parents; faith and worship.

2. Is information conveyed in Miss Rossetti's verses? What substitute for an explicit moral is used? Try to show how some didactic writers might have treated "A Diamond or a Coal?" "O sailor, come ashore," "Dancing on the hilltops," or any other examples which suggest themselves.

3. Read *Goblin Market* for your own renewed delight, and to discover how the author achieved certain poetic effects.

4. Miss Repplier [2] calls attention to the inappropriateness of

---

[1] *Ibid.*

[2] Repplier, Agnes, "The Children's Poets," from *Essays in Idleness.* Houghton Mifflin Company.

"tramp, tramp, tramp" as descriptive of creeping shadows in Stevenson's "Shadow March." Is this a common defect in his poems? Find examples of exceptionally well-chosen expressions of sound, movement, atmosphere.

5. The little boy in *A Child's Garden of Verses* is said by critics to be a solitary and rather introspective child. Make a list of the types of activity in which he and other children in the book engage.

6. Which of Stevenson's poems do you consider most unchild-like?

7. Which of Laura Richards's poems remind most strongly of Mother Goose? Of Edward Lear? How successful was she in poems other than the nonsense type? Which of these in your opinion are the best? How does this New England mother and grandmother treat goblins, bogy-men and similar creatures in her poems for children?

8. Look for poems by A. A. Milne which have distinct beauty apart from any amusing or playful quality.

9. Among the types of healthy emotional appeal for children, are joy, love, wonder, sympathy, mirth, gaiety, and the sense of security — of being cherished. Find excellent examples of these in poetry for children.

10. Offer brief but choice examples of poetic imagery (figures of speech); clear sensory images; tonal beauty; unique ways of looking at common things; concepts calculated to stretch the vision a bit; the consonance of sound and meaning; and passages whose charm consists in the mere enumeration of names.

11. Supplementary to topic 10, make a study of references to sensations of touch and taste which are much less frequent in poetry than images of sight, sound, and smell. A child's violent reactions against rice pudding is the subject of more than one humorous poem. For your own pleasure, read if possible Louis Untermeyer's long poem for adults called *Food and Drink*. (Harcourt, 1932.) It is like a beautiful banquet in the perfection of its array of delectable food.

12. Study the effects of meter and stanza patterns in different authors.

13. Over a period of about one hundred and fifty years, seek for evidences of a growing use of words (real or invented) for the

purpose of conveying impressions of sound or movement. Examples: "And the vessel goes divie — divie — dive" (Stevenson); "Chickle, chackle, chee" (Thaxter); "A throstle piped 'I'm by, I'm by!'" (De la Mare).

14. Compare Rachel Field's fairy poem "The Green Fiddler' (*Taxis and Toadstools*), with Christina Rossetti's *Goblin Market*. See also De la Mare's "A Silver Penny" and, more striking still, "The Pedlar" (*Songs of Childhood*. Also in *Collected Poems*, volume II.).

15. Select about twenty-five of the best humorous poems suitable for children of seven years or younger, exclusive of all anonymous verse.

16. Try to find twelve or more short poems which lend themselves readily to representation by children in the form of improvised dance and rhythms, simple pantomime or tableaux, or spontaneous dramatic action involving little or no speech. There is a wide scope here for artistic and happy interpretation on the part of children who are not ready for much oral expression. The brevity of most poems is a further asset in lower primary grades.

17. Make a collection of modern fairy poetry for children. Seek especially those poems which best accord with the spirit and nature of traditional fairies, their mystery and magic.

18. Make a collection of modern narrative poems — poems which tell a story pleasing to children.

19. Trace the gradual development of nature poetry for children beginning with Watts.

20. Make a collection of poems on quite modern themes and experiences — city sights and sounds, travel, trade, machinery, etc. Be especially alert as to literary quality. The little girl in "The Green Singing Book"[1] suggests the spirit of such themes:

> I sing about the City, too
>   The noises and the wheels;
> The Windows blinking in the sun; —
>   I sing the way it feels.

---

[1] Peabody, Josephine Preston. *The Book of the Little Past*. Houghton Mifflin Company.

BIBLIOGRAPHY

For Adults

The Art and the Craft of Poetry

These references all deal in some measure with the theory and techniques of poetry and the authors have definitely directed their discussion toward enlarging the understanding and quickening the appreciation of readers. The star (*) marks a few references especially serviceable to more advanced students of poetry.

Abbott, Allan. "The Imaginative Element in Poetry." *Teachers College Record*, October, 1926.

Abbott, Allan. "Rhythm in Poetry." *Teachers College Record*, March, 1927.
    The thoughtful reading of these two articles should deepen one's appreciation of poetry and help teachers to avoid some of the pitfalls awaiting those who attempt to teach it.

Abercrombie, Lascelles. *Poetry; Its Music and Meaning.* Oxford University, 1932.
    A small book, only 64 pages — simple but scholarly.

Auslander, Joseph, and Hill, Frank Ernest. *The Winged Horse.* The Story of the Poets and Their Poetry. Doubleday, 1927.
    Inspiring and informing. Calculated to send readers straight to the great poets of all time for a closer acquaintance.

Deutsch, Babette. *Potable Gold.* Some Notes on Poetry and This Age. Norton, 1929.
    Stimulating and original. Chapter III, "Poetry and the Machine."

Dickinson, Edward. *The Education of a Music Lover.* Scribner.
    Chapters VII and IX deal with poetry in relation to music.

*Downey, June E. *Creative Imagination.* Harcourt, 1929.
    Penetrates deeply into origins and processes of the creative act.

Drew, Elizabeth. *Discovering Poetry.* Norton, 1933.
    "... an effort to try to discover in what poetic genius consists and in what ways we may best train ourselves to recognize and to enjoy it."

Eastman, Max. *The Enjoyment of Poetry*. Scribner, 1914–1926.
  Opens up and deepens many channels toward enjoyment of poetry.

*Gummere, Francis B. *The Beginnings of Poetry*. Macmillan, 1901.
  A basic study of origins of forms and modes. Chapter II, "Rhythm as the Essential Fact of Poetry."

*Parkhurst, Helen Huss. *An Interpretation of Art and the Imaginative Life*. Harcourt, 1930.
  This book breaks new ground and enriches old in the field of creative art. Chapter III, "Sensuous Qualities of the World." Chapter VII, "Prose and Poetry."

Pritchard, F. H. *Training in Literary Appreciation*. Crowell, 1924.
  Chapter III, "Rhythm." Chapter IV, "Change and Recurrence."

Stedman, Edmund C. *The Nature and Elements of Poetry*. Houghton, 1892.
  Chapter II, "What Is Poetry?"

Strong, L. A. G. *Common Sense About Poetry*. Knopf, 1932.
  Treats in a simple and readable style of some technicalities of verse forms.

Untermeyer, Louis. *The Forms of Poetry; a Pocket Dictionary of Verse*. Harcourt, 1926.
  A very useful handbook.

*Wilkinson, Marguerite. *The Way of the Makers*. Macmillan, 1925.
  The author lets the poets speak for themselves through quoted passages which tell "how they feel, think, live, and labor."

Young, C. C., and Gayley, C. M. *Principles and Progress of English Poetry*. Macmillan, 1922.
  Introduction excellent on rhythm.

Recent Biography

Brenner, Rica. *Ten Modern Poets*. Harcourt, 1930.
  Very interesting sketches of contemporary poets several of whom have written some verse for young readers.

Mégroz, R. L. *Walter de la Mare*. A Biographical and Critical Study. Doran, 1924.

The best single reference regarding the life and work of a poet who has contributed more than any other living writer to poetry for children.

Stuart, Dorothy M. *Christina Rossetti*. ("English Men of Letters Series.") Macmillan, 1930.

Published in the centenary year of Christina Rossetti's birth. The most important events of her life are set forth, together with a discerning and sympathetic estimate of her place in English poetry.

For other sources of biographical material on earlier as well as contemporary writers see Bibliography.

Suggestion and Criticism

Especially helpful to those who attempt to mediate in any way between children and true poetry.

Barnes, Walter. *The Children's Poets*. World Book Company, 1924.

A very useful text in the study of poetry for children.

Conkling, Grace Hazard. "Children and Poetry," *The Bookman*, November, 1922.

Mrs. Conkling offers some inspiring ideas as a substitute for pedantry.

Conkling, Grace Hazard. *Imagination and Children's Reading*. Hampshire Bookshop, Northampton, Mass., 1922.

A small booklet by a writer who is qualified in every way to discuss children and imaginative literature. An excellent antidote for an attitude of condescension toward children.

Hartman, Gertrude, and Shumaker, Ann, Ed. *Creative Expression*. Edited for The Progressive Education Association. John Day, 1932.

Contributions from a number of writers on the creative aspects of English. One section of this book is a reprint of "Creative Expression through Literature" which constituted one quarterly number of the *Progressive Education Journal*, volume V, no. 1, 1928.

Lamborn, E. A. Greening. *The Rudiments of Criticism*. Clarendon Press, 1917.

Lowell, Amy. Introduction to *Poems of a Little Girl*, by Hilda Conkling. Stokes, 1920.

Lowell, Amy. "Poetry, Imagination and Education," *North American Review*, volume 206, p. 762.

Mearns, Hughes. *Creative Youth.* Doubleday, 1925.
How one school broke away from the formal approach to poetry. Deals chiefly with upper grades and high school and has proved helpful at all levels.

Wheeler, Jean. "Poetry for Children," *Childhood Education*, January, 1930.
A sincere account of the work of one teacher with young children.

Wilkinson, Marguerite. *New Voices.* Macmillan, 1919.
Contains a section called "Children and Poetry."

Wilkinson, Marguerite. "Poetry for Children," *Children*, January 1928.
It is interesting to note that three poets, Miss Wilkinson, Mrs. Conkling and Miss Lowell have a deep understanding of both poetry and children.

A Few of the Earlier Poets

In editions which are of greater interest to adults than to children.

Blake, William. *Songs of Innocence.* Minton.
A facsimile reproduction of the first edition made by hand by Blake and his wife in 1789. Copied from the original in the British Museum.

Rossetti, Christina. *Sing-Song: A Nursery Rhyme Book.* Illustrated by Arthur Hughes. London, Macmillan, 1871.
This is the complete original edition with illustrations which Miss Rossetti liked very much.

Taylor, Ann and Jane. *The Original Poems and Others*, by Ann and Jane Taylor and Adelaide O'Keefe. Ed. by E. V. Lucas. Illustrations by F. D. Bedford. Stokes.
This is the centenary edition and is a beautiful book, but is placed in this group because only the rare child today will care for many of the poems. There is an interesting introduction by Mr. Lucas.

Watts, Isaac. *Divine and Moral Songs.* Page.

Anthologies for the Use of Adults with Children

Gosset, Adelaide L. J., compiler and editor. *Lullabies of the Four Nations.* London, De la More Press.
The four nations are England, Wales, Ireland, and Scot-

land. An unusual collection which includes some rare and charming renderings from the Welsh and Gaelic.

Hubbard, Alice, and Babbitt, Adeline. *The Golden Flute: An Anthology of Poetry for Young Children*. Day.

A large and very inclusive collection of verse for children of nursery age and through early primary years. The compilers have drawn not only from well-known authors but have included many selections from current periodical literature, and from traditional and anonymous sources. One good feature is the large number of short poems.

BOOKS DESIGNED FOR THE USE AND DELIGHT OF CHILDREN
Attractive New Editions of Poetry by a Few Early Writers

Allingham, William. *Robin Redbreast and Other Verses*. Pictures as in the original edition, by Helen Allingham, Kate Greenaway and other artists. (The Little Library.) Macmillan.

A happy restoration of a charming book which children love.

Blake, William. *Songs of Innocence*. Illustrated by Jacynth Parsons. Prefatory letter by W. B. Yeats. Medici Society of America, 1927.

The English artist was only sixteen years old when she painted her exquisitely beautiful pictures for this book. Lambs and babes in her pictures are so young, so innocent! Were pictured lambs ever so fleecy (not woolly) as these? There are nineteen poems, very well chosen for children.

Blake, William. *The Land of Dreams*. Twenty poems by William Blake selected and illustrated by Pamela Bianco. Macmillan, 1928.

Another young, sensitive and highly gifted artist illustrated this beautiful book. She also chose the poems, twenty in number, most of them from *Songs of Innocence*. There is an other-worldly touch throughout the book which is very fitting.

Taylor, Jane and Ann. *Meddlesome Matty*. Illustrated by Wyndham Payne. With an introduction by Edith Sitwell. Viking.

The title is that of one of the best known of these old moral poems chosen from *Original Poems for Infant Minds*.

Children of today are likely to be amused rather than awed by the fate which befell young culprits a century and more ago.

Some Modern "Cautionary" Verse

These rhymes and pictures are certain to amuse children, and by their gay exaggeration they *may* serve the deep-laid scheme of grown-ups to discourage certain infantile tendencies.

Belloc, Hilaire. *The Bad Child's Book of Beasts*. Knopf.

Belloc, Hilaire. *New Cautionary Tales*. Harper.
Burlesques on the dismal fate which once overtook naughty children.

Burgess, Gelett. *Goops and How to Be Them*. Stokes.

Burgess, Gelett. *More Goops and How Not to Be Them*. Stokes.
Clever rhymes and absurd pictures continue to delight children.

Pyle, Katharine. *Careless Jane and Other Tales*. Dutton.
Verses and pictures according to the old formula for naughty children.

Anthologies

With few exceptions these books appeal to children in form as well as content.

Barrows, Marjorie, compiler. *One Hundred Best Poems*. Whitman.
This small volume which has sold at ten cents is a real gift to childhood, for it is as remarkable for the excellence of its contents as for its price.

De la Mare, Walter, compiler. *Tom Tiddler's Ground*. Illustrated by Joan Souter-Robertson. London, Collins.
The range of selections is very wide — from *Mother Goose* to *The Ancient Mariner*. The introduction and notes by Mr. de la Mare are addressed to young readers. A beautiful old-fashioned-looking book.

De la Mare, Walter, editor. *Come Hither*. A collection of Rhymes and Poems for the Young of All Ages. Woodcuts by Alec Buckels. Knopf.
The sub-title well describes this unusual book. While there is not a great deal in it which appeals directly to younger children, it is a treasure to poetry lovers and espe-

cially to those who are trying to foster a love of poetry in others.

Harrington, Mildred, compiler. *Ring-a-Round*. A Collection of Verse for Boys and Girls. Illustrated by Corydon Bell. Macmillan.

A superior collection for younger children and a book which appeals strongly to them in every way.

Hutchinson, Veronica S., compiler. *Chimney Corner Poems*. Illustrated by Lois Lenski. Minton.

An excellent collection well designed for younger children.

Hutchinson, Veronica S., compiler. *Fireside Poems*. Illustrated by Lois Lenski. Minton.

A second collection by Miss Hutchinson, for somewhat older children. Her two books offer a variety of choice selections in attractive form well suited to children from the nursery stage to middle elementary school years.

Hill, Wentworth, and Wood, H. G. *The Land of Poetry*. A Series of complete Anthologies of English Verse for young readers. Books I, II, and III. London, Nesbit.

These very inexpensive books in flexible covers contain well graded selections, old and new, chosen with taste and understanding.

Huber, Bruner and Curry. *The Poetry Book*. In 9 vols. Rand.

Books I, II, and III are suited to kindergarten and primary grades. Excellent material, old and new, is found in this graded series.

Owen, Dora, editor. *The Book of Fairy Poetry*. Illustrations by Warwick Goble. Longmans.

Contains much of the choicest poetry in this field but not a great deal for children below eight or nine years of age.

Stokes, Anne. *The Open Door to Poetry*. Scribner.

A very choice collection which includes many poems not found in other anthologies. It is truly an "Open Door" to children passing out of early childhood.

Thacher, Lucy W., compiler. *The Listening Child*. Illustrated by Nancy Barnhart. Macmillan.

A new edition of this favorite old collection with an added section of modern verse chosen by Marguerite Wilkinson. The range of appeal as regards maturity of readers is rather wide.

Thompson, Blanche J., compiler. *Silver Pennies*. (The Little Library.) Macmillan.

   A small book, and a great favorite with children of elementary school age. Part I is for the younger ones.

Untermeyer, Louis, compiler. *This Singing World.* For Younger Children. Illustrated by Clara M. Burd and Decie Merwin. (Junior edition.) Harcourt.

   A choice collection of modern poetry by an accomplished anthologist and poet. Primary teachers should remember that the term "younger" is a relative one. Mr. Untermeyer uses it to distinguish this book from an earlier edition having the sub-title *Modern Poetry for Young People*. The selections appeal to pre-adolescents with a generous number for children in the lower grades. Children, teachers and others will discover much that is fresh and beautiful.

Wiggin, Kate Douglas, and Smith, Nora Archibald, compilers. *Pinafore Palace*: A Book of Rhymes for the Nursery. Doubleday, 1907.

   Mother Goose, and other nursery rhymes, riddles, games, and lullabies — for the youngest.

Wiggin, Kate Douglas, and Smith, Nora Archibald, compilers. *Posy Ring:* A Book of Verse for Children. Houghton, 1903.

   Excellent selections from earlier writers, for children beyond lower primary grades. These two books are old, but in the matter of discriminating selection they have not been surpassed.

Christmas Verse

Carnegie Library School Association, compiler,
   Christmas in Poetry. First Series.
   Christmas in Poetry. Second Series.
   (Paper covers.) New York, Wilson.
      Old Christmas carols and poems for all ages.

Farjeon, Eleanor. *Come Christmas.* Decorations by Rachel Field. Stokes.

   Christmas poems, carols, and sketches of Christmas customs.

Hyett, Florence B., compiler. *Fifty Christmas Poems for Children.* Appleton.

   Only seven of these poems are traditional and anonymous — the others are by recognized poets.

Individual Poets

It is futile to attempt to define a narrow age level for the enjoyment of poetry. Books in this list are in the main well-suited to children under ten years of age. Those which appeal especially to the five- and six-year-olds are marked with a star (*).

Aldis, Dorothy.
  Everything and Anything. Minton.
  Here, There and Everywhere. Minton.
    Short poems for young children about everyday affairs, domestic and personal.

Conkling, Hilda. *Silverhorn*. Illustrated by Dorothy Lathrop. Stokes.
    Selections from two volumes of poems written when the author was a little girl. This collection is especially intended for children.

De la Mare, Walter.
  A Child's Day. Holt.
  Peacock Pie. Holt.
  Songs of Childhood. Longmans.
    Fully reviewed above. *Peacock Pie* is the most satisfactory single collection.

Drinkwater, John.
  All about Me: Poems for a Child. Houghton.
  More about Me: Pictures by H. M. Brock. Houghton.
    Described above.

Farjeon, Eleanor. *Joan's Door*. Illustrated by Will Townsend. Stokes.
    This English writer draws her subjects from both city and country life. The nature poems in particular are fresh and original.

Field, Eugene. *Some Poems of Childhood*. Selected by Bertha E. Mahony. Illustrations by Gertrude A. Kay. Scribner.
    Excellent selections for a child's own book.

Field, Rachel.
  Taxis and Toadstools. Doubleday. Pictures by the author.
    Charming verses about both city and country experiences.
  The Pointed People. New edition. Macmillan. Silhouettes by the author.
    Experiences of an imaginative child among Maine's pointed firs find expression in genuine poetry.

Fyleman, Rose.
  Fairies and Chimneys. Doubleday.
      The first, and one of the most charming, of the English
      poet's many volumes of verse.
  Other titles are: *Fairies and Friends*, *The Fairy Flute*, *The
  Fairy Green*, all published by Doubleday.
  The Rose Fyleman Fairy Book. Illustrated by Hilda T. Miller.
  Doubleday.
      A very attractive book containing choice selections from
      the volumes listed above.
  Fifty-One New Nursery Rhymes. Illustrated by Dorothy
  Burroughs. Doubleday.
      Miss Fyleman's new departure in the field of nonsense
      rhymes is very successful. This large picture book should
      certainly be added to the "funny books" for little chil-
      dren.

Godley, Elizabeth. *Green Outside*. Decorations by Rex
  Whistler. Viking.
      A quaint and original little book. Pingo, the wee man of
      Pottle Woods, wrote clever verses on scraps of paper and
      stuck them around on thorn bushes. Miss Godley kindly
      collected them and put them into the form which Pingo
      dictated — at least that is his story.

Howard, Winifred. *Out of the Everywhere*. Oxford University
  Press. Illustrated by Elizabeth Montgomery.
      Suited to the imaginative and rather mature child. A
      few poems which younger children will like are "White
      Horses," "The Squirrels' Christmas," and "A Windy Day."

Lear, Edward.
  Nonsense Books. With all the Original Illustrations. Little.
  Lear's Nonsense Songs. Illustrated by Leslie Brooke. Warne.
      Fully discussed above.

Lucas, E. V. *Playtime and Company*. Illustrated by Ernest
  H. Shepard. Doran.
      Most of these poems deal with distinctly English experi-
      ences but one section is devoted to other lands and scenes.

Milne, A. A.
  When We Were Very Young. Dutton.
  Now We Are Six. Dutton.
      Illustrated by Ernest H. Shepard.
      Fully discussed above.

Peabody, Josephine Preston.   *The Book of the Little Past*.   Illustrated by Elizabeth Shippen Green.   Houghton.

A beautiful book, and one of the first collections to present small everyday events in a child's life through the medium of pleasing verse.

Richards, Laura.   *Tirra Lirra.   Rhymes Old and New*.   Foreword by May Lamberton Becker.   Little.

Fully discussed above.

Roberts, Elizabeth Madox.   *Under the Tree*.   Viking.   Enlarged edition illustrated by F. D. Bedford.

Discussed above.

Rossetti, Christina G.   *Sing-Song:* A Nursery Rhyme Book and Other Poems for Children.   Illustrated by Marguerite Davis.   (The Little Library.)   Macmillan.

A very attractive new edition of a much-loved book. Fully discussed above.

Sherman, Frank Dempster.   *Little Folk Lyrics*.   Illustrated by Genevieve Cowles.   Houghton.

Fully discussed above.

Stevenson, Robert Louis.   *A Child's Garden of Verses*.   Illustrated by Charles Robinson.   Scribner.

The same.   Illustrated by Jessie Willcox Smith.   Scribner.

The same.   Illustrated by Marguerite Davis.   Macmillan.

Fully discussed above.

Teasdale, Sara.   *Stars Tonight*.   Illustrated by Dorothy P. Lathrop.   Macmillan.

A small and very lovely book.   In the main beyond the grasp of the nine-year-old but they can enjoy the poetry of the pictures and a few selected stanzas.

Tippett, James S.

I Live in a City.   Harper.

I Go Travelling.   Harper.

Two small books in which little children find short rhythmical narratives of events which are novel or pleasantly familiar to them.

Turner, Nancy Byrd.

Magpie Lane.   Pictures by Decie Merwin.   Harcourt.

Discussed above.

Zodiac Town.   Illustrated by Winifred Bromhall.   Atlantic Monthly Press.

Charming gay little poems related in subject to each month of the year.

Welles, Winifred. *Skipping Along Alone*. Illustrations by Marguerite Davis. Macmillan.
  The black and white pictures are a perfect accompaniment to the melodious verse. Discussed above.

Wynne, Annette. **For Days and Days*. Stokes.
  While Miss Wynne's pleasing little poems take the children around the year in days and seasons, a variety of other experiences are recorded for their enjoyment.

CHAPTER XI

THE MODERN FANCIFUL TALE

Out o'er the tops of highest mountains skipping,
Out o'er the hills, the trees and valleys tripping,
Out o'er the ocean seas, without an oar or shipping, —
Hallo my fancy, whither wilt thou go?
WILLIAM CLELAND, *Hallo, My Fancy*

THE second half of the nineteenth century marks the beginning of a new era in prose stories written expressly for children. The most marked feature of the period is the extensive production in England, and less notably in America, of original fanciful tales or fairy tales by writers of distinction. Although three-quarters of a century has passed since this new type became clearly apparent, such stories are properly called "modern" to distinguish them from the old anonymous folk tales of mystery and wonder. Realistic stories of child-life had already begun to take on a different tone and the mid-century brought no such notable change in them. They were responsive, however, to the same liberalizing influences which launched the modern fairy tale and much that is said in this chapter regarding these causes of change and the resultant effects is applicable in some degree to all kinds of real literature for children.

The term "modern fanciful" is used to cover a very large class of stories representing great diversity both as to type and period of production. In point of time, one must go back nearly a hundred years to Hans Andersen to find the first stories of pure invention in the realm of fancy. Many of Andersen's stories are "modern" in the sense that they are not the old traditional tales, but are of his own original creation. The term "fanciful" is

employed to designate stories which in subject or treatment or both, are imbued with magic and touched by the
supernatural in contrast to "true" or "realistic" stories
which depict figures, events, and situations as they appear
to the senses and to a mind awake in a rational world.   A
careful student will soon come to see that the two types
are not quite mutually exclusive and that an attempt to
separate them leads us into difficulties and tempts to an
academic classification.   For purposes of study, however,
the division seems to be justified for the following reasons.

There is the eternal question on the part of many grown-
ups and some children, "Is the story *true?*"

The offering in children's stories is now so extensive
that a balanced and representative selection is easier when
certain general groupings have been made.

While standards for evaluation may not differ greatly
for different types of stories, the emphasis will certainly
shift considerably.

Genuine literature, no matter how simple, can be
produced only through the operation of creative imagination, but imagination operates differently when engaged
in depicting real life and when in free flight in a world of
fancy.

The mingling of the everyday world and the world of
dreams calls for the very highest art.   Perhaps this art
will be better appreciated by those who can recognize
forms of beauty in the two separate spheres.

The omnibus term "modern fanciful" as already defined
covers stories as divergent in period of production and in
character as Andersen's *The Brave Tin Soldier* and *The
Snow Queen*, Thackeray's *The Rose and the Ring*, Kingsley's
The Water Babies, Lewis Carroll's *Alice in Wonderland*,
George MacDonald's *At the Back of the North Wind*,
Mrs. Craik's *Adventures of a Brownie*, Kipling's *Just-So*

Stories, Barrie's *Peter Pan,* Bannerman's *Little Black Sambo,* Carl Sandburg's *Rootabaga Stories,* Hugh Lofting's *Doctor Dolittle,* Anne Parrish's *Floating Island,* and Wanda Gag's *Millions of Cats.* Different as these stories are, they possess the common element of fresh invention in the limitless ranges of wonder and magic. The authors were not bound by any kind of law except the elastic and variously interpreted laws of artistic writing for young readers which the talented author imposes upon himself.

Stories which thus shook off the domination of literal truth, transcended logical behavior in human beings and typical behavior in animals, and were inspired and guided by free creative imagination, were but little known in England until about the middle of the nineteenth century. Contributions of note in this field came still later in the United States where, at the time mentioned, writers were very much occupied with realistic stories. In fact this country has comparatively little to show in the production of original fanciful tales before 1900, although such stories were received joyfully from other countries and were widely distributed.

The great and rapid development in this field will probably surprise one whose attention is called to it for the first time. The translation into English of Andersen's *Fairy Tales* in 1846 gave impetus to this kind of writing though for some time that influence was felt more in the retelling of folk tales than in original work. The steady waning of Puritan influence, growing consciousness of the unhealthy tone and inartistic quality of many of the books written for children, rebellion against the interdiction of fairy tales, an increased respect for children and a better understanding of them culminated in one of those outbursts of expression not uncommon in the development of the arts. A new and fundamental conception was stirring — the notion that the concern of real literature in relation to the young was not to serve moralistic and utilitarian ends, but to furnish pleasure and delight. Acceptance of this point of view carried with it, of course, the idea that the wings of creative imagination should not be arbitrarily clipped and that fun and nonsense were as legitimate and desirable in prose as in Lear's nonsense rhymes. There was very little theorizing on the subject. Children and parents were ready for something different, and what seems to be now a sudden transformation was made by a few notable books which were published in quick succession in England just past the middle of the nineteenth century. An examination of these books should serve to throw a little light on the vast array of fanciful tales which confronts anyone who today attempts to guide students or help children in the choice of books.

A FEW BOOKS WHICH POINTED THE WAY

Critics point to the publication of *Alice in Wonderland* (1865) as a sort of timely explosion which permanently changed the contour and character of childhood's literary landscape. Harvey Darton calls it "the spiritual volcano of children's books." [1] The idea that literature was primarily for pleasure and delight had been slow in finding effective expression and popular acceptance, and now quite suddenly people of all ages were laughing together at the most irresponsible nonsense written in holiday mood for children. Lewis Carroll made no apology for a lack of serious purpose in the fantastic tale, and it cloaks no ulterior ends.

The centenary of the birth of Lewis Carroll (Charles Lutwidge Dodgson, 1832), which has just been celebrated with great distinction in England and America, brought out every possible phase of his life and work in great detail.

[1] Darton, F. J. Harvey, *Children's Books in England.* Macmillan, 1932.

Our purpose here is merely to call attention again to a few facts which bear particularly on the effect of the "Alice" books in establishing a new point of view regarding stories for children. We recall that in July, 1862, Charles L. Dodgson, an Oxford don and lecturer in logic and mathematics, took three little sisters, daughters of Dr. Liddell, Dean of Christ Church, on a picnic by boat on the upper Thames, and that in the course of the day and according to custom, he told them a story of his own devising. On this occasion the story happened to be the beginning of what was later known as *Alice in Wonderland*, and in it the second little sister, Alice, was made the central figure. Well-known facts and the story itself go to show that the tale throughout its telling was produced in the spirit of fun, by a man who was a great friend of children, especially little girls, and that in inventing and relating it he was having quite as good a time as his eager young auditors. It is easy to read between the lines of this fantastic tale as well as the later *Alice Through the Looking-Glass* (1871) and hear the teasing banter, the challenging jokes, and the merry laughter when the author poured his keen wit and inventive genius into the pleasurable task of entertaining a few favorite children. And so completely did Lewis Carroll enter into the spirit of such occasions that he was able to preserve this attitude and spontaneity in the second book which was written when Alice Liddell was a young lady. The Dedication mentions the intervening years of separation —

> I have not seen thy sunny face
> Nor heard thy silver laughter,

and refers to the beginning of the earlier book —

> A tale begun in other days
>   When summer suns were glowing,
> A simple chime, that served to time
>   The rhythm of our rowing.

Using the utmost brevity in connection with an inexhaustible subject, we may say that the world owes the "Alice" books to a happy combination of circumstances in which a young bachelor of unusual gifts who loved and understood children and enjoyed genuine play with them, turned his wit and his fun-loving spirit into the channel of story production, with a mind wholly free from responsibility for either the instruction or edification of his little friends. He had no facts to impart, no moral lessons to impress, no ambition to improve childish deportment, no fear of confusing young minds in regard to native traits of rabbit, dormouse, and walrus, recognized no dark inhibiting bogy called "the subconscious," and felt no obligation to be either logical or reasonable. *Alice in Wonderland* represents the purest phantasy, with people and animals amusingly distorted, a few fabulous creatures introduced, the familiar world turned topsy-turvy, and not a fairy in the book. There have been many attempts at imitation of what is inimitable and the dream-world of more or less clever paradoxes has become a much-used device in modern fairy stories.

We have mentioned *Alice in Wonderland* first because of the outstanding character of the book and its undoubted influence upon other writers, but there had been some stirrings of free imagination a little earlier.

There were several delightful little books written by Richard Horne who used the pseudonym "Mrs. Fairstar." The stories still seem so fresh and childlike that one wonders that they were allowed so long to be forgotten. *The Memoirs of a London Doll*, first published in 1852, is one of the most delightful doll stories ever written. Every little girl who loves dolls should have an opportunity to become acquainted with Maria Poppet who writes her own Memoirs and tells of many exciting experiences in London eighty years ago. The story now appears in attractive form in The Little Library (Macmillan) with an interesting Introduction by Marion St. John Webb.

Frances Browne deserves special notice for the independence and originality of her work and the genuine charm of her stories which are still greatly enjoyed. She is known today by one book, a collection of stories called *Granny's Wonderful Chair and Its Tales of Fairy Times* (1857), which continues to appear in new and beautiful editions. The author was born in a little village in Donegal, Ireland, in 1816, and was blind from infancy. She was one of twelve children in a family of small means, and no character in her fairy tales ever had to surmount such difficulties as those which she overcame in the long process of self-education and literary achievement. She possessed the imagination of a poet and the playful fancy of a child, and with these she compounded, out of her Irish background of mystery and wonder, stories quite new and charming. Her main purpose was to entertain children, and there is nothing that "dates" her stories except the allegorical names which many of her characters bear, such as Princess Greedalind, Childe Charity, Merrymind, and Wisewit. But this implied ethical meaning is never intrusive, and whatever the lesson, it is conveyed through story-action and without obvious intention. A gentle humor easily sensed by children plays through most of the stories. Separate stories in this collection are often included in anthologies, "The Story of Fairyfoot" being especially popular.

Charles Kingsley followed soon after with *The Water Babies: A Fairy Tale for a Land Baby* (1863). It antedates by about two years the publication of *Alice in Wonderland* and appears to be the first long story of a fanciful nature by an English author, and the first nature-fairy tale. The story is many-sided, but its peculiar feature is the important part played by a great variety of living creatures in their natural habitat and with some deference to their native characteristics.   There are parts of this story which children today find very tiresome, but the adventures of Tom, the little chimney-sweep — his hair-breadth escapes, his transformation into a water-baby, and his remarkable experiences with the little creatures of stream and ocean are features which they enjoy.   There are good abridged editions which omit most of the didactic parts with great advantage to the story.   Kingsley was a clergyman with liberal views, well informed in natural science, and a nature-lover intimately acquainted with the life of field, fen, and ocean.   While *Water-Babies* shows a strong tendency to instruct and to improve behavior, it constitutes a milestone on the way toward stories to be enjoyed wholly for their own sake.

In *At the Back of the North Wind* (1871) George MacDonald portrayed normal human life on a broad stage with a mysterious dream-world impinging so closely upon it that the little boy Diamond moved constantly from one to the other, borne by his beloved North Wind.   Through this little dreamer, beauty and grace are imparted to hard and sometimes bitter experience and an ideal world is brought very near.   There is something in this story for widely different ages and tastes, but it is not for very young children. Some will be held chiefly by the interesting events in Diamond's normal everyday life and others will move sympathetically with him in and out of the dream-world. The next book by this author, *The Princess and the Goblin* (1872), is marked by the same close intermingling of the worlds of reality and phantasy, but there is less philosophizing and the thread of the story is easier to follow.

George MacDonald was a Scotch minister, a poet, and a mystic, with broad human sympathies.   He and Lewis Carroll were intimate friends, and *Alice in Wonderland* in manuscript was read to the MacDonald children, bringing keen delight to them and to their parents. This story may have confirmed MacDonald in a predisposition toward the free range of imagination in the direction of pure phantasy, but, needless to state, it took a very different form in his books.

To this period belong also Jean Ingelow's *Mopsa the Fairy* (1869) and Dinah Mulock Craik's *Adventures of a Brownie* (1872). They are mentioned together because of their proximity to each other in point of time and the contrast they offer in conception and treatment. The first-mentioned shows exuberant fancy unfettered by tradition and unlimited in its range (earth, air, sea, sky), picturing a whole new fairy world with its own rather complicated society. The story barely touches the real world of child-life. It exhibits instead a richness of invention which is perhaps too elaborate and intricate for any but the most imaginative children. For such readers the book is by no means outmoded. *The Adventures of a Brownie* delights children today quite as much as it did their grandmothers. It is of interest to the student of the period as an excellent example of a story which introduces a true brownie of the old tradition into a more modern English home with a careless cook, a crotchety gardener, and six frolicsome children. Mrs. Craik does not fabricate a new fairy world. Her invention consists in creating interesting situations in the affairs of normal family life in which the little elf plays a typically tricksy and amusing part.

In America a few writers appeared in the last quarter of the century who turned their talent toward producing stories of a fanciful type for children. Often these appeared first in the *St. Nicholas* magazine which for several decades set a high standard for all types of literature for the young, and attracted writers of ability.

Julian Hawthorne was one of the early contributors to this periodical. His fairy tale, *Rumpty-Dudget's Tower*, was first published in an English magazine, but a year later (1878) it came out serially in *St. Nicholas*. It has excellent story quality, and in response to continued demands, from parents and grandparents, who remembered it with delight, Stokes and Company produced it in attractive book form in 1928. The tale has originality and it is rather exciting, as the plot is marked by several crises in the rescue of little Prince Henry, in which his sister and brother, Hilda and Frank, are quite active.

Charles E. Carryl also contributed two long fanciful tales to *St. Nicholas* in the eighties. Estimates of the lasting worth of his stories vary considerably, but the liking of children for them has maintained the books in circulation and has seemed to justify new and attractive editions. The best-known tale is *Davy and the Goblin: or What Followed Reading Alice's Adventures in Wonderland* (1884). The sub-title, of course, invites invidious comparisons. Carryl interspersed very clever and amusing verses throughout his stories and some of these are certain of a long life in anthologies of humorous verse.

One very important American writer of this period is Howard Pyle. Strictly speaking, few of his stories can be called "modern fanciful," since most of them are a fresh rendering of traditional material. They are charmingly told in an individual style and the author's very beautiful and distinguished illustrations and decorations place the Pyle books among the real treasures of a child's library. Collections well suited to upper primary and intermediate grades are *Pepper and Salt, or Seasoning for Young Folks*, and *The Wonder Clock*.

Frank R. Stockton made some notable contributions in the field of imaginative literature for young readers. His stories are marked by sincerity and beauty of conception, but in general they are too mature for the age-range with which we are chiefly concerned.

Going back to England and to the turn of the century, we come to Rudyard Kipling's *Just-So Stories* (1902) which furnish something unique and at the same time reminiscent of folk literature. They appeal strongly to widely differing ages and their vivid animal characterization, lively humor, dramatic quality, and amusing language, render them especially suitable for oral presentation.

SUMMARY

Before attempting to scan the crowded shelves devoted to the first three decades of the present century, it may be possible to make a few valid deductions regarding the forerunners which have just been singled out. It would seem that these few books taken together exhibit almost every trait of the best fanciful tales as we know them today. We find pure phantasy, dreamlike in quality and rich in invention; assured entrance into an imaginary world, "behind the moon," in the caves of the ocean, or in enchanted islands; a numerous company of fairy creatures freshly conceived and newly created, as well as a few of the more traditional sort; natural phenomena in the guise of fairy magic; occasional outbursts of nonsense and mirth together with much gentle, whimsical humor; and a vigorous re-creation of the marvelous in animal tales, so popular in traditional literature and long neglected outside that realm.

There are at least two features which have sprung into great prominence recently which were but little used by earlier writers with the exception of Andersen. To find the forerunner of stories in which children's toys and other inanimate objects are treated as active living creatures (a very common device today), one must go back to Andersen. And as for living animals which deport themselves like human beings and even transcend the human race in marvelous performances, they were rare before 1900, though today they threaten to monopolize the entire stage.

Another fact of some importance is that the earlier writers of fanciful tales produced very little which was well adapted to children below seven years of age — always excepting the precocious or highly favored child. It is only in quite recent years that writers of reputation have seemed to take into account the large and eager youngest group.

Following is a list of books mentioned above, arranged in the order of publication. With the possible exception of *Water Babies*, all these books are still favorites with children, although several of them should be reserved for an age-level above ten years.

Richard Horne (pseud. Mrs. Fairstar). *The Memoirs of a London Doll: Written by Herself*. (1852.) Modern edition. Illustrated by Emma L. Brock. (The Little Library.) Macmillan.

Frances Browne. *Granny's Wonderful Chair and Its Tales of Fairy Times*. (1857.) Modern edition. Illustrated by Katharine Pyle. Dutton.

Charles Kingsley. *The Water Babies: A Fairy Tale for a Land Baby*. (1863.) Modern edition. Illustrated by Heath Robinson. Houghton.

Lewis Carroll (pseud. for Charles Lutwidge Dodgson).
Alice's Adventures in Wonderland. (1865.) Illustrated by Sir John Tenniel. Macmillan.
Through the Looking-Glass and What Alice Saw There. (1871.) Illustrated by Sir John Tenniel. Macmillan.

Jean Ingelow. *Mopsa the Fairy*. (1869.) Modern edition. Illustrated by Dorothy Lathrop. Harper.

George MacDonald.
At the Back of the North Wind. (1871.) Modern edition. Illustrated by Francis D. Bedford. Macmillan.
The Princess and the Goblin. (1872.) Modern edition. Illustrated by Elizabeth MacKinstry. Doubleday.

Dinah Maria Mulock (Mrs. Craik).
   The Adventures of a Brownie.   (1872.) Modern edition. Illus-
      trated by Mary L. Seaman. (The Little Library.) Macmillan.
   The Same.   Illustrated by Edna Potter. Harper.

Julian Hawthorne.   *Rumpty-Dudget's Tower: A Fairy Tale.*
      Published in *St. Nicholas* (1878).
         First edition in book form (1928) has an interesting intro-
      duction by the author telling of the writing and reissue of the
      story.   Stokes.

Howard Pyle.
   Pepper and Salt, or Seasoning for Young Folks.   (1885.)
   The Wonder Clock.   (1887.)
      Illustrated by the author.   Harper.

Rudyard Kipling.   *Just-So Stories.*   (1902.)   Juvenile Edition.
   Doubleday.

TWENTIETH-CENTURY FANCIFUL TALES

We have drawn a light imaginary line between the two
centuries for several reasons.   In the first place, a number of
the stories mentioned above have already become classics.
Their beauty and worth are established, and their enduring
interest to children may be predicted.   Only two of the
leading writers of last century are now living (1933), Barrie
and Kipling, and they have written nothing for children
for a long time.   A juster estimate can be made as to the
quality and the influence of work which is finished than
of that which is growing and changing.   The leading
writers of this century are living and producing, and we
are probably too close to their work to get a very true
perspective of it.   Besides, the world itself is changing
rapidly and who can tell how these changes may affect the
interests and pleasures of children?   During such a prolific period as the present there is a vast amount of material
of all kinds which has not yet found its level of intrinsic
merit.   There are many factors which may tend to a
mistaken evaluation — the glamour of the name of author
or artist, beautiful format of the book, hasty, ill-considered

reviews, repeated appearance of a title in published lists, catering to some transient but insistent vogue — these and other more or less superficial influences may tend for a time to give a spurious rank to a book.

The attempt to measure new books by strictly classic standards is just as mistaken as to be uncritically hospitable to innovations.   It may once have been true that the only really worthy books for children to read are those which were not written expressly for them, but the principle has small validity today.   This tenet is held chiefly by gifted literary people who look back upon a fortunate childhood during which they browsed at will in an excellent home library.   In general, it would seem to be much truer to reverse this position and to say that books written for children which prove to be so trivial, infantile, insincere and patronizing that a person of mature years and taste can find no pleasure in them, are likely to be unfit for children.   But it happens not infrequently of late that a book written primarily for children and very popular with them furnishes almost equal delight to adult readers of developed taste, and such unity of response many times multiplied is perhaps the surest guarantee of real excellence and lasting approval.

Few critics would wish to attempt to predict what will live and what will prove to be of only temporary interest. Time and the children themselves are the final arbiters, but in the meantime we must do the best we can to sort and sift, for the books are here in quantity, they are offered with every possible persuasive device, and next year there will be others bidding for attention.   To the student, the main concern should be to enlarge one's own horizon, improve one's taste, get as close as possible to children in their various contacts with chosen books, and thus learn to become more understanding companions in literary pleasures.

On account of the very large offering of fanciful tales, their variety of style and their wide range of appeal as regards the maturity of readers, it is necessary to set some definite limits to the books to be selected for special attention. There are various ways in which this might be done, but any effective procedure will have to make use of the laboratory method by which tentative judgments are made and tested. Such procedures can only be suggested in a published study such as the present one. In print, selections and exclusions always seem to imply some fixed and well established distinctions in value, whereas in class work, quick surveys, brief reviews, and group reports make it possible to get a hearing for a much fuller list of worthy books. One hesitates also to offer in cold print specific negative examples which unquestionably do serve to build up standards of judgment. But in class discussion, freely expressed opinions from students and instructor when supported by evidence from the book itself, the comparison of similar books by different authors or by the same author at different periods, all help to clarify thought and mold opinion, and should be constantly used.

We abandon at this point all regard for chronological order. Within the limits of about three decades, priority in authorship is of little or no consequence. A relatively small number of contemporary authors and books have been chosen for special attention and these selections have been made on the basis of variety of type and what we believe to be their representative quality. We have gauged the importance of the book to children by inquiry among able teachers carrying on progressive work with children, by the published opinions of numerous specialists, by composite views formed from opinions of a large number of college students actively engaged in studies of this kind, from lists prepared by highly competent judges and, no doubt, by the particular tastes and predilections of the present writer. It is intended as a representative list of books in which adults may find common enjoyment with children, become better acquainted with fine types, and discover some of the specific qualities which make for excellence.

A few very elastic divisions are suggested solely for convenience in approaching a large and widely varied class. Such divisions are not intended to apply in any way to use with children except as it may help teachers and others to a better acquaintance with the books. The order of titles under each heading is from the easier to the more difficult. Picture story books are not included in this list unless the story itself possesses a certain degree of merit apart from the pictures.

1. Many modern fanciful tales follow some easily recognizable folk tale pattern. Subject and plot may be quite original, however, as in all but the second of the following stories. All these are of the accumulative type.

Helen Bannerman. *Little Black Sambo*. Stokes.

> One of the very few modern fanciful tales which might easily be mistaken for a folk tale (except for the anachronism of an umbrella!). It has already given unusual delight to two or three generations of small children and is the despair of writers who attempt to imitate it. A [1]

Edith Rickert. *The Bojabi Tree*. Pictures by Gleb Botkin. Doubleday.

> A gaily humorous tale which Miss Rickert attributes in its original form to African folklore. Hungry animals discover a new fruit and it becomes highly necessary to learn and report its name. Every emissary to King Leo forgets the name until at last Tommy Tortoise evolves a memory scheme and is able to report that the fruit is good to eat and that the tree is called "Bojabi." A

Wanda Gag. *Millions of Cats*. Coward-McCann.

> Pictures by the author are inseparable from the story. There is a remarkable quality in the story itself, however,

---

[1] For an explanation of the letters A, B, and C used in this list, see Chapter I, page 9.

with all its brevity and simplicity. It is liked by all ages for different reasons but is usually assigned to younger children.   A

Félicité Le Fèvre. *The Little Grey Goose*. Large colored pictures by Freda Derrick. Macrae.

A little duck has lost her pretty yellow shoes and yellow stockings and cannot go to the Red Hen's birthday party. She is sent in various directions in search of her shoes and stockings, in the course of which she meets several Mother Goose characters.   A

Emma L. Brock. *To Market! To Market!* Pictures in color by the author. Knopf.

A Dutch duck and a Dutch mouse find a gulden and start for Op-Zoom to buy something for themselves. They meet with many adventures on the way and at the market. A true Dutch atmosphere pervades the scenes and incidents. While the pattern of the story is in part accumulative, the whole is told with pleasing variety.   A

2.   Animals of every kind and in many guises occupy an amazingly large place in story books of this century. They were very prominent in folk tales and their appeal is equally strong in modern stories. Puss in Boots was not the last swaggering hero of his race nor were the Bremen Musicians the last mixed company of dissatisfied animals to take to the road in an effort to better their condition.

We are regarding as "fanciful" all stories of talking animals and of such as in other ways far surpass the normal behavior of their kind. Many such tales which depart from the literal truth in some particular such as speech, depict animals with fidelity as regards dominant native traits and natural habitat. To young children (and to many of their elders) animal pets seem almost human. They are the playmates of children who talk to them, translate their language, and interpret their behavior in terms of human thought and feeling. The sympathetic writer of animal stories who has command of his art finds a large audience with a natural readiness to respond imaginatively to his tale.   The super-cat or the super-dog may be represented in his own natural coat or he may appear in human habiliments.   His dress has little to do with his portrayal by a creative artist.   Peter Rabbit would suffer as a beloved character if he should lose permanently his little blue coat, while Good Cat Jupie stands at the door of her little house wearing only her own beautiful fur coat and is the very personification of smiling competence and hospitality.

It would seem that no other type of story has been so invaded by the cheap and tawdry and yet there is a large and excellent offering from which to choose.

Beatrix Potter.   *The Tale of Peter Rabbit*.   Warne.
>   Peter leads the procession of quaint, clever, and appealing little animals who are the celebrated heroes of a long series of small books now justly regarded as nursery classics.   The illustrations in color by the author are exactly in key with the stories.   Beatrix Potter is an English writer who lives on a farm in the Lake district.   She knows rural life intimately as all her work clearly shows.   She is supreme in this particular type of story for small children.   A
>   Other very popular books in the series are:
> *The Tale of Benjamin Bunny.*
> *The Tale of Tom Kitten.*
> *The Tale of Squirrel Nutkin.*

Alice Dussauze.   *Little Jack Rabbit*.   Translated from the French by Allan Ross MacDougal.   Macmillan.
>   As humanized characters, Jackie and his sister Jennie are treated quite seriously and the story has a pleasantly old-fashioned flavor.   After the first few pages it is written in quite a dramatic style and tells of dangers and escapes as well as more peaceful living among animal friends.   A, B

Neely McCoy.   *The Tale of the Good Cat Jupie*.   Macmillan.
>   Simple pleasing pictures in black and white by the author.   This story of a very domestic and hospitable cat and a little girl who keep house together succeeds in creating an illusion

which gives a feeling of delightful reality to the very simple
action.   Jupie is a real character not easily forgotten. A, B
    Children will be eager to hear the continuation in *Jupie
Follows His Tale* — but it is scarcely the equal of the first
book.   A, B

Peggy Bacon.   *The Lion-Hearted Kitten and Other Stories*.   Macmillan.

    The pictures in black and white by the author are wonder-
ful examples of animal portraiture.   A collection of stories
about jungle animals and one tiny stray kitten, not humanized although endowed with more than animal intelligence
and often given to guile.   People who believe that in children's books even animal behavior should always be on a
high ethical plane will disapprove of some of these stories.
Especially entertaining are, the title story, "The Gloomy
Hippopotamus," which is very funny; and "The Little Baby
Zebra."   A, B

Hugh Lofting.   *The Story of Mrs. Tubbs*.   Stokes.

    A small book with amusing pictures in color by the author.
How a dog, a duck and a pig (Punk, Ponk and Pink) circum-
vented a churlish landlord and restored their good friend
Mrs. Tubbs to the cosy home from which she had been
evicted.   A, B

    The Story of Dr. Dolittle.   Stokes.

    The first of nine volumes which concern this clever and
benevolent animal doctor and his astonishing relations to
animals domestic and otherwise.   Mr. Lofting has a real
genius for this sort of thing both as writer and illustrator.
He employs a mock-serious style which delights by its bland
assumption of genuineness in the most amazing situations
and events.   This book is the best of the series for younger
children though all of them have an unusually wide appeal as
regards age.   B, C

Albert Bigelow Paine.   *The Hollow Tree and Deep Woods Book*.
Illustrated by Reginald Birch.   Harper.

    Mr. Paine began writing what are now called "bedtime
stories" before there was such an overproduction of the general type.   The earlier books in his series called "Hollow
Tree Stories" are among the best of the kind.   The leading
characters are a Coon, a 'Possum, and a Big Black Crow
who are much given to sociability.   Their adventures and

misadventures are very amusing and appeal to children beyond the Peter Rabbit stage.   B, C

Walter R. Brooks.
  To and Again.   Illustrated by Adolfo Best-Maugard.   Knopf.
    Instigated by Charles the rooster, some of the animals on
    Mr. Bean's farm decide to avoid the rigors of winter by mi-
    grating to Florida.   Their absurd adventures and hair-
    breadth escapes en route and in residence, and their safe re-
    turn to Mr. and Mrs. Bean bearing rich treasure-trove, form
    a very funny story which arouses hilarious laughter when
    read aloud.   B, C
  More To and Again.   Knopf.
  Freddy the Detective.   Knopf.
    Kurt Wiese's pictures fit these jolly tales perfectly.   The
    same domestic animals undertake further adventure with
    boldness and success, and the author sustains his reputation
    as one who can make the most ludicrous and incredible situa-
    tions seem almost plausible.   E, C

Rachel Field.   *Little Dog Toby*.   Macmillan
    Quite often Miss Field illustrates her own books and she
    has done so in this case.   She has created a most engaging
    dog character in Little Dog Toby who, early in the story,
    flees his vagabond life and attaches himself to a Punch and
    Judy show in the streets of London as understudy to the
    old Toby about to be retired.   Little Toby is hardworking,
    faithful, and a bit romantic in his attachments and these
    traits Miss Field utilizes to give continuity and plot to this
    unusually interesting little story.   Toby converses and
    philosophizes but he is kept true to his character as a trick
    dog.   B, C

Elizabeth Coatsworth.   *The Cat and the Captain*.   Macmillan.
    If it were not for the uncanny behavior of the Cat and his
    more than feline intuitions this story might be considered a
    realistic narrative about the Captain, his colored cook Susan-
    nah and a mischievous pet.   But Miss Coatsworth has
    created a Cat with super-powers which he discharges in in-
    solent independence of action, trying to the soul of Susannah
    and sometimes vexing to the Captain.   There is an exciting
    climax in which the Cat detects and frustrates a thief and is
    forgiven by Susannah for all past offenses.   Miss Coats-
    worth has made animals the central figures in several of her

stories. There is something inscrutable in the art by which she exalts their behavior without distorting their animal nature. Lively incident and humor make this story very popular with children.   B, C

3. Stories in which toys, puppets, and other inanimate objects become living creatures are almost as numerous as animal tales and their popularity has a similar basis. Toy animals often call out a child's deep affection and they are their very own, as living animal pets frequently are not; and everyone knows how truly many little girls are veritable mothers to their precious dolls. Children invent an imaginary life for themselves and their toys and in so doing are creating in substance, fanciful tales and dramas. Their dolls, teddy bears, bunnies, cats, and toy engines are "as real as real" which is of course what makes Christopher Robin with his Winnie-the-Pooh, Piglet and the rest, such a true picture of the universal child. Because of this attitude toward their own toys, children take to their hearts well-drawn toy characters in story books. They follow breathlessly the race of Clever Bill, an ardent and determined wooden soldier, as he attempts to overtake the train which is separating him from his little owner and friend; and to an older child, the Velveteen Rabbit may be almost as real and appealing as the living Peter Rabbit is to a small brother or sister.

While stories of this kind are not peculiar to this century, they have been produced in great quantity of late. They are easy to write but very difficult to write well — with sincerity and without condescension. It is no exaggeration to say that in the finest stories of this kind authors have put the very breath of life into creatures of wood and sawdust in the true spirit of childhood. As stated in an earlier chapter, Andersen was the first great creator of stories of this type, his Brave Tin Soldier standing as an immortal example of the toy which comes alive.

A little later the Italian writer Lorenzini created a universally popular hero in the marionette Pinocchio in whose
wooden head and heartless body a true boy's nature at
last develops.

The following are some of the most successful of the
more recent stories of this class:

A. A. Milne.
  Winnie the Pooh. Dutton.
  The House at Pooh Corner. Dutton.
    Delightful drawings by E. H. Shepard form an important
    part of the story. Author and artist together, aided by one
    little boy's own imaginings, have succeeded in the faithful
    portrayal of a whole family, or rather society, of stuffed ani-
    mals. Each character has a distinct personality and plays
    his part and speaks his lines accordingly. It seems a mis-
    representation to refer to them as "stuffed." No small
    child would ever use that term when telling about these
    loved books.   A

William Nicholson. *Clever Bill*. Doubleday.
    A picture story book in style. Artist and author are one,
    and the story though very short is worthy of the fine full-
    page pictures. It tells of sharp disappointment and final
    achievement when a little girl in the rush of departure leaves
    behind her most precious toy, a wooden soldier, and he with
    his long legs at last overtakes the fast train which is bearing
    her away.   A

Elsa Moeschlin. *The Red Horse*. Coward-McCann.
    A small toy horse, Trott-Trott, red and gaily decorated,
    gradually grew larger in response to the ardent desire and
    the good care of his owner. At last he is able to take the boy
    on a long trip back to the shop of the old peasant wood-
    carver who made him. The story verges on the propaganda
    type as the implication is, eat oatmeal and thus grow big and
    strong, for the boy feeds his small toy the cereal which he
    (the boy) does not want. Otherwise, the story is well writ-
    ten and worthy of the beautiful colored pictures by the
    author.   A

Clare Leighton. *The Musical Box*. Longmans.
    Illustrated by the author, who is a noted English artist.
    The large full-page woodcuts are very beautiful and the

hand-printed text accords with the pictures.   The story tells
of a toy town in a glass case in which all action is suspended
because no outside person remembers to ring the bells.
Priest, beggar, miller, milkmaid, and cow, all stand trans-
fixed until one day the case gets knocked off the stand and
the little actors undergo an earthquake.   At last the case is
restored to position, someone remembers to ring the bells
and the figures resume their animated and orderly lives.

A, B

Ethel Calvert Phillips.   *Little Rag Doll*.   Houghton.
     Many delightful pictures in color and pen and ink by Lois
Lenski.   A neglected doll is befriended by a fairy and the
two find a home in the playhouse of a little girl who understands and loves dolls and fairies.   A, B

Margery Williams Bianco.
     Almost all Mrs. Bianco's stories for children have as their
subject children's dolls or toy animals.   She is very sensitive
to children's feelings about such possessions and in two stories at least, the theme has had to do with the question of
"reality" from the imagined standpoint of the toys themselves.   This gifted writer treads lightly and delicately in
approaching the mysterious border-line between what is, and
what is imagined.   She is a lover of animals and seems to
have been able to transfer some of her knowledge and understanding of living creatures to their nursery substitutes.
Characterization was also aided, as in the case of Milne, by
taking some of the subjects right out of her own children's
toy closet with their characters and dispositions already well
settled by familiar nursery tradition.
The Little Wooden Doll.   Macmillan.
     The pictures for this little book were drawn by Mrs.
Bianco's daughter Pamela when she was about nine years
old, and they fit admirably the simple little story of an old-
fashioned, shabby, neglected doll and her rescue.   The doll
is discovered in a dark corner of the attic and her friends,
the mice and spiders, restore her beauty, supply her needs,
and take her to be a comfort and joy to just the right little
girl.   A, B
The Velveteen Rabbit, or How Toys Become Real.   Illustrations
in color by William Nicholson.   Doubleday.
     An old Skin Horse explains the laws of the toy universe

to the Velveteen Rabbit and he learns how it is that toys sometimes become REAL. His own transformation is gradual up to the time that a Fairy supplies the final touch and sets him down among his brothers, the woodland rabbits. A less artistic writer almost certainly would have allowed a vein of sentimentality to creep into this story and the next one, but Mrs. Bianco is herself too "real" and genuine for that.   **B**

The Skin Horse.   Doubleday.

The illustrations, poetically conceived and beautifully executed, represent the more mature work of Pamela Bianco. The story is a sweet and tender one of the strong bond between a lonely little boy in a hospital ward and an old toy horse who has belonged in turn to several children and now, as he assures the boy, belongs "to the child that needs me most." On Christmas Eve the old toy appears to the child, transformed into a glorious white winged horse and the two take flight, leaving the bed and pain and weakness behind. A reverent and lovely story.   **B, C**

Anne Parrish.   *Floating Island.*   Written and Illustrated by Anne Parrish with Sketches by Mr. Doll.   Harper.

This story of a shipwrecked doll family has been called by one reviewer "the odyssey of a doll family." It has also been called the *Swiss Family Robinson* of the doll world. The author declares she wrote it with the idea of making it as exciting and full of suspense as any mystery story, and she has succeeded. The book as a whole gives evidence of the pleasure Miss Parrish must have had as author and artist. The illustrations in black and white are a true representation of tropical sea-life and jungle-life, not distorted in any way. A further air of "authenticity" is imparted by the learned footnotes. This delightful book will be most appreciated by children old enough to enjoy its mock-serious tone.   **C**

Giuseppi Fanciulli.   *The Little Blue Man.*   Translated from the Italian by May M. Sweet.   Illustrated by H. L. Bacharach. Dent, London.

A little girl paints a picture of a little man as a postman giving him a proper uniform of blue. Her little brother grabs the paper figure and tosses it away, and thus begin his wanderings in the course of which he becomes a marionette. He has many strange adventures chiefly in the woods among

flowers, snails, bees, and ants.   In spite of his tiny stature
and frail substance the little man is quite a character.   C

Marie Barringer.   *Martin the Goose Boy*.   Doubleday.

This is rather a long story (188 pages), with eight full-page
pictures in color and many in black and white, by Maud and
Miska Petersham.   The length permits an interesting development of the story of Gustel and his most precious toy,
the little wooden goose-boy named Martin, who plays an
important part in the fortunes of Gustel and his kind old
grandfather, the woodcutter.   Bimbli, the mischievous goat,
complicates and enlivens the story.   The scene is laid in the
Black Forest and life there is made vivid and interesting.

C

Rachel Field.   *Hitty: Her First Hundred Years*.   Macmillan.

The quite perfect illustrations are by Dorothy P. Lathrop
and in making this book there seems to have been a kind of
inspired collaboration between author and artist.   According to a strict grading, we should have been obliged to omit
this book from our list because it is clearly intended for older
readers.   But it would seem like a lamentable oversight to
omit from a list of stories about dolls, toys and puppets, one
of the most notable doll stories ever written.   Hitty is a very
convincing character with a fascinating history and an uncanny longevity which may extend through another hundred years.   If properly introduced, boys do not scorn this
book.   Awarded the Newbery medal, 1929.

Readers ten to thirteen years

4. Stories in which fairies play a typical and important
part are now to be considered.   They are not so numerous
as one might suppose among so-called "fairy tales."
Andrew Lang in the Preface to his *Green Fairy Book*,
commenting on the fine quality of traditional tales, says,
"There are not many fairy tales, because they [modern
writers] do not believe enough in their own stories, and
because they want to be wittier than it has pleased Heaven
to make them."   New and talented writers have entered
the field since Lang made that comment, and while in
many cases their fairies do not bear much resemblance to

those of English tradition, they are often portrayed with sincerity and beauty, and sometimes convincingly. Among those who are writing extensively in this vein, some of the most successful are Margaret Baker, Henry Beston, Anne Casserley, Padraic Colum, and Ella Young. Other well-known writers have produced single successful books having fairy characters.

We have already seen that the presence of fairies is by no means necessary to imparting an atmosphere of magic and wonder, but they furnish a familiar element of charm and mystery which, happily, the modern child-world is not willing to discard.

Elsa Beskow. *Elf Children of the Woods*. Translated from the Swedish by Zita Beskow. Harper.

One of Elsa Beskow's most beautiful picture books for young children. The story action is scarcely more imaginative than an account of the happy daily life of a simple good-tempered peasant family. But of course household tasks of their own performed by such fascinating elves in lovely woodland scenes carry a delightful play of humor when pictured by this artist. A

Miriam Clark Potter. *Sally Gabble and the Fairies*. Macmillan.

In the small compass of this book is a highly original and delightful story. Helen Sewell's illustrations in black and white are quite unusual also and serve to accentuate the qualities of humor and surprise. The assured and casual manner in which the most astonishing events are narrated, accounts in part at least for the sense of reality which is conveyed. Under the spell cast by Miss Sally readers might almost believe the unbelievable — for she catches a wee, delicate, dainty fairy in a trap, adopts her and names her Mary Jane. She manages to placate a whole tribe of pestiferous fairies who live in the Magic Woods, by granting them certain rights and privileges in return for the undisputed companionship of Mary Jane. B

Margaret Baker.

Two English sisters have collaborated in the production of several delightful fairy stories. Margaret Baker writes the stories and her sister, Mary Baker, illustrates them with delicate, graceful, and humorous silhouettes. Many bits of folklore are woven into the tales but they are quite original in plot, well constructed, rich in imaginative detail, and touched with gentle humor.

The Pixies and the Silver Crown. Duffield.

Danny and Nan on the way to the fair lose a silver Crown which the pixies find and use to draw out the inner traits of various passers-by. These are true pixies as one can see from the clever, merry silhouettes of the artist.　B, C

Other delightful fairy tales by the Baker sisters are:

The Dog, the Brownie, and the Bramble Patch. Duffield.

The Lost Merbaby. Duffield.

Dorothy P. Lathrop. *The Fairy Circus.* Macmillan.

Miss Lathrop, the artist, is also the story-teller in this book. This is one of the few fairy stories in which there are no human beings at all. Miss Lathrop's exquisite pictures in color and black and white tell the story of a miniature circus in which fairies and all kinds of small woodland creatures duplicate the full-sized circus which on one occasion invaded their territory. The text simply amplifies somewhat the delicately humorous pictures. Children of all ages pore over this book picking out with delight every imaginatively realized detail.　B, C

Eleanor Farjeon. *The Old Nurse's Stocking Basket.* Illustrated by E. Herbert Whydale. Stokes.

By an ingenious device the Old Nurse in this book is made to appear an ageless and timeless creature who has been nurse not only to the mother and grandmother of the four children in the story but also to royal children of past ages. Out of such an experience "there was no end to the Old Nurse's stories." The collection contains ten of these, each located in a different country and time. They are pleasing original fairy tales with here and there quite a flavor of the traditional.　C

Henry Beston. *The Firelight Fairy Book.* Illustrated by Maurice E. Day. Atlantic Monthly Press.

A young lad complains that he can never find any new fairy tales among the new books, and Fairy Goldenwand replies that many things have happened in fairyland since the last books were written and promises to tell him some new stories if he will write them down. The boy agrees and so, Mr. Beston says, this is how the stories in his book came to be written. On the whole, Goldenwand keeps her promise about the newness of her tales which involve adventure, sacrifice, magic, clever ruse, gorgeous transformations and laughable situations.   C

Of the writers mentioned in the opening paragraph of this section, the three who are Irish-born seem to succeed most completely in taking the children back into the heart of fairyland. And this is to be expected, for even in legendary lore no other Western race ever lived so close to the "Little People," and certainly none has retained in these sophisticated times so genuine a faith in them. It is in the blood and rooted in the soil of Ireland. Peasants still see and talk with fairies, and poets know how to re-create an atmosphere favorable to their return. Irish literature for old and young is shot through with fairy strands both dark and golden, but we are especially concerned with stories suited to children of ten years and younger. This explains the omission from this section of such names as *Lady Gregory*, *James Stephens*, and *W. B. Yeats* who have written many beautiful things enjoyed by older children as well as adults. For children of the lower elementary school Anne Casserley is most fully enjoyed, but Padraic Colum and Ella Young have also made notable contributions to this period.

Anne Casserley.

Miss Casserley's stories are so uniform in quality and style that they do not need to be considered separately. There is a certain continuity also, as some of the same characters appear in several of the books. She is her own illustrator, using very simple line drawings which are full of character and expressive of mood.

Saturated from early childhood in the beliefs both homely and poetic of a very simple country folk, Miss Casserley has attained high success in weaving these into fresh, original and very entertaining stories. Always hovering near and

frequently mingling in the action are the true fairies of rural
Ireland. "The fairies owned the mountain; rock and cave,
heather and gorse, bog and stream, rushes and bracken, all
belonged to them." (*Brian of the Mountains.*) They are
genuine fairy folk as one can see from their description, with
"their wide laughing mouths, their brown wrinkled faces,
their eyes so bright and cold and old" and "their shrill
malicious laughter." (*Roseen.*) She summons also a group
of fascinating animals from the glens and mountains as well
as from tiny farms in the Donegal hills. There is the Flana-
gan Pig, free, roving and impudent; the little black pig
Roseen, domestic and wise; Little Black Lamb, opinionated
and officious; Drimin, the cow, a would-be adventurer with a
timid soul; Shaugran, the red fox, who consorts with the
Leprechaun — "brothers in deceit and treachery"; the
fussy, domineering Kerry Cow and her calf; Young Donkey
who means well but blunders often; and a score of others,
each revealed vividly through action.

The human characters, Michael, Paudeen and his grandmother, the Clogmaker's wife, the Old Apple Woman, the
Tinker and all the rest, are genuine Irish peasants, generous,
quick-tempered, easily penitent, kind, clever and merry.
Miss Casserley succeeds in giving the effect of Irish speech
in rhythm and idiom without using the brogue which is confusing to children and elusive to all but an Irish tongue.

There is a delightful humor throughout and some scenes
are very funny. Many of the separate stories read aloud
are enjoyed by the seven-year-old but in general they are for
slightly older children.

Michael of Ireland. Harper.

The Whins on Knockatten. Harper.

Roseen. Harper.

Brian of the Mountains. Harper.   B, C

Padraic Colum. *The Peep-Show Man.* Illustrated by Lois
Lenski. Macmillan.

Padraic Colum creates out of the rich lore of Ireland three
original stories having the poetic beauty and the rustic
humor of native fairy tales. An indefinable charm is in all
this author's stories for children. As the sub-titles indicate, each of these stories has a special seasonal significance.
This feature is slight, however, and the book is by no means
limited and occasional in its appeal.

"The Princess Swallow-Heart." (A Story for Midsummer Day.)
"The Twelve Silly Sisters That the Pooka Carried Away with Him." (A Story for Hallowe'en.)
"The White Blackbird." (A Story for Easter.) C

Ella Young.

It is a rare thing to find in a writer of children's stories such gifts and accomplishments as Ella Young possesses. She is a poet of distinction, a recognized scholar in Celtic language and literature, has a thorough and intimate acquaintance with the simple peasant folk of Ireland from whom she obtained much of her material and, as indicated by her stories for children and young people, has retained a fresh and childlike spirit. The scholar in her has never shackled the imaginative, creative artist. An earlier book, *The Wonder Smith and His Son: Celtic Wonder Tales*, possesses a fascination for older children, but happily her latest is addressed to children somewhere around the ten-year level.

The Unicorn with Silver Shoes. Illustrations in black and white by Robert Lawson. Longmans.

All specialists in children's literature and other competent judges hailed this book as one of the most notable contributions of 1932. The author has turned her gifts of imagination, insight, and humor, and her deep knowledge of folklore to the creation of this tale. Apparently it was not written with the complete plan in mind from the beginning for the Foreword says, "It grew out of stories I used to tell to two children who had a fondness for tales about Ogres and Magicians and Strange Beasts. In an unlucky hour I invented Ballor's Son and could never be quit of him after. He especially delighted those children, perhaps because he was not a model of all the seven deadly virtues." And there you have as good an indication of the nature and quality of this unusual book as can be given in a short paragraph. Imaginative children love the story but few below ten years of age are able to get its full flavor. C

5. Some writers bring the real world and the world of dreams so close together, weave them into a continuous pattern so quietly and with such assurance, that the reader scarcely knows at a given moment whether he is

looking upon a stable and familiar world or upon its shifting reflection. This quality is easily recognized in certain books for adults; for example, Christopher Morley's *Where the Blue Begins*, Kipling's *They*, Barrie's *The Little White Bird*, as well as his more recent *Farewell, Miss Julie Logan*, and De la Mare's *The Midget*.

In children's stories, such excursions into the fourth dimension are apt to be accompanied by an intricate plot and subtle implications unsuited to the younger children. George MacDonald's *At the Back of the North Wind*, Greville MacDonald's *Billy Barnicoat*, Hudson's *Little Boy Lost*, and De la Mare's juvenile play *Crossings*, are good examples of this type. The following stories are suited to children of eight to ten years.

Sir James M. Barrie. *Peter and Wendy*. Illustrated by Francis D. Bedford. Scribner.

> This narrative was written by Barrie from the play *Peter Pan* and includes all its most loved features.   C

Georgette LeBlanc. *The Children's Blue Bird*. Translated by A. Teixeira De Mattos. Dodd.

> The wife of Maurice Maeterlinck has in this book put into pleasing narrative form his famous fairy play about the search far and wide, by Tyltyl and Mytyl, for the bluebird of happiness.   C

Christopher Morley.

> This writer makes swift and unexpected changes from the normal and active life of four healthy, lively children into an imaginary world which impinges in a startling way upon the real. But his stories are so full of the spontaneous merriment and excitement occasioned by household pets, childish pranks, and a teasing whimsical father that children can move happily and freely between the real and the make-believe with only an agreeable jolt now and then. The good times of the highly original Mistletoe family with occasional fantastic interludes and accompaniments constitute the chief charm of Morley's stories.

I Know a Secret. Doubleday.   B, C

The Goldfish Under the Ice. Illustrated by Kurt Wiese. Doubleday.   B, C

Elizabeth Coatsworth. *Knock at the Door*. Macmillan.

Miss Coatsworth quite often hovers around the border-line between the everyday world and fairyland, but in this story she has interwoven the two in having as her central figure the lad Stephen who is the son of a fairy mother and a mortal father. He is not lacking in the courage necessary to meet the situations which this heritage entails. Boys who are a little inclined to look askance at fairy tales are likely to find the magic horse, Starling, difficult to resist. Francis Bedford's beautiful and delicate drawings interpret the story perfectly. C

6. Some of the modern mechanical products of man's ingenuity are winning entrance to fairyland because a few writers of imagination are able to sense the fantastic suggestions and inherent romance in such objects as skyscrapers, engines, taxicabs, and airplanes. The pioneer in this type of story and certainly the most uniquely perceptive writer up to the present time is Carl Sandburg. Many others have invented tales about road-builders, derricks, and excavators, but most of them are thoroughly realistic and informational in character, even though human attributes and functions may be added to the machine's own remarkable powers. If not too fanciful, such stories may serve with some children to impart knowledge about machinery and to develop an appreciation of its gigantic service in the work-a-day world. But making machines talk and behave in a purposeful manner does not transform them into veritable actors in the lawless world of magic and they do not belong in this chapter.

Cornelia Meigs. *The Wonderful Locomotive*. Illustrated by Berta and Elmer Hader. Macmillan.

An old broken-down engine, Number 44, is restored by hard work plus magic and takes one last mad flight across the continent with a trustful little boy, Peter, as engineer. Charged with some new elixir of life, and with a little guidance from Peter, the old derelict performs marvelous feats of strength and speed. Miss Meigs's skill as a writer imparts imaginative reality to an exciting dream. This story should not be confused with the many uninspired narratives about machinery intended to convey information about the modern world. This is pure romance of a high order.   **B**

Carl Sandburg.

Sandburg's stories were written wholly for the pleasure and entertainment of children and with no ulterior purpose. Anyone acquainted with *Rootabaga Stories* or *Rootabaga Pigeons* would scarcely accuse him of desiring to instruct. He chooses engines, railroads, skyscrapers, cornfields, chimneys, and dollar watches as actors in his stories because he can make them play picturesque and dramatic rôles on his modernistic stage. Being a poet and a born story-teller with a keen eye for the whole heterogeneous life of today in America, he senses a kind of personality in commonplace things and proceeds to dramatize their life in all kinds of fantastic scenes. His fancy is errant, irresponsible and gay, and it disregards all natural law. Skyscrapers lean toward each other at a dizzy angle but do not topple; crazy, zig-zag railroads take their erratic course across the country; chimneys climb down and dance clumsily; frolicsome jack-rabbits leap over tall skyscrapers and the tallest building kisses the fifth rabbit on the nose and whispers something in his long ears before he disappears in space; the builders of a skyscraper strive to reach the moon and lay plans to eat supper from its shining disc. As the Night Policeman of the Village of Cream Puffs says on one occasion, "'tis marvelish, 'tis marvelish."

Stories of rural objects, haystacks, crickets, pumpkins and cornfields are just as jolly and whimsical as those which concern modern inventions and show both keen and delicate perceptions: "Young Leather and Red Slippers were walking across the Rootabaga Country. And they were walking because it made their feet glad to feel the dirt of the earth under their shoes and they were close to the smells of the earth." A day in spring is celebrated in new and melodious words: "I have heard high in the elm trees the flummy-wisters yodeling their yisters in the long branches of the lingering leaves."

The human characters are as odd an assortment as those ordinarily described as inanimate, and many of them cause "a ticklish laughter" whenever they appear.

Sandburg's stories delight all ages above the lower primary and are ideal for reading aloud to mixed groups at home or elsewhere.

Rootabaga Stories.   Harcourt.

Rootabaga Pigeons.   Harcourt.

Both collections have delightful illustrations by Maud and Miska Petersham who have sensed and interpreted perfectly the droll, comical, wistful and poetic qualities of the strange congerie of characters.   C

Caroline Emerson.   *A Merry-Go-Round of Modern Tales*. Dutton.

Like Carl Sandburg, Miss Emerson regards the modern world as fit subject-matter for stories of lively imagination. She says: "I have tried to look at the world around me with a fancy and a humor which is contemporaneous. I have tried to play with the environment and the ideas of my own day." And she gives an excellent demonstration of her theory in "The Timid Truck," "The Shop That Gave Things Away," and other whimsical tales. The illustrations by Lois Lenski are quite as jolly as the stories.   C

Delicate humor has pervaded more than one of Mrs. Bianco's stories but *A Street of Little Shops* brings laughter as well as smiles. Like all true artists she sees more than meets the eye in common objects all about us and this time Puck gets the better of Ariel in the workshop of her mind. How do young children regard the headless manikins still seen in village "emporiums"? Mrs. Bianco knows, and tells us all about Mr. E. M. Porium's strange family. What does that magnificent creature, the saddler's lay-figure horse, do at night? The tobacconist's wooden Indian can tell. Greatly enjoyed by all who have the background of village life.

There is one charming and original little book which defies even a very flexible classification and must stand by itself. It is intended for children, but grown-ups interested in fairylore will treat it with respect.

George M. Richards. *The Fairy Dictionary*. (The Little Library.) Macmillan.

> With an air of seriousness and in accurate terms, each traditional fairy creature is described in a short paragraph and pictured by the author who is an artist of note. Name, abode, and dominant traits of more than sixty inhabitants of fairyland are included, arranged in alphabetical order according to true dictionary requirements.   B, C

SUGGESTED PROBLEMS AND TOPICS FOR FURTHER STUDY

1. Study a number of stories which convey to you a feeling of reality although they are quite impossible in plot and incident, for the purpose of discovering if possible how the author secures this effect.

   What causes other stories to fall short in this respect? Give examples.

   What do critics mean when they speak of "writing down" to children? Can you identify this style in specific stories?

2. Look for short passages of unusual beauty which you believe children under ten years of age might respond to with pleasure. Of course it is not intended to imply that such passages should be presented in an isolated way to children.

3. Prepare a list of fanciful tales which seem to you distinctly humorous. Test them in an informal way with children.

4. Select a few separate stories by Anne Casserley which seem to you among the most simple and amusing and therefore best suited to children in lower primary grades.

5. Small groups of adult students might enjoy making pictorial maps such as children like to draw and paint, representing the setting of a story, or stories. Suitable subjects might be: Miss Casserley's fairy world with its haunts and huts and striking characters; Miss Parrish's *Floating Island*; Miss Meigs's *The Wonderful Locomotive*; Beatrix Potter's *Fairy Caravan*. There are many others just as richly picturesque.

6. Almost everyone who comments on the work of Margery Williams Bianco points out features of resemblance to the stories of Hans Christian Andersen. Examine several of her stories seeking the basis for this comparison.

7. (*a*) Look for a few short stories in Carl Sandburg's collections which might be read separately to children in lower primary grades.

(*b*) Most of Sandburg's stories are quite robust in character. In contrast to these, look for one or two which have unusual beauty of concept, feeling, and language.

8. Fairy creatures in modern fanciful tales; or, a *Who's Who* of fairyland.   Specify stories.

9. Substitutes for fairies; or, How does the modern writer "make magic"?

10. Prepare for oral or written presentation, an account of the work of leading artists who have developed an individual style in portraying fairy creatures.

11. The use of old fairy-tale patterns in modern stories.   Give examples.

12. The mixture of fact and fancy in modern stories.   Include examples of true local color.

13. Giants ancient and modern; or, Jack the Giant-Killer out of a job.

14. Toys and puppets which come alive.   What are some of the methods used to cast this spell over the reader?

15. Some notable cats and dogs in modern stories.   Extend this to include realistic stories if desired.

16. The effective use of original verse as an adjunct to prose narrative.   Notice especially Elizabeth Coatsworth's stories.
Note.   Several closely related topics and problems will be found at the close of Chapter XII.

REFERENCES

Some of the references on poetry (Chapter X) have a direct bearing on all literature of the imagination.

References on biography of contemporary writers and artists, literary criticism, reviews, and the illustration of books for children will be found under Supplementary Bibliographies.

CHAPTER XII
MODERN REALISTIC STORIES

Oh, certainly, we must send invitations to the Every Day Country, for some of the folks there are just as good as the Dreamland people, only of course they haven't had the same advantages.

SAMUEL McCHORD CROTHERS, *Miss Muffet's Christmas Party* [1]

THE sense in which the term "realistic" is being used in this discussion of stories for children was explained in the last chapter, but it seems advisable to restate the point of view and to elaborate it somewhat as regards three aspects before entering upon an examination of stories which we have chosen as examples.

1. The term is not being used to express the meaning which now attaches to "realism" in adult literature. Stories of good literary quality suited to the age-span under discussion (five to ten years) appear always to be written with a certain degree of idealism and with an imaginative treatment which lifts them out of the crass circumstances and unmitigated hardness of much of modern life. When child-life is the subject, it is usually depicted as normal, healthy, and on the whole buoyant and happy. According to our definition, realistic stories although imaginatively conceived, contain nothing supernatural, nothing beyond the power of human beings to accomplish.

2. This classification is used simply as an aid in becoming better acquainted with a variety of types and styles and has no value in itself; certainly nothing arbitrary or academic is intended. The creative freedom of able writers is shown by the fact that some of the choicest stories defy classification as either "fanciful" or "realistic." They may be both in different degrees. Often where

[1] Published by Houghton Mifflin Company.

nothing supernatural occurs, the tale is so fantastic and improbable as to strain even the elastic definition we are employing. For example, *Snipp, Snapp, Snurr and the Gingerbread Boys* contains no discoverable magic, but it is decidedly fanciful in its "major premise" as well as in subsequent details. It is a delightful and amusing story of three little boys who tumble into a baker's mixing-trough and go triumphantly on their way into other adventures, dripping the dark batter with which they are covered. The audacity of the tale will greatly entertain without deceiving the six-year-old. It was not the author's purpose to present a true picture of child-life but to write a colorful and somewhat exciting story to please little children, and her particular method in the *Snipp, Snapp, Snurr* stories is to carry three attractive little boys through some rather fantastic experiences.

3. Animal stories also fall into these same two general classes, some of them quite clearly and others with less distinctness. Whether certain animal stories are scientifically true or not even scientists themselves sometimes dispute. The old question of "nature-fakir" stories is involved with an implied opprobrium attaching to animal tales which have the air of being true but which are in reality highly fanciful. There are many stories for children in which animals are made to talk. In regard to some of these there is reliable testimony that they are scientifically true in all features of behavior except command of human speech. Thornton W. Burgess writes in this vein. Stories in the *Burgess Animal Book for Children* are frankly intended both to instruct and entertain, and except for the fact that animal characters converse and soliloquize rationally they are truthfully portrayed. Kurt Wiese's *Karoo the Kangaroo* belongs in this class. His intention to instruct is much less obvious, but his knowledge of Australian animals and their ways imparts a sure touch to

his portrayal of a mother kangaroo and her baby. This he accomplishes almost entirely through interesting action. *Bambi*, by Felix Salten (for adults and older children), is a very fine example of the dual quality of faithful presentation and sensitive, poetic interpretation of the life of a forest animal — in this case a deer.

Our intention in this chapter is to use for illustration only those animal tales in which the animal characters lead a perfectly normal life among themselves or in relation to human beings. The one exception is that in some of the stories animals may converse or may have attributed to them certain thoughts and purposes suggested by their actions. In this matter of talking beasts and birds, the small child does not and cannot distinguish with accuracy between the real and the imaginary. They talk to their pets constantly and they interpret animal language and actions in terms of their own thought and feeling. The mature creative artist does much the same thing, the difference being that unless his deliberate intention is to write an animal fairy tale he keeps within the bounds of the animals' known traits and powers and displays these through their behavior.

There are many picture story books for young children about cats, dogs, goats, and ponies in which the animals appear without "make-up" of any kind. In this sense, the effect is realistic. Often the story is so slight that it is useless to attempt to define it. The charm of the book lies in its total effect, the pictures being much more important to little children than the text. Titles of some of the most satisfactory of these books appear in a separate list. (See page 413-15.)

STORIES OF CHILD-LIFE

The outburst of fairy tales and the like which occurred during the second half of the nineteenth century did not have a counterpart in the production of realistic stories, although the quality of the latter type began to improve greatly about that time.   There had been a feeble stream of stories purporting to be drawn from real child-life following upon the period described in Chapter VII when prolific writers of didactic stories held the stage.   But most of these were without literary merit and the authors were very often anonymous.   People of taste and intelligence must have sickened at the mounting pile of mediocre and unhealthy books, commonly referred to now as "Sunday-School books," which had their day both in England and America immediately following upon Mrs. Sherwood's dreary productions.   For several decades after Maria Edgeworth's last work for younger readers, healthy, happy, spontaneous children engaged in interesting activities were very rare in literature.   Almost the only saving grace at this time (from the viewpoint of today at least) is found in the numerous books of an informational character which appeared in great quantity and interesting variety.

It was not until the last quarter of the century in England, with the appearance of Mrs. Ewing, Mrs. Molesworth, and "E. Nesbit" (Mrs. Hubert Bland) as writers for children, that prose tales began to reflect with fullness and charm the changed aspects of family and social life as they relate to the young.   Juliana H. Ewing is one of the best delineators of English childhood at this period. Her relations with children were close and understanding and she makes use of much small detail on a relatively broad canvas.   In a literary way she was able to do two quite different things with equal success, to write tales with elaborated plots and dramatic situations, such as *Jackanapes*, and to construct in a loose and discursive fashion pleasing pictures of country and village life such as *Mary's Meadow*.   Mrs. Molesworth and "E. Nesbit"

mingled skillfully the real and the unreal in several of
their stories but in so doing they presented natural boys
and girls unhampered and freely creative in their excursions into the realm of fancy.

Some of the books by these authors are read today with
enjoyment by children in the upper elementary school
years, but they are not adapted to the ages with which
we are chiefly concerned.   Stories which Mrs. Molesworth intended for the nursery age, *Herr Baby* and *Little
Miss Peggy*, seem quite inane and are strewn with un-
intelligible baby-talk.

This country suffered the same epidemic of utterly
common-place and sickly religious books as did England,
and the vogue of the informational type seems to have had
an equally strong and perhaps even a more persistent
hold upon us.

About the mid-century in America a more childlike
type of realistic story began to appear.   Specific behavior
problems and everyday facts were given an important
place, but they were subordinated to action or made
essential to the natural development of the tale, and the
children were real children having interesting personalities and normal relations with each other and with their
elders.   The Reverend Jacob Abbott, author of the inter-
minable "Rollo" books (twenty-eight volumes) wrote also
three shorter series of very entertaining stories, parts of
which children still read or listen to with pleasure.   The
"Lucy" books published in the fifties — *Lucy's Conversations, Cousin Lucy on the Sea-Shore, Lucy in the Mountains*
— no doubt would seem in places quite tedious to young
readers of today.   For example, when Lucy and Marielle
enter the drawing-room of a rather imposing house where
they are on a brief visit, every single article of furniture
is described in detail and its position in the room is indicated.   But really interesting details of travel, food, play,

and nature experience are also given and these stories offer pictures of life in New England which are true to the period both in fact and spirit. The "Lucy" books are of some importance as being the earliest of their kind which were at all well adapted to the tastes and capacities of children from six to eight years of age. They are found now only in collections of old books. Abbott's *Franconia Stories*, also written in the fifties, continue the tradition, but with new and interesting characters and a quite different style. The lad called "Beechnut" (a playful contraction of his French name) bears a delightful relation to the two children, Phonny (Alphonzo), and his girl cousin Malleville. The older boy's good-tempered teasing mystifies, challenges, and amuses the younger children. Social behavior is sometimes made crucial but the psychology employed will bear modern inspection. These stories are for children a little beyond the "Lucy" stage. The lasting appeal of *Franconia Stories* is shown by the fact that some of them have been kept in constant circulation, whereas the "Rollo" books are long since dead and gone so far as children are concerned. There is a modern abridged edition of *Franconia Stories* published by Putnam.

Two series of books by Sophie May which appeared at the close of the Civil War and were eagerly devoured by little girls of that day are by these same little girls, now grandmothers, seen to be extremely weak and silly. Such reviewers are usually quite surprised to find in the *Dotty Dimple* and *Little Prudy* books so much soft sentimentality.

Louisa May Alcott (1832–1888) influenced greatly the character and quality of realistic stories in America, with her *Little Women* (1868). She wrote very little for younger children, although an occasional short story suitable for them may be found in some of her collections, but for several generations her longer stories when read aloud have offered entertainment to groups of widely varying ages.

The centenary celebration in 1932 of Miss Alcott's birth, brought abundant evidence that *Little Women* is still popular in a world which has undergone so many external changes. It mirrors the uneventful home life of New England with truth and sincerity and creates through a loosely constructed narrative four young girls remarkable for their distinct personalities.

Mary Mapes Dodge (1838–1905) also had a more than passing influence upon fiction for children. She was largely instrumental in founding the magazine *St. Nicholas*, in 1873, and was its editor for many years. Her best-known story is *Hans Brinker, or The Silver Skates*, which set a high standard of excellence and is today a classic for children in the upper grades. Among the numerous stories about children of other lands, few have been written with the rich background of knowledge and understanding which went into this old story of Dutch life.

Almost all the early American writers for children lived in New England and naturally that section became in the main the scene of their stories. Mrs. Mary P. Wells Smith, who wrote *Jolly Good Times, or Child Life on a Farm* (first published in 1875), and many other stories, made the neighborhood of her old home in Massachusetts the center of most of them. Commenting on this particular book a critic says that it contains "enduring pictures of a New England which is no more — simple, happy, human documents of little lives and slender happenings, set in a countryside. And the charm of their days and of the story-teller's manner wins each new generation as it comes." [1] A new and attractive edition of this story was brought out by Little, Brown and Company in 1927.

Any student of nineteenth-century writers for the young will readily discover how barren the period was in the

---

[1] Gulliver, Lucile, "Mrs. Smith and Her Books," in *The Horn Book*, August, 1927.

matter of stories of real child-life adapted to children below nine or ten years of age. No wonder people of taste reached the conclusion that it was useless to look for genuine literary art in books written expressly for small children. But that counsel leaves out of account the child's desire for, and right to, the fictional presentation of his own world and that of other children of about his own age, both near and far. It is a fact, however, that stories of this character having any claim to distinction are of all types the most difficult to write. Why is this so, and along what lines may progress be seen today?

A partial answer to the first part of this question is found in the mistaken attempt to apply to simple stories of normal everyday life the principles which underlie either the dramatic folk tale or well-written fiction for adults. Good folk tales always have clear-cut, well-balanced plot, and fiction for adults shows as a rule not only plot, but a gradual revelation of character through action. Dramatic plot is the result of conflicting desires, and character is best revealed through behavior, especially in crucial situations. But only occasionally will these principles apply very clearly to the realistic story for children and the younger the audience the less appropriate is any set fictional scheme.

Simple childish virtues are not dramatic in their manifestation, whereas naughtiness is often quite spectacular and may readily suggest a theme and plot. Too often in narratives which claim to picture real life to the small child, the writer has sought a crux for his story and has found it in some childish weakness or misconception with its attendant predicaments or catastrophes. This search for a well constructed plot in the relatively uncomplicated lives of small children explains the dominance in the past of the moral tale and its persistence today even though its severity has been much softened. Doubtless the fear

of seeming puerile and uninventive has caused some
ambitious writers to look for the unusual in human behavior and the novel in environment, forgetting that what
is to adults tame and hackneyed may be to small children
fresh and even exciting if suitably presented.

Various methods have been used in the attempt to become better acquainted with what is in the children's own
minds which may tend to determine their attitudes toward
certain subjects for stories and certain types of treatment.
Dr. Jean Betzner [1] conducted an experiment with a somewhat different objective, but her findings throw some light
on the probable predisposition of children toward certain
kinds of story material. She obtained by direct contact
1215 original, spontaneous oral compositions dictated in-
dividually by public school children from five to eight
years of age. Among the many interesting findings in Dr.
Betzner's analysis of these original stories are the following:

As main centers of interest or themes, human beings rank
highest — personal experiences, children and adults total-
ing 76.9 per cent; animals and nature subjects come next
with 18 per cent; while toys, mechanical inventions and all
other inanimate objects account for only 3.1 per cent.
Among the older groups, people were used as main characters more frequently and animal subjects decreased.

Analysis showed that boys and girls at all age levels included in the study made use of both realistic and imaginative treatment of their themes, the difference in amounts
being much less than is quite commonly assumed. A realistic treatment is used somewhat more frequently by all
age groups except one — the eight-year-old boys. This
group employed an imaginative treatment more than twice
as frequently as a realistic. Another interesting fact is

[1] Betzner, Jean, *Content and Form of Original Prose Compositions
Dictated by Children from Five to Eight Years of Age*. Bureau of Publications, Teachers College, Columbia University, 1930.

that five, six, seven, and eight-year-old girls followed a realistic pattern more often than did corresponding groups of boys.

As to conduct, its expression was predominantly normal and wholesome. "There were only four cases in the entire number of compositions in which unpleasant family relations appeared.... There were in all only eighty stories in which wrong-doing was handled.... While the girls show a greater tendency to concern themselves with the effect of punishment on future behavior, the boys leave fewer wrongs unpunished."

Many talented writers have been able to get a true perspective from the child's standpoint and they have broken quite away from traditional story forms and from the exaggerated use of behavior issues in plot construction. They secure unity, variety, color and pleasurable excitement without overstrained emotion and spectacular incident. The result is a great expansion as regards subject, scene, story pattern and style of writing. An informal survey of story books for children under ten years of age reveals a generous use of those subjects which the children employed most frequently in their own original stories.

Subjects from child-life come first. The following five divisions of more recent stories of this kind are intended to indicate certain trends rather than well-defined and mutually exclusive classes. The validity and usefulness of such divisions can be judged by the student only after a careful reading of a number of books in each group. Stories about children of other lands have been grouped under that head not because of any essential difference in them but as a matter of convenience to students.

1. There is a tendency today to furnish stories for children of nursery school age which are entirely without plot in the usual sense of the term. This is in response to a

better understanding of the mental and emotional life of young children. It is argued that the mounting excitement of a dramatic climax is not needed to arouse and hold their interest since the whole world is new and fascinating and that part which touches them intimately holds a strong personal and emotional appeal. Subject-matter chosen from the familiar surrounding world and a very simple narrative style are recommended. Mrs. Lucy Sprague Mitchell has done pioneer work in developing stories of this kind and she tells of extensive experiments and makes a clear statement of underlying theory in the Introduction to her collection of original stories mentioned below. Mrs. Mitchell seeks to give young children "a sense of adventure in the world of today" by recreating in vivid, sensory language, experiences drawn from home life and neighborhood exploration. In her more developed stories she uses rudimentary plot occasionally imitative of simple folk tales, but she avoids issues arising out of mistaken motives and actions of children.

Mrs. Lucy Sprague Mitchell.   *Here and Now Story Book.* Dutton.

This is not a child's book, but a collection of short stories for telling and reading to children from babyhood to about seven years. The subjects are in the main drawn from city life or short excursions — engines, boats, subway trains, delivery wagons, skyscrapers — all are invested with something of the vivid quality which they doubtless possess to eager young eyes and ears. These stories are especially approved by parents and teachers who desire to avoid or greatly reduce the use of folk and fairy tales with young children. The author has sometimes been represented as disapproving altogether of the latter type of story. A careful reading of the Introduction will show that this is not her attitude.

2. Some writers of stories for young children choose a simple experience in real life and break it up into successive

steps with a happy but unforced culmination. Through a simple artistic form they seek to secure a heightened realization of an everyday experience. An earlier writer, Miss Maud Lindsay, was sometimes quite successful in this kind of story. Some of the best examples are to be found among Elsa Beskow's beautiful picture story books. Maj Lindman's stories, which are as much real as they are fanciful, have already been mentioned.

Maud Lindsay. *A Story Garden for Little Children*. Lathrop.
  A small book intended chiefly for the story-teller's use. The subjects are usually well suited to very young children. Notice especially *Thimble Biscuit*, *The Strawberry Short-cake*, and *Ten Pennies*.　　　　　　　　　　　　　　　A

Elsa Beskow. *Pelle's New Suit*. Full-page pictures in color by the author. Doubleday.
  The story is told almost as much by the lovely pictures as by the text. Pelle participates at each step in the pro-duction of his new suit from the shearing of his lamb to the work of sewing and finishing.　　　　　　　　　　　　　A

Maj Lindman. *Snipp, Snapp, Snurr and the Red Shoes*. Albert Whitman.
  A Swedish artist tells in charming colorful pictures and simple accumulative story, how three little boys earned the money to buy red satin shoes for their mother's birthday. Other little boys will envy them some of their occupations. A

3. In longer stories for children from five to seven years of age a very common method is to adopt an un-dramatic narrative style descriptive of the even flow of simple childish experience from day to day with its ups and downs of joy and woe. Stories of this sort are apt to cover at least a few months of a child's life and to be told in several chapters. Often an entire chapter could be taken right out as a separate story without affecting the development of the whole, showing that there was no intention of constructing a unified plot. The personality of child characters is revealed more or less clearly accord-

ing to the skill of the writer, and in the course of the book there may be many interesting and happy events which other children will enjoy in imagination. For the age level mentioned, probably stories of this kind offer the best mirror of life and help children to enter most fully into other homes and other spheres. Many good examples can be found. Among the most successful writers are the following.

Clara Whitehall Hunt.
> *About Harriet.* Houghton.
>> This story covers one week in the life of a lovable little four-year-old and tells of what she did with her mother and Daddy on each of seven days. Children several years older than Harriet like to read for themselves this simple story record. A

> *The Little House in the Woods.* Houghton.
>> This story tells of one summer in the life of a little girl whose sixth birthday is celebrated soon after the arrival of the family in Maine. It describes the delightful and varied play life of a group of natural children at the sea-shore, on picnics, and in a wonderful tree-house. Miss Hunt is particularly happy in her presentation of the relations of adults and children in family and neighborhood groups. A, B

Helen Hill and Violet Maxwell.
> *Charlie and His Kitten Topsy.* Macmillan.
> *Charlie and His Puppy Bingo.* Macmillan.
>> Not all the stories in the first book are "realistic" according to our definition, but that is the general character of most of them. A real little boy has all kinds of interesting experiences with his pets and toys and enjoys the stimulating companionship of understanding grown-ups. Quite commonly, separate chapters constitute a single incident with its own small plot. A

Margery Clark. *The Poppy Seed Cakes.* Doubleday.
> The pictures and decorations by Maud and Miska Petersham add greatly to the delightful story about the little boy Andrewshek and his indulgent Auntie Katushka. A little neighbor, Erminka, "a sweet little white goat," and a greedy goose, add to the lively doings of the children. The animals

are not always strictly realistic in their behavior but only the big green goose is actually a creature from the world of magic.   A

Ethel Calvert Phillips.
    Miss Phillips writes with a good deal of variety, her child characters are natural and unaffected, and she can impart a feeling of life and animation to simple scenes without resorting to exaggeration.
Little Sally Waters. Houghton.
    Six-year-old Sally, her dog Tippy, and her new friend Alice have good times together and a few difficulties for which Tippy is responsible.   A
Wee Ann. Houghton.
    A little Scotch girl goes for a long visit to her grandmother's in the country and the story tells of natural childish play and recounts a few more exciting experiences.   B

Helen Fuller Orton. *Bobby of Cloverfield Farm*. Stokes.
    There are a number of the "Cloverfield Farm" books, all of them dealing in an interesting manner with work and play on a New England farm. They contain a good deal of information of the kind children are apt to seek but it is skillfully subordinated to the story.   B

Eliza Orne White.
    Miss White's first stories were published in the late nineties and she now has some nine or ten books to her credit. Whether she writes of a century ago or of today, the scenes are usually laid in New England and a simple, refined, and quiet family life is portrayed. The difference between the past and present will impress the modern child but Miss White never makes the mistake of deflecting or halting the story for the sake of emphasizing history. Her children are full of life and not always good and she displays unusual skill in carrying a story forward by reproducing natural, animated conversation.
A Little Girl of Long Ago. Houghton.
    The little Marietta in this story is really Miss White's mother who crossed from Scotland in 1826. She is a very interesting and straight-forward little girl and she and her brothers and sisters and her little friend Leonora have many good times in Boston of a hundred years ago.   B, C

When Abigail Was Seven. Houghton.

An attractive edition with scissors-cuts by Lisl Hummel. The story opens with little Abigail at work on her sampler which contains the line, "Abigail Wetmore 1828," so this is another story of a century ago.   Again a refined and whole-some home life is portrayed and two of the children have an interesting visit at Uncle Timothy's in Salem.   B, C

Elinor Whitney. *Timothy and the Blue Cart.* Pleasing illustra-tions by Berta and Elmer Hader. Stokes.

A story of three city children and their summer in the country.   Timothy is a faithful old horse belonging to the farmer who owns the blue cart, and horse and cart have much to do with the happenings of the summer.   There is more variety than is usually found in a story of this kind, including a bit of a mystery which the children help to solve.   B, C

Peggy Bacon.
   The Terrible Nuisance and Other Stories. Harcourt.

The illustrations by the author form a perfect complement to the stories.   The title of the book is somewhat misleading since all the stories concern the doings of a particular family in a suburban neighborhood.   There are three perfectly natural and lively children, several equally genuine grown-ups (parents, cook, and neighbors), and the household pets, among which is Chug the puppy, otherwise "The Terrible Nuisance."   Mrs. Bacon shows the freedom from hampering tradition in this book which she displayed in her animal stories, and readers are taken into the heart of contemporary life in a home where common sense, good breeding, and comradeship prevail.   C

Mischief in Mayfield. Harcourt.

Illustrated by the author.   The same three lively and natural children engage in further adventures in the country.   C

4. Some of the most charming stories of child-life are quite short and tell of a single episode.   In these there is good plot construction in contrast to the more diffuse style just described.   They present a small slice of life well selected and skillfully developed with the beginning,

middle, and end which unity demands. Sometimes they are published in a collection as unrelated stories by a single author, but more commonly of late they have enjoyed the pleasant distinction of appearing in separate books. Often these are of the small size which children love, and publishers are exercising much care and taste in producing them. This format is not peculiar to realistic stories but it seems to accord especially well with narratives which have brevity and completeness. On the other hand, authors who are themselves artists often prefer to use the large picture-book style for their short stories. The following three books are examples of this form:

Elsa Beskow.

    Aunt Green, Aunt Brown, and Aunt Lavender. Translated from the Swedish by Siri Andrews. Harper.

        Three quaint old ladies, two children who have the good fortune to find a home with them, and several friends and neighbors find some strong common interests, the most important being their concerted endeavor to recover a precious little dog which was stolen.   A, B

    Aunt Brown's Birthday. Harper.

        This "Aunt" is a great favorite, and Peter and Lotta succeed in celebrating her birthday in suitable style.   A, B

    The Adventures of Peter and Lotta. Harper.

        The same characters appear in this story, but the children have a more prominent part and they have some surprising and amusing experiences.   A, B

Rachel L. Field.

        Miss Field is one of the most versatile and gifted writers of today, succeeding almost equally well in a great variety of forms. For children under ten years of age, nothing that she has done gives more pleasure than her short and perfect realistic stories which have been bound separately in small books with gay covers. Considering the brevity of the tales, her characters stand out with remarkable individuality. Miss Field selects her central incidents and situations with keen insight into what young readers are likely to consider important and interesting. In each of these little stories there is something which the small actors have set their hearts on and which we see them obtaining through their own efforts and through happy circumstance.

Polly Patchwork. Illustrated by the author. Doubleday.

Polly goes to a spelling match wearing a remarkable new dress made from an old patchwork quilt and it helps her to win the match. **B, C**

Pocket-Handkerchief Park. Illustrated by the author. Doubleday.

A group of children led by small Timothy Toomey take it upon themselves to save a precious little park in their neighborhood and meet with success. **C**

The Yellow Shop. Illustrated by the author. Doubleday.

The twins, Will and Rebecca, "going on nine," are adopted by Aunt Roxanna. They soon discover that their generous aunt is in sad need of money and they conceive the idea of opening a little shop near a frequented crossroads. There they have both exciting and profitable experiences. To keep shop some time is the dear wish of almost every child, and this story appeals strongly to that cherished hope. **C**

Constance Heward.

Most of Miss Heward's charming stories are illustrated in color by Susan B. Pearse and the result is an unusual unity in interpretation. Their books are not of the "pocket-book" size as the pictures which are such an integral part of the amusing little dramas require a somewhat larger page. The stories are short, each is complete in itself, and delightful child characters usually carry through some enterprise or meet some unique experience with directness and originality. Ameliaranne, who appears in several of Miss Heward's stories, is her most original and spirited child character.

The Twins and Tabiffa. Illustrations in color by Susan B. Pearse. McKay.

"Tabiffa" is the nearest approach the twins can make to "Tabitha," the name of their pet cat. To the grown-ups of the family she is an unwelcome member of the household, but she at last justifies the warm championship of the twins and wins a place for herself and her kittens. **B**

Ameliaranne and the Green Umbrella. Illustrations in color by Susan B. Pearse. Macrae.

All the little Stigginses except Ameliaranne are kept at home with "cold in their heads" on the day of a wonderful party. She plays the part of big sister with forethought and

daring and succeeds in bringing a share of the treat to the
five little prisoners, and that is where the big green umbrella
comes in.   B, C

Ameliaranne Keeps Shop.   Illustrations in color by Susan B.
Pearse.   McKay.

Again this faithful and competent little girl is master of
a difficult situation.   This does not mean that she is either
a child prodigy or a "goody-goody."   C

Alice Dalgliesh.   *The Blue Teapot and Other Sandy Cove Stories*.
Illustrated by Hildegard Woodward.   Macmillan.

This is a collection of separate stories all of which relate to
simple child-life in Nova Scotia.   The children are natural
and resourceful and are seen in happy relation to grown
people.   Two of the best stories are *The Blue Teapot* and *The
Seven White Cats*.   A, B

5. With no sharp line of demarcation, the simple,
loosely organized narratives referred to under paragraph
3 above, evolve into the longer and relatively more complex and closely knit stories which are often designated
specifically as "juveniles."   Such stories display a larger
canvas than is required for any kind previously mentioned.
Typically, there are more characters (although the story
centers in one or two), events and scenes are not of independent and equal significance but are calculated to forward the main action, and quite often there are small
sub-plots which enlarge and qualify the whole.

There are not many choice books of this kind for boys
and girls too immature for those written by Kate Douglas
Wiggin, Cornelia Meigs, and Rose Knox, for example.
And yet many children of nine and ten are ready for and
crave the more fully developed presentation of interesting
characters acting and being acted upon in situations not
wholly single and uncomplicated.   Readers at this level
owe much to Johanna Spyri whose stories possess all these
qualities.   Her well-known books beginning with *Heidi*,
published in 1879, have greatly enriched the lives of chil-

dren in the many countries which have had translations of them.

It would appear that there is room for more books of this general description suited to boys and girls of the "middle-age" level — about fourth and fifth grade. Stories which portray life in other lands or seek colorful material in past times are much more numerous than those which attempt to interpret contemporary American life. Is this because writers tend to lean heavily upon the unique and picturesque in the remote, and fail to discover the kernel of romance and drama nearer home? Of course it is more difficult to lift familiar subjects out of the trivial and commonplace and at the same time avoid exaggeration, but our best writers seem to have no difficulty in doing this for children only a little beyond the age-level mentioned.

Of the following recently published stories for younger readers which picture the American scene, three are about pioneer life in the United States and the scene of another is laid in Quebec at the present time

Laura Ingalls Wilder. *Little House in the Big Woods*. Illustrated by Helen Sewell. Harper.

"Once upon a time sixty years ago, a little girl lived in the Big Woods of Wisconsin, in a little gray house made of logs." The life of two sturdy little sisters with their parents is exciting, but Pa adds to the picture of pioneer days by telling stories of his own boyhood. C

Ethel Calvert Phillips. *Gay Madelon*. Illustrated by Ilse Bischoff. Houghton.

A story of unusual charm as regards characters, plot, incidents and scenes. Madelon is a little French Canadian who travels down the Saguenay River to Tadoussac to spend some months with Tante Marie and Oncle Paul, and then on to Quebec in the winter. Boys as well as girls like the book as there are several interesting boy characters and men play important rôles. There is much local color, but it is introduced as an essential part of the background. C

Helen Fuller Orton.   *The Treasure in the Little Trunk*.   With embellishments by Robert Ball.   Stokes.

A story of child-life in the early nineteenth century.   The Armstrongs move in a covered wagon from their well-developed farm in Vermont to Western New York when that section was still a wilderness.   There are many interesting incidents connected with the trip and with getting settled which give an authentic picture of the time and the country.   In that sense it is historical, but first and foremost it is an interesting story.   C

Cornelia Meigs.   *The Willow Whistle*.   Illustrated by E. Boyd Smith.   Macmillan.

This is the easiest of the long stories by Miss Meigs, but still it will require something of a stretch for the average ten-year-old reader.   It is included here because it is an excellent example of what children of that age should be rapidly growing into.   It is a gripping story of pioneer life in the western prairies in which Indians, friendly and otherwise, play an important part.   Mary Anne, eight years old, and Eric, somewhat older, are sure to be admired by young Americans.   Little girls are not the only ones who are likely to marvel at Mary Anne's equanimity in a terrifying situation.   A willow whistle and an old Blue-Backed Speller are important "properties" in the little drama.   C

STORIES ABOUT CHILDREN OF OTHER LANDS AND RACES

Attention has been called to the great number of stories about other countries and peoples as compared to those of equal worth dealing with contemporary life in America. There are several rather obvious explanations of this trend.   It has already been pointed out that the average writer finds it much easier to discover high points of interest in action and scene when these are sought in a remote time or place, or in an alien race.   Deprived of such adjuncts, the story-teller is forced to try to penetrate into what is, to a superficial adult view, commonplace and lacking in story quality.   Another stimulus to the production of stories of other lands is the sincere desire to broaden the sympathies of children by giving them truer and more complete pictures of other lives; and closely related to this is a sharpened sense of the importance of social studies in the reconstructed curricula of our schools. Probably greatly increased travel into all parts of the world is having its effect upon writers in suggesting to them colorful and picturesque story material. This is further accentuated by the fact that many artists are now writing stories for children and naturally they seek scenes and situations rich in pictorial possibilities. Whatever the sources of the impulse, it has resulted in the production of many beautiful picture story books about children of other lands, and some excellent stories.

Perhaps attention should again be called to the fact that many fanciful tales such as "To Market! To Market!" and "Martin the Goose Boy," previously noted, serve almost as well as more realistic stories to give this larger vision.

The value of vicarious experience obtained through well-written, artistic, and authentic books is unquestioned, and happily there has been great improvement of late in these three qualities. The features for emphasis are selected with care, the tendency being to avoid those which would seem very peculiar or unlovely to our children, to accent those which are pleasing and admirable according to our standards, and to show that in some matters we have a good deal to learn from other peoples and races. The most successful writers accomplish these ends without resorting to falsity or admonition, and with no loss of dramatic and colorful elements.

The work of some of the most prominent writers in this field will be mentioned, together with a few outstanding single books by less prolific writers. As in previous lists, the order is approximately from the simple to the more difficult. Books in which the pictures seem to be much more important than the story are included in the "Picture

Book" list, and naturally the larger number of books suited to the youngest children will be found there.

Lucy Fitch Perkins.

Mrs. Perkins is one of the best known writers of stories about children of other lands. She has sustained her reputation in this field over a long period of time and throughout the many volumes of the "Twins" series. She has run less risk of monotony than most writers of a book series because each of her books has a different pair of twins. This writer has the ability to select natural childlike events and to display deep-lying human characteristics along with the unique and picturesque in native custom and scene. Mrs. Perkins illustrates her own books very successfully. The following are among the most suitable of the series for the youngest children.

The Farm Twins. Houghton. A, B
The Dutch Twins. Houghton B
The Eskimo Twins. Houghton. B
The Japanese Twins. Houghton. C

Grace and Carl Moon.

Mr. and Mrs. Moon have collaborated most successfully in writing and illustrating their stories of North American Indians. Most of these are more suitable for older children but the following is well designed for the younger ones.

The Book of Nah-Wee. Doubleday.

Very lovely colored pictures true to Indian life and pueblo scenes. The stories are about Nah-Wee, a little girl, and Dat-say, a boy, who are good friends and have many experiences together. Children like the book but the stories have no real distinction. There is a good deal of accurate information about food, houses and handicraft which is introduced incidentally. B

Zhenya and Jan Gay. *Pancho and His Burro*. Morrow.

A large picture story book with full-page pictures in clear brilliant colors. The story tells of the daily life of Pancho and his sister Lola — especially of their market affairs in which the burro figures. B

Rhea Wells.

This author-artist has made some notable contributions to stories of life in other lands. He seems to be equally accomplished in the two fields of writing and illustrating. In addition to the many delightful pictures in his books he makes use of attractive page decorations. Several of his book titles identify some leading animal character, but each of these stories tells about many interesting and characteristic events and customs among the people concerned, with children always playing an important part. Mr. Wells's stories and pictures are full of unforced humor.

Peppi the Duck. Doubleday.
　　Concerning the adventures and experiences of an ambitious duckling in the Tyrolean Alps. 　　　　　B

Coco the Goat. Doubleday.
　　About a mischievous little goat, his young master Garito, and their life in a small village in Spain. 　　B

Beppo the Donkey. Doubleday.
　　The story of a tiny donkey on the island of Sicily and how he shared the fun and work of a family of children. 　　B

E. Mildred Nevill. *Ah Fu, a Chinese River Boy*. Friendship Press.
　　A small book with many pictures telling in a sympathetic way about life on a house-boat in China. 　　B

Eleanor Frances Lattimore. *Little Pear*. Pictures in black and white by the author. Harcourt.
　　The story of a little Chinese boy in his native village, written by one who knows life in China intimately. Little Pear, his sisters and friends, are genuine children and the stories are lively and colorful but true in incident and setting. 　　　　　B

Dorothy Rowe. *The Rabbit Lantern*. Illustrations are by a Chinese artist, Ling Jui Tang. Macmillan.
　　The author is an American who was born in China and spent her childhood there and her stories are full of the joys of those years. This is a collection of short stories about Chinese boys and girls, their home life and their travels. In more than one of them we hear "the laughings that little boys love." Interesting facts essential to the action are woven into the stories in an artistic way. 　　B, C

Katharine L. Keelor. *Little Fox*. Illustrated by Frederick Richardson. Macmillan.
　　Little Fox is a small Algonquin boy who lived with his

family on the island of Manhattan before Hendrick Hudson landed there. Miss Keelor made a deep study of the life of this tribe and tested her material thoroughly, with children. She has woven many interesting facts into the texture of the story.

B, C

Margaret Loring Thomas. *The Burro's Money Bag*. Abingdon Press.

How Pedro, a little Mexican boy, filled the money bag that bought the coveted burro. Parents and grandparents helped, but Pedro proved himself ingenious as well as independent. A pleasing story with true pictures of Mexican life.

B

May Mulvaney Dauteur. *Joan and Pierre*. Doubleday.

Joan is a little American girl and this is the story of her visit to Pierre in Paris and then in Brittany. It is a gay and colorful little story of simple French life, rural and urban, with many delightful pictures by the author who is thoroughly at home in France.

B

Alice Cooper Bailey. *Katrina and Jan*. Volland.

One of the great charms of this book consists in the beautiful colored pictures by Herman Rosse who has made the most of the gay Dutch scenes. The story makes a strong appeal as the two children are carried through several rather exciting and closely related adventures. The part played by Katrina's remarkable goose may strain the credulity of a nine-year-old a bit, but he adds greatly to the dramatic plot.

C

F. M., and Howard Everson. *The Coming of the Dragon Ships*. Dutton.

An interesting reconstruction of life in Iceland in Viking days with a little girl as the central figure. Edgar P. d'Aulaire's illustrations are, as always, beautiful and revealing. There has been a lack of story material for younger readers depicting this region and period.

C

Barbra Ring. *Peik*. Translated from the Norwegian by Lorence M. Woodside and charmingly interpreted by Robert Lawson's pictures. Little.

There is nothing trite in this story of a sturdy little Norwegian boy, for the situations are somewhat unusual and Peik is a child who possesses a real personality.

C

Johanna Spyri.
  Heidi. Ginn.
       There are several different translations and editions of this
    old and ever-popular story of a lovable little girl and her
    interesting life in the Swiss Alps. One of the most attrac-
    tive is the one published by Ginn, with many delightful pic-
    tures by Marguerite Davis, who spent several months in the
    very region where the scene of the story is laid.
  The same. Houghton.
  Illustrated by Gustaf Tenggren.   C

Margaret Warner Morley. *Donkey John of Toy Valley.* Mc-
  Clurg.
       This is another old story which has been enjoyed by two
    generations of children. It is a sincere and sympathetic tale
    of a ten-year-old herd boy in the Tyrol who is ambitious to
    become a wood-carver and how he develops one unique
    talent — that of carving wonderful donkeys.   C

TRUE AND ALMOST-TRUE ANIMAL STORIES

The general distinctions between fanciful and realistic
animal tales were set forth at the beginning of this chapter,
but before attempting to select illustrations of the latter
type certain traits should be recalled and amplified. We
are seeking animal stories which are true to actual life in all
essential points but which possess true literary quality,
therefore we are not concerned with strictly informational
material of the textbook or factual sort. In this particular
division we have chosen to include only those stories in
which animals are the leading characters, — in some instances they are the only ones.

It calls for high literary art to create an individual animal character which will call forth a peculiar interest and
sympathy beyond that ordinarily aroused by its class; to
respect facts but make them serve in creating beauty; and
to appeal to feeling without sinking into sentimentality.
Animal stories which possess these qualities can be produced only by well-informed, talented and sincere writers.

While the dressed-up animal has an acknowledged and secure place in fanciful stories, such disguise is inappropriate in stories which purport to portray animals as they are. A number of our leading artists are proving how appealing and fascinating animals can be in their own unique forms and ways. Even in the "almost-true" stories here listed, the animal characters do nothing that is really eccentric, nothing which is fabricated out of human behavior.

The fact must not be overlooked, however, that young children can enter into the feelings and experiences of dumb creatures only as these are interpreted through human language, consequently speech must sometimes be accorded to animal characters. Although the pigs in the first story below talk a good deal among themselves their overt actions are wholly pig-like. There are many such stories which, in deference to the precisionists, we are calling "almost-true." Perhaps Miss Brock's story of a young goat with a remarkable homing instinct and Mrs. Kuebler's "Hansel" call for this qualification. It might seem time wasted to attempt these distinctions except for the fact that so many parents and others are demanding some such guidance in stories for young children. We suggest that students become acquainted with good examples of all kinds of stories and then forget all about minor distinctions of subject and treatment except in response to the children's own questions. Listening to an absorbing story, it is the rare child who will ask whether a goat or a gander could really do this or that.

Helen Fuller Orton.
The Little Lost Pigs. Stokes.
A very attractive small book, illustrated by Luxor Price. Two little pigs seized by the wanderlust and feeling themselves imposed upon in Farmer Gray's pigpen, set out to explore the Big World. They are humanized in many of their sensations, hopes and fears, but their acts are all in accordance with pig nature. Very popular with small children. A

The Twin Lambs. Charmingly illustrated by Marjorie Flack.
Stokes.

> The mother of twin lambs rejects them and they are given
> to Joan and Kenley to be raised. They become great pets
> and follow the children everywhere, and thus is developed a
> sort of "Mary's little lamb" story. No more delightful pets
> could be imagined for children in the country.   A, B

Emma L. Brock. *The Greedy Goat*. Illustrated by the author.
Knopf.

> The story of a young goat, Anna Marie, in the high Tyrol,
> her naughty tricks and how she defeated the many attempts
> of the family to get rid of her. "Realistic" only in the sense
> that there is no magic in the events except Anna Marie's
> truly remarkable homing instinct. An amusing story with
> delightful pictures.   A

Katharine Kuebler. *Hansel the Gander*. The illustrations consist of eight lovely soft pastel pictures by Ilse Bischoff.
Morrow.

> Hansel, a great white gander, is the leader of all the geese
> in a Bavarian village. He fails to return one evening and
> his little mistress Elsa has a long search for him. He has
> been stolen and shut up but is at last discovered and re-
> leased. A good plot with dramatic interest.   A

Eliza Orne White. *Sally in Her Fur Coat*. Charming scissors-
cuts by Lisl Hummel. Houghton.

> How twin kittens, Sally and her brother, Oxford Gray,
> find a comfortable home. Clever rhymes are interspersed.
>   A, B

Kurt Wiese. *Karoo the Kangaroo*. Coward-McCann.

> Unusual full-page crayon drawings by the author, who
> spent five years in Australia and knows the background
> thoroughly. The story gives a sympathetic and accurate
> picture of a baby kangaroo and his mother, their life in the
> herd, and the dangers and escapes in desert and bush.
> Other native animals play minor parts in the story and help
> to complete the scene.   B

Eleanor Wheeler. *Jemmie: The Kitten from Maine*. Illustrated
by Marjorie Flack. Smith and Haas.

> A story of nearly a hundred pages about a kitten whose
> real life with his mistress Marjorie is told in much more

detail than most stories of animal pets for small children. All this kitten's ways are described with the detail which only a cat-lover could command, but the style is one which will hold the interest of children. **B**

Zhenya Gay and Jan Gay. *The Shire Colt.* Doubleday.

The first year in the life of a little colt foaled in the Cotswold Hills, England, is beautifully told in story and pictures. Few animal stories are developed so completely from the physical and sensuous life of the animals themselves, and there is no straining after dramatic effects. The entire story, which is not long, is devoted to the way the little creature lives and learns close to his wise old mother in the fields of Penny Farm. **B**

N. Karazin. *Cranes Flying South.* Translated from the Russian by M. Pokrovsky. Illustrated by Vera Bock. Doubleday.

There is much that is fanciful about this charming story but it is placed in this group in order to call attention again to the way facts and fancy, reality and beauty may be linked together in a literary story. The factual side in this instance concerns the peculiarly interesting life of cranes, and the Russian country as seen by them in migration. **B, C**

Allen Chaffee. *Wandy, the Wild Pony.* Illustrated by Richard Floeth. Smith and Haas.

Both boys and girls are certain to like this story about a little wild Devon pony. It is a vivid account of his life, first with his mother and the herd, and later as a trained and clever pet.

Mabelle Halleck St. Clair.

Max, the Story of a Little Black Bear. Illustrated by Lee Townsend. Harcourt.

This is a very unusual story, being a humorous and sometimes exciting account of the ways and wiles of a baby bear adopted as a pet by two children with the assistance of patient and resourceful parents. To one who makes no claim to expert knowledge about bear cubs, the story seems on the whole plausible, and it is highly entertaining. **C**

More about Max. Illustrated by Lee Townsend. Harcourt.

As a two-year-old, Max is scarcely a suitable household pet and he is taken to join the bear colony in Yellowstone Park. The closing scene of the story will delight all readers for it tells how the family to whom he had belonged visit him in the park and are recognized by him. Mrs. St. Clair spent several months in Yellowstone Park before writing the second book and she makes good use of amusing incidents which she witnessed.

C

INFORMATION IN THE FORM OF FICTION

Several times in this chapter attention has been called to the fidelity and effectiveness with which writers have utilized facts about animals in their literary stories, but this section has reference to the artistic presentation of more specific scientific facts which the writers deem suitable for children. Almost all stories of this type assume the form of biography or autobiography and hence contain more information than the purely literary story would need to use in order to work out a compact plot. A faint and not always easily recognizable line exists between such stories as the following and good simplified science books. The one strong point of difference is the manner in which these stories impart a sense of personal significance to the smallest and most obscure creatures. Not every writer can do this without resorting to an exaggerated humanization of them.

Wilfred S. Bronson.
  Polliwiggle's Progress.   Macmillan.
    Numerous detailed drawings by the author form a very essential part of this story of the repeated cycle "from egg to frog to polliwog." Without reading into a polliwog's experience the feelings and sentiments of people, Mr. Bronson conveys vivid impressions of the multitudinous life of the pond and the polliwog's relation to it. Many of the explanatory drawings supply a humorous side-light which helps to relate a fact or incident to something with which children are likely to be familiar.

C

Paddlewings: The Penguin of Galapagos.   Macmillan.
    Penguins with their amusing and unique characteristics have become very popular in story books of late, and Paddlewings is a distinguished member of his species. Mr. Bron-

son uses text and pictures with equal success in relating a young penguin's adventures from his earliest days until he arrives at the New York Aquarium.   C

Fingerfins: The Tale of a Sargasso Fish. Macmillan.

Mr. Bronson was an artist with the Beebe expedition to the Sargasso Sea and this notable book for children is based upon that wonderful experience.   C

Alice Crew Gall and Fleming H. Crew. *Wagtail.* Oxford Press.

An interesting story is supplemented by Kurt Wiese's delightful drawings. The whole relates with fine imagination but no false values, the life and adventures of this little creature from tadpole to frog.   B, C

Thornton W. Burgess.

The Burgess Animal Book for Children. Little, Brown.

A large book with numerous authentic and carefully executed pictures in color by Louis Agassiz Fuertes. This book is devoted to mammals, large and small, from field mouse to buffalo. The author says in the Preface, "The utmost care to be accurate in the smallest detail has been exercised.... No statements which are not confirmed by two or more naturalists of recognized standing have been made." Mother Nature keeps school and teaches many lessons about animals and their ways. These stories are a little more mature than the Burgess *Bedtime Stories*.   B, C

The Burgess Bird Book for Children. Illustrated by Louis A. Fuertes. Little, Brown.

A companion volume to the *Animal Book*.   B, C

MACHINES AS HEROES

The very keen interest which children, especially boys, manifest in machinery, has led to some experiments in story-writing in which machines are treated very much like human beings of gigantic proportions. Story action is wrought out of the machine's characteristic performances, and through the copious use of imitative syllables a kind of language is constructed to serve the new type hero. When the main purpose in writing a story is to present a great many facts about function, structure and process, creative imagination working through literary art is effectively smothered. On the other hand, a gay little book, such as *Little Machinery* by Mary Liddell (Doubleday), has all the appearance and effect of having been made for sheer fun and yet it conveys some interesting facts in a whimsical way.

The present writer knows of only one actually true story possessing distinct literary worth in which a mechanical object is the central figure, and that is *Little Blacknose*. The author had as a basis for this story an historical incident rich in dramatic possibilities, and she was not dependent upon sheer mechanical invention and achievement for character and theme. Until we have more examples on this level it remains to be proved that modern mechanisms can be anything more than clumsy actors in the realm of true literature.

It is true that old and young gaze fascinated at these great giants at work whose actions often bear an uncanny resemblance to those of some powerful and intelligent beast, but such brief observations are quite different from the demand made upon a writer who attempts to construct a consistent and sustained tale with a machine as hero and with no concession to the unreal. Are structure, function and process really made clear, or are they obscured in such stories? Is not the simple, straightforward descriptive style in excellent English which is used by Mr. Lent in *Diggers and Builders*, for example, a better approach in every way?

Another possible medium is poetry. Poets writing for adults are able occasionally to create powerful and sharply etched pictures of some of man's mechanical inventions. Perhaps verse with its brevity, rhythm and sensory images, will be found to be a better medium than prose fiction by which to offer to children glimpses of some of the wonders of the machine age in which they are living.

Hildegarde Hoyt Swift. *Little Blacknose. The Story of a Pioneer*. Harcourt.

Strong simple woodcuts by Lynd Ward fit perfectly this "true and honest story of the DeWitt Clinton Engine, and all that he saw and did." Quaint little "Blacknose" is the first locomotive ever made for the New York Central Railroad and his life story is here told vividly and with delightful humor. There is no false ornamentation and engine "language" is used with artistic restraint. Boys and girls love this book and incidentally they learn a good deal from it.

B, C

Here are a few examples of books which do not attempt a story form, but give a plain straightforward account of some fascinating features of industry and machinery. The authors do not talk down to children but use clear and vivid description. Such books have a very wide appeal from early childhood on, and for that reason we omit the usual symbols indicating age levels. The two easiest are put first, however.

Berta and Elmer Hader. *The Picture Book of Travel*. Macmillan.

A large and gorgeous picture book about all kinds of transportation with a brief text which gives desired information.

Peter Gimmage. *The Picture Book of Ships*. Macmillan.

Ships of long ago and of today are shown together with a clear explanatory text. The pictures are strikingly beautiful.

Henry B. Lent. *Diggers and Builders*. Macmillan.

Labor is not decked out in a sentimental fashion, but is shown to be both dignified and dramatic. Six different kinds of labor with the equipment used, all connected with building, are here pictured and described in a fashion well suited to primary grades.

Adele G. Nathan and Margaret S. Ernst. *The Iron Horse*. Knopf.

Large picture book form with many fine photographs of locomotives and a clear interesting text.

George Buck and Boris Artzybasheff. *What Makes the Wheels Go Round*. Macmillan.

> A fascinating book especially suited to boys of nine and over.

Lewis W. Hine. *Men at Work*. Macmillan.

> "Photographic studies of modern men and machines." For young and old.

OTHER INFORMATIONAL MATERIAL

There are, of course, many other avenues of knowledge which have a strong attraction for children. To attempt to investigate all of them would take us into curriculum-making in social studies and elementary science, and that is not the purpose of this book. We will simply offer a few more examples of books prepared with due regard for scientific and artistic qualities and intended to stimulate and satisfy the intellectual curiosity of children from six to ten years of age.

Berta and Elmer Hader. *The Farmer in the Dell*. Macmillan.

> A picture book of convenient size, profusely illustrated. A brief and simple narrative describes the work and play on a small American farm where modern machinery is not at all prominent. Activities are arranged in the order of the seasons.

Edith M. Patch.

> This author is very skillful in presenting informational material. Her subjects are well chosen and she handles them with simplicity and charm.

Hexapod Stories. Little.

> All about insects.

First Lessons in Nature Study. Little.

> About a variety of nature experiences.

Holiday Pond. Macmillan.

> Plant and animal life in a pond.

Rhea Wells. *An American Farm*. Doubleday.

> Life on a farm in East Tennessee and methods of farming are simple and somewhat primitive, and the account is all the more interesting for that fact. Suited to children of nine years and older.

Frederick Arnold Kummer. *The First Days of Man*. Doubleday.

Well-chosen material, scientifically correct, and presented with clearness, simplicity and charm. Can be read by fourth grade children and contains material interesting to younger ones.

Bertha Stevens. *Child and Universe*. Day.

In the hands of teacher or parent this book offers a rich mine of knowledge and rare beauty. It is too difficult and expensive for general use below sixth grade, but every nature-lover will long to own it. There are many superb pictures well calculated to sharpen the observation of all ages in direct contact with nature.

GENERAL COLLECTION

Morse, Mary L., Editor. *Told Under the Blue Umbrella*. Macmillan.

Thirty-seven stories of child life selected and arranged by a committee representing the Association for Childhood Education and designed for children from five to eight years of age.

SUGGESTED PROBLEMS AND TOPICS FOR FURTHER STUDY

1. Over a period of one hundred years or more, show in what ways the realistic story has been a mirror of the times.

2. Study especially the relation of parents to children. There are three stories about willful little girls which offer an interesting comparison:

"Rosamond and the Purple Jar," Maria Edgeworth, late eighteenth century. (See Bibliography, Chapter VII, for sources.)

Susanna's Auction. Latter half of the nineteenth century. Translated from the French. Macmillan.

Abigail's Private Reason. Weda Yap. A story of today. Macmillan.

3. Notice how very seldom school life is introduced in modern realistic stories for children below high school age. Do you find it even in minor episodes? Why do writers of today tend to reject the entire scene? Notice what a large number

of stories mentioned in this chapter are vacation stories — vacation in the country. Can you find five or six good stories of some length in which children stay at home and find their pleasures and excitement in family and neighborhood life?

4. Select ten or more modern story-book children who seem to you very genuine and characterize each one briefly. Also indicate some of the means by which writers create this feeling of real personality.

5. Read at least ten longer stories about children of other lands and rank them according to your judgment as regards the art displayed in subordinating information to story.

6. It is generally conceded that children do not like long descriptions which retard the action; but should not short vivid description which is well placed afford added enjoyment? Scenes in foreign lands especially call for the judicious use of word pictures. Find good examples of this feature.

7. Study *Gay Madelon* and *The Treasure in the Little Trunk* as showing the interaction of a good many characters, several changes of scene, many colorful incidents, and coherent and plausible plot. These traits are common in fiction for children approaching high school age. Is there any good reason why they might not occur more frequently in stories for the younger ones?

8. Estimate the story quality of ten or fifteen large picture story books in which the pictures are rather notable. What is the literary worth of the stories? How many of them could stand alone as stories to be told? Is this a fair question or is there a fallacy in the implication?

9. Are you able to detect a superior unity or harmony of effect in some picture story books written and illustrated by the same person? Would it be fair to assume that if you do seem to find unusual harmony in such instances you should be able to detect also a less perfect unity in books produced otherwise? Can you offer examples of this type of production in books for adults? Go back as far as you desire historically.

10. Read *Little Blacknose*, *Little Machinery*, and *Diggers and Builders* (see Bibliography) to become acquainted with three quite different but artistic presentations of modern machinery through literature. Look for other stories abou~

machines and examine them critically in the light of the best standards you have developed or accepted.

Watch the tendency to invent a "language" for machines. Is there danger of exaggeration in this style? If you can find a page where there is a good deal of such "talk" in a variety of imitative syllables, try to read it aloud. What do child *readers* make of it? Critical study and informal experimentation seem to be called for here.

Note. In questions 8 and 9, do not limit yourself to stories of a realistic type, but include fanciful as well.

Several of the questions offered above can be better dealt with through the co-operative effort of a small group than by one person.

Several topics and problems closely related to this subject are proposed at the close of Chapter VII, Early Books for Children.

REFERENCES

References on biography of contemporary writers and artists, literary criticism, reviews, and the illustration of books for children will be found under Supplementary Bibliographies. Also some of the references for Chapter VII have a bearing on the subject of this chapter.

SUPPLEMENTARY BIBLIOGRAPHIES

There are some books for children and references for adults which could not be fitted into the chapter bibliographies, and others which for purposes of ready reference seem to call for separate treatment. Such books and reference materials compose the following lists. A few titles have been repeated.

BOOKS FOR CHILDREN

Picture story books

This list is miscellaneous in character and is intended to supplement the many picture story books previously mentioned in connection with specific topics. In most of these books the stories are very slight, but a lively and ingratiating little animal such as Angus or Bingo, for example, requires only a slender thread to tie the delightful and amusing pictures together.

Artists and writers have discovered that the picture-book age does not end at six or seven years. The proverbial appropriation by parents of children's Christmas toys has now extended to their books, and such books as *Millions of Cats*, *The Hole in the Wall*, and *The Painted Pig*, for example, are promptly claimed by the whole family. Because of their wide appeal it is futile and misleading to attempt any close grading of these books, but this list begins with some of the simplest in subject and form, such as are well suited to nursery and kindergarten.

Four and Twenty Toilers. Pictures by Francis D. Bedford. Verses by E. V. Lucas. McDevitt-Wilson.
> A favorite English picture book by a famous artist, showing the simpler forms of labor without much machinery.

A.B.C. Book. Charles B. Fall. Doubleday.
> An animal A.B.C. with very simple clear pictures in bright colors.

A.B.C. Book for Everybody. Helen Sewell. Macmillan.
> Each letter is connected with some everyday activity of small children, even to Z — "Zip into bed." Unusual pictures.

Ask Mr. Bear. Marjorie Flack. Macmillan.
> A wee story ending in a surprise. Delightful pictures of animals, all of them domestic except Mr. Bear.

Karl's Wooden Horse. Story by Lois Donaldson. Pictures by Annie Bergman. Laidlaw.

Beautiful gay pictures and a short interesting story about a toy horse.

Angus and the Ducks. Marjorie Flack. Doubleday.

Angus is a very young Scottie — inquisitive, daring but easily put to rout.

Angus and the Cat. Same.

After some misunderstandings, Angus and the Cat become friends.

A Good Little Dog. Anne Stoddard. Pictures by Berta and Elmer Hader. Century.

Bingo is a puppy of character who on occasion can be heroic.

Here Bingo. Same.

This is a very entertaining story about the same amusing and clever little dog.

Baby Bear. Hamilton Williamson. Pictures by Berta and Elmer Hader. Doubleday.

A baby bear's adventures in a deep jungle. Expressive and amusing pictures, most of them in black and white.

Lion Cub. Same.

Little Elephant. Same.

All of these baby animals appear very real in action and posture and they are appealing, as most young creatures are.

The Life of Baby Animals. In Picture Strip. George F. Morse. Pictures by Don Nelson. Rockwell.

A picture book which portrays actual happenings in animal life. A choice book for small children.

Wallie the Walrus. Kurt Wiese. Coward.

Walruses, polar bears and gulls are seen in brilliant arctic setting.

Tooky. Berta and Elmer Hader. Longmans.

A baby seal, born in the Arctic, is lured away and sold to a circus where he learns to do familiar circus tricks.

The Story of Noah. Clifford Webb. Warne.

A superb animal picture book. It follows in general the Bible story but with as childlike and literal an interpretation as that of "Green Pastures."

The Ark of Father Noah and Mother Noah. Maud and Miska
Petersham. Doubleday.
>A thoroughly "modernized" story with gorgeous pictures.

The Hole in the Wall. René d'Harnoncourt. Knopf.
>An absurd tale of what happened to a very thin man
originally drawn on a wall by an artist. Little children and
older ones as well are highly amused by d'Harnoncourt's
pictures of the predicaments which arise.

E. Boyd Smith has done a number of pleasing picture books in
color. Each has a brief explanatory text which does not serve
the needs of young children very well.

The Country Book. Stokes.
The Chicken World. Putnam.
The Seashore Book. Houghton.
The Railroad Book. Houghton.

The Complete Version of Ye Three Blind Mice. John W. Ivimey.
Illustrated by Walton Corbould. Warne.
>An old rhyme with some additions, and amusing pictures
in color.

Johnny Crow's Garden. Leslie Brooke. Warne.
>An old book and a great favorite, done by an inimitable
English artist.

A Roundabout Turn. Robert H. Charles. Illustrated by Leslie
Brooke. Warne.
>A humorous story in rhyme, with delightful pictures in
true Leslie Brooke style.

The following books might have been listed quite properly
among the stories of other lands, but their exceptional beauty and
distinction as picture books seems to place them here:

Miki. Maud and Miska Petersham. Doubleday.
>A small American boy, Miki, goes for a visit to Hungary
(once the home of Miska Petersham) where he has interesting adventures with Sari, the goose, and Matyi, the shepherd
dog. Numerous richly colored pictures.

The Painted Pig. Elizabeth Morrow. Knopf.
>This book is notable for the fourteen full-page gaily
colored pictures, truly Mexican in character, by René

d'Harnoncourt who used his own famous collection of Mexican toys as his subjects. The story is about one of these toys.

Ola. Ingri and Edgar Parin d'Aulaire. Doubleday.

A large picture story book in which Mr. and Mrs. d'Aulaire have collaborated with great success. The glowing pages display the beauty, gayety, romance and rugged toil of life in Norway as viewed and participated in by the little boy, Ola. Some of the events are half magical but all are "real" in the truest sense.

Our Children. Anatole France. Duffield.
Girls and Boys. Same.

The simple sketches (scarcely stories) of charming little French children written by a great French author are fittingly illustrated by L. M. Boutet de Monvel. These books have a lasting charm.

CHRISTMAS STORIES IN PROSE AND VERSE

Books in the following list are not collections of stories but each contains a single choice story or poem. All are in attractive format and several of them represent the very finest work achieved in books for children. Christmas is a season of family and communal celebration and because young and old unite in so many pleasures they are certain to find common pleasure in books. For this reason it is worse than futile to try to assign any exact age placement to Christmas books. All that can be said is that the first two on this list are for all ages, and that the remainder have been designed for the pleasure and delight of children from about six to ten years of age.

The Christ Child. Maud and Miska Petersham. Doubleday.

This is one of the most beautiful picture story books ever made. The text consists of selections from the Gospels and the wonderful pictures were painted in Palestine and printed in Germany under the supervision of the artists. A reverent and lovely book.

'Twas the Night Before Christmas. A Visit from St. Nicholas. Clement C. Moore.

There are several beautiful editions of this beloved old poem, illustrated by different artists. The following are very attractive.

Title as above. Pictures by Jessie Willcox Smith. Houghton.

The Night Before Christmas. Illustrated by Arthur Rackham. Lippincott.

Same. Pictures by Elizabeth MacKinstry. Dutton.

Little Tooktoo. The Story of Santa Claus' Youngest Reindeer. Marie Ahnighito Peary. Illustrated by Kurt Wiese. Morrow.

The author is the daughter of Admiral Peary and is a true child of the Far North. The theme of the story is original and its development is charming. In an emergency, the little reindeer Tooktoo, takes Cupid's place in Santa's well-seasoned team and comes through with honor.

The Robin's Christmas. C. E. Bowen. Warne.

A favorite old story in verse with fifteen colored pictures by Winifred M. Warne.

Mr. Pickles and the Party. Constance Heward. Illustrated by Anne Anderson. Warne.

A small book containing a delightful story about real children, told in Miss Heward's best manner. Many pictures in color.

The Tailor of Gloucester. Beatrix Potter. Warne.

This is one of the small books written and illustrated by Beatrix Potter. Its size bears no relation to its importance on the shelf of Christmas books.

The Christmas Tree in the Wood. Susan Smith. Pictures by Helen Sewell. Minton, Balch.

This story of an outdoor Christmas party in the Maine woods is conceived with fine imagination and told with a remarkable blending of the happy reality of Christmas and its deeper spiritual meaning.

The Bird Began to Sing. Rachel Field. Pictures by Ilse Bischoff. Morrow.

How a recalcitrant mechanical bird intended as a gift to a small boy was set singing late on Christmas Eve through the voluntary services of a devoted little girl who employed surprising measures.

Little Christmas.   Louise Seaman.   Macmillan.

This lovely little book is worthy of a place among the choicest of its kind.   Miss Seaman has woven into a perfect whole, several old European legends about the Christ Child, here called *Little Christmas.*   Reversing the usual order, the story was written to fit some remarkable Christmas pictures made at an earlier date by a young Czecho-Slovakian artist, Zdnek Guth.

Little Heiskell.   Isabelle B. Hurlbutt.   Illustrated by Alida Conover.   Dutton.

In the uniform of a Continental soldier, Heiskell had perched as a weather-vane on top of the Market House in Hagerstown, Maryland, for many years.   One Christmas Eve he came down from his perch and succeeded in setting straight some matters which were greatly troubling Frieda and Victor.

Saint Nicholas in Trouble.   Felix Timmermans.   Translated from the German by Amy Flashner.   Illustrated by Else Wenz-Vietor.   Harper.

A story of the German legendary Saint Nicholas very different from the Santa Claus of American children.   A pleasing story but some of the references will not be understood by children below eight or nine years of age.   There are ten lovely full-page pictures in color.

There are two books for children which should have a special significance for adults interested in children's literature.   They are therefore included although they belong properly in fifth or sixth grade in a list for children's reading.   One of them happens to be a Christmas story.   Both these books are rich in literary references and possess the element of delight attendant upon the recognition of loved and admired objects, places, and people. Parts of these books children enjoy hearing read aloud long before they are able to read and understand the whole.

Miss Muffet's Christmas Party.   Samuel McChord Crothers. Introduction by Anne Carroll Moore.   Houghton, 1929. First published 1902.

With the able assistance of a friendly spider, Miss Muffet gives a "literary" party, the guests being characters from children's books published before 1900.   One wonders what characters created since that date Mr. Crothers, through Miss Muffet, might have invited to the party had it been given in 1925. Interested readers might like to make a short list of belated guests deemed worthy to join the earlier group.

Nicholas and the Golden Goose. Anne Carroll Moore. Illustrated by Jay Van Everen. Putnam, 1932.

Nicholas, the dream boy of an earlier book by Miss Moore, and his grown-up friend "Anne Caraway" visit well-known writers and illustrators of children's books. Readers are thus introduced intimately to Beatrix Potter, Leslie Brooke, Walter de la Mare, Eleanor Farjeon and other delightful people, and learn many interesting things about them and their surroundings.

REFERENCES FOR ADULTS

General Anthologies for Use with Children

Miller, Olive Beaupré, editor. *My Book House.* 6 volumes. Chicago, The Bookhouse for Children, 1925–1928.

Each book contains a variety of well-chosen material both prose and poetry, well graded, and in a form which is very attractive to children. At about third grade reading level children can begin to use these books independently.

Scudder, Horace E., compiler and editor. *The Children's Book.* Houghton, 1909.

A large collection of the choicest material available at the time of publication. No other single book has taken its place.

Tappan, Eva M., editor. *The Children's Hour.* 15 volumes. Houghton.

An excellent collection, well graded and covering a great variety of material both prose and poetry.

THE ILLUSTRATION OF CHILDREN'S BOOKS

Mahony, Bertha E., and Whitney, Elinor, compiler. *Contemporary Illustrators of Children's Books.* Boston, The Bookshop for Boys and Girls, 1930.

An indispensable reference in this field.

Mellinger, Bonnie E. *Children's Interests in Pictures.* Bureau of Publications, Teachers College, Columbia University, 1932.

The clear account of an experiment in which children from first to fifth grade recorded their preferences for pictures identical in all respects except color and style (realistic or conventionalized).

Owen, Helen Hammett. "Notes on Contemporary Artists" in *The Three Owls, Third Book*, by Anne Carroll Moore, pp. 436–442.

    Brief but very satisfactory paragraphs on each of about forty of the best-known illustrators of children's books of today. This book contains also numerous short articles by different writers about the work of several contemporary artists.

Pearson, Ralph M. *Experiencing Pictures*. Brewer, 1932.

    Does not treat directly of pictures for children. "This book is... an attempt to arrange in an orderly way our available knowledge about the tangible content of pictures so that knowledge may be used to help form intelligent judgments of our own." (Preface.)

White, Gleeson. *Children's Books and Their Illustrators*. Special winter number of *The Studio*. London, The Studio, 1898.

    A very important reference covering the period from early anonymous chap-books to the closing years of the nineteenth century.

James, Philip. *Children's Books of Yesterday*. London, The Studio.

    The whole development of juvenile picture books is told here with numerous plates.

SOURCES OF BIOGRAPHICAL NOTES

For English authors consult:
    Dictionary of National Biography. Macmillan.
    The Cambridge History of English Literature. Putnam.

For American authors consult:
    Dictionary of American Biography. Scribner.
    Volume XI (1933) has now reached in alphabetical order the letter M.

For living authors, English and American, consult:
    Living Authors. A Book of Biographies. Wilson, 1931.
    Includes a great many authors who are contributing to literature for children and gives many interesting and pertinent facts about them.

The Horn Book and *The Three Owls* (see below), also contain much that is timely. Some of the sketches of favorite authors might well be shared in some degree with children.

Publishers of children's books are often able to furnish special book lists which contain brief biographical notes. Although book "jackets" cannot always be relied upon for a just estimate of the book, they often contain interesting information about the author.

AIDS TO THE UNDERSTANDING AND APPRECIATION OF LITERARY ART

Becker, May Lamberton. *Adventures in Reading*. Stokes, 1927. Intended for boys and girls, but profitable and interesting to more mature readers.

Eastman, Max. *The Literary Mind*. Its Place in an Age of Science. Scribner, 1931.

Moulton, Richard G. *The Modern Study of Literature*. An Introduction to Literary Theory and Interpretation. University of Chicago Press, 1915–1930.

Pritchard, Francis H. *Training in Literary Appreciation*. Crowell, 1924.

Quiller-Couch, Sir Arthur. *On the Art of Reading*. Putnam, 1920.

Wharton, Edith. *The Writing of Fiction*. Scribner, 1925.

GENERAL REFERENCES ON LITERATURE FOR CHILDREN

Barry, Florence V. *A Century of Children's Books*. Doran, 1922. Covers the eighteenth century and continues certain features to 1825.

Bone, Woutrina A. *Children's Stories and How to Tell Them*. Harcourt, 1924.

Curry, C. M., and Clippinger, E. E., editors. *Children's Literature*. Rand, 1920.

Dalgliesh, Alice. *First Experiences with Literature*. Scribner, 1932.

Darton, F. J. Harvey. *Children's Books in England*. Five Centuries of Social Life. Cambridge University Press, 1932. The subject is very fully covered through the nineteenth century.

Fay, Lucy E., and Eaton, Anne T. *Instruction in the Use of Books and Libraries*. Faxon, 1915–1928.

Field, Mrs. E. M. *The Child and His Book*. Wells, Gardner, 1895.

Gardner, Emelyn E., and Ramsey, Eloise. *A Handbook of Children's Literature*. Scott, 1927.

Hewins, Caroline M. *A Mid-Century Child and Her Books*. Macmillan, 1926.
A pioneer in children's library work tells of her favorite books as a little New England girl in the 1850's.

Leonard, Sterling A. *Essential Principles of Teaching Reading and Literature*. Lippincott, 1922.

MacClintock, Porter L. *Literature in the Elementary School*. University of Chicago Press, 1906.

Matthews, Florence E., and Coffin, Rebecca J. *Experiencing Literature*. Chicago, Bookhouse for Children, 1931.

Moses, Montrose J. *Children's Books and Reading*. Kennerley, 1907.

Olcott, Frances J. *Children's Reading*. Revised and enlarged ed. Houghton, 1927.

Rawlinson, Eleanor. *Introduction to Literature for Children*. Norton, 1931.

White House Conference. *Children's Reading*. A Study of Voluntary Reading of Boys and Girls in the United States. Report of the sub-committee on Reading. Carl H. Milam, Chairman. Century, 1932.

CRITICISM AND REVIEWS. BOOK LISTS

The Horn Book. Published quarterly by The Bookshop for Boys and Girls. Boston.
A magazine devoted to books and reading for young people. Contains reviews of new books, criticism, annotated book lists and literary news items. An indispensable reference.

Mahony, Bertha E., and Whitney, Elinor, compiler. *Realms of Gold in Children's Books*. Doubleday, 1929.
A suggestive purchase list compiled by the editors of the *Horn Book*. Contains a wealth of material selected and presented with skill and taste. There is no adequate substitute for this book.

Moore, Anne Carroll, author and editor.
  The Three Owls. Second Book. Coward-McCann, 1928.
  The Three Owls. Third Book. Coward-McCann, 1931.
      Contemporary criticism of children's books by one of the
  leading authorities in this field and by other able critics.
  These two books introduce almost every important writer of to-
  day for children and contain original and interesting articles on
  many questions concerning the production of beautiful books.
American Library Association. *Graded List of Books for Children*.
  Compiled by Nora Beust. Chicago, American Library
  Association, 1930.
      Books are graded in a flexible manner and annotations are
  brief but very helpful.
American Library Association. *The Right Book for the Right
  Child*. Day, 1933.
      Books were selected and annotated by a sub-committee of
  the Committee on Library Work with Children. They
  were graded by the Research Department of the Winnetka
  Public Schools. Selection was made upon the basis of interest and suitability in content and literary quality. The
  books were then assigned to certain grades according to the
  results of standardized reading tests widely administered.
  This placement according to reading ability must be kept in
  mind in using this reference, as selections for grades I and II
  are meager and poor in comparison with the pre-school
  list — and some very childish books find themselves in
  strange company in the upper grades.
Children's Catalog. Compiled by Minnie Earl Sears. (Standard
  Catalogue Series.) Fourth edition revised. H. W. Wilson,
  1930. Supplements 1, 2, and 3. 1931, 1932, 1933.

Finding List

Eastman, Mary H. *Index to Fairy Tales, Myths and Legends*.
  Faxon, 1926.

  Lists of new books and new editions of old books are published
at intervals by the children's department of the Public Library in
several of the larger cities. Cleveland, New York, and Pitts-
burgh, among others, have contributed much in this way.
Several of the leading publishers of children's books issue annually
illustrated and descriptive catalogues which are of real assistance
to the prospective purchaser.

INDEX